The ONE YEAR® BOOK OF
Inspiration for
GIRLFRIENDS

...juggling *Not-So-Perfect*, OFFEN-CRAZY, but *Gloriously* REAL LIVES

ELLEN MILLER

TYNDALE™
MOMENTUM

An Imprint of
Tyndale House Publishers, Inc.

Visit Tyndale online at www.tyndale.com.

Visit Tyndale Momentum online at www.tyndalemomentum.com.

TYNDALE, LeatherLike, The One Year, and *One Year* are registered trademarks of Tyndale House Publishers, Inc. *Tyndale Momentum*, the Tyndale Momentum logo, and The One Year logo are trademarks of Tyndale House Publishers, Inc. Tyndale Momentum is an imprint of Tyndale House Publishers, Inc.

The One Year Book of Inspiration for Girlfriends . . . Juggling Not-So-Perfect, Often-Crazy, but Gloriously Real Lives

Designed by Beth Sparkman

Unless otherwise indicated, all Scripture quotations are taken from the *Holy Bible*, New Living Translation, copyright © 1996, 2004, 2007 by Tyndale House Foundation. Used by permission of Tyndale House Publishers, Inc., Carol Stream, Illinois 60188. All rights reserved.

Scripture quotations marked NASB are taken from the New American Standard Bible,® copyright © 1960, 1962, 1963, 1968, 1971, 1972, 1973, 1975, 1977, 1995 by The Lockman Foundation. Used by permission.

Scripture quotations marked HCSB are taken from the Holman Christian Standard Bible®, copyright © 1999, 2000, 2002, 2003 by Holman Bible Publishers. Used by permission. Holman Christian Standard Bible®, Holman CSB®, and HCSB® are federally registered trademarks of Holman Bible Publishers.

ISBN 978-1-4143-7331-7 LeatherLike Dusty Rose
ISBN 978-1-4143-3899-6 LeatherLike Black Patent
ISBN 978-1-4143-1938-4 Softcover

Printed in China

19 18 17 16 15 14 13
9   8   7   6   5   4   3

For Mammaw

CONTENTS

ACKNOWLEDGMENTS

Without you . . .

my Insiders, this book just couldn't have happened. Your support in carrying my business workload enabled me to have the time and mental bandwidth to write these words. Debbie, Jesse, Will, Becky, Mary Jo, Kathy, Carol, Paul, Clay, Christian, and especially Paula—who is also my dearest friend—thank you for your moral and physical support.

Without you . . .

my dear girlfriends, I would not have had the confidence to even begin this journey. Your encouragement energized me and motivated me to do something I never thought I could have done. Elaine, Linda, Susan, Gretchen, Karen, Petey, Kathryn, Dina, Stacie, and all my girlfriend subscribers around the world—you are such a blessing to me. Kim Miller, my editor, and Jan Long Harris and the team at Tyndale—thank you for taking this chance with me.

Without you . . .

LifeNet, including Terry Smart and the other fabulous team of professionals there, I might not have this story of hope to tell. Thank you for giving my son the tools and encouragement to get his life back. I know God must have a very special place in heaven for those of you who selflessly give your time and energy to those in our society who are so deeply hurt and broken.

Without you . . .

my family, there is no story for you are the ones who give depth and meaning to my life. My in-laws Al, Harriett, and Dean who love me like their own daughter; thank you for always being so proud of me. My son-in-law, Adam, who is way more son than "in-law," I thank you for the way you love and care for my daughter and granddaughter. Shauna, my light and best friend since I was eighteen years old, you bring me joy and happiness beyond words; I cannot imagine my life without you. To Ava, your very presence has ignited in me a desire to live intentionally in order to leave a meaningful legacy to you as my grandmother did for me. And, Scott, without you I would not be the woman I am today. Your struggles have humbled me and brought me to my knees, and your courage and determination to fight your way back has filled me with hope and pride. Thank you for so graciously and boldly allowing me to share your struggles so that other moms who are also facing crisis with their children may find hope.

Without you . . .
Steve, I am only a ghost of myself. Your direction, support, and encouragement right me when I fail; your interest, insight and suggestions fuel me when I'm drained. And the way you love me—deeply, selflessly, and passionately—completes me. I am so blessed to have you as my husband. I love you with all my heart.

Without you . . .
my God, I am nothing.

INTRODUCTION

ON A SUNDAY afternoon in 2004, I had an "urging"—a really strange sense of calling—to write some of my girlfriends. I wanted to reach out to those women who I knew were in the difficult life stage of building a career while caring for a family. Since I had passed through that crazy life stage and lived to tell about it (along with my husband and kids), I sent a few of my gal pals an e-mail with a short note and a quote from Andy Andrews's book, *The Traveler's Gift*. On Monday morning, my girlfriends, some of whom I had not even corresponded with in over a year, responded with notes like "How in the world did you know that I needed that? Life is so hard right now. Keep 'em coming!"

Goaded by my dear friend and mentor Elaine Weeter, I agreed to begin compiling and sending out some of my personal stories, reflections, and thoughts. As my subscriber base grew, I launched www.ellenmiller.com, a blog for women seeking to live a life of uncommon joy. My musings, called Truth Nuggets, are sent via e-mail and posted to my blog. This book is a compilation of some of those writings.

In the movie *Shadowlands*, a student tells his professor, C. S. Lewis, "We read to know we're not alone." And, really, that's why I began to write. Over five years later, my audience is global. It includes women of all faiths and no faith. These women range in age from their early twenties to nearly seventy. Some have never worked outside the home; others are high-flying executives. But they all long to live intentionally and to leave a legacy for others.

While my purpose in life is to encourage my girlfriends, my profession is marketing. I am the founder and president of a technology marketing company. Since 1994, Insider Marketing has helped launch some of the most innovative and significant products in the technology industry. Prior to opening the firm, I was an executive with a Fortune 500 company. During that period of life I struggled to maintain any semblance of balance between building my career, securing a new marriage, and raising my children. This was the life stage I refer to as my three-ring circus!

My purpose and profession are just two-thirds of who I am, however. Personally, I am a God-loving sinner saved by grace. While I am deeply spiritual and a faithful follower of Christ, I am not a church lady. I can't pray like they pray; my words are often clunky. My Bible is well worn and read (literally red, with lots of notes written in ink); but I have a hard time recalling Scripture—especially in a pinch! And . . . well . . . sometimes I'm just selfish and prideful and impatient and—I guess you get the idea. I think church ladies are really neat; I'm just not one of them. Going on twenty years of marriage, I am head over heels in love with my husband, Steve. This is his first marriage and my second. Steve helped me raise our daughter, Shauna, and son, Scott. We've added to the crew with the addition of our son-in-law, Adam, and our granddaughter, Ava.

When I first began writing to my girlfriends, our son, who was addicted to drugs, had been missing for three years. Scott's drug dependency and recovery are a significant, if painful, part of our family history. For this reason, 50 percent of my profits from the sale of *The One Year Book of Inspiration for Girlfriends . . . Juggling Not-So-Perfect, Often-Crazy, but Gloriously Real Lives* will be given to LifeNet, a Dallas-based nonprofit that helps people recovering from mental illness and chemical dependency to rebuild their lives.

Scott believes our story can help other families who also live not-so-perfect lives, so he's given me his permission to tell our story. In fact, Steve, Shauna, and Adam have also generously allowed me to share some of their stories with you, since our experiences have been my best teachers for living a life of uncommon joy.

Because I am a real woman, living a real life—sometimes a very messy and complicated life—I face new challenges every day. I have found peace that passes all understanding in my relationship in Christ. I hope this book of inspirations will bring you joy and hope as you journey for the next 365 days through your real life too.

FINDING YOUR JOY

I sometimes wonder whether all pleasures are not substitutes for joy. C. S. LEWIS

ARE YOU HAPPY?

The pursuit of happiness. A final destination so important that our fore-fathers included it in our Declaration of Independence. Millions *trade* their way to happiness—sometimes finding it in a corner office, others with a power-shopping trip to the mall—only to find that it quickly dissolves into discontent. Here today, gone tomorrow. Happiness, in reality, is just the emotion we feel when we are in a state of well-being. But emotions are fickle and can change with the weather or a ten-second hormonal surge! In fact, I think happiness is overrated—after all, it's so dependent on outside influences.

Do you have peace?

When my kids were teenagers, I would have these moments (sometimes hours) when both kids were doing well in school, their social networks humming; my job was going great; my husband was content and satisfied with his work—our little family a Norman Rockwell poster. And then the sun would come up and there'd be an algebra test, a girlfriend's hurtful words, or a boss's unreasonable expectation, and that peace would be a distant memory.

Peace is a state of serenity. But your peace can be interrupted when the tele-phone rings. For this reason, I know that peace is fleeting and, like happiness, should not be our lifelong pursuit.

So that leaves us with joy. Do you have joy?

Better yet—do you have *uncommon* joy? Do you live in a state of contentment that defies all logic in this world gone mad? Regardless of who has harmed you in the past, what circumstances may get in your way today, or what life-blows you'll face in the future, can you say you live in a state of constant, uncommon joy? To live with rich contentment, joy—which cannot be affected by outside forces—is required. Joy is a state of heart and is the only one of these three states—happiness, peace, and joy—that you and you alone can control. No one can mess with your joy unless you let them.

I have told you these things so that you will be filled with my joy. Yes, your joy will overflow! (JOHN 15:11)

Have you maybe misplaced your joy? It's not gone—it's just in a very good hidey-hole. Let's go find it. Over the next 364 pages, I will share with you a few very practical but transforming tips to finding uncommon joy—regardless of how common your life is!

FINDING YOUR JOY
Let's Start with You

To find the good life you must become yourself.   DR. BILL JACKSON

GIRLFRIENDS, now that we're all grown up, we need to get over trying to please others. If you're over the age of thirty-five, you probably know that you're never going to please everyone and that on some days, you'll please no one. The harder you work at it the more impossible it is to gain or to maintain that person's favor. Seeking the approval of others is a surefire (for my out-of-state friends, that's a Texas term for *guaranteed*) way of losing your joy.

I'm not sure if approval seeking is a result of our upbringing; I guess if we were little girls whose self-esteem got a boost when Mom and Dad were well pleased, we are probably more likely to need approval from others today. I think my need for approval is genetic. I was born this way and came out of the womb hoping to dazzle the doctor! No matter how it's acquired, approval-seeking doesn't cohabitate with joy.

For many years, I confused approval with respect. But of course, they are different. I learned, much too late, that people can respect you without always agreeing with your position or your actions. Have you confused approval with respect?

While some women are concerned about what others think, many of us are our own worst enemies. We don't approve of who we are. Of course, there are always things we need to work on. That's okay—we are all works in progress. If you have issues that you know need to be addressed and you don't feel you can give yourself the big Five-Star Approval Rating, give yourself at least four stars; for heaven's sake, recognizing a problem is half the battle!

What is important here is that we be our best for ourselves. No one else. If you're trying to please your husband or boyfriend, your mother, your boss, or your kids—you can forget about it. You won't find joy in that pursuit. Joy is a state of contentment that cannot be affected by outside forces.

Say out loud with me: "Someone will not like something I say or do today."
How do you feel? Not so good?
Say it again, but this time add: "Someone will not like something I say or do today but that's okay—God and I are well pleased with me."

You will show me the way of life,
   granting me the joy of your presence
   and the pleasures of living with you forever. (PSALM 16:11)

Better?
You will find lasting joy only when you decide that others' approval is not important to who you know you are.

FINDING YOUR JOY
Reassigning Your Treasure

I AM A PERSON of joy, and some people think it's because I live a perfect life. Ha! Nothing could be further from the truth. But I have discovered a secret that is the source of my joy: *I have reassigned my treasure.*

My family, probably like yours, is far from ideal. In addition to a wonderful husband and an awesome daughter and son-in-law, our son, Scott, was a non-functioning drug addict for a number of years.

As a matter of fact, when I first wrote this Truth Nugget to my girlfriends, he was missing. Again. We had not heard from Scott in over three years. Could it have possibly been worse? Yes. His drug of choice is methamphetamine. Heartbreaking doesn't even begin to describe what a mother goes through when she knows her baby (yes, at twenty-six, he was still my baby) is in a desperate situation, most likely sleeping on the streets (again), and unable to find his way. My precious little redheaded boy who loved to laugh and play and snuggle was now standing uncomfortably close to the threshold of death.

What mother ever envisions dealing with missing persons officials and calling the morgue on a monthly basis? I sure didn't. You see, we did everything "right." We went to church on Sundays, ate dinner around the table as a family every night, attended soccer games and band competitions. How could this possibly be happening to us? Sometimes I felt like I was playing a part in a bad made-for-TV movie. Whenever the phone would ring—I expected it to be him. I literally held my breath hoping that my one-time saxophone-playing, lovable, huggable, honor-student kid would say, "Hey, Mom! What's up?"

I share my story with you because, like many mothers, my treasure was my children. For many years, I drew my identity, creativity, and self-worth from my children's well-being. My dream of raising healthy, happy children was my energy source. But I've learned through this journey that this doesn't work; I can't commit my sanity, or insanity, to my children. My joy must come from knowing that God's agenda is greater than my own. Thus, I reassigned him to be my treasure by placing my trust in his promise of grace and mercy. Once I shifted my focus from me to him, I realized I could be joyful and strong regardless of this heartbreaking situation. Though darkness had taken my son, I absolutely refused to relinquish my joy to it.

So, what is your treasure? Your home? Your spouse? The quest for money or more stuff? Your children's success? Your position in your church or community? Be careful; it may make finding joy an impossible task.

Wherever your treasure is, there the desires of your heart will also be.
(MATTHEW 6:21)

Of course, reassigning your treasure may not be easy. My only helpful tip: it's easier to let go of something once you recognize it wasn't yours in the first place.

FINDING YOUR JOY
Letting Go of Yesterday

We must accept finite disappointment, but never lose infinite hope.
MARTIN LUTHER KING JR.

SOMETIMES WE HAVE our joy, only to misplace it. There are as many ways for joy to elude us as there are personalities in the world, but one way we lose it is by not being present in the now. We spend so much time thinking about where we should have been, where we need to be, what we need to do, and how we're going to do it that we forget about right now. We're not going to get this second back, so why are we such poor stewards of this moment?

Notice, I didn't say be in *the* moment. I want you to be in *this moment*. I want you to begin to recognize when you have a "this moment" with your family, your peers at work, your friends. I've found that it is very difficult to be in this moment if we're constantly plagued with thoughts of yesterday or tomorrow.

Living a not-so-perfect life, I have experienced the consequences of sin—my own and those bestowed on me by others. I have made mistakes that shame me to no end; sins that if I dwelled on them and failed to receive the forgiveness freely given, would send me into a black hole from which I would never return. And I have also experienced sin on the receiving end: abandonment, betrayal, manipulation, and emotional abuse. Accepting my failures, as well as those of others, is the only way to deal with a fallen world. And moving on is the only way to hope.

Don't let your past haunt your now. What happened yesterday, last month, or when you were twelve years old cannot be undone. It happened; and it was probably sad *and* unfair. Thinking about, dwelling on, and reliving the past—one created by you or for you—will only rob you of joy today. Joy is a state of contentment that cannot be affected by outside forces. Remember: yesterday is an outside force.

> *I cried out to the LORD,*
> *and he answered me from his holy mountain.*
> *I lay down and slept,*
> *yet I woke up in safety,*
> *for the LORD was watching over me.* (PSALM 3:4-5)

Are you willing to let it go? Notice I asked if you were willing. Most of us are capable but have become so comfortable rolling around in our tormented pasts that we've come to relish our "victimhood."

What will you choose? The agony of yesterday or the joy of today?

FINDING YOUR JOY
Being Present

Regret for the things we did can be tempered by time; it is regret for the things we did not do that is inconsolable. SYDNEY HARRIS

I WASTED PRECIOUS "this moments" with my family by not stopping to take in the details of everyday exchanges. Oh, the kids had my full attention when the tears were flowing or when they slammed the bedroom door! (That only happened once. At our house if you slammed the door, Dad would remove it from the hinges to ensure it didn't get in your way again.) But the little things that make a conversation so precious—facial expressions, giggles, or a well-kept secret finally shared—sometimes went by without my full registration of the moment. Why? I was too busy trying to do other things. Were the other things— like cooking dinner or folding towels—more important? No, of course not. So why didn't I stop whatever else I was doing to be in that moment?

There will always be challenges with the kids, issues with the boss, home appliances that break down, or a girlfriend whose feelings were hurt. If we are constantly thinking about the next moment and what we need to do, how can we possibly enjoy and be in this one? You will have another moment to deal with life. Life's stuff is not going away—it will wait for you.

To excel at being in this moment, you will want to turn off the stove when your kids are in the kitchen with you after school. (It's okay—dinner can be late.) You'll switch off the TV when your grown kids come over. You will turn off your mobile phone when you go to lunch with a girlfriend. You will learn to *ssshh* the constant chattering in your head. Being in *this moment* will allow you to see, hear, and feel in a whole new way. And that, my friend, is pure joy.

> *Please, LORD, rescue me!*
> *Come quickly, LORD, and help me.* (PSALM 40:13)

Choose to make *this moment* a priority for you and the ones you love. Pure, uncommon joy awaits you.

FINDING YOUR JOY
Give Something Away Every Day

Be careful how you live; you may be the only Bible some people ever read. UNKNOWN

I BELIEVE we rob ourselves of joy by not giving something away—every day.

There's nothing in the world like the feeling you get when you perform a random act of kindness. I almost feel guilty for the pleasure *I* gain when I am helpful to someone. If it feels so good, why do we stop to think before we just *do*? Are we afraid we'll look too soft? Are we afraid we might be embarrassed if the offer for help is refused? Or do we talk ourselves out of helping by drawing a fact-less conclusion that the person will be fine and doesn't really need our assistance?

Most people limit their gifts to money or time. Both are critical, but I've discovered joy by looking for other things to give, such as:

- *Encouragement.* Let's admit it—we're all faced with challenges every day. That's why I started writing my blog. Girlfriends need encouragement. Many of you give away encouragement by forwarding my notes on to your girlfriends, and some of you write me to cheer me on. What inspiration I gain from you!
- *An extra pair of hands.* Ever see a mom struggling at the grocery store or at the airport with her kids, bags, doors, car seats, etc.? I always smile, ask gently if I can lend a pair of hands—and have never been refused. The mother looks at me like I'm some sort of angel. What brings me joy about this? I usually get to hold the baby!
- *Your seat.* This one gave me my biggest jolt of joy ever. I had the opportunity to give my first-class airline seat to an army private coming home for leave from the war in Iraq. Every minute I sat in his middle seat from Dallas to Portland was pure joy. What an honor it was for me to serve him, if only for three hours and fifty-nine minutes. Wow! I could have floated off that plane. (And he was pretty tickled too.)
- *Forgiveness.* I give forgiveness. Because I make mistakes, I know others do too. I've found when I give forgiveness, it's me—not the other person— who benefits. Forgiveness is freeing, and being free is joyful.

The generous will prosper;
*   those who refresh others will themselves be refreshed.* (PROVERBS 11:25)

Some people confuse this type of generosity with being nice, but it's much more than that. There's nothing like the rush of joy you get when you give something away. So what will you give away today?

FINDING YOUR JOY
Glory in What You Have

Contentment is not the fulfillment of what you want, but the realization of how much you already have. ANONYMOUS

LIFE IS FULL of blessings we take for granted.

Yet so often we dwell on what we don't have. I think the more we dwell on that, the harder it is to come by joy. So if yearning for things robs you of your joy, the opposite must be true. Glory in what you have, and the joy will come flowing through!

This is the Ellen version of "stop and smell the roses." Don't just be happy about the things or people in your life . . . take *glory* in them. *Celebrate* them. Be in *awe* of them. This isn't about the stuff—it's about how your heart *thinks* about the stuff! One important note: in order to glory in what you have, you will need to have mastered being in *this moment*.

So what do I glory in?

- *A walk.* I glory in the fact that I have feet and that I can walk. I walk every day. It's good for my heart, my mind, and my derriere. What a blessing!
- *My Dean Martin CD.* Dean Martin is pure joy. My mom, who died several years ago, loved Dean Martin and played his albums almost every Saturday evening when I was growing up. Warm, fond memories are good for joy.
- *Cut flowers.* I pick up a bouquet of cut flowers at the grocery store every week. Girlfriend, $6.99 can't buy anything else this good! Every time I look at them I am amazed at the creativity of our God. Joy in a six-inch vase. How cool is that?
- *Dancing.* I just dance and dance and dance . . . usually in the kitchen and usually to Dean Martin. I'm not very good but it seems to provide great entertainment for my husband—he gets joy from watching my joy!
- *Sunshine.* I'm fueled by sunny, warm days. How can sunlight possibly be free? Well . . . I guess if you live in California you pay for it in property costs. But for the rest of us, it's free. Sunshine brings me joy.

O our God, we thank you and praise your glorious name!
(1 CHRONICLES 29:13)

What do you glory in? Take a few minutes to make your own list. Once you *recognize* what you glory in and you learn to be in *this* moment—you'll glory in it *more*. And that will bring you joy.

FINDING YOUR JOY

FATHER GOD, you have spoken to me and I realize that joy awaits me when

- ☐ I stop allowing others' disapproval of me to disrupt my sense of well-being;
- ☐ I let go of those things I hold on to so tightly and reassign you as my treasure;
- ☐ I choose to let go of yesterday;
- ☐ I am fully aware of being in this moment with you;
- ☐ I give something away;
- ☐ I glory in what I have.

ACTIONS I WILL TAKE:

Example: I will let go of my pain of yesterday by reminding myself each morning that I have accepted the forgiveness Christ has so freely given.

1. _____

2. _____

3. _____

God of glory and lover of my soul, I thank you for caring so much for me that you would want me to live with uncommon joy. Thank you for this life you have given me and for the delights you have awaiting me today, tomorrow, and in my life with you ever after. Amen.

SPREAD TOO THIN

Freedom means choosing your burden. HEPHZIBAH MENUHIN

MY HUSBAND, Steve, and I are serial remodelers. We often finish a project (or sometimes an entire house) only to move immediately on to the next room, or even the next place of shelter, to provide a little TLC (tender loving construction). Because our professions rarely afford us even a small glimpse of some tangible result from our daily toil in the office, I think it's our way of feeling productive and creative. When we remodel, we actually get to see the fruits of our labor.

During one of those makeovers, this time of the master bathroom, I especially enjoyed the rapid progress of the work. Steve, being the visionary as well as the general contractor for these projects, always looks forward to my critique of our craftsmen's handiwork (not!). One day, I arrived home to find that the painters had applied their magic. But . . . in one tiny area, over in the corner, the paint was spread too thin.

Although the work (paint job included) was spectacular overall, in this one confined space, the work looked sloppy. It lacked the crispness and the detail that surrounded it. It wasn't as fresh. It actually looked a little worse than before. I thought I could ignore it—but when I went back to the bathroom to take in the sight of the beautiful tile work—all I could focus on was the wall peeking through the Sherwin-Williams, Rope #SW8011.

Like the paint job, I'm often spread too thin, coming across a bit sloppy—in my relationships, in my work, and in caring for myself. I'm not fresh. I'm not creative. I'm not detailed. I'm not present. I'm just a mess.

> *You are the salt of the earth; but if the salt has become tasteless, how can it be made salty again? It is no longer good for anything, except to be thrown out and trampled under foot by men. . . . Let your light shine before men in such a way that they may see your good works, and glorify your Father who is in heaven.*
> (MATTHEW 5:13,16, NASB)

Are you overcommitted too? Uh-huh. I thought so.

There's tangible fallout when we overschedule our lives, and the majority of the time, that fallout occurs in the depth and breadth of our relationships. We cannot fulfill our life purpose if we become like salt that is tasteless and dull.

You have the right and the power to choose between those things that are causing you to be spread too thin. You also have the obligation. Those in your world are looking for your light to shine. What things can you eliminate today that will allow you to glorify your Father?

SPREAD TOO THIN
An All-about-Me Life

DO YOU FEEL like the weight of the world is on your shoulders? Are you stressed out because there's just not enough of you to go around? If so, you'll be able to relate.

It was a bit uncharacteristic of me, but not too long ago, I had a total meltdown. Yep—driving down the road—I couldn't see a thing for all the rain (and there wasn't a cloud in the sky).

Here's what had happened just minutes before: I was running late to a meeting. Not just any meeting. This one was with our adult son, Scott, who had recently returned after being missing for over three years and was going through rehab. As I headed out the door, it dawned on me that I was double booked—in addition to the commitment with Scott, I had two conference calls scheduled for the afternoon.

On top of that, my head was swimming, as mothers' heads do—when had I last called our daughter? It's always the child who is *not* in crisis who seems to get the short end of the stick. My cell phone was ringing off the hook as I fished around my purse for my keys and headed to the car. Steve was pulling up the rear as we headed out to lunch.

It was while we were standing there in our office parking lot that Steve and I had a major communication snafu on a very minor issue (isn't that how it always is?). I needed to take my car; he suggested we should drive together. I snapped back a thoughtless response about my lack of "me" time and the state of my personal energy crisis. He implied that I was having an "all about me" moment.

Oh . . . puuhhlllleeeeeaaassseeee.

All about me? *All about me?*

It took me until about seven that evening to realize he was right. I was having an all-about-me *life*, because I had encouraged others to depend and rely on me to the point that it wasn't healthy—for any of us. Nor was it fair.

How often we needlessly, selfishly carry the burden alone—not allowing those who care for and love us to shoulder part of our load. How egotistical we must appear; how others must feel that we don't value them or trust them to help us resolve issues or fix problems. By 3 a.m. I had surrendered my hold on the weight I'd been dragging around.

> The LORD helps the fallen
> and lifts those bent beneath their loads. (PSALM 145:14)

Are you carrying a burden alone too?

SPREAD TOO THIN
An All-about-Me Life (Part Deux)

I don't know the key to success but the key to failure is trying to please everybody.
BILL COSBY

AFTER TOSSING and turning in bed the night after my meltdown, I awoke to a new day. And with a new attitude (after finally giving over my problem in the wee hours of the night).

I took our daughter, Shauna, up on her previous offer to play a bigger role in the family as we encourage Scott back to a healthy life. Because Scott doesn't drive and has limited opportunities for entertainment, she and her husband, Adam, saw to it that Scott got out more and spent more time with them at their house. Her unconditional love for Scott has proved to be far more motivational than anything I could ever say or do, and she loves being helpful to me.

I delegated major projects at work, those that originally I thought only I could do, to my team members. My previous efforts pale against the creativity and energy they're bringing to these projects.

I rearranged conference calls and my workload to allow me a more sane schedule, one in which I was not always running late. It seems to be totally illogical, but I'm actually accomplishing more, not less.

I forfeited my role as family social director. I found that other family members are happy to call and make a reservation for Sunday brunch.

Your wisdom and your knowledge, they have deluded you; For you have said in your heart, "I am, and there is no one besides me." (ISAIAH 47:10, NASB)

I know from experience that I cannot be all things to all people. And when I try—I fail them all. Instead of being light, energy, and a positive force to anyone, I become a drain. By spreading myself too thin, I had been making a mess of my relationships. Now, instead of being stressed that everyone needs me at once, I can truly glory in the blessing for *all* the people I love and who love me.

Are you choosing to live as everyone else's "center"? Have you said in your heart, "I am and there is no one besides me"? Maybe you haven't said it, but could you be living this out loud?

There was one *other* thing I did the morning after my meltdown. I made an appointment with my colorist. The next day, I spent twenty precious processing minutes under a heat lamp with nothing more than my solitary thoughts. This is why I'm a bottle blonde. Every six weeks, come rain or shine—it really *is* all about me!

SPREAD TOO THIN
The Sin of Multitasking

IS YOUR TYPICAL DAY best described as spinning plates, herding cats, and juggling knives, while simultaneously dancing *en pointe*? Yes, mine too.

Samuel Johnson wrote that "he who waits to do a great deal of good at once will never do anything." Well, clearly Sam wasn't a working mother! I *can* get everything done at once! But is getting stuff done the end game? Is ticking thirty-four action items off my to-do list the measure of a day well lived?

I confess. I am a bona fide, professional, ace multitasker. I can solve business dilemmas, arrange for home deliveries, cram for my Bible study, and work through family *opportunities*, all while running on my treadmill. It's not that I feel my roles are in conflict or that I'm overextended; on the contrary, I feel that having a multidimensional life is critical to my state of emotional health.

However, I fear that if I'm not careful, my hamster-wheel mind will fail to give the important elements of my life the focused time each deserves. If multitasking keeps me from arriving at the best conclusion or investing my best energy in those people and projects that really matter, then my state of constant hum is no longer a positive but a negative. For this reason, I no longer consider this skill and state of mind an attribute, but a character flaw. Actually, I'm beginning to think that *my* multitasking might even be sinful!

I'm afraid we often confuse being busy with being fulfilled; we have placed more value on doing more than doing with excellence; and we have aligned our days with being productive rather than living with purpose.

Sin is no longer your master, for you no longer live under the requirements of the law. Instead, you live under the freedom of God's grace. (ROMANS 6:14)

If you're fulfilled, doing an excellent job, and living a purposeful life—congratulations! You pass the test.

However, if you're like me—busy and productive, but with a to-do list that never ends . . . well, you might be suffering from multitasking too.

SPREAD TOO THIN
The Sin of Multitasking (Part Deux)

We should readjust our priorities to be proud not of how much we get done but what we're able to achieve with a sense of enjoyment.[1] ALEXANDRA STODDARD

MULTITASKING, as defined by *Merriam-Webster's*, is the concurrent performance of several jobs by a computer.[2] So here's the problem! Multitasking isn't something that was even designed for us; it's a function of a computer—not a *human being*. No wonder we're spread too thin. We need a reboot.

A life well lived is clearly a life lived with thoughtfulness. So in order to harness my tendency toward multitasking, I now plan my day knowing that I will reflect back on how I invested my fixed time and energy. The helmet of protection against my sin of multitasking is knowing that, at the end of each day, I will ask myself these questions:

- What did I accomplish today that brought me great satisfaction?
- Specifically, what was one thing I delighted in?

- What did I accomplish today that was excellent?
- What did I do to the very best of my ability that I am proud of?

- What did I accomplish today that will have a profound effect on another human being?
- What did I do today that is bigger than me and my personal agenda?

I pray that God, the source of hope, will fill you completely with joy and peace because you trust in him. Then you will overflow with confident hope through the power of the Holy Spirit. (ROMANS 15:13)

Doing less could mean more—not only for others but for you. Focus your attention on the few things that will really matter at the end of the day: your personal delight, your achievement of excellence, and your contribution to other people.

SPREAD TOO THIN
Positive Thoughts

I'M OFTEN SPREAD too thin—not because of my workload, to-do list, demands from my family, or volunteer work, but from sheer brain overload caused by the negative voices in my head.

We don't have to be diagnosed with schizophrenia to know that we deal with a barrage of nasty voices that spread us too thin. Things we literally make up, conclusions we jump to, and fantasy "showdowns" we have to *set the record straight*. I know you know what I'm talking about: the articulate positioning, perfect timing, and final zinger you "share" with that person who harmed you; the venting that happens *over and over and over*—but only in your head.

Spending time dwelling on hurts, wrongs, and misfortunes is a waste of time. How many hours each week do we squander, pondering how we've been wronged and how we should defend our honor? Consider the outcome if we took that same amount of time and did something useful with it. Like maybe read a book; call someone who makes us laugh; listen to upbeat music; or better yet—pray. Imagine the positive energy we would gain by putting a stop to our negative thinking.

When I fixate on something hurtful someone has said or done (or hasn't said or hasn't done), my spirit is drained. My enthusiasm, loveliness, and *spunk* are nowhere to be found. This lack of positive life force only hurts those who *haven't* wronged me. How unfair is that?

Starting a quarrel is like opening a floodgate,
  so stop before a dispute breaks out. (PROVERBS 17:14)

But when I purposefully replace my brooding thoughts with positive observations, I am joyful; I am at peace; and I can only imagine I am a lot more fun and engaging to be around. To purposefully transform my thoughts I have to first recognize that I am in a negative state of mind. Then, I take a few minutes to count just a few of my *hundreds of blessings* to move myself out of my pity-me party. No, it's not always easy, and it typically requires me to be conscious of my thoughts and diligent in my actions. But the effort is worth it.

It's time to choose the positive over the negative. Put a stop to those fantasy showdowns and replace them with a power walk, a good tune, or something that makes you giggle. Don't waste another minute listening to those nasty voices. You're spread too thin as it is.

SPREAD TOO THIN
The Disappearing Act

I KNEW I was spread too thin before my meltdown in the car. I had been fantasizing for months about taking a sabbatical because I knew in my heart that I was burned out. I knew I needed to spend time cocooning.

A few years before, I had learned about cocooning from my former pastor. I had adopted the process, leaving home every twelve months (for a period between a few days and a week) to read and study, rest, dream, and plan in order to hear God's calling—and to be prepared to take action.

This time, because I was so burned out, I elected to take a monthlong recess from the office. While some might go to a spa or on a Caribbean vacation, I elected to stay home during this cocooning event to work on my three Rs: resting, renewal, and rededication. But I quickly realized I was rusty on all three! My first challenge: relearning to rest.

Resting. We're not very good at this, are we? We get one hour at home, alone, and what do we do? Start busying ourselves in the name of productivity. Are we bored? Or could we actually fear time alone with our thoughts? Quiet time is a requirement to renewing one's mind, body, and soul, but I found myself in the first two weeks of my "holiday" keeping the same pace I had when I was heading into the office. It finally dawned on me, about eight days into this intermission, that I would need to *plan* my rest as I plan anything else of importance to me.

So, a question for you: when was the last time you had eight continuous hours of shut-eye? When cocooning, I am one of the chosen few who gets a full night's rest, because I plan it. Are you burned out too? I feel safe in prescribing rest for you. Easy to say, hard to do. Yet I learned during my month of cocooning that our lack of sleep is less about available sleeping hours and more about our unwillingness to make sleep a priority.

Once rested, it's amazing how our rewired minds can process information much more clearly. And it's not just sleep that refreshes us. While cocooning, I also learned to rest from

people—my social calendar was closed;
problem solving—the focus was listening for God's will for me, not trying to solve everyone else's problems;
spending—shopping sprees are not part of the cocooning process.

Those who live in the shelter of the Most High
will find rest in the shadow of the Almighty. (PSALM 91:1)

Are you spread too thin? Before you disappear for good, consider a few days of cocooning. And if you're a mommy with kiddos still bouncing about the house, just hide in the closet for fifteen minutes. A break is a break.

SPREAD TOO THIN
The Disappearing Act (Part Deux)

REST IS THE mind-and-body stage of cocooning. During the first couple of weeks, I had rested my mind from thinking and then begun filling it with new perspectives by reading books and other material recommended to me. Once my foggy state of mind began to clear and my hormones began to stabilize, it was time to begin the more formal process of cocooning. The heart work came next: it was time to renew.

During the renewal cycle, I reflected on what was working in my life and what was not. As I thought back on the past twelve months and considered those things that worked well in our marriage, with our finances, in our business, and in our family, I knew what actions I wanted to repeat. Likewise, I found some room for improvement in every area of life. So the assessment also allowed me to consider those things that didn't work.

Next I considered the only two things I can control—my thoughts and my actions. How was I doing? This part of the renewal process is always hard for me, because I quickly realize that I often do not live a life of grace. When I'm spread too thin, I tend to become harsh and judgmental.

When renewing our hearts, we must be gentle with ourselves; after all, no one is perfect. At the same time, to really make positive changes we must be honest so we can avoid repeating mistakes. Something as simple as acknowledging an unhealthy pattern or reaction can be a powerful tool in stopping the insanity of repeated mistakes.

Life assessment is not something most of us do without being prompted, but it is critical to intentionally living the life God has called you to live. When you're so overwhelmed that you can no longer extend grace to others, it's time for a break.

Since you judge others for doing these things, why do you think you can avoid God's judgment when you do the same things? Don't you see how wonderfully kind, tolerant, and patient God is with you? (ROMANS 2:3-4)

Are you constantly disappointed by others? Are your expectations so high that when they fail, you judge them harshly? If you're slow to forgive and move on, you might need to disappear for a few days to reflect on the grace that's been extended to *you.*

SPREAD TOO THIN
The Disappearing Act (Part Trois)

Decide that you want it more than you are afraid of it.   BILL COSBY

THE ASSESSMENT STAGE was only part one of renewing my heart. And, for me, it was actually the hardest part of cocooning. After resting, reading, and assessing, I was ready to get on with my cocooning process—dreaming. Big honkin' Barbie-pink dreams. Like we had as little girls. You know the one . . . where we come bouncing to the door, our long beautiful blonde hair falling perfectly to the small of our back as our gorgeous hunk of a boyfriend sporting a cardigan and perfect white teeth sweeps us off our feet to drive us in his racy Corvette to our future home—the two-story pink dream house. Yeah. That one.

What was your last dream? To graduate from college? To get married? To have children? To buy a home? Yeah. I thought so. You're rusty too. I think women get so busy with the nits and nats of life that we fail to be still and allow God to fill our minds with possibilities. That's why I think the part of cocooning God must really love comes when you're finally quiet enough to hear him. You see, when you pray for his guidance and wisdom, you find that most of those "harebrained" ideas you came up with are actually his.

For example, I opened a marketing consulting firm in 1994, and from day one, it was an instant success. Where did I get such a brilliant idea? Sitting in church, asking God to guide me to find a way to balance my professional career and talents with the needs of my family.

Another dream I had while cocooning was of having a close relationship with my adult children and a family unit that continued to thrive after they left home. God showed me how to do it.

And this book—another dream God laid on my heart while I was cocooning several years ago. I thought it pretty strange, not being a writer or having anything to say, that I would dream of having a book published. But here it is. A dream come true.

> *Trust in the LORD and do good.*
>   *Then you will live safely in the land and prosper.*
> *Take delight in the LORD,*
>   *and he will give you your heart's desires.* (PSALM 37:3-4)

So, when was the last time you dreamed big honkin' Barbie-pink dreams? It might be time to be still and listen and allow the Lord to fertilize your imagination.

SPREAD TOO THIN
The Disappearing Act (Part Quatre)

An unexamined life is not worth living.   SOCRATES

THE LAST PHASE of cocooning for me, once my dreams are well documented, is the planning stage. I develop a three-step plan for each of my dreams as a way to begin bringing them to fruition. While some people might write detailed journals that rival a Harvard business plan, I opt for an easy, 1-2-3 outline of the next steps I need to take. These action plans aren't always actionable; sometimes they will sit idle for years at a time.

After my planning, it's time to rededicate my life and soul. I give my dreams over to God, thanking him for the opportunity to play a role in his master plan. I now realize that this time of prayer and rededication is the point of the cocooning.

Interestingly, this culmination of the cocooning process came as a surprise to me. I couldn't have articulated my purpose in taking such a luxurious extended break from work, but today I know I was looking for rededication even more than rest or renewal.

During the first twenty-one days of this retreat, I made a new commitment to my spiritual growth and development; I am more deeply committed than ever to my husband and my precious family; and I look forward to new and wonderful adventures in my professional life. I have to be honest with you—it had been a couple of years since I had last rededicated my mind, body, and soul to higher purposes.

> *And God will generously provide all you need. Then you will always have everything you need and plenty left over to share with others.*
> (2 CORINTHIANS 9:8)

I know that not everyone can enjoy a thirty-day hiatus from work. I've been a professional for over twenty years, and this was a first for me. But I do know that you can choose to take a couple of days (no, you can't do this while visiting Disneyland with the family) to consider mastering the three Rs of rest, renewal, and rededication.

SPREAD TOO THIN
Time and Money

We make a living by what we get, but we make a life by what we give.
NORMAN MACEWAN

IF THERE'S ONE THING we all have in common—regardless of age, income, or profession—it is that we are all spread too thin when it comes to time and money. Especially when it comes to investing our volunteer time or our cash in organizations and charities.

Women are hardwired to care deeply, and we are inspired to bring about change for our children and grandchildren. But the problem comes when we take our many passions and spread them too thin—making little difference to any one cause. Or worse, we fail to invest in the programs we care about the most. I know because my own charitable giving has been spread too thin.

Not long ago, as the guest of my financial advisor, Carol Meyer, I attended an event called The Power of the Purse, sponsored by the Dallas Women's Foundation and underwritten by Merrill Lynch. The topic: women in philanthropy.

This event was an eye-opener for me. I realized my giving was often more what one presenter called an "honored obligation" than a "passionate investment" to create change. My honored obligations were competing with my passions, and more often than not, those things I felt "required" to give to often won out over the things I cared most deeply about.

Both men and women came, all whose hearts were willing. They brought to the LORD their offerings of gold—brooches, earrings, rings from their fingers, and necklaces. They presented gold objects of every kind as a special offering to the LORD. (EXODUS 35:22)

I realized it was time to give as much consideration to *why* I was giving as to *how much*. In fact, it was essential if I wanted my gifts of time and money to matter, not just to others, but to me.

SPREAD TOO THIN
Time and Money (Part Deux)

The man who dies rich dies disgraced.   ANDREW CARNEGIE

AT THE POWER OF THE PURSE event I learned important questions to ask myself to help me prioritize where to give.

- What bothers you?
- Are you giving to organizations that can bring about change to those issues that concern you the most?
- What do you want to see changed in your lifetime?
- Can the organization, given time and money, effect the change?
- What are your passions?
- Can you link your passion to what bothers you?

The second set of questions empowered me to track the results of those gifts:

- How do you determine if the charity will be a good steward of your gift?
- How do you ensure they are managing their resources well?
- How do they measure the results of the services they deliver?
- How do you shift your gifts when your concerns evolve over time?

Over the past couple of years, Steve and I have shifted our giving—aligning it to those causes we feel impact our society. By more thoughtfully investing in organizations we believe in, our giving is more than cheerful—we're downright giddy when we write the check.

So what bothers me? The fact that mentally ill people often turn to drugs to self-medicate, leaving them homeless. How can I contribute in a meaningful way? Write a book.

As I mentioned in the introduction, 50 percent of my profits from this book will go directly to LifeNet, a nonprofit organization that provides mental and emotional services, substance abuse programs, housing, food, and jobs to "the least of these" in Dallas. Aligning my God-given dream of writing a book with a God-given call to help the homeless seems like a God-given solution to stretching my money, which is spread too thin. Isn't it just amazing how God provides?

You must each decide in your heart how much to give. And don't give reluctantly or in response to pressure. (2 CORINTHIANS 9:7)

Are you giving . . . *cheerfully?*

SPREAD TOO THIN
Time and Money (Part Trois)

THE CONCEPT OF "checkbook" philanthropy—writing lots of small checks without having a deep concern for the cause—was raised by more than one speaker at the conference. That made me think as much about *why* I give as *how* I give.

One day, as I was visiting with the vice president of marketing for LifeNet, he mentioned in passing that, due to a temporary cash flow challenge, the organization was no longer providing coffee for the caseworkers, doctors, nurses, or other staff. I heard him when he said it—and then I heard his words echo in my ears every morning for the next five days as I walked into our office kitchen and poured myself my third cup of Starbucks. It was like being haunted by the ghost of Christmas past.

Finally, I marched down the hall to Steve and told him that the good people up the road, who were working for wages far below what they could earn in other fields, were sitting in their offices without coffee because the organization refused to cut back on any of the services for their needy clients. Steve said, "Call Ross now. Tell him I am writing a check—we're calling it the Coffee Grant."

Give, and you will receive. Your gift will return to you in full—pressed down, shaken together to make room for more, running over, and poured into your lap. The amount you give will determine the amount you get back. (LUKE 6:38)

A week later, Steve and I received a poster-sized, custom thank-you card with a picture of the staff at LifeNet lined up for their coffee and tea. That card is invaluable to us. Our gift was returned in smiling faces!

We can't be all things to all people, and when we try, we fail to be important to anyone. I believe the same holds true of our charitable giving. If your time and money are spread too thin, determine whether you're "passionately investing" in those charities that can bring about change. I bet that will make your giving so much sweeter!

SPREAD TOO THIN

FATHER GOD, I hear you speaking to me and I ask that you teach me to

- [ ] recognize when I'm spread too thin;
- [ ] delegate and then let go;
- [ ] put multitasking in perspective;
- [ ] focus on those few things that really matter;
- [ ] replace my brooding and negative thoughts with positive ones;
- [ ] rest my mind, my social calendar, and my pocketbook;
- [ ] renew my heart;
- [ ] dream, again;
- [ ] rededicate my life and dreams to you;
- [ ] be a more thoughtful steward of my time and money.

ACTIONS I WILL TAKE:

Example: I will rest my mind, my social calendar, and my pocketbook by reserving Sunday as a true day of rest. No work. No parties. No shopping.

1. _____

2. _____

3. _____

God of peace, I pray that you will teach me to slow down and to rest in knowing that you're in control. Thank you for teaching me to re-center on those few things that matter. Amen.

LIVING INTENTIONALLY

The wise don't expect to find life worth living; they make it that way. ANONYMOUS

OVER THE PAST several months, I've found truth in some counterintuitive principles. Take this one for example: *To get more done—stop working.*

Once I shortened my workday, I began to accomplish more. By limiting my working hours, I became both more focused and more efficient, and the result is a far more productive workday. And not only do I complete a greater volume of work, the quality of my labor investment has improved as well. *Stop working* to get more done. Who woulda' thought?

I think the concept of living intentionally is a bit counterintuitive too. Although many of us grasp the big picture, sometimes we're a bit foggy on how best to go about living *on purpose* rather than just having life happen to us.

So, if you're up for it, we're going to dig in on the topic of *living intentionally*. The counterintuitive principles will include:

1. Fake it
2. Scrap your priorities
3. Stay behind
4. Break a hip
5. Whine
6. Be confused
7. Disappoint someone
8. Spend it all today

No, these are not the topics you usually find in a self-help book, but I hope as we delve into them you'll be able to recognize and live out some truths of living intentionally.

I pray that your hearts will be flooded with light so that you can understand the confident hope he has given to those he called—his holy people who are his rich and glorious inheritance. (EPHESIANS 1:18)

LIVING INTENTIONALLY
Fake It

The only normal people are the ones you don't know very well.   JOE ANCIS

HERE'S A NOVEL IDEA for some of us: Fake it for a change. Be yourself.

I have a darling child in my life named Samantha who, I have no doubt, you will someday watch as she accepts her Academy Award for Best Actress. At four years old, this little gal can *become* a character faster than you can load a DVD. She changes from costume to costume, scene to scene, accent to accent, as she entertains you with her incredible wit and conviction (on cue). But Samantha knows who she is when she takes off her Cinderella dress. She doesn't stay in character so long that she forgets who she really is. Unfortunately, many of us do. We have put on an act for so many years that we're out of touch with our authentic selves.

I have lived my life in two very different worlds, both of which I am deeply grateful for. It's because I have lived in these two worlds that I can state, as fact, that I know there are at least six groups of women who suffer from an inability to be genuine. They are (in no particular order):

- women who live in an upper socioeconomic class: rich girls
- women who live in depressed financial circumstances: poor girls
- women who aggressively climb the corporate ladder: working girls
- women who invest their hearts and souls in the raising of their children: mommy girls
- women who spend their Sunday mornings in church: good girls
- women who spend their Sunday mornings in some Joe's (what's his last name?) bed: bad girls

Did I leave anyone out? Nope. I think this about covers us all.

Being a totally authentic person is absolutely frightening for some of us. It means we can't hide behind a fantasy to guard our heart. It might mean becoming transparent, which equates to putting away the status; the piety; the Botox; the executive title; the perfect kids; the money; the reckless behavior; the Gucci bag. . . . It means we have to forfeit our props so that our real character can be known.

In his kindness God called you to share in his eternal glory by means of Christ Jesus. So after you have suffered a little while, he will restore, support, and strengthen you, and he will place you on a firm foundation. (1 PETER 5:10)

Are you ready for your true self to be restored?
I hope you will consider a coming-out party.

LIVING INTENTIONALLY
Fake It (Part Deux)

We are what we believe we are.   C. S. LEWIS

THE PROBLEM IS we want to be accepted. We want to be admired. We fear ridicule—to our faces or behind our backs. Thus we create a fictional character that we believe is more engaging and attractive than our true self. But she's not; she's just the opposite. The fictional character we create is usually plastic and shallow, and an authentic woman can smell a fake before her first hello.

If you've been in character too long, you may have forgotten how to fake it and be yourself. If that's the case, here are my three best tips:

Reveal: Tell others something about yourself that is deprecating but humorous. Others love to hear that you're not perfect, that you make stupid mistakes, and that you don't take yourself so seriously that you can't laugh at your own nuttiness.

Respond: Authentic people listen with their hearts and respond with their eyes. Sometimes simple eye contact alone says a thousand words. The eyes are indeed the window to the soul.

Relax: Get comfortable. A few years ago, I led a women's Bible study. As a matter of course, we took off our shoes during our meetings. Pedicure or no, together we walked barefoot through the book of Daniel—and it was amazing to watch the walls come down when the heels were kicked off.

> *But you belong to God, my dear children. You have already won a victory over those people, because the Spirit who lives in you is greater than the spirit who lives in the world.* (1 JOHN 4:4)

So who do you believe you are? Is she a different woman than you allow others to know? If you've been in character too long, you may have forgotten how to fake it and be yourself.

You can't live intentionally until you fake it; try being yourself for a change.

LIVING INTENTIONALLY
Scrap Your Priorities

THE SUCCESS and prosperity we enjoy in this great country have come at the expense of millions of men and women who, over the past two hundred and thirty-four years, refused to give up. We're a tribe of dogmatic individuals who strive 24-7 to have it all. We are not sissies. But as a society we haven't a clue how to live intentionally because we don't know when to throw in the towel.

That phrase comes from the sport of boxing. When the fighter is just too exhausted to continue and his coach realizes he can't succeed, the coach throws a towel into the ring to indicate that the fight is over. I love the imagery here—the boxer, too close to his own struggle, doesn't make the call, but his coach, who sees the situation objectively, makes the decision for him. The priority to win is scrapped to fulfill the priority to live. I think to live intentionally we have to know when to throw in the towel—when to scrap some of our priorities—and rarely can we make this call on our own.

One of the most popular Truth Nugget series I have written was the one titled "Spread Too Thin." The response from women, coast to coast, in all stages of life was overwhelming. But the single most-oft repeated message was, "My husband has been telling me this for years." And all of these women wondered why their husbands or boyfriends could see what they couldn't.

Like the boxing coach, sometimes your best friend or your partner can see when you've put yourself in a position where you can't possibly succeed at living; they can see that you're only existing.

> Trust in the LORD with all your heart;
>   do not depend on your own understanding.
> Seek his will in all you do,
>   and he will show you which path to take. (PROVERBS 3:5-6)

Can you have it all? Of course you can! Just not *every* day. And not in *every* life stage.

LIVING INTENTIONALLY
Scrap Your Priorities (Part Deux)

The key is not to prioritize what's on your schedule, but to schedule your priorities.
STEPHEN R. COVEY

IF YOU'RE READING this book and know in your heart you're not living intentionally, there's an excellent chance that your priorities are out of whack. Assess your situation to determine what self-imposed duties are robbing you of joy. Then develop a vision and a plan to get to the place where you're experiencing life, not just moving from task to task. It's a destination worth planning for, and if you won't listen to your significant other, maybe you'll take a tip from your girlfriend (me).

Following are just a few of the priorities I scrapped when I was raising children, building a career, and dealing with a three-hour daily commute:

- *Exercise.* I gained fifteen pounds as I climbed the corporate ladder. I sacrificed a firm fanny for a firm foundation for my career.
- *Dinner.* To complement my healthy lifestyle of no exercise, we picked up fast food two nights a week. Not an organic vegetable on the table, but we enjoyed our meals together at the kitchen table every night. Spinach was sacrificed for quality time with the family.
- *Laundry.* I bought pink towels for Shauna and blue towels for Scott and taught them both to do their own laundry at the ages of eleven and fourteen. If they didn't wash it, they wore it dirty. Saturday became a fun day, not a work day—and no one turned me in to Child Protective Services.
- *Bible study.* I traded my daily Bible study for Christian CDs and books on tape during my long commute, to gain thirty precious minutes of sleep. I'm pretty sure Jesus still loved me.
- *Continued self-development.* My continued learning consisted of helping with science projects, slogging through eighth-grade algebra, and keeping up with the teen lingo. Self-development was sacrificed for self-preservation.

So think clearly and exercise self-control. Look forward to the gracious salvation that will come to you when Jesus Christ is revealed to the world.
(1 PETER 1:13)

You're in the ring, sweat dripping from your brow. You feel the blow. Are you down for the count? It might be time to throw in the towel.

LIVING INTENTIONALLY
Stay Behind

MOST MOTIVATIONAL SPEAKERS, self-help gurus, and professional mentors will tell you that to live a successful life, you must be aggressive and "get out front." I think this is flawed thinking. If you really want to live a life of difference, get behind someone who knows the track.

Several months ago, Steve and I took up bicycling. Most weekends we log between thirty and fifty miles on the trails around Dallas atop our sleek silver street bikes (complete with riding gear—it's *so* about the outfit). Sometimes my confidence kicks in and I take the lead, but most of the time, I hang back. I've found there are some significant benefits to staying behind.

More knowledgeable about the sport and more familiar with the course, Steve serves as my guide. Often I hang back several feet, watching him zig and zag—alerted in advance that the path is about to become more difficult to navigate or that a gaggle of marathoners has congregated. He provides a "heads up" when the path becomes tricky and it's time to put on the brakes. Do you allow someone to help you navigate the potholes? Or are you heading toward a wipeout? Girlfriend, ask for direction or get behind someone who has successfully dealt with life's blows; such a person makes a great trail guide.

There's a common practice in bicycle racing known as drafting that provides a perfect picture of what I mean. When you are drafting, you are following only inches behind the lead biker's back tire (yes, this can be disaster with one wrong move by either of you—which, of course, is a Truth Nugget topic for another time). The lead biker faces the resistance, allowing you to keep up while exerting only a fraction of the energy.

The godly offer good counsel;
*   they teach right from wrong.*
They have made God's law their own,
*   so they will never slip from his path.* (PSALM 37:30-31)

When the winds are blowing hard in life, many high achievers try to face it alone. How often do you let someone block the headwind for you? Girlfriend, allow someone the privilege of helping you face your adversity—you'll both be better for the experience.

LIVING INTENTIONALLY
Stay Behind (Part Deux)

WHEN WE'RE CYCLING and Steve's out front, he's usually cookin'—thus, I have to pedal like there's no tomorrow just to keep up. But his pace makes me a better athlete (although I'm not so sure his Speedy Gonzales impersonation is doing much for our marriage). He sets goals for us. He encourages me to make it to the next mile marker.

So who is your personal life trainer? Who's pushing you to become a better, stronger, wiser, more balanced person? Get behind someone who can inspire and motivate you. If you get too comfortable with this scenic ride of life, you're going to miss out on the adventure.

Self-reliance is important, but to live intentionally, you need to surround yourself with quality people—people who are wise because of experience gained; honorable people who are strong in character and who can provide you a buffer zone when you're tired; and people who can be objective enough with you to say, "Get your fanny in gear." Even as a grown-up, you're still only as good as the company you keep.

In the sport of tennis, the athlete is encouraged to find an opponent who is ranked higher (thus better at the game) to practice with. While I'm sure it is discouraging to lose every week, I completely understand the concept. In order to reach the next level, you need someone who has played this game before to push you to become the champion you can be.

In contrast, if you have chosen a weaker opponent or partner to practice with just to appear to be the winner, you're really only cheating yourself. It is the same in biking. And in life.

> Walk with the wise and become wise;
> associate with fools and get in trouble. (PROVERBS 13:20)

But just a quick note of caution to you as you're riding around the track of life: while you're biking behind those who are motivating you, don't forget that someone may be on your back wheel too.

We're in this race together.

LIVING INTENTIONALLY
Break a Hip

Anyone who has never made a mistake has never tried anything new.
ALBERT EINSTEIN

IT ALL HAPPENED in slow motion. I could feel myself falling, but for the life of me, I couldn't catch myself. I was going down, and I was going down hard. Lying on the ground, I was bewildered, frustrated—and embarrassed. And I was mad at the world.

No, I didn't trip. This was a full-fledged, self-induced fall. I fell off my bicycle while learning how to "clip in."

To take my bicycling to the next level, Steve introduced me to the concept of clipping in. In order to optimize the strength and power of the quadriceps and glutes, many bikers buy a unique type of shoe that actually attaches to specially designed pedals. The problem is, it's not natural! It's tricky to get started and almost impossible to stop—without the help of asphalt. So there I was, starting, stopping, and falling. After three tries, my right hip looked like hamburger meat!

Clipping in, like living intentionally, is not for sissies, those afraid of failure, or those who are willing to pass on the fabulous adventures that come with optimizing life. Counterintuitive to conventional wisdom that says play it safe and you'll live happily ever after, I believe we need to go out on a limb and be willing to fall a time or two if we want to live intentionally.

I have met many women who have so much to offer but fail to take their skills and talents to the next level. As a result, they never enjoy the abundant life God intended for them. When the road gets hard, obstacles get in our way, or we fail, we tend to say, "Oh, it must not be God's will." *Really?*

How do you know that he didn't intend for you to have to work hard, fail, try again, practice, and dedicate yourself to a dream? Why do you think it should always be easy to be in the middle of his will?

> *Put your hope in the LORD.*
> *Travel steadily along his path.*
> *He will honor you by giving you the land.*
> *You will see the wicked destroyed.* (PSALM 37:34)

I fell three times and it hurt like the dickens but know what? It was not God's will that I not succeed—it was God's will that I keep trying and stop being a sissy.

LIVING INTENTIONALLY
Break a Hip (Part Deux)

Without risk, faith is an impossibility. SØREN KIERKEGAARD

OUR SOCIETY has us all paralyzed with fear that we're going to get hurt—or worse, fail and then be embarrassed. Well, sometimes we might. But to truly experience life rather than just tick down the days until we die, we have to be willing to fail; to fall; and to succeed. To live intentionally means we take risks while walking in faith, allowing life's surprises to mold us into interesting people rather than bitter, boring ones. I'm not saying you should be reckless: I'd hate to hear that you went out Saturday night and got a Harley tattoo. But I am saying that many of us miss out on rich experiences because we're not willing to explore new things.

So what new experiences might make life a little more flavorful this month?

Go to a play.
Travel someplace new.
Research a new line of work or industry.
Take dancing lessons.
Go on a mission or humanitarian trip.
Take golf lessons.
Join a choir.
Go to the symphony.
Take an art class.
Try tennis.
Go back to college (or go for the first time).
Join a book club.
Take up bicycling.

Try just one new thing. You don't have to adopt it as a lifestyle. You only have to adopt the philosophy of experimenting, with the understanding that it's okay to fall.

For every child of God defeats this evil world, and we achieve this victory through our faith. (1 JOHN 5:4)

Girlfriend, I don't know about you, but I don't want to be ninety-three and gray, telling a sad story about breaking a hip as I fell on the way to the bathroom. I want a tale of adventure, and I want it now . . . complete with the success. Yes, my failures (and bruises) were all worth it; clipping in has taken my cycling to a whole new level. And my falls made the success all the sweeter.

LIVING INTENTIONALLY
Whine

"IF YOU KEEP that up, I'm going to give you something to *really* cry about!" Yes, we all heard those biting words from our mothers and fathers fed up with our carrying on. But let's be honest: whining isn't just a youthful exercise. When was the last time you thought:

- This weather is crummy.
- The traffic is ridiculous.
- The kids don't call.

Whining. That's what I was doing not long ago. I spent precious moments complaining about the most minute things.

When I caught myself, I felt ashamed. What was going on that was really all that bad? Summer heat on a November day? But then, just as my mother promised, I got something to really whine about.

At the time, Shauna was pregnant with our first grandbaby and due to deliver on January 11—but on Thanksgiving Day, she went into premature labor. She spent two weeks in the hospital, pumped full of drugs on bed rest. We were all on pins and needles as she tried to keep her little critter in the oven a few more weeks.

When Shauna did go into labor on December 7, her emergency C-section and the baby's resuscitation was nothing short of pure drama. As we prayed through the night for Shauna's recovery and the health of our sweet granddaughter, Ava, I realized I had not a complaint in the world. I had something new to refocus my attention.

Your parents might drive you nuts. Your job might be the pits. Your husband might not be the most romantic or the best gift giver. But really, is life all that bad?

I think to live life intentionally we must have a really good whine every now and then. Complain (to yourself, please) for no less than sixty minutes, once a month, about the lousy hand you've been dealt or the unfairness of it all. Get it out. Rant and rave. Wave your hands. Stomp your feet. And then I want you to *drop it*. Or else you might get challenges much bigger than a bad hair day to distract you from your personal pity party.

> *Dear friends, don't be surprised at the fiery trials you are going through, as if something strange were happening to you. Instead, be very glad—for these trials make you partners with Christ in his suffering, so that you will have the wonderful joy of seeing his glory when it is revealed to all the world.*
> (1 PETER 4:12-13)

As I sit here this afternoon with baby Ava in my arms, I have no complaints. Just pure gratitude for the gift of life, sweet family and friends, and second chances to take in the miracle of life.

LIVING INTENTIONALLY
Be Confused

DON'T BE A flip-flopper. Make up your mind. Stick with your story.

We're told that to be people of influence we must dig in our position and stay the course.

Hogwash.

I think to live intentionally we must be confused. Because confusion, coupled with a compass, ultimately results in personal clarity.

At the tender age of sixteen, I took marriage vows before God and man, and I took them seriously. Two years later, I began asking the questions I should have asked before the wedding. *Are we really "one"? What principles and philosophies do we share that will bind us for the rest of our lives?* Frightened and disappointed, I was failing miserably in the relationship. Confusion became my constant companion for nearly eight more years until, unfortunately, the marriage finally failed.

Confusion in marriage can sometimes result in separation, but it doesn't have to. I think that a state of confusion can actually be healthy at times. Some relationships and aspects of a relationship "need" to die in order for a new stronger union to be resurrected. Confusion in marriage, when coupled with the compass of counseling and communication, can lead to renewed commitment. But first a couple has to have the courage to admit they're confused and the ability to properly communicate the source of the confusion. And they have to have a good imagination to envision what could be.

Dear brothers and sisters, when troubles come your way, consider it an opportunity for great joy. For you know that when your faith is tested, your endurance has a chance to grow. So let it grow, for when your endurance is fully developed, you will be perfect and complete, needing nothing. (JAMES 1:2-4)

Are you confused? Your willingness to shine a new light on your partnership might be the best thing that ever happened to your marriage. Imagine finding out that there's more than just those two kids that bind you together. Ahhhhh. Living · intentionally—together.

LIVING INTENTIONALLY
Be Confused (Part Deux)

I'D LIKE TO SAY that I've never been confused about my spiritual beliefs. But that wouldn't be true.

I accepted Christ at the innocent age of ten (back in 1969, fourth graders were still innocent) during my Wednesday evening Bible study course called Girls Auxiliary. As my leader prayed, I made a commitment to follow Christ. Having a treasured secret, I didn't share with Mrs. McBroom or my classmates that I had just made the single most important decision of my life. Nor did I tell my parents—at least not right away.

Arriving home, I went straight to the bathroom (notice the word *the*—one bathroom, four people—who knows how we made that work), locked the door, and drew my bath. Singing all three stanzas of "I've got that joy, joy, joy, joy down in my heart" I completed my personal praise and worship service with my baptism. I said aloud, "I baptize thee my sister Margaret Ellen Haralson in the name of the Father, the Son, and the Holy Spirit" (I'd seen these baptisms a time or two—so I was pretty sure I had my lines right). Rinsing the shampoo from my hair I was confident that I had been cleansed of the white rock dust from our front road *and* my sins.

My parents? Well, yes I'm sure they were amused when I sprang forth from the bathroom wrapped in towels, proclaiming in a loud voice "I've been saved." And yes . . . they required I participate in proper baptism by our minister. But for me—it was all for show. The real one was done in the bathtub.

So you can imagine my shock when in my midtwenties a good friend of mine challenged me on my spiritual beliefs. "Where did you get these facts? How do you know this is true? *Why* do you believe this?" The girl with all the answers (me) was left speechless. Even with my profound conviction and personal experience, I couldn't tell my friend the *why* behind my faith. I only knew that I believed what I believed because I had always been told to believe it.

As her challenge morphed into my confusion, I sought answers. I began to question everything and journeyed not just toward a confirmation of my belief system but an even deeper renewal. I realized, as I dared to question the tenets of my faith, that my confusion ultimately allowed me to live my beliefs more intentionally.

If the Son sets you free, you are truly free. (JOHN 8:36)

Are you confused? That's okay. Your willingness to shine a new light on your belief system might be the best thing that ever happened to your relationship with Christ. Imagine finding out that there's more than just rules and requirements—there's a relationship. Ahhhhh. Living intentionally—with him.

LIVING INTENTIONALLY
Be Confused (Part Trois)

HOMOSEXUALITY. Anyone confused about this one?

When I was in my midthirties, I had to face the reality that our son is gay. This didn't come as a complete surprise to either my husband or me. I had wondered about Scott's gender orientation for years; still, I hoped for a miracle. Every night for over ten years I prayed that "this cup would pass from him."

Nature or nurture? As his mom, I had a front row seat in the developing movie called "Scott's Life." Watching him in his size 3 Toughskins make a beeline for his sister's Barbie over his trucks and cars was only the first sign that he might be struggling with his gender identity. A little later, any sport involving a ball was treated with the same disdain as spinach; and well—he was a sweet, tender-hearted boy. To counter these inclinations, we enrolled him in contact sports, bought him manly boy toys, and encouraged him to "toughen up." But it didn't work. With every passing year, I became more sure the day was coming when he would tell us he was gay.

Condemned or forgiven? Well, here's where I struggled. My pastors and church friends clearly condemned homosexuality. But sometimes when they spoke about those who struggle with this tendency, I felt as if they were vilifying my sweet seven-year-old.

Conditional acceptance or unconditional love? Oh, have I ever flip-flopped on this one. Scott was fourteen the night we finally addressed the elephant in the room. I told Scott I loved him unconditionally—that if his eyes were purple and his hair was green, he'd still be my baby. But honestly, I flip-flopped. When he matured and became sexually active I had to set new boundaries; I shut things out and I cringed. It was a harsh awakening for me to realize that I love him, yes—but my ability to deal with this lifestyle is very conditional.

If you need wisdom, ask our generous God, and he will give it to you. He will not rebuke you for asking. (JAMES 1:5)

Are you confused about how to deal with your child's sexual orientation? I firmly believe that God was with us in our family's struggle, and it's okay if you are struggling too. Living intentionally is sometimes very complex.

LIVING INTENTIONALLY
Be Confused (Part Quatre)

True wisdom is to . . . change with good grace in changing circumstances.
ROBERT LOUIS STEVENSON

I GUESS I'M REALLY weird when it comes to politics. Rather than viewing flip-flopping as a negative, I find it refreshing to hear that politicians and voters consider new views and then are open-minded enough to admit they've taken a new position. At least I know they're thinking.

When I was in my midforties, I became confused about my position on all things political. I would make a fabulous senator, since I changed sides on everything from the war in Iraq to our city's position on the homeless. But my confusion brought clarity.

By reading, listening to commentary (both conservative and liberal), discerning facts from the press (as best one can), and being open to the fact that "I might not be right," I have arrived (for now) in a place where I feel comfortable holding to my own positions, not the popular opinion.

My point is this: in order to live intentionally, we must have the courage to be confused and be willing to carry a compass in the form of research and learning. We must desire to dig for the "why" behind our opinions. We must have the maturity to look beyond our closed minds and the independence to think for ourselves. And the stamina to do it all again. Because if we are truly wise, we must be willing to change our minds as the circumstances change.

In a time when our country is split red and blue, I wish we could, at least on the most important issues, become a bit more purple.

> *How wonderful to be wise,*
> *to analyze and interpret things.*
> *Wisdom lights up a person's face,*
> *softening its harshness.* (ECCLESIASTES 8:1)

Are you confused with politics? I sure hope so. Your willingness to shine a new light on the issues of the day might help us all find a middle ground of bipartisanship. Imagine a system where we address issues and get something done. Ahhhhh. Living intentionally—as one country under God.

LIVING INTENTIONALLY
Disappoint Someone

DO YOU SERVE OTHERS—either organizations or people—from your heart or your head?

If you're serving from your heart, you know it. Your investment of time and talent doesn't drain you—it acts like rocket fuel; you soar with a "done good" feeling. You gals who've figured this out can skip today's reading. (Just kidding. Don't you dare turn to tomorrow's entry.) However, if you're one of my girlfriends who feels obligated, burned out, or frustrated by your selfless service, today's devotional reading is just for you.

Self-sacrifice is not always a noble thing. Service rendered out of a sense of expectation or obligation rather than an expression of gratitude, talent, or love is rarely pleasing either to the soul of the recipient or the do-gooder; the service can actually have the opposite effect on our spirit. I recognized this in myself as I drove reluctantly to meetings or events, dreading the next two hours of selflessness.

For this reason, I believe it is important that we ensure that every good deed, every favor, and every act of service be done from the heart—not the head. This means, of course, that from time to time, in order to live intentionally, you will disappoint someone.

I have experience here.

I have found that high achievers not only expect a lot of themselves, but others often have unreasonable expectations of them too. Moral indignation flashes across the face (or worse, spews from the mouth) of the disappointed individual because I did not _____ (fill in the blank) the way the wounded party thought I would, I should, or I could. How selfish of me! Well, yes. That's the point.

In our world others constantly clamor for us to give more, do more, invest more, and allow more when there is little time for us, as individuals, to *be* more. To get ahead financially, we all know that we must pay ourselves first (in the form of savings). But few of us acknowledge that to achieve a well-balanced life, we must make the commitment to pay ourselves first in the form of *time* and to be extremely conscious of those we invest time with and for.

> Commit everything you do to the LORD.
> Trust him, and he will help you.
> He will make your innocence radiate like the dawn,
> and the justice of your cause will shine like the noonday sun.
> (PSALM 37:5-6)

If it takes you a half hour to spin up a positive attitude for your volunteer service and a half hour to relax your forced-smile muscles once you're home, you might be serving from the head. To live intentionally, you must serve only from the heart.

LIVING INTENTIONALLY
Disappoint Someone (Part Deux)

To refuse a request for just cause is as praiseworthy as to grant a request that is worthy. It is for this reason that the "no" of some people pleases more than the "yes" of others. A refusal accompanied by sweet words and a civil manner gives more satisfaction to a true heart than a favor given with bad grace. MARQUISE MAGDELEINE DE SABLÉ

SEVERAL YEARS AGO, a girlfriend told me that in addition to her COO position for a major corporation, she served as a board member for the city symphony; was the local chairwoman of fund-raising for not one, but two, of the largest nonprofits in the country; and was required to attend social, civic, or political functions nearly every night of the week. She wrote: "I'm exhausted. I'm miserable. I'm worn out."

Her glamorous, selfless life of service had resulted in burnout—not just toward the organizations she served, but toward life itself. My girlfriend realized she was not living intentionally because she didn't want to disappoint.

I am a huge proponent of service—to community, school, or church—and feel that as a collective society we could do a lot more than we do. But I don't think service should be left to just a few. And this is where high-achieving women often struggle to maintain balance. Because they *can* do it (and others haven't or won't), they feel obligated to jump in and get the job done. But service from obligation rarely fulfills and usually drains.

If your gift is serving others, serve them well.
(ROMANS 12:7)

Are you extending a favor or service with bad grace because you feel obligated to do so? Endeavor to serve those projects that are true to your heart's calling and say no to the rest. Yes, you will disappoint someone, but the service you do render will be a blessing—both for you and that special person on the receiving end. Now *that's* living intentionally.

LIVING INTENTIONALLY
Spend It All Today

When I stand before God at the end of my life, I would hope that I would not have a single bit of talent left, and could say, "I used everything you gave me." ERMA BOMBECK

WHAT'S IN YOUR ACCOUNT? Spend it all, every last penny. Today.

I can hear the shrieks of financial advisors from coast to coast. But I'm not talking about your bank account. I want to explore the more important things that we hide, hoard, and ignore—our talent, our network, and the impact we have on others.

I am a marketing gal. I'm not a writer or a motivational speaker. These are not what I consider my core strengths. So how did I end up writing a blog and speaking? I (finally) recognized that my talent is encouraging women through my ability to share my life experiences. Coupled with my courage to examine tough topics, I began writing my Truth Nuggets and speaking to inspire women to achieve balance and live intentionally. Never in a million years did I think these two somewhat nebulous talents would emerge in the form of a biweekly newsletter to thousands or this book. But they did. And I do not take these gifts for granted, nor will I waste them.

But what other talents should I be utilizing? According to the test I took after reading Marcus Buckingham's *Now, Discover Your Strengths*, I have the following gifts:

1. WOO (Winning Others Over)—I make a good first impression.
2. Relator—I naturally empathize with others.
3. Positivity—My glass is never half-empty.
4. Maximizer—I can get the most out of my projects and my team.
5. Activator—I don't procrastinate; I can get projects started quickly.[3]

Knowing what comes naturally to me has helped me clarify achievable goals. And understanding how I am hardwired has allowed me to leverage my talents in both my business and personal pursuits. God presents us with opportunities every single day to make a difference on this earth. Like Erma, I don't want to stand before him and whine, "Well, I wasn't sure if I could really do that. . . ." Yuk.

You are the light of the world—like a city on a hilltop that cannot be hidden. No one lights a lamp and then puts it under a basket. Instead, a lamp is placed on a stand, where it gives light to everyone in the house. In the same way, let your good deeds shine out for all to see, so that everyone will praise your heavenly Father. (MATTHEW 5:14-16)

Can you articulate your top five talents? Are you sharing them? Or are you hiding your light under a bushel? "This little light of mine, I'm gonna let it shine . . . let it shine, let it shine."

Spend your talent today. You might not get a tomorrow.

LIVING INTENTIONALLY
Spend It All Today (Part Deux)

Be a Lovecat: amass and share knowledge, amass and share your network and be compassionate.[4] TIM SANDERS

DO YOU KNOW someone who might be a great contact or friend to someone else?

Many of us waste our network, hoarding contacts in case we need a favor. I say spend your network on your friends and colleagues. Tim Sanders, in his book *Love Is the Killer App*, encourages us to use our network generously for the benefit of others. Some people understand this concept intuitively—they are "connectors" by nature.[5] My girlfriend Donna is a master connector. She is generous with both her time and contacts, constantly working to ensure that people who need each other know each other.

But some of us must be reminded that our success is never entirely of our own making but is due in part to the goodness, kindness, and generosity of others. What goes around, comes around. And I'm afraid that what's coming around for some women is a whole lot of ugly.

Let's just call a spade a spade. Some women are downright stingy with their network. Seeing other women as competition, rather than collaborators, they cheat themselves of the joy that comes from working with other gals. They miss out on celebrating with other women when those women succeed. Is it jealousy or envy that prevents women from embracing their peers? A lack of confidence? Or is it this type of thinking: *If you achieve a certain degree of success you might drain the available market. We might run out of success!*

Girlfriend, just because you achieve some level of success doesn't mean that I won't. God's world of possibilities is infinite for us all.

Dear friends, let us continue to love one another, for love comes from God. Anyone who loves is a child of God and knows God. (1 JOHN 4:7)

Reach out and extend your network to friends and colleagues looking for a job, a business lead, or a housekeeper. Take a look at who is in your network. Are you sharing it? Spend your contacts.

LIVING INTENTIONALLY
Spend It All Today (Part Trois)

The true measure of a man is how he treats someone who can do him absolutely no good.
SAMUEL JOHNSON

HOW MUCH TIME did you spend yesterday thinking about how someone hurt your feelings?

How much time did you spend yesterday thinking about how unjustified that situation was?

How much time did you spend yesterday thinking about what you should have said when she said . . . yeah, you get the point. Okay. Next set of questions:

How much time did you spend *collectively last week* thinking about how you could improve the morale at your office?

How much time did you spend *collectively last week* thinking about how you could encourage your husband?

How much time did you spend *collectively last week* thinking about how you could show love to your next-door neighbor (the one with the yapping dog)?

I think if we all spent just half as much time thinking about creative ways to show kindness as we do dwelling on how to get even, the world would be a nicer place and we'd all have less nausea. Kindness seems to be out of sight and out of mind.

I believe most of us underestimate the impact we have on others (from family members to total strangers). Either positive or negative—nothing is neutral—you made a mark on someone's life today. Did you inspire or motivate? Did you leave that person more confident than when you found him or her? Did you extend generosity or kindness or mercy? Did you make someone laugh? Did you leave someone with hope? One thing I'm sure of: as you checked out at the grocer, ate at the diner, instructed your child, passed your husband at the door, or sat in a boardroom—you left something in your wake. What did you leave?

"And you must love the LORD your God with all your heart, all your soul, all your mind, and all your strength." The second is equally important: "Love your neighbor as yourself." No other commandment is greater than these.
(MARK 12:30-31)

Spend your kindness.

LIVING INTENTIONALLY

FATHER GOD, reveal to me

- [ ] the props I use to disguise my true self;
- [ ] how to receive your gift of self-confidence in order that I might be more open, responsive, and relaxed so I can be the authentic witness you have called me to be;
- [ ] when the time has come for me to throw in the towel in order to better live by my priorities;
- [ ] when I need to allow others to help me face the headwinds of life;
- [ ] a quality mentor who can teach me and challenge me to live with excellence;
- [ ] steps I can take to fortify my courage in order to persist—even when I keep falling down;
- [ ] when I whine too long and too often;
- [ ] wisdom brought through my confusion;
- [ ] those areas where I am serving from my head rather than my heart;
- [ ] kind and truthful ways to say no;
- [ ] new ways to spend my talents and contacts today.

ACTIONS I WILL TAKE:

Example: I will kindly and respectfully decline to serve on the PTA board by saying, "Thank you for asking, but I must decline at this time."

1. _____

2. _____

3. _____

Father, open our hearts and minds with your light; open our eyes to the rich life you have abundantly given us. Help us, O Lord, to live each day for you, intentionally. Amen.

WHEN THERE'S A HOLE IN YOUR SOUL

WE ALL HAVE good days and bad days, right? But have you ever had an entire bad year? I remember one stretch of about three years when, for the life of me, I couldn't get out of my own way. Everywhere I went and everything I touched ended in disaster.

Looking back now, I see that during that three-year stint, I had a hole in my soul. Of course, no one was brave enough to point this out to me at the time. I don't know if anyone even hinted to me that my situation might be self-induced or that I was headed down a path of self-destruction. I had become a regular little rainmaker of difficulties. Being the overachiever that I am—let me tell you—I had produced a real frog-strangler! (For my girlfriends in states east of the Mississippi and west of the Rockies, that means a hard rain.)

So what is a hole in your soul? It is a deep, dark well that resides in the core of your being. And the harder you work to fill it with stuff, the bigger the doggone thing gets! Maybe you know what I'm talking about. Perhaps you've even tried to fill your hole with

Clothes. But standing in your closet, you realize that designer suit doesn't bring you the contentment you thought it would—it just makes your butt look big!

Romance. But after six months, you see the situation for what it is. Your poor attempt to use him to fill your void has failed miserably and now you have to deal with him *and* a hole in your soul!

Status. But if that's working, why are you most lonely when you're surrounded by friends and associates who so respect you?

Wine. Yes. This works pretty well for about three hours. And then the hole starts growing, getting bigger and bigger and bigger . . . along with your headache.

How are you filling your soul? With food? work? a baby? busyness?

Looking back at my disaster years, I realize that most of my poor—and sometimes sinful—choices were made because I didn't trust that God had my best interest in mind. I thought I could choose those things that would fill the hole in my soul, but I always chose wrong.

And this same God who takes care of me will supply all your needs from his glorious riches, which have been given to us in Christ Jesus.
(PHILIPPIANS 4:19)

Is it time for you to get whole in your soul to find uncommon joy? Choose Christ.

WHEN THERE'S A HOLE IN YOUR SOUL
Needing Control Is Controlling You

IN MY YOUTH, I needed to be right. But being right takes a tremendous amount of energy—from you and the other people in the room. Also, needing to be right can almost ensure that you will alienate others. And really, when you think about it . . . who in the devil will even care next Tuesday if you were right or not?

As we mature, our need to be right morphs into the need to be in control. I have a news flash: none of us are in control. Just pick up the local newspaper, watch the world news, or try to reason with a two-year-old. Honey, you're not in control.

This is a fairly easy concept to grasp; however, understanding it doesn't make life easier when you like to be in charge but things are not going your way. During one four-month stint, I worked with a team of professionals to develop a corporate Web site. On a scale of one to ten, my frustration level on any given day was about nineteen! Why? Because the development of the code was beyond my control. I'm a "get-it-done" gal—I don't like to fool around waiting for things to happen or for people to take action. So my frustration over my lack of control ate a hole in my soul (and probably my stomach lining). I finally decided one morning that I was fighting an invisible army and it was time to lay down my shield. God's timing is much more perfect than Ellen's timing—so I took a chill pill. (And I took one the next day, the next day, and the day after that!)

Some women want to control their friendships, the PTA board, the neighborhood association, the church bake sale, their daughters-in-law, *and* the yard boy. Strangely enough, we're totally out of control when we're driven by the need to control, which is always at conflict with finding uncommon joy anyway. The ultimate in self-control is knowing you need not be in control at all.

Don't worry about anything; instead, pray about everything. Tell God what you need, and thank him for all he has done. (PHILIPPIANS 4:6)

The best kept secret is the one you keep in your heart. And that's the one where you know your position but no longer require others to agree or approve. How much of your life and energy are you wasting on trying to control circumstances and other people? Choose to give him control.

WHEN THERE'S A HOLE IN YOUR SOUL
Work Could Be Eating You Whole

WORK IS VERY IMPORTANT to filling the hole in our soul. Regardless of what our work is or where it is, it is critical that we hone our gifts in order to find true harmony *within* ourselves. There is a tremendous pressure on us all—men and women alike—to just do the work and get over it. For one reason or another, many of us are in roles that don't match our talents.

I know many stay-at-home moms who are so gifted, so perfectly poised for their role, that they should be on the cover of *Parenting* magazine. I know others who are not. I believe that if you get up each morning dreading the minute you must start your workday (whether at home or a workplace), it will absolutely eat a hole in your soul. I know this personally.

I once had a job that left me physically ill every Sunday evening as I anticipated walking back into the environment come Monday morning. Girlfriends, this type of disconnect with work affects both our health and our family dynamic.

I think work eats us whole, first, when we feel unproductive. We were not put on this earth to be slugs or to fight an unending political battle that results in negligible progress. We were put here to accomplish stuff! to engage! to commit! to impact! Don't you just love when, at the end of the day, you can say to yourself, *Wow! That was fun! I moved the needle. I used my talents. I was 100 percent on!* Yes, we were designed to be productive. When we're not—when we're not engaged with our work or our workplace—it eats us whole.

Second, if our value system is at odds with our work, we will slowly begin to disappear—mentally, emotionally, and physically. It's easy to comprehend this when we're talking about ethics and moral issues. It's a bit more complex if we are trying to find lasting meaning pushing papers around for eight to ten hours a day. All work is important—especially if it is work *we were uniquely created to do.*

The questions to ask yourself are: Does my job, output, or company align with my value system? Do I know I make a difference, and is that difference important to me as an individual (not as an employee)?

> *God has given each of you a gift from his great variety of spiritual gifts. Use them well to serve one another. Do you have the gift of speaking? Then speak as though God himself were speaking through you. Do you have the gift of helping others? Do it with all the strength and energy that God supplies. Then everything you do will bring glory to God through Jesus Christ. All glory and power to him forever and ever! Amen.* (1 PETER 4:10-11)

Are you using your gifts? Are you committed? Are you making an impact? If not, what are you waiting for?

WHEN THERE'S A HOLE IN YOUR SOUL
Work Could Be Eating You Whole (Part Deux)

ON THE FLIP SIDE of making an impact is total boredom. Are you bored? often restless? mostly frustrated? even a bit sad?

You must be engaged in your job, the company, or the outcome of the work process. When you are fully engaged in your job, you're productive and content. When you're engaged with your company, you feel like you're part of a team. And when you're engaged with the outcome of the work, you know you contribute to something greater than yourself. If you're not engaged in any of these areas, you might consider choosing another line of work. Yes! *You can choose!* Don't you just love living in America? I am amazed by the number of people who complain for years on end about their work or company but do nothing about it, draining the energy of those around them.

In his book *Artful Work*, Dick Richards says: "The degree to which we seek joy within our work is the degree to which we invite artfulness. We deserve joy, every one of us, but we don't expect or seek joy in our work when we believe the reward for work lies in approval, external rewards, and celebrations."[6]

The days of working thirty years at the same company are over. You probably won't be getting a gold watch or company appreciation retirement party. Nor will your mug shine brightly in the People section of your hometown newspaper. The celebration, however, should still happen—but it should be internal, for a job well done, for success in meeting a goal, for overcoming incredible odds. The party that happens in your heart will result from knowing you have done a good job—for him.

And whatever you do or say, do it as a representative of the Lord Jesus, giving thanks through him to God the Father. (COLOSSIANS 3:17)

Girlfriends, one way that the hole in your soul is filled is by the sense of accomplishment you gain when you know you're doing what you were uniquely gifted to do. There's neither a big enough paycheck nor enough stock options in the world to compensate for anything less. The choice is yours.

WHEN THERE'S A HOLE IN YOUR SOUL
Yep! You Were Cheated!

IT'S BEST if we admit out loud that *we were cheated*. Cheated out of a happy childhood. Cheated out of a loving relationship. Cheated out of the wonder of motherhood. Cheated out of a corner office. Cheated out of good health. Cheated out of financial security. The list goes on.

Sometimes we were cheated by people who intended us harm, but more often we were cheated by people who were oblivious to the destruction they caused. People who just weren't taught better. People who were previously cheated by others and knew no other way to act. People who were just plain stupid. The list goes on.

We blame the people who hurt us. We blame the people who didn't come to our aid. And sometimes we blame God.

There is not a man, woman, or child walking on the face of the earth who has not been or who will not be betrayed. The question is, have you let your anger and disappointment fester into bitterness that is now eating a hole in your soul? Will you let the past or present define your future? Will you continue to try to fill the hole in your soul with stuff? Girlfriends—designer shoes, Twinkies, and sex will not fill that very sad, lonely place where you have been deeply wronged.

I know; it's hard. I've been there too.

I had to forgive my mother for planning a suicide attempt so I would be the one to find her. I was fifteen years old when I came home from school and found her lying on the floor. I was too young to know that my anger would subside only to be replaced by something far more destructive. Over a period of 5,475 days (that's fifteen years), bitterness ate a hole in my soul.

I did not excuse my mother for disregarding how her young daughter might feel or react in finding her and reading the note, alone at home. I did not excuse her—but as I tired of my own bile bitterness and recognized my own short-comings as a mother, I did choose to forgive her. She made a terrible mistake, and fortunately, her suicide attempt failed. I did not forgive her for her well-being but for my own. I realized that forgiveness was the only way I would find peace.

What about you? Do you have people or circumstances you need to forgive? As Joel Osteen says in *Your Best Life Now*: "Forgiveness is a choice, but it is not an option."[7]

> *Be kind to each other, tenderhearted, forgiving one another, just as God through Christ has forgiven you.* (EPHESIANS 4:32)

Feeling cheated results in anger, and over time, anger turns into bitterness. Bitterness is a poison that slowly eats a hole in your soul. Forgiveness works as your antacid.

WHEN THERE'S A HOLE IN YOUR SOUL
Guilt and the Hole in Your Soul

I WONDER if you relate to any of these:

- You drop your three-year-old off at day care on your way to work. Your work is important to you and your family needs your income, but guilt eats a hole in your soul.
- Your husband wants you to be available for him emotionally and physically but you have nothing to spare. You know you're not holding up your end of the relationship, and guilt eats a hole in your soul.
- You know your mom needs you to help her more because your dad's health is declining fast. But you're stretched so thin you want to cry; guilt eats a hole in your soul.
- Your teenager takes a nosedive and is making every wrong decision in the book. You blame yourself, and guilt eats a hole in your soul.
- You tell your boss you have to leave early to pick up your son from day care. The project is due tomorrow, and guilt eats a hole in your soul.
- Your eighteen-month-old is precious—but you can't stand another minute of his clinging! You need a breather, and when you finally get it, guilt eats a hole in your soul.
- Your "organization" is calling for volunteers, but you don't raise your hand. You know they need you to contribute; guilt eats a hole in your soul.
- Your brother wants to borrow money. You say no, or you say yes. Either way, guilt eats a hole in your soul.
- You're lucky—you get to stay home with the kids—but you're miserable. Other moms would kill for this opportunity, and guilt eats a hole in your soul.
- You're supposed to love him. Guilt eats a hole in your soul.

Guilt is a tricky topic. On the one hand, guilt is a valuable tool used by the Holy Spirit to help develop our characters. It pulls us out of our self-centeredness. It ensures that our moral compass is always pointing due north. Thus, the dictionary's definition of guilt—remorseful awareness of having done something wrong[8]—is critical to the shaping of our person and our society.

However, the guilt I'm writing about is more in line with the dictionary's other definition of guilt—self-reproach for *supposed inadequacy* or wrongdoing.[9] Girlfriends, sometimes things are not good or bad. They just are . . . at least for today.

> *I am leaving you with a gift—peace of mind and heart. And the peace I give is a gift the world cannot give. So don't be troubled or afraid.* (JOHN 14:27)

Your self-reproach for your supposed inadequacy is eating a hole in your soul. Tell the voice of guilt to be quiet—you're doing the very best you can. *Ssshhh.*

WHEN THERE'S A HOLE IN YOUR SOUL
Good Deeds Turned Sour

OUR UNREALISTIC EXPECTATION of others can inhibit us from living life with joy and contentment. This is a hard one for me. I have only recently learned that I cannot hold others to the *Ellen Standard*. It is unfair to them and often results in my disappointment.

Did you ever do a favor for someone only to discover that, when you needed a favor in return, she was nowhere to be found? You too? It's hurtful, isn't it? But our thinking is twisted. Why in the world would we ever do a favor for someone and then expect something in return? That wasn't an act of kindness—that was a loan with interest! The change in my expectation (considering my favor a loan) turned my good deed sour.

Perhaps you subscribe to the "Pay It Forward" concept—that if you perform a random act of kindness for someone, someone else will do something nice for you. I think this really does happen, but this idea also will lead you to *expect* something from someone else as a result of your kindness. When you don't see the payback in a relatively short period of time, well, you begin to wonder why you're the *only one* making the sacrifice. Hmm . . . that kind of thinking turns the good deed sour.

Or maybe you don't expect anything other than a polite acknowledgment for your selfless act. This is the mind-set I'm most often guilty of, but it too robs me of living fully. I don't expect anything in return from the person I served or from anyone else; I'd just like a little *gratitude every now and then*! This is my bad. Many times those who most need our kindness are incapable—due to worry, fear, grief, confusion, exhaustion, or embarrassment—to respond at all. I *finally* figured out that it's not an issue regarding *their* poor manners. It's more an issue regarding the condition of *my* heart. Expecting gratitude turned my good deeds sour.

Love your enemies! Do good to them. Lend to them without expecting to be repaid. Then your reward from heaven will be very great, and you will truly be acting as children of the Most High, for he is kind to those who are unthankful and wicked. You must be compassionate, just as your Father is compassionate.
(LUKE 6:35-36)

We set ourselves up for a life of disappointment when we create rules and expectations for *others* to live by. We must be willing to give unconditionally with no expectation for our return on investment. I love the philosophy of John Bunyan, author of *The Pilgrim's Progress*: "You have not lived today until you have done something for someone who cannot pay you back."

WHEN THERE'S A HOLE IN YOUR SOUL

FATHER GOD, I recognize I have a hole in my soul, and I realize that I have sometimes

☐ not trusted that you have my best interest in mind;

☐ used clothes, status, romance, food, or other substances to fill the hole in my soul;

☐ tried to control others or circumstances that are not mine to control or manipulate;

☐ allowed work to eat a hole in my soul;

☐ wrestled needlessly with guilt;

☐ allowed my unfulfilled expectations of others to turn my good deeds sour.

ACTIONS I WILL TAKE:

Example: I will let go of trying to control the desires and actions of my sister.

1. _____

2. _____

3. _____

Father, only you and your Son, Jesus, can fill the hole in my soul. I thank you for the gift of life eternal and the love you have poured out through the life of your Son. Remind me that you are the beginning and the end to filling my emptiness. Amen.

ONE BREATH AWAY FROM BURNOUT

EXHAUSTED. Bored. Frustrated. Unfulfilled.

These are the words that best describe me when I'm burned out. When I'm used up. When I'm at the end of my rope. Or when I feel like I'm trying hard but not getting anywhere.

I can feel it coming on like a bad cold. I get cranky. I'm short with people. I'm anxious. And I don't sleep well.

But rather than pull the covers back over my head, I know I should fight this malady. I must counter this condition of discontent or frustration before it's too late, before it takes me and my family down. So how do I revive myself?

I take my cue from the online encyclopedia *Wikipedia*, of all places. In describing resuscitation, *Wikipedia* says "CPR is unlikely to restart the heart, but rather its purpose is to maintain a flow of oxygenated blood to the brain and the heart, thereby delaying tissue death and extending the brief window of opportunity for a successful resuscitation without permanent brain damage."[10] Yes. Exactly. I want to thwart any more brain damage when dealing with family, work, and self!

If the objective is to stop our physical or emotional exhaustion—or worse, apathy—before it occurs, I think we should consider and address a few of the root causes that fuel the symptoms of our personal, spiritual, professional, and relational burnout. Over the next few days, we'll examine some of the driving forces behind burnout and discover new ways to reinvigorate a bored body, a frustrating job, an unfulfilled spirit, and an exhausted heart.

So humble yourselves under the mighty power of God, and at the right time he will lift you up in honor. Give all your worries and cares to God, for he cares about you. (I PETER 5:6-7)

As handsome as they might be, I'm not waiting for the paramedics to begin my resuscitation.

ONE BREATH AWAY FROM BURNOUT
An Exhausted Heart

SOME OF YOU will be able to relate when I say, "He wears me out."

It's hard to admit, but sometimes we come to the end of our rope with family. Parents, spouses, siblings, or kids drain the life out of us, which results in relational burnout and an exhausted heart. So what's often the driving force behind our burnout with the people we love the most? Control.

Picture a little girl running on the beach with her kite. She has great expectations for how her kite will soar. She runs fast, pitching the kite of relationship into the air and up, up, and away it goes! She's thrilled. But after a period of time, the wind takes a turn and the little girl must focus hard, strategize, and manipulate the string to keep her kite flying. After a while, flying the kite becomes a lot more work than fun. I think many of us are little girls who need to let go of the string.

Trying so hard to control the "state of their union," my girlfriend burned out. Her marriage dissolved before her eyes. Regardless of how many times she told her husband what she wanted from him, he couldn't seem to deliver. She knew she was on her last breath when she began using Google to search for divorce attorneys. Her arms were tired and her heart was exhausted from attempting to control her husband's actions, desires, and commitment.

Some of us fly the kite of control when it comes to our children. Investing all her energies to ensure her daughter made the honor roll and the cheerleading squad, a mom I know suffered from an exhausted heart when her daughter rebelled. "I don't know what happened. She's nothing like she was as a child. I gave her everything and did everything I could for her." She knew she was on her last breath when her eighteen-year-old daughter left home, yelling, "I'm not coming back" as she slammed the front door behind her. The mom was distraught and heartbroken that her kite wouldn't sail.

I know all about flying the kite of relationship because I'm a master at tugging on the strings. Like my two girlfriends, I also watched my kite crash as I tried to control my son's addiction and recklessness. At one point during Scott's rehabilitation, his promises of sobriety morphed into a tangled web of lies, leaving me, again, with a totally exhausted heart. I knew I was on my last breath when I realized I was working harder for his sobriety than he was.

Each time he said, "My grace is all you need. My power works best in weakness."
So now I am glad to boast about my weaknesses, so that the power of Christ can
work through me. (2 CORINTHIANS 12:9)

How are your kite-flying abilities? Are your arms tired too?

ONE BREATH AWAY FROM BURNOUT
An Exhausted Heart (Part Deux)

WOMEN COME by this kite-flying thing pretty naturally. Many of us like to hold on to the kite strings of our relationships. We really like the feeling of control this gives us. Crazy as it sounds, I think it all starts while we're still in pigtails.

Men, throughout their formidable years as little boys, set up battlefields and rescue scenarios, strategizing how to best control situations. They look to be the protectors; they feel their role is to provide answers and solutions. Little girls, however, become the control mavens we are through our fastidious placement of a perfectly formed family in the perfectly decorated rooms of our perfectly proportioned dollhouse. We are in *control* of this family! Good grief—no wonder we're twisted.

I was in my office working when Scott called and said he had something to tell me. After he admitted he had been deceptive with me and had relapsed, I hung up the phone. My heart was so exhausted, I couldn't even hold my head up. As I put my head on my desk, I let go of my kite.

I was so disappointed and disillusioned that I didn't talk with Scott for three weeks. Finally, I called him and invited him to lunch. Over a plate of chicken fried steak (how can kids eat like this?), he told me about his recent success in getting back on his plan. I told him how proud I was of him.

Wanting Scott to understand that our relationship would be different from then on, I shared with him that I had let go of our kite of relationship. I explained that I couldn't hold on anymore. That I loved him but he'd have to sail on his own now.

His reply? "Mom, I'm proud of you!" You see, Scott was also exhausted—*he* was worn out from me tugging on his string.

> So the LORD must wait for you to come to him
> so he can show you his love and compassion.
> For the LORD is a faithful God.
> Blessed are those who wait for his help. (ISAIAH 30:18)

Are you holding on too tight to your kite of relationship? It might be time to let it go.

ONE BREATH AWAY FROM BURNOUT
An Exhausted Heart (Part Trois)

There is only one way to happiness and that is to cease worrying about things which are beyond the power of our will. EPICTETUS

AS OFTEN AS WE peg others as the source of our burnout, the problem usually is not with the people we love. Even the irregular people in our lives are not to blame for our state of frustration. The driving force behind our relational burnout is our need to "fix" another person. Trying to control the desires, wills, habits, motivations, conscience, and futures of those we care for is what really wears us out.

Although Scott was twenty-seven the day he called me at the office to tell me of his relapse, I realized I was still parenting him like he was five. Without intending to, I had continued my "control tower" brand of parenting: I'm looking down—watching you, protecting you, guiding you—because you don't have the ability to take care of yourself. I came to the conclusion as I let my kite go that I had undermined my son's confidence, indirectly communicating to him that he wasn't bright enough, strong enough, or man enough to take care of himself. When I let go of my kite, I watched a man unfold before my eyes. Almost immediately, his self-worth soared.

If you're suffering from burnout with someone you love, you might try what I did the day I let the kite go (which so far seems to be working much better than my old ways of intervention and prodding):

Let go; give the person space.

Allow the other person to make his or her own way, even if it's not your way.

Give opinions or counsel, but only when asked.

Allow your family member or friend to stumble; you have not been called to walk upright for others.

Refrain from swooping in to rescue; you can't fix someone else.

Let the movie roll; you're only a supporting actor. Leave the directing to God.

Be patient.

And pray.

I have fought the good fight, I have finished the race, and I have remained faithful. (2 TIMOTHY 4:7)

By trying to mold the ones you love into what you want them to be, you're only setting yourself up for frustration—and an exhausted heart.

ONE BREATH AWAY FROM BURNOUT
A Frustrating Job

"I'M DONE. I am absolutely done with this job." How many of us have gotten to a breaking point in our careers? Or a better question might be: how many of us are at that point today?

Once we really begin to analyze the cause of burnout at work, we discover that the actual job or task we perform is rarely the issue. Most of us enjoy doing the work. And while our bosses, subordinates, or coworkers can sometimes be a bit wonky, for the most part they're good people with good intentions. Eliminating the work itself and the people we work with leaves us with only three other possibilities: me, myself, and I.

I was my own worst enemy at the age of thirty-one. Managing a $750 million business unit for a soon-to-be publicly traded company, I threw myself 110 percent into every initiative that crossed my desk. No project was too big or too small for me to take on. My boss warned that I couldn't sustain my pace or perfect record, and he predicted I would crash and burn. And I did. Four years later I left the company and job I loved because I was physically and mentally burned out.

Looking back I see that the root cause behind my burnout was perfectionism. Driven by the need for acceptance and validation, I drove myself (and I'm pretty sure everyone else around me) absolutely batty trying to get a project or job done perfectly. But something else fueled my perfectionism: fear. Having neither the education nor the experience to run such an important piece of the business, I was afraid management would discover I wasn't as smart as they thought I was. Over time, my twisted thinking, not my lack of intelligence, caused my burnout.

So where does this perfectionism stem from? I have a theory. First of all, some of us are genetically inclined this way. My mother was a perfectionist, so I think I got a touch of it from her gene pool. But for some of us, it is a reinforced philosophy. If you excelled in solo sports such as swimming or tennis, if you were a trained gymnast, if you were a seasoned dancer, or if, like me, you were a classically trained musician, there's a good chance that a perfect performance was expected. Before my behind hit that piano bench, I knew that I had to perform my music perfectly. There would be no stage performance without a perfect practice.

Do not waste time arguing over godless ideas and old wives' tales. Instead, train yourself to be godly. "Physical training is good, but training for godliness is much better, promising benefits in this life and in the life to come."
(1 TIMOTHY 4:7-8)

If you're suffering from professional burnout, consider the source of the fire. It might not be a thing to do with your job, the gal in the next cubicle, or a stinky boss.

ONE BREATH AWAY FROM BURNOUT
A Frustrating Job (Part Deux)

One of the symptoms of an approaching nervous breakdown is the belief that one's work is terribly important.   BERTRAND RUSSELL

CLOSELY LINKED with perfectionism is ego.

If you are a girlfriend who takes great pride in what you do, your self-worth might be closely linked to what you produce at work. This is not all bad, in and of itself.

Ego can be a great asset for one's profession when it propels a well-grounded sense of self-confidence; but it can be extremely dangerous when we allow it to get out of check, draining our vision, ambition, creativity, and sense of balance.

- It is ego, fanned by the flames of fear, that drives our compulsion to check our BlackBerrys every five minutes.
- It is ego, driven by a Superwoman complex, that compels us to take responsibility for failures (and successes) for which we have been given no authority or accountability.
- It is ego that throws the crushing blow to our sense of self-worth when we define ourselves only by our outcome measures at work.
- It is ego, slapped silly day after day by the nonsense that occurs as a matter of course in the halls of corporate America, that convinces us that we have little to offer our coworkers, subordinates, or senior management.
- It is ego, fueled by our need to be validated, that convinces us that if we work hard enough and long enough, we can single-handedly save the corporation from itself.
- It is ego, driven by need for acceptance, that clouds our judgment of our own limitations.
- And it is ego, generating enough stress to stop the heart, that kills. Literally, we can work ourselves to death trying to satisfy the ego.

So don't be afraid; you are more valuable to God than a whole flock of sparrows. (MATTHEW 10:31)

If you're not saving lives (as a doctor or volunteer for a suicide hotline); saving souls, literally or figuratively (as a clergy or social worker); or saving our next generation from illiteracy (as a teacher)—you can relax. Your work is not *that* important.

If you *are* a doctor, social worker, minister, or teacher, there's a good reason for your high anxiety. I think I'm fairly safe in saying that it's probably not ego that's fueling your stress, as lives literally rest in your hands. The rest of us ego-driven maniacs will be lifting you up in prayer.

ONE BREATH AWAY FROM BURNOUT
An Unfulfilled Spirit

ACCORDING TO The Barna Group, the adult population in the United States grew by 15 percent between 1991 and early 2004. During that same period the number of adults who did not attend church nearly doubled, rising from 39 million to 75 million—a 92 percent increase![11] But I have a theory: it's not always the place of worship that we're burned out on. I surmise the root cause of our unfulfilled spirit is not corporate worship but a far more personal dilemma. I believe our emptied spirits are the result of despair.

I was twenty-two when I realized my first business was failing. I was one breath away from burnout; my spirit was drained. I was so worn out with praying and waiting for a specific outcome that I just could hardly stand to pray or wait anymore. Day by day, my faith wasted away a little more. I was running out of time, money, hope, and solutions. My mind-melting despair trumped my faith and destroyed my gratitude and desire to praise the almighty God for who he is . . . rather than what he could do for me.

When everything around me was falling apart, I could only cry out to God to save me. During that most difficult time, not once did it dawn on me to praise him, as Job of the Old Testament did.

As is our nature, our world revolves around ourselves—our hopes, our dreams, our problems, and our disappointments. And this self-concern flows daily, or sometimes hourly, into our prayer life. We say "all about me" prayers, moaning our pains, problems, disappointments, and needs to God to the point that I'm just amazed he's not burned out with us! But amazingly, he's far more patient with his needy children than we are with him. Frightening when you stop to think about it, isn't it?

> The righteous person faces many troubles,
> but the LORD comes to the rescue each time. (PSALM 34:19)

I don't know where you are right now. Life may be perfect, and if it is, praise the Lord with all that is within you. But if it's not perfect, if you're struggling with all your might to get through each day, drop to your knees (that's what they're for) to bow down and let him know how much you love him just for who he is.

He'll show up again—you can count on it.

ONE BREATH AWAY FROM BURNOUT
An Unfulfilled Spirit (Part Deux)

AFTER MY FIRST business failed, my life—and my faith—eventually returned to normal. I continued to have a love affair with Christ while being totally baffled by how he works (or sometimes doesn't). I still wondered what exactly had happened. I was not sure why he hadn't come to my rescue when I was so sure he would. I wouldn't be clear about my role in our relationship for nearly twenty years.

My "aha!" moment came early one morning in 2003. I was at a very good place in my life—my marketing company was thriving, my family was happy, our marriage was humming, and Steve and I were preparing to move to a beautiful new home. On a whim, I had purchased a book I saw on an endcap display at the airport just days before. The title had grabbed my attention; it looked like a must-read.

As I read the opening page of Rick Warren's *The Purpose Driven Life* early that morning, I could hardly breathe: "It's not about you," Warren wrote.

> The purpose of your life is far greater than your own personal fulfillment, your peace of mind, or even your happiness. It's far greater than your family, your career, or even your wildest dreams and ambitions. If you want to know why you were placed on this planet, you must begin with God. You were born *by* his purpose and *for* his purpose.[12]

Hmmm . . . are you sure it's not all about me? *Because I really think it should be.*

It took a while for this concept to sink in, but once it did—it changed my approach and recharged my faith. Today, rather than repeatedly asking God, "Why haven't you? Why can't you? When will you?" I humbly place my desire at his feet, thanking him in advance for his favor. Laying a quiet, tender request before the Lord with a heart of gratitude is a marked contrast to running out of faith because he hasn't granted my every wish according to my Day-Timer.

Are any of you suffering hardships? You should pray. Are any of you happy? You should sing praises. (JAMES 5:13)

If your spirit is drained and you're one breath away from spiritual burnout, consider a change in your prayer life from "I need you to . . ." to "I praise you for . . ." Your circumstances may not change immediately, but your heart will.

ONE BREATH AWAY FROM BURNOUT
A Bored Body

"WHEN THE OXYGEN masks drop from the overhead compartment, pull firmly and secure the mask over your nose and mouth first; then assist children and those around you." Do you think this is a self-centered act? No, of course not. We all know that in a case of airline emergency, we must ensure we receive oxygen so we can care for those who depend on us. So why don't we apply this same thinking when it comes to our health and fitness?

We're only about eight weeks into the new year, and I'll bet you a dollar to a salmon sushi roll that you've already given up on your "healthier you" resolution. I have a proven theory (or at least I've proved it to myself) that we're not burned out with sweating; the driving force behind our burnout with our fitness and healthy eating habits is time. We don't have time to go to a gym. We don't have time to invest in learning more about health or fitness. And we don't have time to make stir-fry tofu (even if we like it). Our time crunch causes us to sacrifice ourselves, leaving our bodies bored, begging for some attention.

If you're suffering from workout burnout, I'd like to share with you seven quick tips (three today, four tomorrow) to get you back on track—because you, my girlfriends, are important. And important people must stay fit in order to care for all the people who depend on them. Let's start with tip number one:

1. If you can't work a thirty-minute walk into your day, walk ten minutes, three times a day. This slight change could help you get back on track, and soon you'll feel so good you'll be "making" time for that thirty-minute walk.
2. Load new tunes on your iPod or Nano every four to six weeks because boredom can set in quickly. What's new on my iPod this month? Shelby Lynne. Her music is snappy and fun—"Restless," "10 Rocks," and "Don't Mind If I Do" are a few of my favorites.
3. Once you get the walking down, alternate a slow one-minute jog with a brisk one-minute walk. Before you know it, you'll be ready for the Boston Marathon. (Well, maybe not—but you'll feel better.)

Work brings profit,
    but mere talk leads to poverty! (PROVERBS 14:23)

Okay. Stop talking about it. Put on your sneakers. At least it's a start.

ONE BREATH AWAY FROM BURNOUT
A Bored Body (Part Deux)

IF YOU'RE NOT careful, you'll get as bored with your workout routine as your body is with you. So make sure that you add some variety to your daily workout. Yesterday I offered three tips to jump-start your fitness routine. Today I offer four more:

4. Alternate walking days and weight lifting days. This is the very best fitness advice I can give you—it's good for burning fat and fighting osteoporosis. Purchase leg weights and do a few exercises with the weights strapped to your ankles. You won't believe the results! Also, buy small dumbbells; I started with two-pound weights and then graduated slowly to heavier ones. I lift nine-pound dumbbells (mine are pink) for fifteen minutes, twice a week. See my video at www.ellenmiller.com to see the results. Pretty good biceps for a grandma, eh?

5. If you don't like walking, dance. Turn the music up loud, be a Disco Dolly, and dance for fifteen minutes straight. The results: a heart that is pumping and a happier disposition. No way can you dance for fifteen minutes and not walk away absolutely giddy. Do you have a daughter? Ask her to join you—it will be good both for your health and your relationship.

6. Don't diet. Everyone wants to attribute women's fussy attitudes to hormones, but I disagree. I think women are out of sorts because they suffer from low blood sugar! Is the whole world on a diet? There are two books on my Web site about "diets" that I recommend: *French Women Don't Get Fat* by Mireille Guiliano (follow her advice and you'll never have a weight problem) and Peter J. D'Adamo's *Eat Right 4 Your Type*. The philosophy shared in this book is very interesting—it explains why different people burn different foods in different ways. It worked like a charm for me, and I get to eat.

7. When you're tempted not to work out or eat right, watch a documentary on the Special Olympics. Ladies, you are in possession of precious gifts: a healthy heart, strong lungs, and two good legs. Be a faithful steward of the body you have been blessed with and take care of it.

Women tend to the needs of their families and professions, ignoring their own well-being and fitness. If you really love your family and your profession, demonstrate it by investing in yourself first. You'll be much better prepared for the day when those oxygen masks fall.

Commit your actions to the LORD,
and your plans will succeed. (PROVERBS 16:3)

I'm taking care of me for the people I love. What about you?

ONE BREATH AWAY FROM BURNOUT

FATHER GOD, hear my cry:

- [ ] I am exhausted.
- [ ] I am bored.
- [ ] I am frustrated.
- [ ] I am unfulfilled.
- [ ] I know it is time to let go of my relationship kite.
- [ ] I know I am trying to play a starring role in someone else's movie.
- [ ] I know my ego, driven by perfectionism, is driving me (and everyone else) nuts.
- [ ] I know my spiritual confidence is drained.
- [ ] I know I need to rededicate myself to you for who you are—not for what you can do for me.
- [ ] I know I have been a poor steward, sacrificing the care and feeding of my physical body.

ACTIONS I WILL TAKE:

Example: Today, I will put my BlackBerry away for two hours.

1. _____

2. _____

3. _____

Father, I come to you with an exhausted heart: bored with my body, frustrated with my job and—forgive me, Lord—unfulfilled in my spiritual walk. I know I am only one breath away from burnout and pray that you will send the Holy Spirit to breathe new life into my body; new energy in my work; new perspective in my relationships; and a merciful welcome as I return home to enjoy fellowship with you. Amen.

PLAYING THE SCALES

ALTHOUGH YOU'D NEVER know it to hear me play, I took piano lessons for twenty years, with the exception of a two-year hiatus that I call my "blunder years." During that twenty-year stint—if my math is right—I played the scales about twelve thousand times (thank you, Mrs. Morgan, Mrs. Spindle, and Aunt 'Cil).

Playing the piano for me was, and still is, both engaging and relaxing. But playing the scales is worse than monotonous. Besides some interesting finger work in the minor key, it's pretty much mind-numbing—especially when you are required to play the same scale *over and over and over*. Just poke my eyeball with a straight pin.

Sometimes our work, love affairs, or relationships with our families and friends can become so routine that—like playing the scales—we sort of zone out and ultimately miss out on the music. Our planning is by rote, lacking creativity. Our responses are mechanical, lacking thoughtful replies. Our engagement in the moment is void, lacking wonder. Life becomes b-o-r-i-n-g.

Always be joyful. Never stop praying. Be thankful in all circumstances, for this is God's will for you who belong to Christ Jesus.
(1 THESSALONIANS 5:16-18)

Regardless of what you call it—playing the scales, running the drill, or going through the motions—we all do it. Our goal: to snap out of it in order to return to the melody at hand. God has created some beautiful music for us; it's time we listened.

PLAYING THE SCALES
The Scale of ME Major

Do not think that love, in order to be genuine, has to be extraordinary. What we need is to love without getting tired. MOTHER TERESA

I LOVE THINGS that are extraordinary. I have "extra" highlights in my hair. I'm "extra" excitable. I speak with exclamation points. Even my husband has been blessed with "extra" patience to deal with his "extra" high-maintenance wife. But all this being extra makes me tired.

As a sophomore music major, I became "extra" burned out. So I took a break from my standard classical repertoire and enrolled in a class called Two Pianos, Four Hands. For those not familiar with this concept, you're partnered with another pianist to play duets. However, instead of playing together on one piano, as you might have done as a child, you play on two pianos. This is a total hoot!

Of course, I had to make many adjustments in order to play this "team sport." The most important: accepting the fact that I was dependent on my performance partner to be "on her game" and likewise, accepting that she depended on me to perform at peak. I realized that to honor my teammate I had to show up—on time, well prepared, and with an attitude of mercy. But interestingly, the class breathed new life into me, and I could play for hours without getting tired.

The lessons I learned from Two Pianos, Four Hands served me well many times throughout my life, but never did they play such a profound role as in December 2006. I was enjoying life and gearing up for the holidays when my dear friend and backdoor neighbor, Karen James, began her journey through grief. Her husband, Kelly, was one of three mountain climbers who died, a week before Christmas, during a horrific storm on Mount Hood. For days the nation watched, and I, along with my family and friends, prayed without ceasing that Kelly would live to share his testimony of faith.

Karen would call in the middle of the night, and we'd whisper our prayers of hope and mercy into the phone to one another. We were both playing a tune that was totally foreign to either of us—nothing monotonous about this one; each word of each prayer was carefully chosen. We needed a miracle.

Dear children, let's not merely say that we love each other; let us show the truth by our actions. (1 JOHN 3:18)

But God had different plans. Karen and the children returned home without Kelly. For me, the music didn't stop—but a new score was being written. Is God rewriting your tune too?

PLAYING THE SCALES
The Scale of ME Major (Part Deux)

OVER THE NEXT several weeks, two of Karen's other girlfriends joined me in a three-piano concerto. No one had to give us the music or direct us—we just instinctively knew the parts we were to play. Total strangers, challenged with solving problems in areas unfamiliar to us, we could have disagreed on direction or temporary solutions. Instead, we played three-part harmony as if we'd known each other all our lives. We were doing what Christ called us to do—faithfully minister to our sister. But that's not what was unique about this song. The awesome part of this score was played by *my* girlfriends.

While I was in the bowels of despair with Karen, and as my husband, Steve, and I grieved for the loss of our dear friend and neighbor, five of my other girlfriends came to our rescue. Shoring us up with resources, contacts, prayers, daily calls, and even food for our family, my friends *fueled me* so that I could invest in someone else. "My" ministry became "our" ministry.

Usually the one who fetches the water for another thirsty soul, I found myself on the receiving end of the Perrier this time. And just as Aaron and Hur supported the arms of Moses as he played his role in the battle between Israel and Amalek, these girlfriends brought relief to my weary soul as I worked to fulfill my mission. Like Aaron and Hur, my friends were:

Proactive: I never called them—they reached out to me. When you're caring for someone else, you have no bandwidth to reach out for help for yourself.

Authentic: Their concern for our family went beyond material things; they were there to talk with us—and more importantly, to listen and to pray for us, becoming an extension of our service.

Creative: There were things I needed before I even realized a need. This is critical when your "thinking energy" is used for someone else.

Understanding that I could have gotten tired or burned out during the most important ministry of my life, I knew that to play my part, I had to allow my other performance partners to back me up. Together, we had a mission.

All of you together are Christ's body, and each of you is a part of it.
(I CORINTHIANS 12:27)

If you're currently serving someone in crisis, expand your ministry by allowing others to participate by ministering to you. Or if you know of a girlfriend who is caring for someone else, reach out and take care of *her.* Love doesn't have to be shown by doing extraordinary things; we just have to choose to prop each other up so we don't get tired.

PLAYING THE SCALES
I Hate This Key

If you can't be thankful for what you receive, be thankful for what you escape.
ANONYMOUS

JUST A COUPLE of months before Kelly left for Mt. Hood, changing Karen's life forever, I was driving home from work while wallowing in a pity puddle. I was in the midst of the most complex, difficult consulting engagement of my career, frustrated to the nines, and bone tired. I had worked 110 days straight—some days putting in twelve- to fourteen-hour days. Work/life balance? I had lost my way.

As I drove home, in the pouring rain no less, I was lamenting how bad my work situation was. Then I came upon an old, white, beat-up pickup truck loaded with construction supplies. The truck was heaped high with shovels, bags of "something," and other tools. Then I saw a leg. No . . . two legs. No . . . four.

Buried amongst the construction and debris were day laborers trying to protect themselves from the weather as they headed home from *their* day of backbreaking work. Girlfriends, this was inhumane: these men had to provide hard manual labor for something below minimum wage and then ride home while exposed to the elements. The sight of these men lying in the back of the pickup knocked me right off my pity potty.

As I drove in my four-door luxury sedan, nestled on my heated seats, listening to Frank Sinatra via my satellite radio, God snapped me out of my mind-numbing scale of "This job stinks." With one crystal clear visual on a stormy night, he reminded me of the charmed life I live.

Regardless of the corporate rat race we run; regardless of our struggles to be heard; regardless of the political maneuvering within our organization, we are a privileged lot and must stop playing in the key of "I hate this job."

> *The faithful love of the LORD never ends!*
> *His mercies never cease.*
> *Great is his faithfulness;*
> *his mercies begin afresh each morning.* (LAMENTATIONS 3:22-23)

Switch keys from self-pity to gratitude. You are a richly blessed person (whether or not you have heated seats in your car).

PLAYING THE SCALES
Round and Round

DURING MY PIANO-teaching days, I would introduce a particular duet, titled "Round and Round," to my fourth-year students. It was a very entertaining little ditty, as the children actually got up and walked around the piano bench and traded places at the keyboard . . . while continuing to play without ever losing a beat! Yes—it was a real crowd-pleaser at the annual spring recital!

I've come to the conclusion that marriages would be more fulfilling if the partners would sometimes consider playing a different part. Due to changes in the job market or our professions, due to unexpected health challenges, or due to shifting life stages of our children or parents, sometimes it is imperative that we trade places in our duet with our significant other, if only temporarily.

Steve and I recently traded places when we agreed to take on the horrific consulting engagement I mentioned yesterday. We discussed the situation before signing the agreement, because I knew that I could not possibly manage the demands of the client while also managing those responsibilities that normally fall to me in the running of our business and our home.

Prior to the engagement, Steve and I sat down and went over everything from dinner (he would be in charge on the weeknights) to how I would stay connected to our other business and clients (I would work on dual e-mail platforms to stay connected to what was happening in our office while I officed across town). By brainstorming about all the day-to-day machinations that take part in our lives, we were able to come up with a plan that kept our family, business, and personal lives humming; I took on greater responsibility with the consulting project, while Steve picked up family and home obligations.

Because we were honest and clear in our mutual expectations and because we discussed the role shift in advance, we continued to play our duet without ever losing a beat. Not once did I ever feel overwhelmed. And not once did that man fail to serve me a hot meal; even when I dragged in at midnight, Central Market takeout was in the oven.

> *In the same way, you husbands must give honor to your wives. Treat your wife with understanding as you live together. She may be weaker than you are, but she is your equal partner in God's gift of new life. Treat her as you should so your prayers will not be hindered. Finally, all of you should be of one mind. Sympathize with each other. Love each other as brothers and sisters. Be tenderhearted, and keep a humble attitude.* (1 PETER 3:7-8)

What's going on in your life? Could you benefit from trading places at the piano bench? Consider developing a plan via calm communication before the storm hits.

PLAYING THE SCALES
Round and Round (Part Deux)

I find that it is not the circumstances in which we are placed, but the spirit in which we face them, that constitutes our comfort. ELIZABETH T. KING

SO WHEN SHOULD you consider getting up and walking around the piano bench? I suggest you and your spouse do it *before* one of you completely flames out in the middle of the performance. If you can plan proactively, that's great. But sometimes life happens and situations sneak up on you.

Here are just a few areas that you might consider discussing with your mate before the next crisis hits:

- At some point, the primary caregiver for the kids or aging parents, regardless of how nurturing he or she is, will—I promise you—*will* burn out. Trade places with him or her for one week. (Caution: please do not attempt this for more than one week at a time; I don't want to hear that any children or elderly grandparents were broken during this brief intermission.)
- Managing the finances can be extremely stressful in families with limited income. While one of you may be more mathematically gifted, at least sit together and discuss options as you pay the bills. It's not fair for one person in the family to bear the banking alone.
- Everyone in your family eats, so why should the meal planning and preparation always fall to one person? In our family, I typically plan the meals, shop the market, and prepare dinner. However, due to the extreme hours I was working during our recent consulting gig, this was out of the question. For five months, Steve planned and picked up every meal. What a blessing to come home late at night to warm food and a thoughtful husband. It was such a small thing in light of the larger business burdens he took on during that time—but nothing meant more to me.
- Our professional lives can be unpredictable, volatile, and frustrating, leaving us drained of energy and desire. Before you burn out, ask your mate for help. It may be time for one of you to pick up part or a greater part of the earning burden for your family. It cannot always fall to one person to keep the household afloat. Besides, one of you might be missing out on the career of a lifetime!

I take joy in doing your will, my God,
  for your instructions are written on my heart. (PSALM 40:8)

Before the bench gets crowded or you get bored with the arrangement, choose to trade places—if only for one song.

PLAYING THE SCALES
Same Song, Fourth Verse

Change is inevitable. Growth is optional.   JOHN MAXWELL

ON JANUARY 12, 2007, I was sitting in a client's office when my cell phone rang. As usual, I turned the ringer down and let the call go to voice mail in order to focus my attention on my client. Just moments later the phone rang for the second time, and I realized from the customized ring tone that it was Steve.

Thinking someone from the office needed me urgently, I excused myself and answered. Steve said, "Scott's at the office." I asked, "Scott who?" He said, "Our son. Scott." I was speechless.

Scott had been missing for three years, one month, and nineteen days.

Upon my reunion with Scott and for several days afterward I realized I was most likely playing the same song, fourth verse with him. Our family has memorized this tune and we know the repeats and the crescendos; we just can't find the place where it resolves.

Many women who write me in response to Truth Nuggets share the challenges they endure with their mentally ill or chemically dependent family members. It's an interesting three-way tightrope we walk between our boundaries, our unconditional love, and our hope. The only way we can help is by fully recognizing that we're not playing this song alone—we didn't write the score, we can't change the tempo, and we can't control how the final chord will be played. We can only pluck out a few new notes, hoping to appropriately accompany the one whose concerto this really is.

I know that Scott has big challenges. I'm not sure he will ever be mainstreamed. And I know there is a chance that he'll "wander off" again, drawn to the dark side where drugs medicate his pain.

But there is something interesting about our song this time. Maybe it's Scott's life experiences. Maybe it's the incredibly long pause in our song. Or maybe it's our mutual acceptance of this situation and the reality of what is and what will never be.

We had to celebrate this happy day. For your brother was dead and has come back to life! He was lost, but now he is found! (LUKE 15:32)

This melody—even if it repeats—is sweeter this time around. Hope springs eternal and puts feeling back into playing the scales. One more time—from the top—with gratitude.

PLAYING THE SCALES

FATHER GOD, awaken me by

☐ shocking me out of my boredom with life;

☐ allowing others to minister to me when I'm ministering to someone else;

☐ snapping me out of my self-pity thinking;

☐ providing me with the motivation, talent, and means to trade places with _____;

☐ strengthening me to play the same song, fourth verse, with grace.

ACTIONS I WILL TAKE:

Example: I am so tired and could use some ministering to myself. Today I will call _____ and share with her my burden.

1. _____

2. _____

3. _____

Father, I come to you asking for forgiveness—forgiveness for failing to live the full life you have waiting for me. I ask you to awaken my every fiber to live the life and be the witness you have called me to be. I am humbled by your love and interest in my every thought, my every move. Amen.

CUTTING THE CLUTTER

ARE YOU SOMETIMES so overwhelmed with family, life, home, and work that you feel as if you're drowning in "stuff"? I once felt that way too. My list of responsibilities, both at home and away from home, was all-consuming. I realized I wasn't picking my priorities—they were picking me!

One of the first places my obligations began to burden me was in our home. This was strange to me at the time because we lived in a lovely abode. But that lovely abode was filled to the gills with lots of *stuff*.

Steve and I determined that the obligations that came along with a nice home and a large lot in the suburbs (in Texas, both homes and parcels of land are sometimes ridiculously large) were creating a mental and physical burden for us. We decided less was more at our life stage and sold our home—furnished. Yes, someone loved our stuff so much that they bought our house intact. It was pretty scary leaving all our furniture behind, but it was totally liberating!

We moved to a modern-style home where simplistic design rules. Yes, less is *so much* more.

We have fewer plants to water; less special occasion decorations to put up, take down, and store; and no knickknacks to dust. The result is a fuss-less, worry-free environment that allows me to *breathe* at home. Because there's less competing for my time and attention, I can finally do the one thing I had never really been able to do at home: sit. Because I'm no longer accumulating and arranging, I can do what you're supposed to do at home: relax.

> *Don't copy the behavior and customs of this world, but let God transform you into a new person by changing the way you think. Then you will learn to know God's will for you, which is good and pleasing and perfect.* (ROMANS 12:2)

After four years in our modern, downsized home, we have decided to do it again. High-rise condo, here we come!

Is it possible that your physical and mental "stuff" is the source of your energy drain too? If so, it might be time for you to discover that less is more and learn to identify those things that clutter your world. But then you have to do something about it—like throw things out!

CUTTING THE CLUTTER
Getting the Stuff out of Your Eyes

Before you try to keep up with the Joneses, be sure they're not trying to keep up with you.
ERMA BOMBECK

COULD THE PEOPLE you watch and measure yourself against be a source of clutter in your life? I think we have too much "stuff" in our eyes.

When you watch the actors on the Golden Globes, what do you see? Women with fabulous frames in gorgeous dresses? Do you feel a bit frumpy lying on the sofa in your faded nightgown and old fuzzy house slippers? Know what I see? I see women who look *hungry*. Get those girls some mashed potatoes—they're wasting away!

When you drive through beautiful neighborhoods with perfectly manicured lawns and houses bigger than the Mall of America, what do you see? The end-all, be-all for having "arrived"? I see homes with baggage—too much upkeep and too many rooms to keep straight!

When you watch the other ten-year-old kids running out on the soccer field while your son sits on the bench, what do you see? Potential stars with college scholarships? Are you convinced that your son's future earning power has been quashed before he hits fifth grade? I see a child whose substance and patience are being formed while sitting on the bench, allowing him to grow into a man of character, not a self-absorbed, "all about me" adult.

When you watch a female coworker make her way up the corporate ladder, what do you see? A woman who seems to get all the breaks? I see a woman who has vision, determination, discipline, and diplomacy to hold her own in the corporate arena.

I think the "stuff" in our eyes and how we perceive life on a day-by-day basis has everything to do with *what* we compete for. Not *if* we compete; most people compete on some level for something every day—a tennis match, a 10k run, or to be the first in their company to hit their sales quota. The type of competition I'm referring to is the kind that affects our self-esteem. It's the competition to be on par with others in order to fulfill one's self-worth. But those who look to their Creator for validation and significance replace that desperate need to compete with peace.

> *But the worries of the world, and the deceitfulness of riches, and the desires for other things enter in and choke the word, and it becomes unfruitful.*
> (MARK 4:19, NASB)

What are you competing for? And when you win—what will be your reward? There's no earthly tiara or trophy at the end of the game. We all end up in the same place: a pine box with handles.

Set your eyes on the prize.

CUTTING THE CLUTTER
Getting the Stuff out of Your Ears

Happiness is good health and a bad memory.   INGRID BERGMAN

I READ an interesting editorial in the *Dallas Morning News.* The writer was exploring a controversial subject, as well as addressing the negative—no, *nasty*—e-mail she had received from a reader. She went on to explain, exposing her vulnerability, how this really affected her.

Is it not amazing that we hold so tightly to that *one* voice—one from our distant past or maybe an opinion expressed just yesterday? Regardless of the number of accolades and positive reinforcement from others, that *one* statement, sometimes made in passing and sometimes not even meant to be hurtful, shapes our perception of our self or our performance.

I don't believe employee annual reviews are helpful. Many times, I have carefully considered the ten objectives for the employee review and marked "Excellent!" on seven of the objectives, "Very Good" on two, and "Needs Improvement" on the *one* remaining. What do you think the employee hears during the review? Yep. *Only* the one thing that needs improvement. All of the "atta boys" and "atta girls" go right out the window, right along with their self-confidence.

I dropped an e-mail to the news columnist after reading her article, sharing with her my respect for her deep thinking, her courage for stating the facts, and her authenticity in exposing her vulnerabilities. She let me know how wonderful it was to get "love" mail rather than hate mail. I wondered, *How many love mails does it take to negate that one nasty-gram?* From my experience with employee reviews, I know it's greater than 9 to 1.

> The LORD is close to the brokenhearted;
>   he rescues those whose spirits are crushed. (PSALM 34:18)

Girlfriends, we have to be determined to get the "nasty stuff" out of our ears. Focus on those who appreciate you and respect your efforts. Don't let that *one* voice undermine who you're supposed to be or what you're destined to accomplish.

CUTTING THE CLUTTER
Picking Your Stuff

ARE YOU HABITUALLY late? I'm not talking about occasionally running behind schedule; I mean, if you arrive at your girlfriend's party on time, would she ask you your mother's maiden name because she'd be sure aliens had kidnapped you and taken over your identity? If this is you, then there is clutter in your schedule.

Or maybe you ask yourself every day, *Why can't I get more done?* I don't mean an occasional one-too-few things scratched from the to-do list. I mean you're the last person anyone ever calls to help get a project accomplished. Is this you? If so, then you may be the poster child for procrastination.

Girlfriends, running late and procrastinating mess with your mental freedom. You may not know it, but one or both are likely a major contributing factor to the stress you feel each day.

Here's what I have learned: if you choose your priorities *purposefully*, you will be doing only stuff that matters to *you*. If you're doing only stuff that matters, you will be on time and you will get the things accomplished that you have deemed important. All the other stuff will just fall away. And it all starts with your personal daily list of priorities.

Each Monday, list those things that are important to do that week; then, put them in priority order. The first thing on your list of priorities this week will be to arrive at your destinations five minutes early. Why? Because this is a priority. Arriving on time is a direct reflection of your respect for the person or people you have committed to meet. In addition, you will have on your list several activities that must be accomplished. If you have seven items on your list to do this week, do three of them by 5 p.m. Tuesday. Absolutely no excuses. Then take the remaining four on Wednesday morning and reprioritize or add new action items to your list; do three of these by 5 p.m. on Wednesday. Keep a running to-do list, but refresh it every two days, since priorities can change. Just make sure that you keep a list so you can see that things are moving off, not just piling on! You're going to feel so accomplished and in control.

I have told you all this so that you may have peace in me. Here on earth you will have many trials and sorrows. But take heart, because I have overcome the world. (JOHN 16:33)

You know, it's usually not the *doing* that overwhelms us as much as *thinking* about the *doing*.

CUTTING THE CLUTTER

FATHER GOD, I praise you for revealing to me that

☐ physical and mental stuff are contributing to my positive energy drain;

☐ the competitive stuff of _____ is in my eyes and robbing me from living with uncommon joy;

☐ I am allowing the negative words of _____ to affect what you have called me to accomplish;

☐ my procrastination is affecting my mental freedom.

ACTIONS I WILL TAKE:

Example: I will honor my friends and family by arriving for appointments and commitments five minutes early.

1. _____

2. _____

3. _____

Father, I thank you for revealing truths to me—truths that when addressed will lead me to a life of uncommon joy. I thank you for showing me how my competitive nature and need for worldly things affect my peace. I thank you for helping me realize that words said hurtfully—from years ago—are affecting my purpose. And, Lord, I pray that you will help me manage my schedule in a way that brings glory to you. Amen.

WORK/LIFE BALANCE AND THE DEBIT CARD

If a person gets his attitude toward money straight, it will help straighten out almost every other area in his life. REVEREND BILLY GRAHAM

POLITICS. Religion. Money. Of the three, which are you least likely to discuss with close friends? Money, of course. Your close friends probably already know how you vote and what you believe from a spiritual standpoint. But I bet they don't know how much money you make or how much money you have.

Money is a topic that is fraught with emotion—both good and bad. I'll show you. When you read the word money, how do you feel? Disinterested? Frustrated? Anxious? Panicky? Angry? Depressed? Engaged? Intrigued? Hopeful? Secure?

Depending on your age and experience, you might have experienced all these emotions at one time or another. When I was a young single mom, you could say the word *money* and I'd break out in a cold sweat. Pure panic was what I felt, 24-7. But that was just for a life season (which felt like the winter that wouldn't end).

I'm embarrassed to say that for most of my adult life, I have been rather disinterested and somewhat neutral when it comes to money; it just never mattered much to me. I always wanted to be paid a fair wage for the value I contributed to the corporation that I served, but that was more about the work and honor— less about the accumulation or the spending of the green stuff. I only became interested in money when I realized it would play a significant role in my ability to choose balance.

Making the decision to leave the safety net of my monthly income and stock options was actually a nonevent when I decided to open my own company in 1994. Was it scary to launch my own business? Oh, sure. But I had something working in my favor that some folks don't enjoy: Steve and I had been living far beneath our means. We had managed our finances in the early years of our marriage as if we lived on one salary. What did that look like? For starters, we bought a far less expensive home than what we qualified for (allowing us to pay it off early); we didn't drive impressive cars (we often bought used); our kids didn't get everything they wanted (they survived); and I didn't wear designer clothes (but Steve said I looked cute anyway). We were into building financial *security* for our family, not a financial *facade* for our friends and neighbors.

Because of a few basic financial principles we followed early on, I had the opportunity to make a life-changing choice. And, girlfriends, having the opportunity to choose your career path and alter your lifestyle to find balance is *liberating*!

Such is the fate of all who are greedy for money; it robs them of life.
(PROVERBS 1:19)

Have you considered living beneath your means? Uncommon joy is the payoff.

WORK/LIFE BALANCE AND THE DEBIT CARD
Why It Really Matters

Many people live their lives going nowhere and doing nothing, not because they like where they are but simply because they are afraid of change. Overcoming this fear takes real motivation. It has to hurt so much that finally you can't take it anymore and you say, "Enough is enough! I want my life to be different!"[13]   DAVID BACH

IF YOU ARE disinterested (as I once was) in the topic of money and think it doesn't apply to you or affect your sense of balance, consider these stats:

- In 2008, Hewitt Associates consultants surveyed nearly 2 million participants in large-company 401(k) plans the company manages and found that women had an average of $56,320 in their accounts, compared with over $100,000 for men.[14]
- The average age of widowhood, according to *BusinessWeek*, is fifty-six. The typical widow exhausts her husband's life insurance within 2½ months.[15]
- Only 5 percent (one in twenty) of us will have annual incomes of $25,000 or more a year at age sixty-five.[16]
- During the last ten years, midlife divorce has tripled.
- One year after divorce, the average midlife woman remains single, with an average income of $11,300.
- Over 58 percent of female baby boomers have less than $10,000 saved in a pension plan or 401(k).[17]

Girlfriends, hormone replacement therapy is a women's issue—and so is money. Just as we learn and take responsibility for our physical health, so we must also learn and take responsibility for our financial well-being. It is a cop-out to delegate the arduous role of managing our money to spouses; you *both* need to know what is being managed and how because there is an excellent chance that one of you will be left alone to manage your affairs at some point in your future.

Finding and maintaining balance doesn't happen by accident. It is a purposeful, well-planned mission, one in which finances often play a pivotal role. Financial stability enables you to live your vision. If you are on solid financial footing, somewhere in life you made and executed a plan—allowing you the freedom to make choices today.

The master said, "Well done, my good and faithful servant. You have been faithful in handling this small amount, so now I will give you many more responsibilities. Let's celebrate together!" (MATTHEW 25:23)

Choose a plan and be faithful to the plan.

WORK/LIFE BALANCE AND THE DEBIT CARD
Do You Have Any Clue Where You Are?

When I asked women about their top five nightmares, winding up a bag lady featured in almost all their scenarios, right along with not having enough money to retire safely.[18]
LIZ PERLE

A FEW YEARS AGO, Steve, Shauna, Adam, and I drove down to Austin for the weekend. We ventured out of town on a winding ranch road and got lost. Our car has a navigation system, but it was preprogrammed to display our final destination. Well, that didn't help. I knew where home was! What I wanted to know was, *Where am I right now and how in the devil do I get on the right road to take me to the interstate?* It took several minutes to figure out what was wrong and reprogram our preferences. In the meantime, we were driving farther away from I-35 . . . not closer!

Just as you need a map or GPS on a road trip, you need a financial plan to help you get where you want to go. You begin by pinpointing where you sit at this moment (your financial assessment) in contrast to where you want to wind up (your desired financial state for retirement). Younger adults also need to identify road stops—things like a home purchase, having children, and saving for their college education. But here's the kicker: you can't drive around for days, months, or years without knowing where you are. Otherwise, you could be headed in the wrong direction—further from your financial destination.

Steve and I finally stopped "driving around in circles" financially. Why did we wait so long? No one told us that this is a critical step toward securing our final financial goal. I asked our financial advisor, Carol Meyer, why people (like us) procrastinate in having a financial assessment done. She said, "Many people are afraid of what they're going to find out. So they just put it off." *What?* That's just plain crazy! It's like skipping your mammogram because you could get bad results.

For God has not given us a spirit of fear and timidity, but of power, love, and self-discipline. (2 TIMOTHY 1:7)

If you really want to live intentionally, assess where you are today to determine how to best reach your final destination. Choose knowledge and discipline over timidity.

WORK/LIFE BALANCE AND THE DEBIT CARD
It's Not about How Much You Make

I CAN TELL YOU right now that you're not going to like this topic. Why? Because it's about saving money, not spending it. And that's hard for many of us (me included) when there are so many cute shoes crying out for my feet and handbags calling my name! But if we want to be women who live a life of uncommon joy and who are secure about our future, we have to dive into this icky topic.

I hosted a think tank of twentysomething women to learn more about the things that challenge and concern young women most when it comes to living a life of balance and contentment. The most common questions from this college-educated, articulate, already successful group of women were: How do we get smarter about money? and, How do we save more? They intuitively knew their finances were tightly coupled with their sense of balance and well-being, but they also knew something was amiss.

After the young women exchanged stories and further shared their financial frustrations, they came to the unanimous conclusion that they felt peer pressure to spend too much money on things like evenings out. Nine out of ten admitted they didn't really grasp the concept of delayed gratification. How could they? They were raised by parents like me who never wanted their children to go without; in addition, they live in a society where there is *so much stuff* competing for their hard-earned dollar. When I was their age, we didn't have a Starbucks or Ann Taylor Loft on every corner!

Later it dawned on me that what these gals really need is a goal. A tangible financial destination would help them develop self-discipline and measure their success along the way to their desired result.

The earnings of the godly enhance their lives,
but evil people squander their money on sin. (PROVERBS 10:16)

Do you know where you're headed financially? Pray that God will give you the desire to be a good steward.

WORK/LIFE BALANCE AND THE DEBIT CARD
It's Not about How Much You Make (Part Deux)

According to a survey from the National Center for Women and Retirement, of those women who say they feel in control of their lives, 56 percent of them saved and invested monthly. Of the 42 percent who said they felt out of control, only 17 percent made savings and investing for retirement a priority. There's a direct correlation between how well a woman takes care of herself financially and how good she feels about herself.[19] LIZ PERLE

IF YOU'RE UNSURE how to set financial goals, consider this example.

Let's say that you're thirty years old, earning $55,000 per year, and your goal is to amass one million dollars by the time you're sixty-five. In order to do this, you'll need to save about $467 per month. Wow! That seems like a lot of money when you're probably not at the top of your earning game. But we all know there are a few things we really *can* do without:

Eliminate 2 foamy iced coffee drinks	$7.00
Pass up that trendy new shade of lipstick	$7.00
Skip that new blouse	$32.00
Cook Saturday night rather than dine out	$45.00
Wear last year's necklace	$16.77
Total weekly savings	$107.77 per week
X 52 weeks per year = $5,604.04	

Invested over thirty-five years, $5,604.04 saved annually (about 10 percent of your salary) with a compounding interest of 8 percent will net you a smidge over a million bucks. Is this too aggressive for you? Start by saving $53.54 per week; at the same compounded interest and term, you'll net $500,000 . . . that's fifty times more than 58 percent of female baby boomers have saved today.[20]

I often hear women say that they *deserve* that new blouse. Really? I think what you deserve is something that will last long after any blouse has gone out of style. *What you deserve is peace of mind.* Consider the greater sacrifice: not going shopping on Saturday or anxiously scrimping for the last thirty years of your life.

> *But divide your investments among many places, for you do not know what risks might lie ahead.* (ECCLESIASTES 11:2)

If you really want the freedom to choose, develop a goal and a savings plan; then stick to it. You *deserve* it; and the smaller jean size that accompanies kicking the high-cal drink habit is a bonus.

WORK/LIFE BALANCE AND THE DEBIT CARD
When We Don't Walk the Talk

I'd never made as much money before in my life, but I'd never traded more of myself for it.[21]   LIZ PERLE

GIRLFRIENDS, when I read this statement in Liz Perle's book, I groaned out loud because I could totally relate.

I realized in the midnineties at the height of my corporate career that I had a disconnect. I was a walking, talking contradiction of my values when it came to money. I wanted more time with my family; I needed less stress for my health; I desired a more fulfilling career; but I wrestled for months with the idea that I made too much money to quit. Night after night, I thought myself crazy for staying in my job and crazy for even considering leaving the financial security behind. Finally, logic prevailed.

We all have our own built-in, deeply held value systems, but it's interesting how they're not always supported by the way we handle our money. Women who wouldn't dream of stealing a pencil at the office will sneak twenty-dollar bills from their husbands' wallets or will "disguise" new purchases in the closet. *H-e-l-l-o?* Does this seem healthy to anyone out there?

We work in jobs we hate to buy stuff that fills us emotionally for only days (and sometimes hours). We purchase things to fill a void, only to be awakened at 4 a.m. guilt-ridden about our spending extravaganza. We buy stuff for our kids to entertain them while we're physically or emotionally absent. Something's gotta give.

At some point we must all make an honest assessment and compare what we really value with how we *really* live. And then we must decide to align our walk with our talk.

Those who love money will never have enough. How meaningless to think that wealth brings true happiness! (ECCLESIASTES 5:10)

Are you happy? Or miserable—even with the big fat paycheck?

WORK/LIFE BALANCE AND
THE DEBIT CARD
Could You Take Control Tomorrow?

MOST WOMEN are surprised to learn that even though I run my own businesses, I haven't paid a bill since 1997. This situation leaves me in a precarious position. If something happened to Steve—my chief financial officer for Insider Marketing, ellenmiller.com, *and* the Miller household—not only would I be devastated to lose the love of my life, I would be paralyzed financially. Recognizing this vulnerability recently, we scheduled a family meeting for a little tutorial.

I admit I was totally lost when Steve opened Quicken. But after a few minutes of hunting and pecking, I was pretty confident that I could pay the electric bill again. Of course, managing the finances and dealing with payroll for the companies is a bit more complex, but at least I know I could cobble things together in case of an emergency. Could you? Or could he?

In many families, one spouse or the other takes care of managing the family budget. But it is the one who has forfeited this task that suffers greatly in a crisis. Talk about compounding a problem! If something happened to one of you, don't you agree that managing the budget and locating your investments should be the last thing that surfaces as a worry or a challenge?

I'm not a detail person. To me, balancing the checkbook and paying bills are like watching paint dry. I don't plan on taking over this duty (much to Steve's relief), but I'm comforted to know I can if I ever have to.

Could you use a refresher course? What about your mom or dad? Could they benefit from a quick walk-through of their investments, statements, and commitments?

Common sense and success belong to me.
Insight and strength are mine. (PROVERBS 8:14)

It might be time for you to reengage in financial discussions. Liberate yourself from ever saying, "I don't know how. He took care of the money."

WORK/LIFE BALANCE AND THE DEBIT CARD
What You Leave to the Kids

WE ARE IN THE MIDST of the largest transfer of wealth in our nation's history. The "greatest generation" is dying away. As good savers and investors, they're leaving trillions of dollars to their baby boomer heirs. So that leaves me really scratching my head . . . if they were such great savers, why didn't they pass this legacy on to their children? And if we didn't learn how to step up to the plate and take charge of our own financial security, how will our own kids learn?

I worry about today's younger generation. Kids today are bombarded with marketing messages at an astronomical rate. Did you know that by the time a girl is seventeen, she'll have been communicated to by a quarter of a million advertisements (specifically directed at her to improve her appearance)?[22] If you think the message you're sending your kids to save, wait, or even do without is being drowned out by Madison Avenue, you're right.

Fact number two: kids today have unprecedented access to cash. As reported in 2002, Teenage Research Unlimited says that, on average, teens spent $101 a week.[23] Regardless if a teen earned this money or was given this much cash to manage as part of an allowance, it is a huge responsibility. *Oh. My. Goodness.* We're talking 5,252 bucks a year! Couple this access to cash with the subliminal messages we send because of our own money management challenges, and we may be setting our kids up for disaster.

> *Wisdom is even better when you have money.*
> *Both are a benefit as you go through life.* (ECCLESIASTES 7:11)

So my question is: How do we leave a legacy of good financial stewardship to our children? How do we impart powerful and liberating lessons in money management and fiscal responsibility to them as they grow?

Let's start today by praying that we all get our priorities in place to better pass on the important lessons of money management to the next generation.

WORK/LIFE BALANCE AND
THE DEBIT CARD
What You Leave to the Kids (Part Deux)

ONLY RECENTLY have I begun to pray for wisdom when it comes to investing and counseling our kids about money. However, even without divine intervention, Steve and I did have some "teachable moments" with our kiddos. You might find a few of our tips—and some we learned from other parents along the way—helpful as you lay the foundation of wise money management for your little ones.

At age 2: Introduce the concept of delayed gratification. Begin when they're old enough to sit in the shopping cart. I don't care how loud they scream at Target—just smile sweetly at the mother standing in line behind you and tell her your child is embracing the concept of delayed gratification.

At age 3: Introduce the concept of giving. Hoarding money is as unhealthy as refusing to take financial responsibility for yourself, so instill the habit of giving. The average three-year-old will clearly understand the concept of sacrificing a toy in order to buy one for another child in need; as a matter of fact, they seem to enjoy the act of sacrificial giving. Get them in the habit now of giving of their first earnings in the form of a tithe or contribution. Explain how such gifts are used and why the organization depends on their financial help.

At age 4: Introduce the concept of pay yourself first. Encourage your child to pay themselves 10 to 20 percent of their allowance or earnings before shopping. Children as young as four should have three piggy banks—one for spending, one for saving, and one for charitable giving. As they get older, replace the physical saving bank with a passbook savings account. Now is the time to get them in the routine of stopping by the savings piggy bank before heading to the toy aisle. It will make the drive-through at the bank second nature by the time they're fifteen.

At age 7: Introduce the concept of the 401(k). For every dollar your children save, match it dollar for dollar. This concept can be grasped by the average seven-year-old, but let me tell you, by the time they're teenagers (and eyeing a new jacket or electronic equipment), they will totally embrace this plan! And there will be no question about how a 401(k) works when they're twenty-five.

At age 7: Don't introduce credit. If you teach delayed gratification, you will not be tempted to allow your kids to "pay you back later." This is a bad habit to start; it just gets them comfortable with borrowing and debt.

Tell them to use their money to do good. They should be rich in good works and generous to those in need, always being ready to share with others.
(1 TIMOTHY 6:18)

WORK/LIFE BALANCE AND THE DEBIT CARD
What You Leave to the Kids (Part Trois)

IF YOUR KIDS are older and you missed the first teachable moments, remember that it's never too late. Of course, if you haven't yet started teaching the discipline of delayed gratification, you might really be embarrassed when your seventeen-year-old throws a hissy fit at the mall. But stand your ground. Just smile at the other mothers and explain it's a teachable moment. They'll be inspired to follow suit.

Other important money disciplines to convey at this life stage include:

At age 16 or 17: Introduce the concept of balancing a checkbook. Do this while your teenagers are still at home. I know from experience that this can be a nightmare if you try to do it long distance after they've headed off to college. Better yet, introduce your teens to Quicken so they can actually see where their money goes in the form of pie charts! What an eye-opener.

At age 18: Introduce the concept of eating beans. Before they leave for college, explain they will be given a set living allowance and you won't make extra little deposits when they run low. Our daughter, Shauna, called home from college once, complaining she was running low on money. After a little interrogation, she admitted she had bought a few items that weren't exactly necessities. How did she make it through the month? Refried beans and tortillas. She was proud of making it to the end of the month and for coming up with a meal that cost just 28 cents.

When they're engaged: Introduce the concept of making choices and sacrifices, and managing money as a couple. Let the nearly-weds manage their own wedding budget. Set up a checking account and make one deposit based on what you're willing to spend on the wedding. Whatever they spend over the budget, they have to come up with; whatever they save, they get to keep. No time like the present to see how they manage money *together*.

When they're married: Offer your experience and counsel. Young married couples are often confused by all things money related—from 401(k)s to buying their first home. Don't insert yourself where you're not appreciated, but offer to share your advice if and when they're interested in learning more. My bet: they'll be interested. Do you think they *want* to be poor?

Direct your children onto the right path,
and when they are older, they will not leave it. (PROVERBS 22:6)

Work/life balance means liberating yourself today from caring financially for your grown children tomorrow. Not sure about you, but I'm planning to leave a lot more advice than cash.

WORK/LIFE BALANCE AND THE DEBIT CARD

FATHER GOD, I realize I could use some help when it comes to money matters, and I ask you to guide me as I

- [ ] develop a rightful attitude toward money;
- [ ] work to create a long-term financial plan;
- [ ] develop new disciplines in order to follow my financial plan;
- [ ] align my value system with my spending system;
- [ ] learn more about the tactical execution of managing our finances;
- [ ] instill in my children a healthy attitude toward and good habits of financial stewardship.

ACTIONS I WILL TAKE:

Example: This week, I will schedule an appointment with a financial planner to determine my fiscal fitness.

1. _____

2. _____

3. _____

Father God, all gifts are from you. Thank you for all you have provided me. Guide me as I work to improve my attitude toward money and material things. Help me to become a faithful steward of all you have entrusted to me. I pray that you will enlighten me with ways to leave a legacy of healthy attitudes and God-honoring ways to manage money to my children. Amen.

IF THEY WEREN'T THE CLEAVERS

MOTHER'S DAY. Father's Day. Birthdays. These special dates on the calendar cause me to reflect on my parents—both what was and what could have been.

I came from a "normal" family—one where there were huge issues, dark secrets, major imperfections, even addictions. I say this is normal because I now realize that the "abnormal" family is the one where everyone gets along well, has a healthy emotional bond, and is quick to forgive one another's shortcomings. If you hail from such a family, consider yourself blessed. If you grew up in a "normal" family like mine, well, girlfriend, this series is for you!

My father had just turned fifty-five when I was birthed by his twenty-nine-year-old wife. Needless to say, this was before the young trophy wife arrangement became fashionable. Dad had three daughters by a previous marriage—all within a few years of my mom's age—and nine grandchildren. Mom had been married once before, too, and had an eight-year-old son when I came along. Thus, we were a "blended" family, although back then there was no catchy marketing phrase designed to make us all feel better about our unique state. No, my family was different, and I quickly realized this as I was the only child in my first-grade class who had a half brother and half sisters; I wondered for years, *Where's the rest of them? When do they get to be whole like me?*

Many of us must deal with a history of hurt, confusion, rejection, and sometimes abuse caused by our families. But we don't have to be held hostage to them. In *Women Who Think Too Much*, Susan Nolen-Hoeksema says, "A critical part of growing into a mature, fulfilled adult is to acknowledge our past and the foibles of our families, and to decide what aspects of our heritage we wish to reject and what aspects we wish to embrace."[24]

I love this! We get to choose to reject or accept what we will remember, take forth, and use in the development of our adult selves.

> *I waited patiently for the LORD to help me,*
>   *and he turned to me and heard my cry.*
> *He lifted me out of the pit of despair,*
>   *out of the mud and the mire.*
> *He set my feet on solid ground*
>   *and steadied me as I walked along.*
> *He has given me a new song to sing,*
>   *a hymn of praise to our God.*
> *Many will see what he has done and be amazed.*
>   *They will put their trust in the LORD.* (PSALM 40:1-3)

I think it's a good idea to explore our "normal" families so we can choose what we will embrace from our past. It could be the difference between joy and pain as those special dates roll around—again and again and again.

IF THEY WEREN'T THE CLEAVERS
Who's Loved Most, Wally or the Beav?

SIBLING RIVALRY EXISTS. So does favoritism. We've all been someone's favorite. Felt it in our bones. Maybe it made us feel special or maybe we felt embarrassed for others who didn't feel as prized. But we've all also been disliked; or at least felt that way. Reality or perception—it doesn't really matter. If you felt like the odd one out as a child, you've probably had to be extra diligent in developing your self-worth.

My girlfriend Anne told me that she felt less valued in her family of seven children. Her mom suffered from "issues," and as Anne was growing up, the duty to care for her younger sister fell to her. Only in the past year, nearly three years after her mother's death, did her siblings confirm that yes—their mother told them before she died that she didn't love Anne the same as she loved the other children. Needless to say, it's one thing to suspect, but something altogether different to have it confirmed that you were not as cherished as your siblings. When I asked Anne how she felt about this revelation she said, "You know, the hardest thing now is for me to know how to love her. I'm supposed to love my mother. She's gone. I can't confront her but I must love her. I'm *supposed* to."

Anne didn't feel threatened or competitive with her siblings—her contest was only with herself. But many siblings take their rivalry to their grave, creating root rot in the family tree. At some point, future generations in the family have to stop the insanity. Someone has to fertilize those roots!

Blessed is a man who perseveres under trial; for once he has been approved, he will receive the crown of life which the Lord has promised to those who love Him.
(JAMES 1:12, NASB)

Were you loved less? I hope not. But if you were, I hope you can find a way to give those who just didn't know better—or those who could have done better and didn't—a pass. Not for them. They most likely don't deserve it. But you do. You deserve to have the peace and freedom that come from letting it go.

IF THEY WEREN'T THE CLEAVERS
She Wasn't Exactly June

I WAS ALWAYS a bit embarrassed by my family. Oh, not that my father was old enough to be my grandfather—au contraire! The man treated me like his little princess! What did I think of him serving as a room mother? How cool! Instead of cupcakes for our class party or event, he brought homemade chili! Yes, the man was Ward in the flesh.

But Mom wasn't exactly June; she would have been better suited for a role on *ER*! We never knew exactly what was coming next at our house, since Mom suffered from bipolar disorder. In *those* days it was diagnosed as manic depression, and let me tell you, the manic episodes were way interesting. I never learned if it was her personality or the disease that caused her to be self-absorbed, easily angered, manipulative, and thoughtless, but I went from walking on eggshells as a child to stomping on them as a teenager. By the time I was thirty I had become an angry, judgmental, full-blown nonhonoring daughter. But thanks to maturity and honest reflection on my own shortcomings as a mother (yes, girlfriends—we make mistakes too) I came to realize something important: she didn't pick this role, nor did I. We'd have to deal with it together. Mom wasn't perfect.

During my period of self-examination, two things occurred to me: first, I realized that I'm a better person due to the challenges I faced as a child, and later as a teenager. Had I grown up in a home without drama, I'm sure I would have become a self-absorbed spoiled brat! The second thing I realized was that regardless of my position as the child, it was my responsibility now to act like the grown-up. No, it doesn't exactly seem fair.

Mom made some really bad choices; things which made it difficult for me to honor her. But the fifth commandment, "Honor your father and mother," has a period at the end—not a disclaimer. It took much prayer and years of wrestling with God for me to allow him to soften my heart.

God provided no disclaimers and Moses didn't edit:

Honor your father and mother. Then you will live a long, full life in the land the LORD your God is giving you. (EXODUS 20:12)

Stop making excuses for your inability to follow this commandment. Two wrongs don't make a right.

IF THEY WEREN'T THE CLEAVERS
She Wasn't Exactly June (Part Deux)

I HAVE TO BE honest with you. Even as an adult, honoring Mom on a good day was difficult. And, on her bad days, well, let's just say that I was shocked that God didn't strike me dead before midnight.

Still, I was determined to do two things: (1) be an obedient daughter to God my Father, and (2) be a respectful daughter to my mother. So I had to get creative.

To start the process I decided to select those things I *wanted* to remember about her instead of the situations that were not so lovely. Consider this an exercise of selective amnesia on steroids! And as I get older I'm amazed at all the little things stored in my memory bank that allow me to remember her fondly and with great honor:

Orange sherbet Push-Ups. During a brief stint as a stay-at-home mom, Mom took me almost every day to our local small-town grocery store for a push-up ice cream. Remember the orange sherbet in a little cardboard container with the stick on the bottom? It was my favorite, and she treated me to it often. I can still feel the "sticky" on my fingers!

"Santa Claus Is Coming to Town." This was my theme song, and my mom sang it to me year-round. She had to sing really loud to be heard above the whir of the window air conditioner in July! She didn't have a very nice voice, but she knew every word. Did you know there are two stanzas?

Homemade dill pickles. Mom wasn't really into cooking, but every summer she packed fresh garlic, fresh dill, and homegrown cucumbers in her Ball jars. The house smelled rank with vinegar boiling on the stove, but the temporary sacrifice was worth it. She was known among my friends not for her "issues," but for her fabulous pickles. Her pickles made me very proud.

> *Then Joshua told the people, "Purify yourselves, for tomorrow the LORD will do great wonders among you." (JOSHUA 3:5)*

What you choose to remember about your parents *can be* their legacy and *your peace.*

I wish you peace.

IF THEY WEREN'T THE CLEAVERS
June Vacuums, Ward Reads the Paper

YOUR MOTHER is a pessimist.

Your father is a narcissist.

June vacuums in her pearls (what's *that* all about?), and

Ward hides behind the paper.

Some things are not going to change. Specifically, *your parents* are not going to change. Why? Because there was likely too much baggage left on their personal doorstep by their own parents. Too much "stuff" has happened to these people—primarily, *their* abusive or absent or controlling parents! But you can change. Am I suggesting that you lower your expectations of your family? Absolutely. They will never live up to your definition of what you need today or what you required yesterday.

When your parents are still very much in your life and display destructive tendencies toward themselves and others, it can drive you nutso. But let me ask . . . what if you knew the source of their pain, their addiction, or their other issues? Would you be more kind? Would you be more patient? Could you be more tolerant?

As my grown cousins and I sat and visited one day, we developed a fascinating theory as to why my mother and their father grew into such dishonorable people. Among their parents, grandparents, aunts, uncles, and a slew of cousins, they were an anomaly. Everyone else was totally normal (well, mostly). But this theory, which I'll briefly explain tomorrow, gave us all some comfort that they didn't wake up each day with hate in their heart for no good reason.

Like us, you may never learn with certainty the underlying cause of your parents' issues. Because many of them came from a generation that does not share or divulge family secrets, they may take their nightmares to their grave. Knowing that might not make you feel better about your childhood—it certainly doesn't change the fact that you were mistreated—but it might help you be more tolerant. And maybe it will help you begin your healing.

I pray that from his glorious, unlimited resources he will empower you with inner strength through his Spirit. Then Christ will make his home in your hearts as you trust in him. Your roots will grow down into God's love and keep you strong.
(EPHESIANS 3:16-17)

Are you willing to consider there might be more to their story?

IF THEY WEREN'T THE CLEAVERS
June Vacuums, Ward Reads the Paper (Part Deux)

DEVELOPING A THEORY, a reason why my mother behaved as she did, became an important tool as I began to rebuild a semblance of a relationship with her and become emotionally able to honor her. It wasn't always easy, nor was I always successful, but I hope my discoveries might help you develop your own tools for coping.

First, I decided that no one wants to be like this. No one gets up in the morning wanting to be unpleasant. Because I didn't know the circumstances or the details that caused my mom so much pain, the theory that my cousins and I concocted was about something that might have happened to her when she was a child. This event would have been so destructive to her self-esteem that she knew no way to deal with her pain other than to deflect it onto others. This was step one in helping me to put my feelings aside in order to be a kinder, more patient daughter.

By sticking with my story and replaying it in my mind, I was able to get through our weekly phone chats with the grace I needed just to sit and listen (and not fume, steam, or scream . . . at least not until I got off the phone).

Second, I limited my face-to-face visits with my mom to no more than forty-five minutes. Yes—some people can do some serious damage in that amount of time, but I found this worked for us. Go to sixty minutes and I promise something was going to blow—because hard as I tried, my patience just couldn't be stretched another quarter hour!

Last, I would choose to forgive my mother for anything and everything she said—*before* I even stepped in her door. I reset my expectations knowing her history as I did. I knew I would be hurt, embarrassed, or disappointed by her, but I refused to harbor these feelings. I imagined that this traumatic event early in life had hurt her so badly that she had forgotten how to be kind to others. Even to me.

Then you will experience God's peace, which exceeds anything we can understand. His peace will guard your hearts and minds as you live in Christ Jesus. (PHILIPPIANS 4:7)

Need better coping skills? You might consider that there is something more to your parent's story.

IF THEY WEREN'T THE CLEAVERS
They Might Make a Good Coen Brothers' Film

A GIRLFRIEND (we'll call her Mary) and I were recently talking about our mothers. Like mine, her mom was a Valium junkie. As we shared our stories, it appeared we had lived one another's lives—until I asked her if her mother had ever been shot.

Mary laughed out loud. "Shot? Are you kidding? Your life sounds like a Coen brothers' movie!" As sad as the event was at the time, years later, I, too, can see a plotline that would make Joel and Ethan envious.

The story goes that my stepfather and mother, during a night of heavy drinking, had decided it was a good time for a shooting lesson. I have always had my doubts (along with the investigating sheriff). I'm not sure what type of lesson includes two rounds to the heart at midnight, but I'm pretty sure Mom figured out firsthand how a gun gets fired. Unfortunately, she refused to press charges. After surgery and an extended stay in the hospital, she returned to the man who had pumped her full of lead. This, of course, gave me a new reason to be concerned for the woman's state of mind. And again, I was put in an awkward situation.

Steve and I had been dating for only a couple of months, but we knew our relationship was for keeps. As he drove me to the hospital after the shooting, I sat in shock. As he drove me home, I sat in embarrassment. How in the world was I going to explain this situation to my soon-to-be mother-in-law? The Southern belle who *was* June in the flesh. I already had one strike against me: I had been married before. Now I had to explain *this*?

Of course, Harriett, Steve's mother, was understanding . . . of what I'm not sure. I didn't understand it! How in the world did my mother get herself in this situation and then fail to get herself out of it? All my pleading, brainstorming, offers, bargaining, and (finally) ultimatums fell on deaf ears.

It was so sad, Steve and I couldn't help but laugh. The old girl had taken two bullets to the chest and was still kicking—and calling her own shots (pun intended). Christmas rolled around a few months later and what do you think— she wanted the family to come over for a Christmas celebration! Steve agreed that it would be the right thing to do, as long as bulletproof vests were passed out at the door.

> *As pressure and stress bear down on me,*
> *I find joy in your commands.* (PSALM 119:143)

Sometimes, all you *can* do is laugh.

IF THEY WEREN'T THE CLEAVERS
You're Not Exactly June Either

It's not until you become a mother that your judgment slowly turns to compassion and understanding. ERMA BOMBECK

PEOPLE WHO LIVE in glass houses shouldn't throw stones. Translation: if you're a mom, there's a good chance you're messing up too.

My point: ain't none of us perfect.

My heart breaks for you girlfriends who came from extremely abusive or neglectful homes; I can't tell you how to overcome the hurt and anger caused by those who robbed you of a safe childhood. I cannot imagine because I was not a child of abuse or neglect. Even though my mom was emotionally crippled, I was deeply loved and cared for. But I can relate to those who feel that their parents were missing some important pages from their parenting instruction manual!

I laugh at myself while writing this and think about my own grown children and wonder what damage I have done to their psyches over the years. Shoot! My kids might wonder how I could have missed entire *chapters* in my guidebook! Since we all know how hard it is to be a good parent (perfect parents do not exist), maybe—for all our sakes—we should consider letting go of the past. And because we're not June either, maybe we should ask our children to forgive us for the parenting mistakes we have made.

Forgive us our sins, as we have forgiven those who sin against us.
(MATTHEW 6:12)

If you are not a mom, looking beyond your own mother's failings may be even more difficult. Forgiving your parents doesn't mean you accept or excuse their poor behavior—it just means that you no longer wish to be a victim or to hold the hurt in your heart. You have to let go and forgive . . . sometimes over and over and over.

IF THEY WEREN'T THE CLEAVERS

FATHER GOD, only you know the experiences I have been through and the hurt I have felt. You have spoken to my heart, and I know that

- ☐ I can choose what I will reject or what I will embrace from my family;
- ☐ I was loved less by them, but not by you. I choose to forgive them;
- ☐ I have not honored my _____ but will now carefully choose positive things to remember—those things that will allow me to extend respect;
- ☐ I may not have all the facts that caused my _____ to be this way;
- ☐ laughter is sometimes the only medicine; bless me with a sense of humor;
- ☐ I am not a perfect parent either.

ACTIONS I WILL TAKE:

Example: Three positive things I will choose to remember about my childhood include: 1)_____ 2)_____ 3)_____.

1. _____

2. _____

3. _____

Father, my heart breaks today for the child I was yesterday. Only you can heal the brokenness. Help me to consciously choose what to remember. Help me to consciously choose to forgive. Help me to realize that although I think I know my parents, there may be many aspects to their story and their history of which I am unaware. Father, pour your blessing onto my children by helping me be a better parent to them. Amen.

WHAT'S IN YOUR PURSE?

I USED TO CARRY an industrial-size tote bag. It was good for holding everything I might need on a given day—and the next two weeks as well! The problem was that everything I needed for the day seemed to sift to the bottom and get lost in a pool of pens, breath mints—I swear those things reproduce on their own—and paper clips. To compound the problem, when I carried my big bag I got this terrible knot in my right shoulder. So I decided less is more and started buying only small bags.

But last week my pocketbook (as my grandmother would call it) felt like it was packing a brick! I thought *what in the world* can possibly be in this tiny purse to make it so heavy? After digging around, I found not one, not two, but *five* tubes of lipstick, $16.32 in change, and enough reward cards to feed the city of Dallas. How did I manage to let this stuff creep into my precious little accessory? I carefully unloaded the excess I didn't need for *that day*, and my handbag once again was light as a feather as I slung it over my shoulder and bounced out the door . . . looking rather chic, I must say.

I've decided that life is a lot like my handbag. We don't always collect all the distractions, stress, and schedules intentionally. But we do allow them to creep in. And it's this stuff that often gives us a knot in our right shoulder or a splitting headache. Things like crazy, ridiculous schedules. And family and friends with dependency problems or other issues. Or sometimes our inability to take control and set our own boundaries is what makes our lives feel like a seventy-pound ball and chain.

Then Jesus said, "Come to me, all of you who are weary and carry heavy burdens, and I will give you rest. Take my yoke upon you. Let me teach you, because I am humble and gentle at heart, and you will find rest for your souls."
(MATTHEW 11:28-29)

You know . . . you choose what you put in your handbag, and you have the power to take things out. Carry only those things you need for today. It's time to start carrying that snappy little clutch!

WHAT'S IN YOUR PURSE?
Turning Off That Stylish New Phone

SOMETIMES OUR PURSES get too heavy because we let other people drop things in them. We don't do a good job of setting our own boundaries. We allow others to invade our space, which makes us frustrated and angry. Can we be honest with each other? Some of us talk too much. I know, because I'm a talker. In the past, whenever someone called to chat, I'd launch right into the conversation.

However, now I know there are times when I don't talk, won't talk, can't talk to anyone. Now this may sound harsh, but I usually take this stance during the weekend. I need quiet time to recharge my batteries. Just because someone wants to chat doesn't make me obligated to visit with them.

I learned this the hard way. I used to be available to anyone and everyone 24-7. They would call and I would listen—well, sort of—until I realized I was being unfair to them and to myself. The telephone was making my purse heavy. So I let the calls go to voice mail. After trying this once, I realized the world did not end when I delayed a conversation until a better time. When I called back, I found that one of three things happened: a) the problem was still there, waiting for me, b) the problem had worked itself out without me, or c) the sale was over and I didn't need to spend the cash anyway! This is a boundary I have set for myself. I talk when I'm in a position to have a *meaningful conversation*. Now my purse is much lighter.

> For the LORD your God is living among you.
> He is a mighty savior.
> He will take delight in you with gladness.
> With his love, he will calm all your fears.
> He will rejoice over you with joyful songs. (ZEPHANIAH 3:17)

This techno-savvy world where we're connected to everyone every minute is draining us of our creativity. Turn off your phone. Put the BlackBerry in a drawer. Close your notebook computer. Choose to be quiet. You'll be amazed by your renewed enthusiasm for and patience with others come Monday morn.

WHAT'S IN YOUR PURSE?
Whose Picture Can We Take Out?

DRAINERS. We've all got them—you know, people who can suck the oxygen out of the room, people who invade your physical and mental space with their ongoing issues, people whom you know you've been commanded by God to love—but it's really, *really* hard.

And it's not always a nosy neighbor or the relationally challenged woman sitting in the next cube. Sometimes it's a close friend or family member. I know because my family has "issues."

Sometimes such people create conflict because they enjoy drama. I'm sure you know the type—someone who seems to get a "high" when there is dissension among friends or family members. I'm the opposite. Discord burdens me.

Friends or family members who generate drama can drain your energy and make your purse so heavy that you can't drag your fanny out of the house. Codependency is a big word with big meaning that can extend from enabling someone with a drug habit to enabling someone to gossip. Want to get that heavy purse off your shoulder? Then put up the hand.

If someone is pushing your buttons, it's not that person's fault . . . it's your fault for not setting your own boundaries. It's your fault for not shutting down the negativity.

Most important of all, continue to show deep love for each other, for love covers a multitude of sins. (I PETER 4:8)

You can't remove some people's picture out of your purse—especially when they're family—but you sure can choose to pull their issues out of there! You can also take out the concealer—you'll have far fewer circles under your eyes from fretting all night!

WHAT'S IN YOUR PURSE?
How Many Lists Do You Have in There?

I'M SURE WE ALL agree that health scares are not fun. However, they seem to bring about one positive effect. Some of my friends and family members have been diagnosed with the big C, and with the exception of one precious soul, they all beat it. Many have said their cancer fight helped them reconsider their priorities.

I got my wake-up call in 2002 when my doctor told me he thought I had multiple sclerosis. For seven days, awaiting the final diagnosis, I had the opportunity to assess my life as it was and what it might be like for the next many years living with that dreaded disease. That time of reflection gave me the opportunity to realize that my hectic schedule was burdening my handbag.

I had a weakness for committees, boards, and baking brownies for the bake sale. My problem is that I don't feel *obligated* to serve . . . I *want* to help! But when I found myself grousing about the very thing I had volunteered for, I had to stop and ask myself if I was overcommitted.

During that time of self-reflection, I was serving on three boards, running two companies, teaching Sunday school, serving as a Stephen minister, and traveling all over the country—in addition to my most important roles as wife and mother. Doing a hundred-pound bench press was easier than carrying my purse around!

Slowly, I began to remove things from my schedule, one by one, so I could find what I needed for each day. And what I needed was to wake up feeling joyful, not burdened. It's a mature, self-aware woman who learns to say, "Thank you for asking, but no I can't . . ."

We have not stopped praying for you since we first heard about you. We ask God to give you complete knowledge of his will and to give you spiritual wisdom and understanding. Then the way you live will always honor and please the Lord, and your lives will produce every kind of good fruit. All the while, you will grow as you learn to know God better and better. (COLOSSIANS 1:9-10)

Caution: those of us who are triple-type A will fall off the wagon within months if we're not alert. Be careful that you don't let too many volunteer efforts sneak back into that precious, but limited-capacity, handbag.

And a health update: while I did suffer from SOS (stressed-out schedule), I did not have MS.

WHAT'S IN YOUR PURSE?
How Many Lists Do You Have in There? (Part Deux)

IN ADDITION to obligations, something else in our handbags may be weighing us down: kid stuff. This topic is touchy for some women, but I think we should at least *explore* the idea that maybe our kids' commitments are *wearing us out*. Some kids' schedules rival those of the average CEO!

I'm not a child expert, but I'm fairly certain it will not damage children's psyches nor will it thwart their opportunity to be the next Bill Gates if you tell them "not today." Actually, our children might benefit from a bit of downtime themselves. What do you need for today? Children who are thriving. And they will thrive without dance lessons, piano lessons, soccer practice, and French lessons—all *before* Tuesday!

I'm sure I'm showing my age here, but I thought most people subscribed to the "one extracurricular activity per semester" rule—not ten! I was in a very different space and time when my kids were younger. First, we didn't have the money to pay for tutors, coaches, music teachers, dance instructors, and camping fees at the same time. Second, I worked. I didn't have the flexibility (or inclination) to shuttle my kids around. When I was off work, I wanted to be with my children, not sitting in the parking lot waiting for them to come out of a lesson. I fear we have traded the value of our teaching and time with our own children for the promise that they can tap out a good "shuffle-ball-change" at the spring dance recital, play the trombone on Friday night, and kick a goal on Saturday. Multidimensional kids are great—but have we taken it too far?

> *Wisdom is enshrined in an understanding heart;*
>   *wisdom is not found among fools.* (PROVERBS 14:33)

If tomorrow you learned that something was going to seriously alter your lifestyle or health, what would you change? Where and how would you spend your time to better nurture your children? I bet it would not be sitting behind the wheel of a car. It's a mature, self-aware mom who learns to say, "no."

WHAT'S IN YOUR PURSE?
How Many Lists Do You Have in There? (Part Trois)

AS LONG AS I'm on a roll and ragging on the kids' schedule, let's discuss weekends. I have listened to women tell me what's on their schedule for their days off, and I swear—I get exhausted before they tell me what they're doing on Saturday evening!

Families, and husbands and wives in particular, don't have enough downtime these days. And they certainly have no downtime together. From demanding careers, to the aforementioned kid stuff, to packed social calendars, there seems to be no time just to *be still*. Do you even remember how to just sit and talk with your husband over a leisurely dinner? What about taking a Saturday morning to sit outside and read the paper together? Does that sound like pure fantasy?

Steve and I sometimes overcommit our weekends, and when we do I don't feel refreshed on Monday. However, I found if we reserve one night (Friday or Saturday) and one day (Saturday or Sunday) for "quiet time," we're totally renewed by Sunday evening. Some women I've talked to feel guilty about this. Girlfriends, give yourself a pass! You don't have to be productive 100 percent of every minute of every day.

> *But the Lord said to her, "My dear Martha, you are worried and upset over all these details! There is only one thing worth being concerned about. Mary has discovered it, and it will not be taken away from her."* (LUKE 10:41-42)

On the contrary, if you can learn to afford yourself this "luxury," your productivity will soar over the next seventy-two hours.

Girlfriend, that knot in your right shoulder may be there because your purse is too heavy with excess burdens and commitments. What can you choose to eliminate? Uncommon joy is waiting.

WHAT'S IN YOUR PURSE?
Girlfriend, You Need a New Purse!

ON THE FLIP SIDE of hectic schedules are routines that bore the life right out of you. I have a love-hate relationship with the daily grind; I am a creature of habit and enjoy my "rituals," but every now and then, I just need a break from the same-ole, same-ole things!

Interrupting your routine takes some planning and a little creativity, but it is a great way to lighten your handbag. Here are a few easy ideas:

- This weekend, serve dinner on your good china and crystal. Dinner might consist of KFC and grape juice—but hey—life is short! Get out the good stuff. Every now and then, I serve Steve our light Friday night dinner of smoked salmon, cheese, and crackers on china. He gets a big kick out of it. Young children really enjoy this. Have everyone "dress for dinner" the way families did in the old days. You can also gently use this event as a teachable moment to reinforce eating with the correct utensil and proper table manners. What do you need today? A chance to celebrate life with those you love the very most.
- Visit with your girlfriend. Women are so busy tending everyone else, they let their friendships flounder. Pick up the phone. Don't always expect your friend to initiate coffee on Saturday morning. Emerson said, "Go oft to the house of thy friend, for weeds choke the unused path." Hmm. Ralph clearly knew something about friendships. What do you need for today? Giggles with your girlfriend.
- And my all-time favorite: Take a pretend vacation (recently coined *staycation* by the media) some weekend. Steve and I do this every few months. We don't go out of town—we just do the same things we would do if we went to another city. We go to brunch. We go to the museum. Then we take in a local site we've never visited. We don't watch TV. We don't answer the phone. We don't do laundry. We're on vacation! If you're a stay-at-home mom with small children, you may need an overnight getaway at a hotel in town; just having the opportunity to go to the potty alone without two sets of eyes staring up at you can make you feel like a new woman! What do you need for today? To get away without packing a bag.

A glad heart makes a happy face;
a broken heart crushes the spirit. (PROVERBS 15:13)

Choose to take the common out of your common life, and your handbag will be so much lighter!

WHAT'S IN YOUR PURSE?

FATHER GOD, you have empowered me with the freedom to choose. Remind me to

☐ turn off my phone;

☐ lay down the burdens of my friends and family;

☐ occasionally say no to obligations so that I don't overextend myself;

☐ occasionally say no to my children in order to preserve family time;

☐ occasionally say no to social engagements that can become taxing;

☐ occasionally interrupt my routine in order to have fun.

ACTIONS I WILL TAKE:

Example: I will set and maintain better boundaries with _____ for my own emotional health.

1. _____

2. _____

3. _____

Father God, my handbag gets so heavy with obligations. Thank you for the freedom you have given me to make choices. Speak to my heart and mind that I might limit my obligations to live each hour of each day with uncommon joy. Amen.

WHAT MAMMAW SAID

UNTIL I WAS WELL into my thirties, I didn't realize that not all women are exposed to an extremely wise older woman. I was lucky and doubly blessed. I not only knew such a woman, she served as my personal and professional mentor and hero. She was my master teacher. She was my Mammaw.

Now, you city girlfriends who come from well-to-do families will ask, "What's a Mammaw?" I realized when I moved from my small, country town to the city over thirty years ago that city girls have this loving, trusted older woman in their families they call Grandmother or something really snazzy like MiMi. Well, in the country, we just call her MAM-MAW. There's a heavy accent on the MAW (let your jaw drop "a-ways") if you want to say it properly.

Mammaw was a very unusual woman for her time. She was a banker for over thirty-five years—in an age when women weren't supposed to enjoy successful careers; she raised a family (including my mom); she was the church treasurer and a champion forty-two domino player; and she could dance the Charleston like a professional (although she was a closet dancer; my Methodist grandmother married a Southern Baptist). But she was something else: she was a near master at living in peace even when her life was in turmoil. As I think back on her life of grace and the beautiful legacy she left her grandchildren and great-grandchildren, I thought perhaps you would enjoy getting to know her too.

John Maxwell, in his book *Thinking for a Change*, says this about creating a legacy: "If you are successful, it becomes possible for you to leave an inheritance *for* others. But if you desire to do more, to create a legacy, then you need to leave that *in* others. When you think unselfishly and invest in others, you gain the opportunity to create a legacy that will outlive you (emphasis added)."[25]

A good man leaves an inheritance to his children's children.
(PROVERBS 13:22, NASB)

Mammaw died with not a penny to her name, but I am dripping with jewels and riches beyond belief because of her influence. Because she unselfishly invested in me.

WHAT MAMMAW SAID
It's Comin' Up a Cloud

Forgiving is required when excusing or condoning or tolerating or accepting are not big enough to do the job. JOHN ORTBERG

MAMMAW LOVED the weather. She'd get worked up over any minor change, but nothing got her attention like an evening spring thunderstorm approaching from the northwest. She'd stand on her front porch, hands on her hips, feeling the wind shift and say, "Ellen, run home quick and get your parents; it's comin' up a cloud."

We lived about seventy-five yards to the south, so I'd trot my short fat little legs home and get my parents. Mammaw would pick up the phone. (We had a party line—know what that is? Telco purgatory to a teenager.) She'd call my aunt, who would bring my three cousins from across the street to join us in the storm cellar. It was stinky, dark, and damp—so she'd light the kerosene lamp and there together, huddled up close, we'd ride out the storm. Telling stories. Singing hymns. Laughing. Together. As a family.

Mammaw's family was far from perfect; both her son and daughter had issues. But regardless, Mammaw knew one thing for sure: no matter the problems we faced as a family—sometimes caused by circumstances, sometimes created by poor choices—when life's storms come, and they will, it's far better to ride out the weather with your family, than alone. Mammaw's own children would sometimes do or say things that she couldn't condone. They made some choices she couldn't accept.

Because Mammaw couldn't tolerate or accept some of their decisions, she was left with forgiving them. I saw firsthand what unconditional love looks like—by a kerosene lamp in a cold, dark storm cellar.

Such love has no fear, because perfect love expels all fear. If we are afraid, it is for fear of punishment, and this shows that we have not fully experienced his perfect love. We love each other because he loved us first. (1 JOHN 4:18-19)

Girlfriends, it's comin' up a cloud. Get over the hurt feelings and call the fam. Let your family's legacy begin with forgiveness.

WHAT MAMMAW SAID
In the Sweet By and By

MAMMAW WAS A GREAT cook who loved to prepare meals for her family. Meatloaf. Fried okra. Mashed potatoes. Icebox pie. (Why would anyone name a pie after an appliance?) One of my favorite memories is standing at her counter as she gave me strict instructions on how to mash the potatoes (*by hand*) without leaving lumps.

Mammaw's house was a two-bedroom frame house with a good-size kitchen. But it was hot in the summer. She relied on a window-mounted watercooler, one of those early refrigerated air units that would occasionally spit water on you, to compete with her circa-1955 Tappan stove. It was hotter than you-know-what when she had all four burners and the oven going. And the woman didn't know how to cook a meal without providing three or four side dishes.

But I don't think it was the steam bath she endured from the heat of that kitchen that she enjoyed—I think it was the reflective time, the worship time she savored while stirring the beans. And this is what I would hear her singing as I ran through the back door to help set the table:

There's a land that is fairer than day,
And by faith we can see it afar;
For the Father waits over the way
To prepare us a dwelling place there.

In the sweet by and by,
We shall meet on that beautiful shore;
In the sweet by and by,
We shall meet on that beautiful shore.[26]

Mammaw's philosophy was simple: our challenges on this earth—as ugly and hard as they sometimes are—are temporary. In the light of eternity, most things are not important at all.

Let us hold tightly without wavering to the hope we affirm, for God can be trusted to keep his promise. (HEBREWS 10:23)

Girlfriends, in the sweet by and by it all works out. Our Father awaits us. Just keep stirrin' your beans and let your walk of faith be the story your grandchildren share about you.

WHAT MAMMAW SAID
Kill 'Em with Kindness

LIKE ALL PRETEEN GIRLS, I had my share of hurt feelings growing up. Whenever I had issues with my friends, I would go to Mammaw for comfort. I'm not sure why I kept doing this, because she never once allowed me to wallow in my brokenness or swim in my despair. She wouldn't be my accomplice in fantasizing on how to get back at those hateful little pigtailed brats either.

When I wanted to be avenged, she would only say, with a sweet smile and soft voice, "Kill 'em with kindness."

Mammaw's theory was that we must—every day—take the high road. Mammaw had lived her entire life in one little country town and had an impeccable reputation. This is a hard thing to do—live in one place for over ninety years without anyone ever saying one bad thing about you. I know I couldn't do it. But Mammaw accomplished this because she always took the high road. She believed that doing so left your adversaries with nothing to attack you with and left your conscience clear.

> *Never pay back evil with more evil. Do things in such a way that everyone can see you are honorable. Do all that you can to live in peace with everyone. Dear friends, never take revenge. Leave that to the righteous anger of God. For the Scriptures say, "I will take revenge; I will pay them back," says the LORD.*
> (ROMANS 12:17-19)

Mammaw explained to me that those who have given their lives to Christ are highly blessed to be called his lambs. We have an obligation to act as Jesus would act, she told me, not as we're tempted by the world to act. Mammaw instinctively lived by the old saying, "Be careful how you live. You might be the only Bible some people ever read." At the same time, she told me about the bonus of being kind to those who attacked me: my adversaries would be frustrated to no end.

I never said that Mammaw wasn't strategic.

WHAT MAMMAW SAID
Actions Speak Louder Than Words

ONE SUMMER I was honored with an invitation to speak at a women's event at a large church in the north Dallas area. Some of the women who were leaders in the congregation had become my "girlfriends" as a result of subscribing to Truth Nuggets. They asked me to speak on the Proverbs 31 woman.

Now the Proverbs 31 woman is the Bible's version of today's "alpha mom." A real got-it-all-going-on type of gal.

I responded to my modern-day "church ladies" that, yes, I was very familiar with the Proverbs 31 passage and would love to dialogue with other women about who she is, what she represents, and how she is relevant to us today. And to boot, I told them, "I even know what she looks like; I have a picture of her!" You see, Mammaw was the Proverbs 31 woman in the living flesh.

Reading the Proverbs 31 passage can give even an ultra-high-achieving woman a complex, since this woman appears to be absolutely perfect. But she's not—the Scripture just doesn't dwell on her shortcomings. The description is merely that of a woman who contributes to her household and values her family—a woman just like you. Proverbs 31 defines those characteristics that a godly gal desires to embrace.

I won't take you through the entire passage—you should read it for yourself—but I will share with you a few of the attributes that Mammaw had in common with the be-all, end-all woman of Lemuel's dreams:

Who can find a virtuous and capable wife?
She is more precious than rubies. (PROVERBS 31:10)

To me, Mammaw sparkled with the brilliance and the elegance of the Logan sapphire. How would you like your grandchild to describe you?

WHAT MAMMAW SAID
Actions Speak Louder Than Words (Part Deux)

ONE OF THE many things that Mammaw had in common with the Proverbs 31 woman was the confidence of her husband.

Pappaw's trust
The heart of her husband trusts in her, and he will have no lack of gain.
(V. 11, NASB)

Pappaw died when he was only fifty-six years old, but I'm sure he had every confidence in Mammaw's love. Although I was always trying to fix her up with the widower in town, Mr. Purdle, Mammaw wouldn't even think about another man. She spent nearly twice as many years as Pappaw's widow as she did his wife. Pappaw gained much as the result of the love and dedication of Mammaw. Her actions spoke louder than words—love your man.

Meaningful work
She . . . works with her hands in delight. (V. 13, NASB)

Mammaw's hands were always busy. She was a banker by profession—you should have seen that girl go on a ten-key adding machine—and a mother and grandmother by calling. Mammaw was also a devoted friend and the church treasurer for over thirty years. She worked but never complained. She was delighted to contribute to any and all who needed her. Her actions spoke louder than words—and what she said was to contribute with a joyful heart.

Mr. Arthur and Mrs. Oni
She rises also while it is still night and gives food to her household and portions to her maidens. (V. 15, NASB)

So get this. When Pappaw was alive, Mammaw would get up *before the sun* and put food on to cook before she went to the bank. She would then come home at lunch to feed my grandfather's field workers. She and Pappaw forged a deep bond with Mr. Arthur and the other African Americans in our town, and she treated them with great dignity (in a region and during a time when that was not the most popular thing to do); in return, Mr. Arthur's bride, Mrs. Oni, would deliver a gorgeous homemade chocolate cake to Mammaw each year on her birthday. The portion Mammaw gave to these workers was returned in the form of respect and honor until the day she died.

Her actions spoke louder than words. I hadn't a clue what racism was.

You were cleansed from your sins when you obeyed the truth, so now you must show sincere love to each other as brothers and sisters. Love each other deeply with all your heart. (1 PETER 1:22)

WHAT MAMMAW SAID
Actions Speak Louder Than Words (Part Trois)

BUT IT DIDN'T stop there. Mammaw's legacy of living like the Proverbs 31 woman was also found in things like:

Certificates of deposit
She considers a field and buys it; from her earnings she plants a vineyard. (v. 16, NASB)

Mammaw, being a banker, understood the importance of investing. Although she was never a wealthy woman, she was a good steward of her money—not only in her tithes and giving but in the manner in which she saved. It was my Mammaw who taught me the importance of taking an active role in the management of my personal finances and the power of compounding interest. Her actions spoke louder than words—don't be a spendthrift; prepare to take care of yourself.

Physical fitness
She girds herself with strength, and makes her arms strong. (v. 17, NASB)

Mammaw was not a wimpy woman. Although she was small in frame and stature, she was strong. That woman could hoe a row, pick a bushel, and shell a quart of peas before I could get my garden shoes on. She was also a walker. Long before Jane Fonda hit the airwaves, Mammaw knew that being physically fit was good for the mind and soul. Her actions spoke louder than words—keep moving.

Presenting a consistent brand
She makes coverings for herself; her clothing is fine linen and purple. (v. 22, NASB)

Mammaw wasn't vain, but she always looked like a million dollars. When she took up sewing after retiring from the bank, we both benefited from her new hobby. Mammaw made sure we always looked nice (and she could control the length of my skirts!). Mammaw never dressed up to go to the grocery store, but let me tell you—she never dressed down, even to go to the garden. Mammaw was true to her brand as a Proverbs 31 woman and always looked like the godly woman she was. Her actions spoke louder than words—you're God's representative wherever you go; look the part.

Girlfriends, as you read Proverbs 31 think about how these characteristics apply to your life today. You'll see you're not so far off from the woman whose children will rise up and call her blessed.

She is clothed with strength and dignity, and she laughs without fear of the future. When she speaks, her words are wise, and she gives instructions with kindness. . . . Her children stand and bless her. (PROVERBS 31:25-26, 28)

Yes. I call her blessed.

WHAT MAMMAW SAID

FATHER GOD, I desire to live out the principles of a godly woman. Bless me so I can live and leave a legacy that

- ☐ enriches the lives of all I touch;
- ☐ instills a strong value system to the next generation that I influence;
- ☐ communicates living a life of peace by living in the middle of your will;
- ☐ models repeat forgiveness and grace;
- ☐ instills peace today through confidence expressed in the sweet by and by;
- ☐ embodies the beauty of the Proverbs 31 woman;
- ☐ kills 'em with kindness.

ACTIONS I WILL TAKE:

Example: Today, I will put my desire for revenge aside and will "kill my adversaries with kindness."

1. _____

2. _____

3. _____

Father God, I thank you for blessing me with _____. She has been a role model and a living example of your Word. Thank you for the guidance you have given me in Proverbs 31. Remind me, Lord, that each day I am writing my legacy. Amen.

THE PUSHMI-PULLYU OF PERFECTION

IN HIS WONDERFUL children's tale about Dr. Doolittle, Hugh Lofting introduces readers to a unique creature called a Pushmi-Pullyu (pronounced *push-me; pull-you*). Do you remember?

> [Pushmi-Pullyus] had no tail, but a head at each end, and sharp horns on each head. They were very shy and terribly hard to catch . . . because, no matter which way you came toward him, he was always facing you. And besides, only one half of him slept at a time. The other head was always awake—and watching.[27]

I am convinced that a pushmi-pullyu haunts most high-achieving women. We are often controlled by something that is pushing and pulling us, causing us to miss lasting joy in our lives. And that something, which I've touched on before, is perfection. While hitting on all cylinders at all times is what takes many women to the pinnacle of success (both professionally and personally), it is this drive for excellence that sucks the *contented* life from that same self-motivated gal.

Of course I know many high-achieving women who are not pursued by the pushmi-pullyu of perfection—but all who come to mind are over the age of sixty. Maturity seems to enable women to finally corner the beast after years of dealing with its sharp horns. These women are living their best lives right now.

If my AARP card-carrying girlfriends can do this, why can't we? I don't want to wait one more day to grasp life and live it to its fullest—I want to do it *now*!

And so I tell you, keep on asking, and you will receive what you ask for. Keep on seeking, and you will find. Keep on knocking, and the door will be opened to you. For everyone who asks, receives. Everyone who seeks, finds. And to everyone who knocks, the door will be opened. (LUKE 11:9-10)

Is your drive driving you crazy too? Well, put on your safari hat—we're going huntin'. We're going to bag us some pushmi-pullyus of perfection.

THE PUSHMI-PULLYU OF PERFECTION
Sweating, Sweets, and Tummy Tucks

IT WAS A WARM afternoon in May; I was fourteen years old. Mammaw, who had carefully sewn my junior high graduation dress, gazed over my shoulder as we studied my reflection in the mirror. The tailor-made "gown" of polyester fell to my ankles—my first long dress (*with matching shoes*). Amazed at the girl looking back at me, I remember telling Mammaw, "I look so pretty." This must have come as a revelation to me, as I had always been a heavy child. But puberty had turned my metabolism around, and for the first time, I was pleased with the girl in the mirror. But I'm embarrassed to share with you that this was the first and the last time I can remember thinking such flattering thoughts about my physical appearance.

Sometime in my early twenties, my self-critique of my appearance moved from observant to painfully critical. I became obsessed with my weight and every calorie I consumed. I wouldn't have defined myself as anorexic because anorexics never do. But I spent as much time and energy keeping my weight at ninety-seven pounds as I did almost anything else. The pushmi-pullyu of perfection had me on the run, and to be honest, I'm not sure, even today, who's chasing whom. You too?

Why can't we be pleased—even better, be *thrilled*—with our healthy bodies and faces kissed with the engaging stories of character and experience? Why is it we're always striving to look younger and be thinner? Why don't we invest the same thought and energy into becoming smarter and kinder? I think our pushmi-pullyus of perfection have us cornered.

Several months ago, the beast of perfection returned and began driving me to increase my workouts. The mach-seven metabolism that I have enjoyed throughout my life is finally beginning to slow. Hormones and age are beginning to have their way with me. (A side note for my cousins: *you can stop that laughing right now—I can hear you.*) More and more outfits in my closet seem not to make it into my wardrobe rotation, if you know what I mean. To maintain my muscle tone, I'm now lifting ten-pound dumbbells. The beast has me on the run, literally.

> You must not have any other god but me. You must not make for yourself an idol of any kind or an image of anything in the heavens or on the earth or in the sea. You must not bow down to them or worship them, for I, the LORD your God, am a jealous God who will not tolerate your affection for any other gods.
> (EXODUS 20:3-5)

What about you? Are you spending too much time thinking about your weight, diet, or wrinkles? Has your physical appearance become your idol?

THE PUSHMI-PULLYU OF PERFECTION
Sweating, Sweets, and Tummy Tucks (Part Deux)

IDOLATRY? The last thing I wanted was to put anything or anyone ahead of my love for my God. But it wouldn't be so easy to put the beast in its place.

I realized I can either embrace my body's changes and delight in my good health or I can spend more time on the treadmill. Not wanting to give in so easily and still trying to catch my pushmi-pullyu of a perfect appearance, I hit the endless rubber belt and stretched my weekly workouts by another two hours. After about four weeks of running fast and going nowhere, I decided that I was going about this all wrong. Instead of dreading my workouts and hyperfocusing on my weight, I decided to embrace my exercise routine, not for what it could do for my fanny, but for how my time invested at the gym could contribute to my flexibility, agility, and energy.

Experts believe that the value our society places on youthful beauty is at the heart of our problem. They're right. But here's the kicker: *we're* society. We're the ones who have stood back and allowed, even encouraged, this focus on appearance. Our obsession has produced a generation of vanity that is shameful and—for many families with young women suffering from eating disorders and mothers disfigured by plastic surgery—painful. Ladies, what are we doing? What if we invested the time, money, and energy we expend on our appearances into making the world a better place for our children and grandchildren, for our communities? I think we need to reassess:

- Would losing a few inches make my jeans fit better? Absolutely.
- Would dropping five pounds allow me to squeeze the ever-lovin' life out of the next sixty seconds? Not likely.
- Would a perfect appearance make me a woman of substance? Not in a million years.

So encourage each other and build each other up, just as you are already doing.
(1 THESSALONIANS 5:11)

I know I haven't yet caught my pushmi-pullyu of a perfect appearance, but this week I have her cornered. When you catch yours, we can corral them together; and we'll all be better off as we provide a healthy example for the next generation of women.

THE PUSHMI-PULLYU OF PERFECTION
Perfect Parenting

SIT UP STRAIGHT. Put your feet on the floor. Use your fork. Say please and thank you. Wait your turn. Tell the truth. Chew with your mouth closed. Do your homework. Be kind. Save your money. Say your prayers. Eat your veggies. Don't interrupt. Don't point. Don't whine. Don't smoke. Don't judge. Don't do drugs. Don't say bad words.

Parenting—arrrgh, there's nothing like it. The endless rules; the endless joys; the endless laundry; the endless laughter; the endless nights spent in prayer.

But did I miss something on the list? I thought my perfect parenting would lead to perfect kids—or at least fully functioning adults. What did I do wrong? Do you think you missed something on the list?

There are millions of mothers out there who, like us, did everything "right" but whose success rate is 50/50 or less. Their children—regardless of the amount of direction given and love dispensed—did not turn out to be enthusiastic contributors to society. Many of us share the burden of knowing that, despite our every effort to be perfect parents, our children failed to thrive.

During the years that Scott was missing, my pushmi-pullyu of perfect parenting drove me mad as I lay awake, night after night, wondering what I had done wrong. As I prayed into my pillow one night, a soft voice reassured me that my parenting was in every way complete; I had fulfilled with great enthusiasm and energy the calling of "mom"; I had embraced with my every fiber my children's physical, emotional, and mental development. Christ told me that I could no more take credit for Shauna's beautiful, honorable character than I could for Scott's poor judgment. What I came to understand and finally accept was that the outcome is not controlled by me, but falls to a force called free will that is even stronger than the mightiest mom.

When I think of all this, I fall to my knees and pray to the Father, the Creator of everything in heaven and on earth. I pray that from his glorious, unlimited resources he will empower you with inner strength through his Spirit.
(EPHESIANS 3:14-16)

If you hit a grand slam with your child rearing, count yourself lucky (but forfeit your pride); we're cheering for you and your children as they round the bases. If you're like me and still have one in the dugout, count yourself blessed. You, my girlfriends, have been blessed with humility; you are mothers who are living examples of tremendous faith; you are mothers who never give up; you are mothers who know not to judge; you are mothers who know to pray for other mothers' kids without them even asking.

THE PUSHMI-PULLYU OF PERFECTION
Mr. Perfect

I CONSIDERED including only three words in this entry: *He doesn't exist.*

But I decided that some of you clearly need a bit more explanation. I know this because I've read your want ads:

> Single, thirtysomething female looking for tall, dark, and handsome; must be well educated; professionally successful with six-figure income; cooks—preferably gourmet—and grocery shops; is the life of the party; longs to father our three perfect children; loves a good chick flick.

I've read the want ads from my married girlfriends too:

> Married, fortysomething female looking for someone else (but this time with a sub-forty-inch waist); demonstrates his tolerance for debt by looking the other way after my Saturday afternoon shopping frenzy at the mall; enjoys meatless dinners; knows better than to answer honestly when I ask, "Does this make my butt look big?"; adores the three rude teenagers I will bring into this marriage; watches anything other than sports.

Whether single or married, the pushmi-pullyu of perfection can turn a high-achieving woman's quest for Mr. Right into a never-ending search for Mr. Perfect. I'm afraid we often rule out or *wring out* our Mr. Rights as we look for the perfect man to fulfill our vision of a perfect relationship.

Am I asking you to settle? You know I never would! But our pushmi-pullyu of perfection in our relationships is often way out of control, with expectations that can never be filled. What I'm asking is for you to consider rewriting your want ad, taking into consideration those attributes that *define* your man more than those that would *refine* him. What would happen to your love affair if you wrote:

> Self-confident but not-so-perfect woman looking for a man who is looking for the love of his life; silly enough to make me laugh and strong enough to challenge me when I'm out of line; willing to help me support our family; daring enough to put up with our out-of-control children; fights bigotry and hatred; demonstrates his love for God through his display of humanity for those who are down and out; will watch a chick flick under extreme duress.

And I will give you a new heart, and I will put a new spirit in you. I will take out your stony, stubborn heart and give you a tender, responsive heart.
(EZEKIEL 36:26)

Rewrite your want ad and take another long look at Mr. Right. Don't let your pushmi-pullyu of perfection drive *him* crazy too.

THE PUSHMI-PULLYU OF PERFECTION
The Perfect Job

If you have a job without aggravations, you don't have a job.   MALCOLM FORBES

JUST THE IDEA of perfect work makes me laugh out loud. Yes, I enjoy running my own marketing company, but let me tell you, even when it's your own business—it ain't perfect.

As a young professional, my pushmi-pullyu of perfection required that my work be exhilarating in every way. I thought my daily labor should be intelligent and interesting; I wanted a job where I could provide strategy. I thought the people I worked with should enthusiastically accept my direction and input; I thought I was the answer to the world's management problems. I thought the customers I served would appreciate the daily investment I made to ensure their success. Instead I found that they expected me to walk on water *every* day. And I thought my superiors would recognize and congratulate me on a job well done by promoting me to a role with more authority. Oh, and the job would pay mega-bucks as I make a difference for mankind. Ha. Ha. Ha.

As it does with most high achievers, the pushmi-pullyu of perfection was stalking me at the office. Regardless of my position or the strides I made, she continued to follow me from floor to floor. The epiphany would not come for several years, when I finally realized that it was not the work itself but my expectations that were warped. So just as I accepted that Mr. Perfect didn't walk the face of the earth, I finally came to the conclusion that perfect work doesn't exist either. By accepting the fact that the projects would not always be challenging, that many of my positions would not be fulfilling, and that the tasks I was expected to complete would not always be perfectly aligned with my greatest strengths, I achieved much greater satisfaction without having to change my career.

So, my dear brothers and sisters, be strong and immovable. Always work enthusiastically for the Lord, for you know that nothing you do for the Lord is ever useless. (1 CORINTHIANS 15:58)

Do you need to get your pushmi-pullyu out of the workplace too? Pray that God will allow you to adopt a new way of thinking.

THE PUSHMI-PULLYU OF PERFECTION
The Perfect Job (Part Deux)

TO TAME MY pushmi-pullyu at work, I transformed my old pushmi-pullyu thinking into more constructive thinking:

The Pushmi-Pullyu Thought:
My work must be purposeful and, in the grand scheme of life, make a difference.
Constructive Thinking:
It's not likely that marketing technology products will change the course of anyone's life, but my profession allows me the flexibility to fulfill my purpose, which is to encourage my girlfriends. My hobby, not my work, fulfills my passion and allows me to contribute to something greater than myself.

The Pushmi-Pullyu Thought:
I am not fairly compensated for my contributions to the organization.
Constructive Thinking:
Compared to people who really do make a difference—teachers, clergy, social workers, police officers—I'm grossly overpaid for what I contribute. Rethinking this, now I'm embarrassed by what I earn compared to those who have given their lives to careers that I wouldn't do for all the tea in China.

The Pushmi-Pullyu Thought:
I am bored with this work—I think I have outgrown the organization.
Constructive Thinking:
Since I can complete my tasks more efficiently than others, I can further contribute by helping my coworkers with their workload. Aha, maybe I can contribute to mankind and work here after all!

The Pushmi-Pullyu Thought:
I'm sick of my peers and their terrible attitudes.
Constructive Thinking:
I love my iPod, and these new headphones are great! Praise God for those engineers at Apple!

So I saw that there is nothing better for people than to be happy in their work. That is why we are here! No one will bring us back from death to enjoy life after we die. (ECCLESIASTES 3:22)

If you work in a job that you have chosen, if you serve in a role where you're competent, if you provide a service to employees or customers, and if you feel good because you've done an honest day's work for an honest day's pay, that's about as perfect as it gets. Congratulations.

THE PUSHMI-PULLYU OF PERFECTION

FATHER GOD, you have spoken to me and I realize that I am dealing with a pushmi-pullyu of perfection that has

- ☐ caused me to curse my physical body more than praise you for my health and agility;

- ☐ caused me to hyperfocus on my shape and weight rather than my substance;

- ☐ plagued me with guilt and shame over my parenting skills;

- ☐ caused me to be judgmental of other parents who are dealing with difficult children;

- ☐ caused me to generate and communicate unrealistic expectations of my partner;

- ☐ plagued my mind with destructive thinking at work.

ACTIONS I WILL TAKE:

Example: I will not weigh myself this week, nor complain about my weight, but rather will praise God every day for my health and agility.

1. _____

2. _____

3. _____

Father, I know that I am wonderfully and uniquely made by you. I thank you for giving me a desire to achieve at exceptional levels. But I pray that you will help me tame the beast of perfection that often thwarts my ability to live fully in the moment and to be content with the gifts I have been given. Teach me, God, to corral the pushmi-pullyu of perfection. Amen.

DUE TO CIRCUMSTANCES BEYOND OUR CONTROL

PROFESSIONALLY, I'm a marketing gal. I have owned my own marketing firm since 1994. Our specialty is consumer marketing; specifically in the area of technology. For those of you who have not worked in or who might not be familiar with the field of marketing, I define my function as this: to deliver a message to you that compels you to buy something. Now that message might be delivered in the form of a TV commercial, on a Web site, or in a magazine. The message could be as short as one word or might consist of thirty or so. But regardless of the delivery vehicle or the number of words, I will probably rely on FUD to motivate you.

FUD is a marketing term that was coined by Gene Amdahl in 1970 and is still widely used today. It stands for Fear, Uncertainty, and Doubt, and it is the primary tactic used by marketing organizations and advertising companies to persuade you that you need—no, you *must have*—a certain product or service. You can easily recognize the tactic; just watch any commercial on women's skincare products featuring a model who is sixty but looks forty. That's FUD.

I am often plagued by FUD—but not as a result of commercials or beautiful print ads. No, I allow fear, uncertainty, and doubt to enter my psyche when my insecurity gets the best of me or when I believe there are unpleasant circumstances beyond my control moving in my direction. Worry, of course, is the result.

Do you battle FUD too? Okay—then we should explore how worry can constrict us and thus prevent us from attaining our true vision and mission in life.

> The LORD is my light and my salvation—
>   so why should I be afraid?
> The LORD is my fortress, protecting me from danger,
>   so why should I tremble? (PSALM 27:1)

Because you can't worry *and* move forward at the same time, we know one of them has got to go! You can probably guess which one *I've* had enough of.

DUE TO CIRCUMSTANCES BEYOND OUR CONTROL
Fear

Whether you think you can or whether you think you can't—you are right.   HENRY FORD

OF THE THREE—fear, uncertainty, and doubt—fear is probably the state of mind that most often keeps us from living to our full potential and with joy. Living in fear and living intentionally are mutually exclusive.

What you and I fear, of course, are different, but I bet we share at least a few things that degrade the value of our days.

Do you ever fear you will fail?

Let's start with a big one. You're so afraid of making a mistake that you won't even try something new. Even if you've never really experienced a huge, ugly, embarrassing failure, you're still paralyzed. Just the thought of what others will say about you or think of you is enough to make you break out in a cold sweat. If that's the case, you might be a teensy-weensy bit pessimistic.

I am an eternal optimist. Dr. Dan Baker and Dr. Cathy Greenberg, authors of *What Happy Women Know*, ask readers to consider who they'd rather have lunch with: Chicken Little or the Little Engine That Could.[28] For those of you sketchy on the plot, Chicken Little was a freaked-out, pessimistic bird who was always getting everyone worked up because the sky was falling, even though it wasn't. That bird did nothing but stir up trouble. In the story of *The Little Engine That Could*, whenever faced with a big challenge, the little engine told himself, *I think I can, I think I can, I think I can.* Now that's my kind of choo-choo. But my question to you is not who you want to have lunch with. My question is: Whose philosophy will you adopt today?

When I'm in a position of needing to take a risk, I always ask myself, *What's the worst thing that can happen?* By identifying, measuring, and working a plan to mitigate my risks, I can move fear aside in order to focus on the incredible opportunity at hand. The plan boosts my confidence.

I don't believe that a spirit of timidity is a gift from God but instead is something that Satan conjures up in us to keep us from living the abundant life. Are you afraid? Pray for the strength to put Satan's Chicken Little call in its place.

> *You are my refuge and my shield;*
> *your word is my source of hope.* (PSALM 119:114)

Girlfriends, there is always a chance that our dreams might not see the light of day. But it won't be the end of the world. We'll just have paid our dues and become somewhat more interesting.

DUE TO CIRCUMSTANCES BEYOND OUR CONTROL
Fear (Part Deux)

All I have seen teaches me to trust the creator for all I have not seen.
RALPH WALDO EMERSON

HERE'S A BIG FEAR that I've seen plague a lot of women: you will not get something that is rightfully yours.

Many people are anxious that they're not going to get what they deserve. That, somehow, someone else's good fortune will eliminate their chance to be successful too. Trust me: you're going to get exactly what you deserve. Nothing more. Nothing less. It disappoints me to see women begrudging a sister's success in the workplace, envying her financial status, or being jealous of her love life. Girlfriends! Just because she got the promotion, cool house, or diamond ring doesn't mean you can't get it too!

Another area this plays out is in families—especially after a parent's or grandparent's death. It breaks my heart to see the family circle dissolve over silly disputes. In the grand scheme of the family's importance, does it really matter who gets Nanna's china or Poppa's watch? If you didn't get the house, your rightful share of the life insurance, the crystal, or the whatever—relax. Something better is bound to come (or perhaps has already come) your way.

A similar fear you may battle comes from "victim" thinking, fearing that your life is a bigger mess than everyone else's. If you think you have been dealt a raw deal, I challenge you to do this: gather a group of ten women together and ask them to share 1) their greatest heartbreak, 2) their biggest concern for their family, and 3) an unrealized dream. I promise you—regardless of your own troubles—you will be praising God that you don't have their problems and you will become much more content with your own.

> *Don't let your hearts be troubled. Trust in God, and trust also in me.*
> (JOHN 14:1)

Everyone is given both blessings and burdens. You will get the blessings that are perfect for you; likewise, you will be granted only those burdens that *you* can carry with grace.

DUE TO CIRCUMSTANCES BEYOND OUR CONTROL
Fear (Part Trois)

The way in which we think of ourselves has everything to do with how our world sees us.
ARLENE RAVEN

REGARDLESS OF HOW self-confident we appear to others, at our core, we are all deeply insecure. We so desire to be accepted and so fear rejection that we often do things we don't want to do, deal with people we do not respect, and make appearances when we'd rather stay home. Why? We fear others will not be pleased, and if they're not pleased, they will reject us.

- I don't really *want* to go to that party tonight, but I *must* go. What if I'm not invited to the next celebration?
- They said I don't have to attend today's meeting and I don't *want* to but I *must* go. What if they go forward with the project without me and I'm not asked to serve next time?
- I don't *want* to spend another holiday with my in-laws; I'd like to spend one with my own parents, but I *must* go. What if my mother-in-law gets mad at me?

Have you ever wondered how much time you spend each year doing things you don't want to do because you're afraid of the rejection that might come later?

The aforementioned situations are all personal examples. I hate to admit how much time I have spent at parties, events, gatherings, and meetings due to my fear of ridicule or rejection. Insecurity drove my time investments; not desire.

I failed to have faith in my sustaining value to my family, my friends, and the organizations I served.

I can testify that

my family still loves me;
I still have friends;
the organizations I serve still need me; and
I no longer sit in committee meetings where I'm bored stiff.

What is the price of five sparrows—two copper coins? Yet God does not forget a single one of them. And the very hairs on your head are all numbered. So don't be afraid; you are more valuable to God than a whole flock of sparrows.
(LUKE 12:6-7)

Take a chance: when you really don't want to do something—don't do it.

DUE TO CIRCUMSTANCES BEYOND OUR CONTROL
Fear (Part Quatre)

Fear knocked at the door. Faith answered. And lo, no one was there.   ANONYMOUS

OF ALL OUR FEARS, this is my favorite. It just cracks me up.

We fear something that is only in our minds.

It's true. Some of us are afraid of stuff that only exists in our heads. Can you believe it? Of course you can. You're probably afraid of stuff you're making up too! We all do this. I estimate that over 90 percent of our fears and worry are pure fantasy!

Girlfriends, what could we do with this energy and mind power if we turned all the worry from stuff that hasn't even happened *and will probably never happen* to thinking positively about our next sixty minutes of living on this earth?

When I was pregnant, I worried Shauna would be born with a birth defect. She wasn't.

When Scott was nine years old, I was worried he would die from Lyme disease. He didn't.

When I was engaged to Steve, I was worried our marriage would fail. It hasn't.

I could list thousands of scenarios I have feared, could paint you grizzly images of Shauna or Scott dead in a ditch, could tell you of the nights I have tossed and turned. The one thing I can't tell you is how many days of my life I have forfeited to fear—made-up fear. What a waste.

Let's take the *F* out of FUD. Every time you begin to worry about something as the result of fear, think instead what a blessing it is to have one more hour to live and make a difference. Why waste that hour worrying? You're not going to get that time back.

Though I am surrounded by troubles,
    you will protect me from the anger of my enemies.
You reach out your hand,
    and the power of your right hand saves me.
The LORD will work out his plans for my life—
    for your faithful love, O LORD, endures forever.
Don't abandon me, for you made me. (PSALM 138:7-8)

Eleanor Roosevelt was a woman who wouldn't bow to fear. She said, "Do one thing every day that scares you." Yes, she knew that to conquer fear you have to stare it down. And I'm not blinking.

DUE TO CIRCUMSTANCES BEYOND OUR CONTROL
Uncertainty

Today is the tomorrow you worried about yesterday. ANONYMOUS

I THINK WOMEN, in general, have a bigger issue with uncertainty than they do with either fear or doubt. So often I hear, "I just want to know what's going to happen; I want to know what to expect." We want a crystal ball, and we want our mates to have one, too, but that's impossible when there are circumstances beyond our control. And this is why we worry.

I think, as women, we most often worry that we will not have what we need in the future: Love. Friendships. Family. Financial security. Health.

Do you find this as interesting as I do? We worry about what we might not have in some distant future when we've never really gone without. I know there are exceptions—and trust me, I've been in some tight financial situations in my life. I know what it feels like to have to seriously scrimp on groceries in order to take the kids to the doctor. But I still had what I needed each day.

So I ask you: Have you ever gone hungry? Have you ever had no clothes to wear? Have you ever lacked a place to sleep? Have you ever gone a day without someone who cared for you? Me neither. God has always provided. Then why do we fret about the uncertainty of tomorrow? It is robbing us of our ability to live intentionally today.

> *That is why I tell you not to worry about everyday life—whether you have enough food and drink, or enough clothes to wear. Isn't life more than food, and your body more than clothing? Look at the birds. They don't plant or harvest or store food in barns, for your heavenly Father feeds them. And aren't you far more valuable to him than they are?* (MATTHEW 6:25-26)

I'm with you, girlfriend. I think I'll try to give up worrying about my future because there is one thing I can be certain about—today I am alive and well.

DUE TO CIRCUMSTANCES BEYOND OUR CONTROL
Doubt

What worries you masters you.   DR. HADDON ROBINSON

DOUBT IS MY NEMESIS. Of the three—fear, uncertainty, and doubt—doubt is the one that most often keeps me from living the life God intends me to enjoy.

Most women are very surprised to learn this about me, an optimist, but it's true. I suffer from sweaty palms, sleepless nights, a racing heart, and self-accusation: *Ellen, what are you thinking? What makes you think you can do this? Who in the world wants to read this silly little book?* Girlfriends, I have a screaming match with doubt every morning before I write one word.

Compounding my problem, I can see that other people sometimes have their doubts about my ability to succeed too. They don't come right out and tell me, but I see it in their eyes. I see it flash across their faces. Do you know the look I'm talking about? It's frustrating, isn't it?

However, you cannot allow your doubt or the skepticism of others to diminish your dreams and aspirations. Other people's small thinking, past failures, and fears—that's their baggage, not yours. Your vision and mission have nothing to do with their ability to properly forecast your outcome. Do not let the doubts of others diffuse your passion. Stand confident.

Here's what I tell myself (maybe it will help you too) to get some perspective: If my sights are set too low, there's nothing for me to be concerned about—no doubt, no worry! But setting my goals too low means I'm not fulfilling my *full* mission. On the flip side, if every now and then I wake up in the middle of the night with stinging doubt and have to wrestle with the Ugly One—well then, my goals must be set about right.

> *What shall we say about such wonderful things as these? If God is for us, who can ever be against us?* (ROMANS 8:31)

Yes, I know that the spewing of accusations in my head is most likely Satan's device to keep me quiet; to ensure I don't share the source of lasting peace, joy, and contentment. But I won't be that easy for him to stifle. I know God is on *my* side, and I'm getting pretty good at those internal debates.

DUE TO CIRCUMSTANCES BEYOND OUR CONTROL

FATHER GOD, when it comes to fear, uncertainty, and doubt, I pray for your divine intervention that I might overcome

- [ ] my paralyzing fear of failure;
- [ ] my fear of not getting what I feel is due me;
- [ ] my victim thinking;
- [ ] my fear of rejection;
- [ ] my fantasies and the terrible things I make up in my mind;
- [ ] my worry and obsession with the future;
- [ ] my self-doubt.

ACTIONS I WILL TAKE:

Example: When fear grips me, I will remind myself that my loving Father is in control.

1. _____

2. _____

3. _____

Father, you are the giver of all good gifts. I pray that you will bless me with courage to overcome timidity. I pray you will bless me with a sense of abundance that I will not be concerned with things I feel entitled to receive. I pray for your blessing of confidence and assurance in myself. And I pray for the blessing of increased faith— that I might trust that you securely hold my tomorrow in your hands. Amen.

WILL YOU BE MY FRIEND?

To find a friend one must close one eye. To keep him . . . two.   NORMAN DOUGLAS

UNTIL WE ADOPTED Scott when Shauna was three, she was an only child. Although she never seemed to mind being the sole focus of our attention, she was always on the lookout for a playmate.

I would often take Shauna to the park in town to allow her to run off some of that boundless energy that little kids are born with. She'd no more hit the sand at the swing set when, without fail, she'd approach another little girl or boy and enthusiastically ask, "Do you want to be my friend?" As I watched her establish a bond with a total stranger standing in line at the slide, I marveled at the ease with which these children could connect.

We're born wanting and needing a connection to others. But unlike children, we take our prejudices, past failures, hurts, expectations, and disappointments to the playground with us, making it difficult and sometimes impossible to establish or keep meaningful friendships.

I've noticed a deep yearning in our culture for something more than a passing acquaintance. First, I get a large number of e-mails from both men and women seeking connection. Also, I see churches and synagogues developing numerous programs to encourage the building of community among total strangers. Both signs tell me there's an epidemic lurking out there. I've come to believe that loneliness may be something for us to fear much more than swine flu.

How can we volunteer at the school, belong to a book club, work in a large enterprise, attend weekly religious services, and live in a country of nearly 250 million adults and still feel alone?

In this chapter, I hope you'll explore with me the challenges, frustrations, and expectations that keep us, not only from developing deep, lasting friendships, but from inviting new friends to join us on the playground.

If someone says, "I love God," but hates a Christian brother or sister, that person is a liar; for if we don't love people we can see, how can we love God, whom we cannot see? (I JOHN 4:20)

How wide is your circle? How deep is your love?

WILL YOU BE MY FRIEND?
Backdoor Friends

RED ROVER, red rover, will someone come over?

Steve and I lived in the same beautiful suburban town for over ten years before we developed a backdoor friend. We lived in three separate neighborhoods during that time and eventually decided something was really wrong with us. We asked each other, "Why don't we have any friends in this town?" The answer: because we weren't available. We both worked, and although we had children in school then, we were not involved in community projects that afforded us the opportunity to get to know others.

I was determined to connect with my neighbors, so finally Steve and I threw a party. Though it had a Key West theme, the underlying message was "Will you be our friend?" I put invitations, each addressed simply to "Neighbor," in the mailboxes lining our street. And guess what? The neighbors came! Just a few weeks after the party, we had invitations for dinner, we visited with folks while out for evening walks, and we connected with those who lived next door. One couple, the month before we moved away, even became backdoor neighbors—friends who would call and say, "Wanna come over for dessert?" That's right; no formal two-week-in-advance invitation. Just a five-minute warning that the cake was about to be cut.

We left our beautiful neighborhood and our wonderful neighbors to move to the hard, cold city of Dallas. I was heartsick that we might end up in the same lonely place—not knowing those who lived next door. But something very strange happened. Before we even spent our first night there, neighbors came by. They welcomed us. They visited with us. While we didn't form friendships right away, at least we could put faces with names and houses! We threw another "Will you be our friend?" party and invited neighbors to come over to get to know us. We had a blast, and again—it worked like a charm.

Within weeks, we had met all our neighbors, developed a wonderful backdoor friendship with our backdoor neighbors (literally), and felt as if we belonged to the community.

Never abandon a friend—
*   either yours or your father's.*
When disaster strikes, you won't have to
*   ask your brother for assistance.*
It's better to go to a neighbor than to
*   a brother who lives far away.* (PROVERBS 27:10)

If you want a backdoor neighbor, you're going to have to make, if not the first step, a considerable step in getting to know those around you. Throw a "Will you be my friend?" party under the guise of any theme you desire (Memorial Day, holiday open house, backyard BBQ), and then unlock the back door.

WILL YOU BE MY FRIEND?
Refrigerator Friends

Each had his past shut in him like the leaves of a book known to him by heart; and his friends could only read the title. VIRGINIA WOOLF

I WAS INTRODUCED to the concept of refrigerator friends many years ago by a *Wall Street Journal* article. I can't find reference to the writer to give him (or her) credit, but here's the idea: a refrigerator friend is that person who is so comfortable with you that she will come into your house, open the fridge, and help herself to whatever she needs. You know—the kind of friend you see on TV sitcoms. Do you have refrigerator friends?

I have this theory: if you have one, you probably developed that friendship when you were younger. When you were *messy*.

When I was a child, my friends would run into our house and throw open my parents' refrigerator door. Whether hungry or thirsty, they were welcome to whatever refreshment they found. Likewise, if I was on their street, I never hesitated to run in their houses and grab the handles of their Frigidaires.

I made my first adult refrigerator friend when I was a young mother. Still in my teens, I was a mess. As I was struggling to make a living, learning to change diapers, and dealing with a new husband, a woman ten years my senior came into my life and opened my refrigerator door. Ina raced me through Kmart to the next Blue Light special, she taught me to make homemade bread, and she was always my biggest fan. Our time together was brief; she soon moved back to her home in St. Louis. But she's still—thirty years later—my refrigerator friend. When we call or e-mail, she always tells me I haven't changed a bit. And she's right. With *her*, I'm a messy kid all over again.

Ina and I became refrigerator friends in about three months. When I met Karen I was in my midtwenties, and it took me nearly a year to open up and be the *messy me* that I am. It took me even longer to find my next refrigerator friend. In fact, I almost starved and dehydrated my refrigerator girlfriend, Paula, because it took us nearly ten years to form this bond! Why did it take so long? As we get older we're more protective of our hearts and our pride; we fear the judgment of others. We want to look like we have our acts together when, in reality, the perfectionism we work to portray is the very thing that keeps others from opening up to us.

Love never gives up, never loses faith, is always hopeful, and endures through every circumstance. (1 CORINTHIANS 13:7)

Like all good relationships, a refrigerator friendship takes two. Two souls who are willing to share their biggest fears, deepest secrets, and future dreams. You can't open my refrigerator door if I can't open yours.

WILL YOU BE MY FRIEND?
Making Dinner Friends

MOST OF US, the old saying goes, can count our true friends on one hand; yet another maxim reports that if you have five true friends, you have four more than most people. So what about the other nine fingers on your hands? If those represent possible friends, don't they matter?

I think the other nine are incredibly important to our overall state of happiness and intellectual development. I call these my *dinner friends*. These are guys and gals that I just enjoy hanging out with. They make me laugh, they are interesting, they are kind, and they like to eat. (Eating is a big plus for me.)

Many people don't have dinner friends, and I think I know why. It takes time and patience. To make and keep dinner friends, I've learned three important things:

- First, you have to be flexible and call in advance. Unlike your backdoor friends, dinner friends need a call a week or two in advance. Also, if either one of you has children living at home, you might feel you can commit to only one Saturday night per month with your dinner friends. That's okay. The important thing is that you're developing new friendships for your next life stage.
- Second, dinner friends require that you accept them as they are. Be prepared, in advance, to accept that they are going to have vastly different political, religious, and social views from your own. If you can embrace this, instead of being disappointed, or worse, challenging their views, you'll probably come away a bit more enlightened. Remember, you're just having dinner—you don't have to adopt one another's philosophies.
- The third thing you have to do: you have to do the calling and the planning. Most people are poor at making arrangements in advance, and though they would greatly enjoy an evening out with you, they just aren't gifted in making the call, selecting the restaurant, making the reservation, etc. Many people are even more uncomfortable entertaining in their homes. So if you're waiting around for an invitation—don't. Pick up the phone and make the call yourself.

How wonderful and pleasant it is
when brothers live together in harmony! (PSALM 133:1)

Our busy lives, hectic kids' schedules, and that noisy TV are robbing us of something that is critical to our health and well-being: dinner friends.

WILL YOU BE MY FRIEND?
Give Her a Pass

A woman wants her friends to be perfect. She sets a pattern . . . lays a friend out on this pattern and worries and prods at any little qualities which do not coincide with her own image. BETTY MACDONALD

GIRLFRIENDS, I want to close this series by asking you to pray with me on a sensitive subject: the reality that women are just way too hard on one another. Too often we expect far more support from a friend than any human *can* or *should* give.

I believe that, just as male and female opposites often attract, the same is true among women friends. We're sometimes attracted to a woman who is very different from ourselves; we admire or hold in high esteem the qualities that we feel we lack. As an example, I have a girlfriend who is a bit reserved, self-effacing, thoughtful of others, and sometimes doubtful. I am attracted to her because I lack these important attributes. She says she is attracted to me because I am typically outgoing, bold, busy, and optimistic. We work well together as a team.

But we don't always embrace our differences when we're faced with a disappointment or crisis. The minute our girlfriend doesn't respond to us the way we would have responded to her, our feelings are hurt—which, when you think about it, is totally nuts. The reason you found her attractive as a friend in the first place was because she was different from you. She can't possibly have your qualities and hers too. Can you *really* love her just for who she is?

> *Don't just pretend to love others. Really love them. Hate what is wrong. Hold tightly to what is good. Love each other with genuine affection, and take delight in honoring each other. Never be lazy, but work hard and serve the Lord enthusiastically. Rejoice in our confident hope. Be patient in trouble, and keep on praying. When God's people are in need, be ready to help them. Always be eager to practice hospitality. Bless those who persecute you. Don't curse them; pray that God will bless them.* (ROMANS 12:9-14)

Your friend will never be perfect. For your sake and hers, give her a pass.

WILL YOU BE MY FRIEND?

FATHER GOD, I am surrounded by people but find myself lonely and longing for friendship. I come before you expressing my desire to

☐ learn how to develop deep, lasting friendships;

☐ have the courage to reach out to my neighbors to establish a connection;

☐ open myself in a true and authentic way in order to become a refrigerator friend;

☐ check my judgments and expectations at the door in order to make new dinner friends;

☐ expect less from and love my girlfriends more.

ACTIONS I WILL TAKE:

Example: I will reach out to our new neighbors and invite them over for dessert.

1. _____

2. _____

3. _____

Father, I thank you for each person on this earth whom you have wonderfully made. I praise you for the concept of fellowship and the joy that friendship can bring. I pray that you will bless me with discernment and wisdom as I choose good friends and as I model Christian values to casual acquaintances. As you bring me friends, Lord, make me friendly. Amen.

THE PIANO LESSON

MY FIRST PIANO LESSON—I was so excited! Five years old, heart thumping, I carried my new music books in a little red satchel (I've always been "all about the bag") to Mrs. Lucile Booth's house. Well, to the other children she was known as Mrs. Booth, but to me she was my great-aunt, whom we called Aunt 'Cil.

Aunt 'Cil was not a pushover for any of us—especially me. She had my number from day one and promptly burst my bubble by explaining to me that, no, I would not be prepared to perform on stage anytime in the near future—I had work to do. *Work?* I thought this was called *playing* the piano, not working it! Besides, what was the point if I couldn't sit on the stage, under the bright lights, with everyone applauding my magnificent performance? "We have to prepare," she explained. And prepare I did. Yes, there would be annual spring recitals in my future, but I wouldn't perform on a real stage (for me that meant a college auditorium) for twenty more years.

But those two decades of piano lessons, theory classes, and the endless ticking of the metronome gave me the foundation I needed for the day when I finally hit the stage. I was a nervous wreck that day, knowing my final grade depended on a flawless performance. The heat was on.

I suspect that for about half of you reading this today, the heat is on for you too. Life is hard; tragedy is staring you in the face, or at best, disappointments are mounting. If you're part of one subset of the other half of our readers, maybe you've not yet had your face-to-face with despair. Well . . . you won't be left out. I don't mean to worry you, but I'm also not going to sugarcoat the reality: None of us escape the pain and suffering that accompanies the gift of life. Every one of us, women of all faiths and no faith, single and married, rich and poor, will live through the season when suffering seems to have no end. The question is—how well have you prepared for it?

But Jesus told him, "No! The Scriptures say, 'People do not live by bread alone, but by every word that comes from the mouth of God.'" (MATTHEW 4:4)

And my second question for you is this: Are you listening to God's direction as he works today to prepare you for tomorrow?

THE PIANO LESSON
Preparing for the Performance of Your Life

IF LIFE as you know it today changed tomorrow, where would you find your strength?

Or, perhaps, did life change for you yesterday?

Carolyn Custis James, in her book *When Life and Beliefs Collide*, explains why we must prepare now. "Life has a way of crashing down on us without warning," she writes. "Whether we like it or not, sooner or later all of us end up in the war zone, where life ceases to be tidy and the pain threshold goes off the charts. Women are not spared this kind of active combat, which makes it all the more urgent for us to think through our theology so our views of God will sustain us when the battle begins to rage."[29]

Perhaps one of the following is your reality today:

A business is failing and bankruptcy looms.
A nursery stands empty.
A son is arrested.
A husband is missing from his side of the bed.

Life is hard. The heat is on.
Do you feel like you're sitting on the stage alone? You're not.

As hopeless, as empty, as tired, as frustrated, as sad, and as angry as you may feel, I want you to know you're not going through this alone. God is sitting right there on the bench beside you. The question is: Will you let him play too? Or will you insist on making this a solo performance?

Whether you're facing your biggest nightmare or living the big life, I hope you will consider how great it would be to have God on stage with you. Only he can fortify you with confidence, hope, and peace as you play the hard notes.

Put on all of God's armor so that you will be able to stand firm against all strategies of the devil. For we are not fighting against flesh-and-blood enemies, but against evil rulers and authorities of the unseen world, against mighty powers in this dark world, and against evil spirits in the heavenly places.
(EPHESIANS 6:11-12)

We have work to do if we're ever to experience joy in the pain.

THE PIANO LESSON
Finding Middle C

I WAS ON MY KNEES, head to the floor, furiously screaming: "Where are you? Don't you care? Why have you totally abandoned me?"

He was nowhere in sight. Day after day, my Savior had failed to show up in my crisis—and now the situation had reached an all-time climax. I was heart-broken, and I was furious. He was missing in action, and I was completely disoriented. Joy? I had no concept of it.

To find my way back, I had to rely on two principles I learned during my first year of piano.

After Aunt 'Cil burst my bubble by informing me that there would be no Carnegie Hall in my near future, we got down to business. The very first thing she taught me was the principle of middle C: here is where it is, and this is where you find it on every piano. If you ever get lost looking at all the black and whites, head home to middle C.

I learned another critical lesson later that first year. Because I was very small, I found it difficult to reach the lower and upper octaves (the next sets of eight to sixteen keys on the keyboard). To get there, I had to "scoot" up and down the piano bench. However petite I was, Aunt 'Cil informed me, there was no excuse for such poor performance behavior. Scooting on one's behind was not allowed! No, if I wanted to be an accomplished performer, I was told I must learn to stretch.

There are some interesting parallels between finding middle C, scooting around, and losing sight of God. First, just like middle C, God is always in the same place. Regardless of what piano we're playing, regardless of whether our life is on the upswing or spinning out of control, he's there and willing to be our center when we get lost. On every piano, and for every person—regardless of age or origin, history or future—middle C and God never move around; when we get disoriented, we can always head home.

If you look for me wholeheartedly, you will find me. (JEREMIAH 29:13)

Are you looking?

THE PIANO LESSON
Finding Middle C (Part Deux)

JUST LIKE ON THE PIANO, circumstances in our lives often lead us into hard-to-reach places. Sometimes we scoot around, trying to make life sound better or feel better than it really is. Rather than stretching and staying close to God when the music turns dissonant, we develop some bad performance habits. We act self-reliant; we become self-absorbed; we attempt to self-medicate; and ultimately we self-loathe. We ask again, *Where are you?*

On one Thursday evening in 1998, my grief was more than I could handle. My cries turned into haunted wails as the reality of our situation with Scott became evident. He had run away again, but this time was different. Scott wasn't upset with us because he had been punished for breaking curfew. There had been no heated exchange. As a matter of fact, I thought he was doing great and believed everything was going to be fine. I was convinced that whatever had come over him during the summer had worked its way through his psyche. We were heading into his senior year of high school with anticipation of good things to come. I came home one evening to find a short note. He was gone—with a man he had met on the Internet.

I knew in that instant that all I had hoped for my child was not going to come to fruition. I knew in that instant that my fevered prayers for Scott had not been answered according to my desire. I knew in that instant that I was in a war zone. My life was crashing down. And I was so hurt that my *Lord* would abandon me. Where had he gone? How could he not hear the pleas of a mother who loves her child so dearly?

> *Come close to God, and God will come close to you. Wash your hands, you sinners; purify your hearts, for your loyalty is divided between God and the world.* (JAMES 4:8)

That night, as I lay on the floor alone in our home (Steve was hosting, solo, an outing for our office members), I found middle C somewhere between the sofa and the TV. That experience proved to be a turning point in my acceptance of God's sovereign plan. In the dark of night, with not a light on in the house, I took the first step in building an unwavering faith that sustains me today.

To find middle C—to find God again—you will need to head home. He hasn't moved. He hasn't abandoned you. He's just waiting for you to get off the bench so he can play the encore.

Today I can see God clearly in his silence. And it's pure joy.

THE PIANO LESSON
Hitting the Wrong Notes

To sit alone with my conscience will be judgment enough for me.
CHARLES WILLIAM STUBBS

THE YEAR WAS 1970. I'll never forget that particular spring recital.

It was warm and muggy (and a bit smelly) in the old high school auditorium. There were about fifty of us in Ms. Hester's class (I'd moved on from Aunt 'Cil's tutelage), and the recital seemed to last FOR-EVER. I was bored out of my gourd.

About three-quarters into the event, a little boy, maybe ten years old, sat down at the piano and began to play with tremendous energy and passion. I was in awe. I didn't know this kid, but I certainly looked forward to congratulating him for a fine performance over cookies and punch.

But then, all of a sudden, he just stopped playing. Right in the middle of a measure, he stopped and put his hands in his lap. After what seemed like an eternity (but in reality was probably thirty seconds), he reached up for his sheet music and turned it 180 degrees. His music was *upside down*. Well, the audience roared with laughter—as did he. I realized that day that mistakes happen, and it is our attitude and the attitude of others that will help us move beyond our errors.

You cannot learn to play the piano if you're afraid of failure. You will hit wrong notes. Learning a new piece of music takes time, patience, practice, discipline, and determination. The same is true of playing life. We all make mistakes, but none are so bad that they can't be righted. My mistakes are usually huge, and I call them sins. So how do I right *those*?

Most religions have a moral code; some actually agree that when you die, sin will separate you from God (heaven). End of story. Well, if that's the case, I'm in big trouble. I try hard to be saintly, but sometimes I'm just bad to the bone.

In the Christian faith, we believe that, because of Jesus, our sins can be forgiven and we can spend eternity with God—even though not one of us is perfect. Now this I can handle. A forgiveness that doesn't depend on my ability to try harder, but forgiveness that's given *because* of my flaws. I just love this thing called grace.

> *"And they will not need to teach their neighbors, nor will they need to teach their relatives, saying, 'You should know the LORD.' For everyone, from the least to the greatest, will know me already," says the LORD. "And I will forgive their wickedness, and I will never again remember their sins."* (JEREMIAH 31:34)

I love the fact that my God is forgetful when it comes to the sin I confess before him.

THE PIANO LESSON
Hitting the Wrong Notes (Part Deux)

SINCE I DIDN'T KNOW the little boy who played with the upside-down music, I never knew what the personal fallout was for him, if any. I know that if I had made such a goof, I would have punished myself for days, weeks, months. Who knows—I might have written about it in a Truth Nugget thirty years later! I'm afraid that the effects of hitting the wrong notes, even when I know I'm forgiven, take a toll on me.

I have committed some big sins—sins I have repented of; sins I have turned away from; and sins I know God has forgiven. Even though Scripture says, "He has removed our sins as far from us as the east is from the west" (Psalm 103:12), I have a hard time forgiving myself. Memories of the events and the hurt I know I have caused my Lord revisit me from time to time, overwhelming me.

When these times come (usually in the middle of the night when a hormonal surge has awakened me), I have learned to turn my guilt and self-loathing to praise for the One who gives life—both on earth and in eternity. I have come to understand that if I allow it, my past sin will create a chasm between God and me. I swear this is Satan—he always sneaks up on me at night, and those hormonal surges are clearly heat from the devil. He knows when I'm vulnerable and how embarrassed I am that I hit those wrong notes. But I now refuse to give in. I will not shortchange the redemptive powers of Christ.

Guilt is a component of some religions, and while that may work for some folks, it's no longer helpful to me. If I continued to feel guilty about every wrong note I have hit, I would have thrown in the piano towel by the time I was six! Instead, it comforts me to know that my audience (my God) delights in my performance on earth and forgives me—even when I hit the wrong notes or when my music is upside down.

Once we, too, were foolish and disobedient. We were misled and became slaves to many lusts and pleasures. Our lives were full of evil and envy, and we hated each other. But—"When God our Savior revealed his kindness and love, he saved us, not because of the righteous things we had done, but because of his mercy. He washed away our sins, giving us a new birth and new life through the Holy Spirit." (TITUS 3:3-5)

I don't know about you, but I think I'll turn my music right side up. Forgiveness. Pure joy.

THE PIANO LESSON
Practice, Practice, Practice

PRACTICE MAKES PERFECT? I'm not sure about that, but daily practice was essential to learning to play the piano. As I matured, I sometimes approached my practice sessions with very different objectives. But one thing was for sure; the more I practiced, the better I got at practicing!

Daily prayer is as essential to growing spiritually as daily practice is to learning to play an instrument. And just as you might have different objectives and approaches when practicing, so might you have them in prayer. Let me explain— but first, let's remember to whom we're praying.

I played the same piano almost every day of my life for twenty years. The name etched over middle C never changed; it was perfectly clear that I was playing a Bradbury baby grand. But when it comes to prayer, some folks seem confused as to whom they're praying to. God is God. Not the Good Fairy, Santa Claus, or a Falling Star. When you're communing, realize that you're speaking directly to the almighty Creator. If that doesn't humble you, I don't know what will.

Once you get it clear who the Lord is, the next thing you'll want to clarify is the objective of your prayer each day.

At times I approached my piano with one goal and one goal only: to relish the music and allow the melody to wash over me. Pure joy—that was my only objective for my practice time.

So also should you set aside a time just to worship God for who he is. That's right—no requests—pure praise. Think of it like one of the times one of your kids runs in to say, "Mom, you're the best mom in the world" without adding, "Can I have twenty dollars?" Just take time to acknowledge the Designer of heaven and earth—and *your* Creator—not for what he can do for you but for who he is to you.

All praise to God, the Father of our Lord Jesus Christ. God is our merciful Father and the source of all comfort. (2 CORINTHIANS 1:3)

Praise God from whom all blessings flow.

THE PIANO LESSON
Practice, Practice, Practice (Part Deux)

TICK. TICK. Tick. Tick. The metronome would sit on my piano waving her little hand at me, taunting me. For years, I thought she was just evil.

As I matured and technology improved, I replaced the wicked little thing with a sleek black compact electronic baby. You could turn off the sound on this one and just watch the light blink to help ensure you were playing to the correct tempo. This one was only a wee bit mean compared to her predecessor.

When I pulled the metronome out for practice, I meant business. I was focused, and the objective of my practice was to improve my performance. Once I set my metronome, I would focus intently on each note, each beat—striving, desiring to become a better musician. Sometimes I was successful. Sometimes I was not.

Likewise, there are times when you go to God with a specific desire. You mean business too. And like the results of focused piano practice, you might get the outcome you want or you might get the outcome he intends for you to have. In her book *I Told the Mountain to Move*, Patricia Raybon shares a story about her daughter's conversion to the Muslim faith. She writes:

> My prayers for her salvation in Christ continued daily. But God's orders, in the meantime, were to trust him always and to show her love right now. . . . But I still didn't understand what was happening. When I prayed, God still spoke to my spirit with one answer: Love her. Trust me. And have some peace. Stop turning yourself inside and out, trying to run *my* business.[30]

O my people, trust in him at all times.
Pour out your heart to him,
for God is our refuge. (PSALM 62:8)

Are you turning yourself inside out with your prayer life? Are you getting out the metronome every time you pray? Might be time to put that baby up for a while and just trust him.

THE PIANO LESSON
Practice, Practice, Practice (Part Trois)

WHEN YOU'RE READING new music, searching for keys, counting the rhythm in your head, and thinking about your date come Friday night, it's hard to hear yourself play. You hear the notes, but you don't always get a full grasp of the melody. And if you've been working on a particularly difficult score for a while, you're often unsure if you're making any progress. Thus, one of the most productive things you can do when you practice is to tape yourself playing.

Sitting quietly and listening is enlightening. And so it is with prayer.

God speaks to me. Quite often. No, I don't hear the big booming voice that Charlton Heston heard as Moses in the movie *The Ten Commandments*. It's more of a big booming thump of my heart accompanied by thoughts that I know didn't get in my head all by themselves. But I only get these thoughts, accompanied by this percussion, when I have asked God for clarity, direction, and discernment. Then I go for a run. And listen. Sometimes he answers pretty quickly; other times he doesn't talk back to me for weeks (or at least I perceive that he hasn't yet given me direction). But eventually, he makes his will and desire known to me.

A couple of my girlfriends told me they were confused and a little jealous that God never speaks to them. They would say, "I can't tell what God's trying to say to me." Speaking the truth in love, I encourage them to shut up for a while. If you stop asking over and over and over and then whining, again and again and again, you might get some clarity in the form of direction.

You can be sure of this:
The LORD set apart the godly for himself.
The LORD will answer when I call to him. (PSALM 4:3)

But you have to be listening and prepared to listen when he picks up the phone. Glory be!

THE PIANO LESSON
Practice, Practice, Practice (Part Quatre)

MY PIANO TEACHERS balanced my seasonal repertoire by including both music that could be easily mastered and scores that were nearly impossible. Having a few numbers that I could get my arms around kept me engaged, entertained, and confident. Having a few that challenged me—well—that mostly just made me nuts.

I would refuse to be beaten by a piece of music. So sometimes when I practiced, I would concentrate my entire practice time on one piece of music—the hard one. The one that challenged me; the piece that made me feel inadequate; the score that threatened my self-esteem. I would sometimes literally yell out loud in total frustration.

I think we should know it's okay to do the same with prayer. It's okay to be honest when you've had a bad day, when you're not sure of God's direction, when life has you pinned up by your ears. And I think it's okay that you sometimes express your anger and frustration with God. At times prayer is a clearing of the air. And if you can't be honest with him, can you really be honest with anyone?

Pray, then, in this way: "Our Father who is in heaven, Hallowed be Your name. Your kingdom come. Your will be done, on earth as it is in heaven. Give us this day our daily bread. And forgive us our debts, as we also have forgiven our debtors. And do not lead us into temptation, but deliver us from evil. For Yours is the kingdom and the power and the glory forever. Amen."
(MATTHEW 6:9-13, NASB)

Practice makes perfect? I have no proof of that. But I do have proof that prayer delivers direction, joy, peace, and contentment—especially if you take the direct approach.

THE PIANO LESSON
Music Appreciation

HIP-HOP. Jazz. Ragtime. Ballads. Contemporary. Classical. The blues. Baptist hymns.

With the exception of hip-hop, I've played them all. Not all classifications could I fully understand, and only a few can I play well. But I grew to *appreciate* and *respect* the socioeconomic conditions, the geographic locales, and the eras that served as the genesis to these diverse genres of music.

When it comes to music appreciation, one is required to have

- an open mind—leave your prejudices behind; you're to listen based not on what you once liked, but on what you might come to respect.
- an open heart—listen for a melody that speaks to you; not all sounds that are dissonant are made up of wrong notes. But to listen with your heart, you have to be quiet.
- an open soul—music is an international language that communicates regardless of history, culture, or class. Music can bridge great divides and create commonality where there was none before.

There is a profound parallel between the mind/heart/soul conditions required to appreciate music and to those needed to live like Christ. But, I fear if Christians were graded for our performance in music appreciation class, well—we'd flunk. We're doing little to inspire appreciation and respect for our beliefs.

For this reason, I rarely offer up that I'm a Christian. During the first two years of writing via e-mail to my subscribers, I did so without expressing my beliefs. Not because I'm ashamed or feel the topic is taboo; I don't openly share because of the damage we Christians have caused to our collective reputation.

Christians sometimes carry deep prejudices. Steve Stroope, pastor of Lake Pointe Church in Rockwall, Texas, once said, "We should be known for what we're for; not for what we're against." If our world, our coworkers, our neighbors, and our family are to appreciate Christianity, I think we're going to have to shift the paradigm and leave the judging to God. It's past time to let the world see that we're known for love, not condemnation.

Brothers and sisters, we urge you to warn those who are lazy. Encourage those who are timid. Take tender care of those who are weak. Be patient with everyone. See that no one pays back evil for evil, but always try to do good to each other and to all people. (1 THESSALONIANS 5:14-15)

I think it's time we all act out our faith in a more thoughtful, tender manner.

THE PIANO LESSON
Music Appreciation (Part Deux)

NOT EVERYONE needs their soul saved today. Some just need lunch.

Steve and I belong to the First Presbyterian Church of Dallas. We made the decision to join the church based on two important facts: (1) Pastor Joe is not only a straight shooter, he's brilliant, and (2) our church feeds people. Hundreds of people, three times a day.

The First Presbyterian Church of Dallas is famous in our community for the Stewpot that began in 1975 to feed a hot meal, once a day, to our city's homeless. Situated in the heart of downtown Dallas, the congregation couldn't look past the least of these, because they were their neighbors. When Dallas opened the Bridge, a shelter for these poor souls, the Stewpot stepped up and said, "We'll feed 'em." In fact, in May 2008 we moved our food service to the Bridge's new facility and began serving three meals a day. By the middle of that July, we'd served a total of 100,000 meals—all because an associate pastor opened the door to a homeless person and listened with his heart.

Now, I'm not dissing evangelism. I believe that we're to "go therefore and teach all nations" and all that stuff. Shoot! I've led numerous children and adults to Christ. But first, I made sure their stomachs weren't growling and they trusted me as their friend. And to get to that point, I had to listen with my heart, bite my tongue, and meet them where they were that day.

Rather than allowing a lost or hurting soul the opportunity to be heard, Christians sometimes jump in too quickly with our own point of view. We usually mess up when we start talking before we've fed the growling stomach. Why, as a group of people, are we so determined to have the first and the last word . . . and every word in between?

Live wisely among those who are not believers, and make the most of every opportunity. Let your conversation be gracious and attractive so that you will have the right response for everyone. (COLOSSIANS 4:5-6)

Not everything needs to be said in every encounter. In Colossians 4:6 (NASB), Paul said, "Let your speech always be with grace as though seasoned with salt." Chili powder is not mentioned in the recipe, but I'm pretty sure offering a bowl of chili wouldn't hurt.

THE PIANO LESSON
Music Appreciation (Part Trois)

SOME CHRISTIANS believe they are superior to other people. Don't believe me? Let some tattooed girl with ratty jeans come sit down next to you, and let's see how you react.

This is a true story: I was flying home from a business conference. The last night of the event, one of the manufacturers hosted a Harley party, and we were each given these very cool—very real-looking—tattoos. I had mine put on my left bicep so I could surprise Steve coming off the plane. Walking up the aisle (looking a bit disheveled and weary from my hard week of work), I reached my row to find a very sweet-looking woman sitting in the middle seat. I said, "Good morning!" She glared at me with disdain and contempt. I was really taken aback as I thought, *What in the world did I do to this chick?* I spoke to her a few minutes later, but she pretended not to hear me. After the flight took off, I reached in my briefcase for my Bible and Beth Moore study book. You should have seen this woman's expression!

She literally turned sideways in her seat, and her mouth flew open like a bass catching flies. *What?* I thought. Within seconds, Ms. Prickly Pious became my new best friend. It took a few minutes for it to register, but then it came to me: this good Christian woman wanted nothing to do with a tattooed girl in jeans until she realized I was "one of her own."

Open your soul; real tattoo or fake—we're not *that* different, and we're all the *same* in God's eyes.

Do not judge others, and you will not be judged. Do not condemn others, or it will all come back against you. Forgive others, and you will be forgiven.
(LUKE 6:37)

I call those who are my Christian sisters to arms today. Let's save the reputation of Christians so that people of no faith and other faiths can appreciate and respect who we are and the truths we believe. Let us be known for what we're for, not for what we're against. Let's be known for joy.

THE PIANO LESSON

FATHER GOD, I confess before you that I

- [ ] am not spiritually prepared to live through a season of suffering;
- [ ] often feel like I'm sitting on the bench alone;
- [ ] have moved around and can't find middle C;
- [ ] have been hitting all the wrong notes;
- [ ] have failed to come to you with a prayer of praise;
- [ ] am prayed out;
- [ ] have been doing all the asking and none of the listening;
- [ ] have not prayed honestly;
- [ ] have prejudices.

ACTIONS I WILL TAKE:

Example: I will begin my prayer life each day with a spirit of grace and praise, rather than supplication.

1. _____

2. _____

3. _____

Father, I come to you today in need of your forgiveness, as I have much to learn about you. I praise you for being the Holy God of all creation and the lover of my soul. Transform my mind that I might take in your ways; transform my heart so I look to glorify you, rather than tend to my selfish needs. And build a fire in my soul, Father, that is pure in its longing for you. Amen.

OUR SECRET SAUCE, MY RECIPE

I ONCE HAD what the Centers for Disease Control calls a marital disruption. That's government lingo for a divorce. My first marriage ended after ten years of both of us trying very hard, and even though I was the one who asked for the separation, I was devastated. I had failed myself and had failed him, completely.

As heartbreaking and damaging as this event was to us individually and as a family, life did go on and love would visit me again. But this time I was determined that I would succeed; I would learn from my past failure and do everything within my power to build a relationship that was true, respectful, fulfilling, and enduring.

By the time this book makes it to press, Steve and I will have celebrated nearly twenty years of pure marital bliss. I know it sounds like I'm bragging (or lying)—and I apologize if I come across as boastful—but I think it's important for you to know that fantastic marriages do exist.

Both men and women have found Steve's and my relationship unique, and many have expressed great curiosity as to how it is that we're *still on our honeymoon* after all these years of working together and raising a blended family. So I thought I'd share with you what we believe are our ingredients for an authentic relationship that lasts—what Steve and I call our secret sauce. And that secret sauce begins with the state of our hearts.

Guard your heart above all else,
    for it determines the course of your life. (PROVERBS 4:23)

As you think about your marriage, be honest with yourself so you can determine the state of your own heart. I am praying for you.

OUR SECRET SAUCE, MY RECIPE
Four Parts Friendship

It is not a lack of love, but a lack of friendship that makes unhappy marriages.
FRIEDRICH NIETZSCHE

STEVE AND I MET on the phone. Because my employer sold and supplied products to the company he worked for, we transacted business for several months, becoming business buddies before we ever met face-to-face at a Christmas party. Then, out of the blue, Steve started showing up at our offices to pick up sales materials. (So much for the honesty factor; he was putting this stuff in the *trunk of his car*! He was using this errand as an excuse to see me. How naive I was—it took six weeks and two male coworkers to clue me in.) But we first became friends during our phone time.

Everyone talks about love being the center of a relationship, but Steve and I disagree. The first ingredient in our secret sauce is friendship. And two of the most important elements of friendship are taking turns and using your kind voice.

Take turns. Steve and I love to hang out together. We enjoy most of the same things. Notice I said *most.* But we do just about everything together because time is required to build a strong relationship. Steve is a music nut and enjoys live entertainment. I'm not crazy about late-night concerts, since the main act comes on way past my bedtime. Steve goes to fewer concerts than he'd probably like and picks venues that he knows will be congenial to me. We go together and have a great time. That's what friends do.

Remember when you were ten? Sometimes you played what you wanted to play; the next time your friend got to pick. It's Friendship 101: in order to build and maintain a solid friendship you must (a) spend time together, and (b) do things that are important to each of you.

Use your kind voice. We speak to one another as we would a dear friend. We never yell. We never attack. We never nag. We never chastise or embarrass one another in front of friends or family. That doesn't mean we always agree—sometimes we agree to disagree, as friends do. Respect is a key component of friendship, and we demonstrate our respect for one another with the words, tone, inflection, and body language we use. We *always* say please, thank you, and could you?/would you?—just as we would with a friend.

> *Love is patient and kind. Love is not jealous or boastful or proud or rude. It does not demand its own way. It is not irritable, and it keeps no record of being wronged.* (1 CORINTHIANS 13:4-5)

Looking to change the dynamics in your marriage? Try consideration.

OUR SECRET SAUCE, MY RECIPE
Four Parts Friendship (Part Deux)

IN ADDITION to taking turns and using your kind voice, there are two other critical components of friendship that should be injected in every marriage: celebrating one another and holding hands.

Cheer enthusiastically. I love watching a good game of kickball being played by a group of third graders. As their teammate rounds the bases, they jump up and down like little jumping beans, arms waving enthusiastically, ready to congratulate the runner as she crosses home plate. What a celebration—you'd think the kids had won the gold medal at the Olympics! Do you and your husband celebrate one another?

Just as you have your doubts about your value and abilities, so does he. Even when he's hitting on all cylinders and at the top of his game, he needs your support. He needs to know you're in his cheering section, so, girlfriends, get your pom-poms out (uniform optional). Let him know that you believe in him and that you're with him come rain or shine. Because sooner or later it will rain, and he has to know that your admiration is not conditional.

Hold hands. In kindergarten, I loved the buddy concept. Always an affectionate child, I loved getting to hold hands with someone. It made me feel connected. And so it is for your husband.

Reach for his hand, whether you're sitting in your family room, in your place of worship, at the movie, in the car, at the restaurant, walking to the car, or walking from the car. Anytime, *every time* you are next to each other (this means the kids can't be walking or sitting in between you—they should never do that; put them to each side), reach for his hand. Women often underestimate the power of touch and the importance of making the move to reach for your husband. Reaching for his hand is a quiet, simple gesture that tells him you care without your ever saying a word. It serves as a nice "I'm sorry" gesture too.

> *Instead, it is you—my equal,*
> *my companion and close friend.*
> *What good fellowship we once enjoyed*
> *as we walked together to the house of God.* (PSALM 55:13-14)

As you're cooking your secret sauce, make sure you begin with friendship. Show God how grateful you are for the man he gave you.

OUR SECRET SAUCE, MY RECIPE
Say What You Mean and Mean What You Say

I'M ONE OF YOU, so don't get all bent out of shape when I say this but . . . we're weird. When it comes to communication, women are total enigmas to men (and sometimes even to each other). Have you ever gotten off the phone with a girlfriend and asked yourself, *What did she mean by that?*

I spent my entire corporate career working with men in a male-dominated industry. Men are very black-and-white, never speaking in a foreign tongue or requiring that we (women) decipher the clues they are dropping. They're pretty straightforward. And I like that.

However, in general, women do just the opposite. They think they're dropping clues, they expect everyone (men and women alike) to read their minds, and they often send very mixed messages. Girlfriends, we must say what we mean and mean what we say. And we can't change our minds by nine tonight! That drives the boys nuts!

Steve and I believe that one ingredient of our secret sauce is our ability to communicate clearly with one another. Here's how we do it, especially when there's something significant that must be addressed.

First, timing is everything. We make sure we have scheduled a time that is convenient to both of us, when both of us are in a frame of mind to solve problems. Second, we turn off all noise devices (computers and TVs): neither of us needs the distraction of the outside world when "our world" needs addressing. Before speaking, I think through *in advance* what I need or want, why it's important to me, and when I need it. I am clear on my position, as is he. We listen—we don't debate the other's position. This takes a bit of self-discipline on my part—Steve's great at it. But by listening instead of discussing, I learn better how a situation is affecting him, and he me. Together we can begin to see and understand one another's position so that we can begin to solve or work through problems we face. Yes, this is very adultlike.

Many of my friends believe that arguing is good for a relationship. Maybe it is good for some people. But Steve and I are better suited to calm conversations. Yes, we have disagreed on issues and approaches, but we have managed to come to a conclusion or next steps without blaming anyone, yelling about anything, or hurting the other person.

The wise are known for their understanding,
and pleasant words are persuasive. (PROVERBS 16:21)

Girlfriends, are you clear, calm, and considerate with your mate when issues arise?

OUR SECRET SAUCE, MY RECIPE
Don't Say Everything You're Thinking

OH, THIS IS SUCH a tough one for a lot of us—especially with our mates. And I'll be honest with you, this is not one I come by naturally. I tend to say what I'm thinking, and when I'm not thinking something pleasant—well, you know—it's not good.

So I learned this secret sauce ingredient from Steve. His diplomacy and timing have taught me that I don't have to share every stinkin' thing I'm thinking. As an example, I got real worked up one day over an injustice dealt us in a real estate transaction. My list of grievances went from here to yonder as I practiced the oral summation I would present to the development executives, aka scoundrels, on Steve. He smiled, sat quietly for a moment, and then said, "Why don't you just politely tell them that you're pulling your offer? They know the mistakes they've made. You don't have to tell them again." With Steve's assistance and a bit more maturity, I've learned that there are some things that fly into my head that are merely a reaction to the moment, the challenge, or a hormone surge. I've learned that by practicing *say what you mean and mean what you say*, I must stop and actually *think* about my position rather than just react emotionally.

When you take the time to really think about your position, the heat of the moment dissipates, allowing you to get a new perspective on your thoughts, maybe hours or even days later. Once the adrenaline drops or your hormone levels return to something close to normal, you most likely will decide that the topic is not worth the emotional exercise.

I have never regretted holding my tongue, but I sure have deep remorse for things I've said that I wish I could take back.

> *Kind words are like honey—*
> *sweet to the soul and healthy for the body.* (PROVERBS 16:24)

Girlfriends, to really have a great secret sauce, you must choose to let some things go. In the grand scheme of your life together, some things *really* don't matter and should be left unsaid. Don't use all your words today; try to save some for tomorrow.

OUR SECRET SAUCE, MY RECIPE
Know When to Back Off

LADIES, this one is for your husbands: encourage your menfolk to figure out when to back off. Steve brings some pretty special ingredients to our secret sauce that we'll get into later, but this one needs to be mentioned now. Men need to add a little discernment to the sauce. Girlfriends, feel free to pass the book over to your partner for this one.

When I get an idea about something, I go full throttle. I am an optimistic Energizer Bunny on steroids when I decide I want to do something, whether starting a new business or spring cleaning. You can only imagine how strong-willed I can be when I get a harebrained idea that I feel needs to be implemented tomorrow.

I have this theory that applies to work *and* family: I believe each of us is hard-wired to be either a *what* person or a *how* person. I'm a *what* person. A visionary. I see clearly what needs to be done and when. I love coming up with new ideas for books, events, and products. I'm an idea person.

However, I'm much less clear on the *how*—even though most of the time, anxious for progress, I plow ahead. Steve is the *how* person on our team. He knows the logical and methodical steps to help me achieve my hand-waving, pie-in-the-sky, big-idea plans. But . . . he allows me to work it out.

Okay, for the men reading this entry, this is key: you might know *exactly* what she needs to do and see clearly that she is likely to make a mistake if she doesn't. However, you don't need to lecture her or give her advice on day one. Tell her what you would do and why and then back off. When Steve tells me how he'd approach something, *over a period of time* I have come to the exact same conclusion—100 percent of the time. There's never been a cross word between us, just a total meeting of the minds.

A gentle answer deflects anger,
but harsh words make tempers flare. (PROVERBS 15:1)

Beautiful, eh? Gentlemen, are you dispensing a little too much advice, too often? Back off.

OUR SECRET SAUCE, MY RECIPE
Adoration, Not Desperation

I DON'T NEED my husband. Never have. Never will.

I make my own money. I have my own ideals. I build my own confidence. I design my own dreams. I don't need Steve—except when it comes to running the complex stereo system in our house! I swear he keeps it difficult just so I will be a little dependent on him.

But I *want* him. I choose him. Steve is my everything. And he knows it. Of course, *he* doesn't need *me* either. He *wants* me. He chose me. I'm his everything. And I know it. This reciprocal affection is what enables our relationship to be incredibly balanced.

In the early years of our marriage, I think Steve was a little taken aback by my independence. He wanted to feel needed until I showed him that it was so much better to be desired.

Relationships work at their peak when they are balanced, when there is a constant, consistent hum of adoration between two people. Desperation on the part of either party can be the beginning of a serious unraveling that may leave either or both of you with nothing but a small thread to hang on to; *it's hard to be the one who is needy and equally difficult to be the one needed.* What makes our relationship work—and other successful partnerships I have witnessed—is balance; we don't look for the other to fill what we lack but desire the other simply for who he or she is.

Three things will last forever—faith, hope, and love—and the greatest of these is love. (1 CORINTHIANS 13:13)

Women (or men) who look to be rescued or taken care of, or who look to their mates to fill their empty vessels, create unbalanced relationships. Let adoration define your relationship, not desperation.

OUR SECRET SAUCE, MY RECIPE
We Love Us More Than Stuff

AT ONE TIME, money was reported to be the number one cause of divorce. New studies say no—it's not money but incompatibility that is the root issue. I always maintained that it was never money or the lack thereof that caused issues in a marriage—it's what you *do* with the money that creates friction. And the more you make, the more opportunities you have to focus on your $tuff, instead of your love.

Money is a tricky subject, and as with all things, you and your mate have to find your own way. I'll tell you our secret sauce ingredient: we love *us* far more than $tuff. And we believe in cash.

Get out of debt and stay out of debt. Steve and I had a goal when we first married: we'd get out of debt and stay out of debt. In order to pay off our home early, we would not buy the things many of our friends were purchasing; we would not go on elaborate vacations; and we would often tell our children no. This singular focus put us in a comfortable cash position as thirtysomethings. The delayed gratification for other stuff only made the nicer home, luxury cars, vacations, and art more enjoyable when we did purchase them. Even today, Steve and I pay for things with cash.

We believe in having a cash reserve (savings). We do not believe in hoarding, which can be as damaging as overspending; we simply pay ourselves a reasonable amount for a rainy day. For some reason, the average American has discounted the power of a savings account. I read recently that we're saving less today as a society than ever before. In 2004, for every $100 earned, the average American saved $1.80; in January 2005 that number dipped below a dollar and then dropped to zero, according to the Bureau of Economic Analysis. The September 2, 2005, *Wall Street Journal* reported that U.S. households actually spent more than they earned in July, sending the personal-savings rate to minus 0.6 percent. *Yikes!*

> *Thrift is not, as many suppose, a self repression. It is self expression, the demonstration of a will and ability to raise one's self to higher plane of living. No depression was ever caused by people having too much money in reserve. No human being ever became a social drifter through the practice of sensible thrift.* HARVEY A. BLODGETT

In our secret sauce, thrift and financial peace are key ingredients.

She has no fear of winter for her household,
*   for everyone has warm clothes.* (PROVERBS 31:21)

Plan now. A cold front is on the way.

OUR SECRET SAUCE, MY RECIPE
We Love Us More Than Stuff (Part Deux)

A LOT OF THE FINANCIAL success Steve and I have enjoyed is due to the fact that we talk, in advance, about our spending. Because just as we save, let me promise you, we spend, too!

We believe in treats. We enjoy our money and make very deliberate decisions about what we will buy and what we won't. This takes some planning and ongoing communication. Girlfriends, don't wait until you're at the car dealership or at Best Buy to *begin* this conversation—it will be too late.

We believe in peace (the wedding day). We've proactively planned for major expenditures. After our daughter and son-in-law's engagement, my husband came up with a fabulous idea. Shauna and I are very close, and Steve could predict the wedding planning and expenses might get out of hand. Thus, he proposed we research what a nice wedding would cost and give that figure to Shauna and Adam in cash. Yes!

We wrote our daughter and future son-in-law a check, and they opened their first joint account. This gave them an opportunity to work through important issues, prioritize their wants and desires, and make their own decisions regarding their big day. Not once during the yearlong planning was there ever a tear. *My husband is a pure genius.*

We believe in gifts. I think you can tell a lot about a person from the way they think about their money—and how much of it they're willing to give away. I don't really consider money mine in the first place. Everything I have belongs to God. The air; the grass; the sun; the moon; the stars. How do you ever repay him for that cool stuff? I am blessed with a healthy body and a strong mind, and I can work—these, too, are gifts. Thus, I believe in giving back. We give more than 10 percent of our income because we feel called to do it; I'm not sure everyone is. But when you can learn to give it away, I have found it always makes its way back to you. Simply amazing.

> *Don't love money; be satisfied with what you have. For God has said, "I will never fail you. I will never abandon you."* (HEBREWS 13:5)

Our consolidated position on matters of money is not an accident. We strategized before we married as to how we would treat our money and what type of priority we would put on stuff. We've not once had a disagreement on money matters, because we developed a plan and have stuck to it. We love *us* more than $tuff. Now that's something to be grateful for.

OUR SECRET SAUCE, MY RECIPE
Did You Feed Frankie?

OUR FELINE FAMILY member, Maggie, passed away several years ago. It was a big loss, and replacing her seemed impossible. When we moved into a new home soon after, though, the neighborhood feral cat took up residence in our yard.

Steve and I were intrigued by Frankie (I named him Frankie because he looks like a "Frank"), but he had *issues*. He didn't make eye contact, he wouldn't allow us to pet him, and his social graces were deplorable. But we loved Frankie, so we fed him—every day, twice a day. Because he didn't interact with us like a normal pet, Steve and I had to check with each other—"Did you feed Frankie?" We knew that *neglect* would surely kill the cat. Same goes for your relationship.

One of the most important ingredients in our secret sauce is our commitment to feed our relationship *every day*. Women and men both tell us they don't have time to invest like this. Well, pay now or pay later, because you'll have more time on your hands than you know what to do with in another ten years when the kids are gone! I'm not saying you have to have a two-hour conversation, every day, but you can invest meaningful minutes. You must connect. *Someone* has to feed Frankie!

Let's give this a try today: call your honey and tell him you miss him. Yes, he might have to look at caller ID to be sure it's you, but let him know that you are in *serious like* with him. Did you feed Frankie? He's looking mighty hungry!

Or leave him a voice mail at the office and let him know you're thinking about him and his "whatever" that's going on at work (there's always something). Did you feed Frankie? He seems stressed.

Maybe you could write him an e-mail and tell him you're crazy, crazy in love with him; yes, for a minute he might think you're just plain crazy. But *feed Frankie*!

Then do it again tomorrow, and the next day, and the next. Okay. Close this book and do it now. Then come back for step number two.

Good job, girlfriend! Now, try this:

Set your alarm thirty minutes early. Share a cup of coffee together before the kids are up or before either of you run out the door for work. Now you're *really* feeding Frankie—he might even start purring!

Take a vacation day during the middle of the week. Have friends pick up the kids from school. Spend the day having lunch, hanging out at a park, and maybe . . . just maybe . . . you might even spend some "bedroom" time in the middle of the day! The cat might die of shock, but oh, he'll be happy!

> Place me like a seal over your heart,
>   like a seal on your arm.
> For love is as strong as death,
>   its jealousy as enduring as the grave.
> Love flashes like fire,
>   the brightest kind of flame. (SONG OF SONGS 8:6)

OUR SECRET SAUCE, MY RECIPE

FATHER GOD, we need a new recipe for our love affair. You have spoken to me, and I realize that I

- [ ] need to invest in the rekindling of our friendship;
- [ ] am not spending enough alone time with my husband;
- [ ] often use a disrespectful tone or disparaging words with him; I am not always kind;
- [ ] could be a better cheerleader for my husband;
- [ ] could connect with him by reaching for his hand more often;
- [ ] could improve our communication by calmly and clearly stating my position; and then, in turn, listening politely to his;
- [ ] need to stop saying every stinkin' thing I'm thinking;
- [ ] need to gently let him know when he's dispensing too much advice;
- [ ] need to replace my feelings of desperation with adoration;
- [ ] need to place a higher value on us than on other stuff;
- [ ] need to feed Frankie.

ACTIONS I WILL TAKE:

Example: Tonight, as we watch TV, I will move to the sofa and reach for his hand.

1. _____

2. _____

3. _____

Father, I thank you today for my husband. You have given me a precious gift, and I praise you for allowing me to spend my life with him. Take control of my will Lord, that I might be the wife to him that you want me to be. Give me patience, determination, and, Lord, help me be kind. Amen.

OUR SECRET SAUCE, HIS RECIPE

WELL, WE KNOW it takes two to tango, so what about our recipe from *Steve's* perspective?

Now that you know how to spice up your secret sauce, I thought maybe the man in your life could use a few cooking tips as well. So, with Steve's permission, I'd like to share with you those ingredients he adds to our secret sauce.

What comes first, the chicken or the egg? This has been Steve's and my dilemma for a while as we have tried to analyze what makes us work so well as a team. He says it's because I'm always positive, happy, and content. He loves the fact that I never nag. But I'm convinced that I am this positive, happy, and contented woman because he's such a great husband. As I continued to think about what makes our relationship work so well, I realized there are things Steve intuitively knows that some guys have never thought about. It's not that they're uncaring or dumb—they're just not wired to naturally know how to make the most of their marriage through the honoring of their wives.

Girlfriends, my hope is that this chapter will help you begin an objective, honest dialogue with your mate if you find that any of these ingredients are also important to you. And, if your man is in touch with his "softer side," pass the book over to him for the next few pages. I promise I'll be gentle. Well, sort of. *Heeheeheehee . . .*

I am my lover's, and he claims me as his own. (SONG OF SONGS 7:10)

Oh, we're stirring the sauce now!

OUR SECRET SAUCE, HIS RECIPE
My Success Is His Success

WHEN I WAS YOUNG I was taught that it was my duty to support my husband's career and his success. I accepted that his success would be my success and thus our success. Well, that was then, and this is now. Our relationship is so unique because Steve also believes in *my* success. My success is his success; thus it is our success. Wow. A real partnership. Who would of thunk?

At every turn in *my* career, Steve has made sacrifices. One sacrifice was absolutely huge. Due to my promotion as a corporate officer of a company to which he sold technology products, he gave up his largest customer—all to ensure there would be no appearance of conflict of interest, which might have blemished my professional reputation. Even though he was making more money than I was, he sacrificed, recognizing the role my professional development played in my overall state of contentment, maturation, and self-worth.

Today, he helps me run my marketing firm—I couldn't possibly lead the company without him—and he has encouraged, yes, cheered me on to write this book. He is not a passive spectator. Steve is an active participant in every part of my professional life. He supports me by encouraging me, researching opportunities and technology solutions, managing the finances, and praying. Before every presentation, as I travel to and fro, as I prepare for every meeting, my husband is standing in my corner, lifting me in prayer. How cool is that?

In the same way, husbands ought to love their wives as they love their own bodies. For a man who loves his wife actually shows love for himself.
(EPHESIANS 5:28)

Gentlemen, if you're bold enough to be reading this, there is no better way to honor your mate than to support her in endeavors that are important to her personal and professional development. Her success is your success, too, so get out your pom-poms!

OUR SECRET SAUCE, HIS RECIPE
Great Sex Starts in the Kitchen

I'VE GOT YOUR attention now, don't I?

Husbands, do you serve your wife? I'll bet a dollar to a doughnut that you haven't provided an act of service to her this month. Shoot! Some of you boys haven't even considered the *concept* of proactively tending to her needs. Steve is a man of service. My girlfriends know that he brings me coffee each morning—that's pretty amazing, isn't it? But that's only the beginning.

Steve recognizes that managing our home is an equal opportunity proposition. As an example, in our nearly twenty years of marriage, he's not once left me alone to do the dishes and clean the kitchen. And how about this? I can't remember ever having to *ask* him to take out the trash.

So, you ask, What's in it for me? Guys, I have never once (well, maybe once) nagged my husband. Why would I? *What is there to nag him about?* But actually, there's something even better in this arrangement than a less-fussy wife: sex. Yes, believe it or not, great sex starts in other rooms of the house—not in the bedroom.

Women, especially those who are maxed out with kids and/or a demanding career, get the most "turned on" when their husbands are engaged at the kitchen table helping with homework, on the phone ordering Chinese for dinner, or waiting for them in the living room. There's nothing, I mean *nothing*, like arriving home from a stressful week to find the fireplace lit, my favorite CD playing, and my husband waiting there, looking forward to talking *with* me, not *at* me. Replacing our quick flurry of exchanges on schedules, honey-do's, and family updates, we slow down to share the important events of the day and our dreams for tomorrow. Gentlemen, I promise you if you try this you'll have a much better chance of getting lucky tonight than you did last night when you arrived home from work at 9 p.m. after your wife had helped with the Algebra II homework, cooked dinner, rocked a crying baby, and planned the holiday menu for your family.

Want your wife to be pleasant and cheerful? Get your rear end in the kitchen. Want her to be "into" you? Get into her and pick up that toilet brush.

> Let your wife be a fountain of blessing for you.
>   Rejoice in the wife of your youth.
> She is a loving deer, a graceful doe.
>   Let her breasts satisfy you always.
>   May you always be captivated by her love. (PROVERBS 5:18-19)

There's nothing like a man who serves his wife. And he's the man who is satisfied, since his wife tends to be much more into "servicing" him too!

Okay. That's enough of that.

OUR SECRET SAUCE, HIS RECIPE
Let Her Be the Momma Bear

I WAS A promotional bride.

The deal that month was "buy one; get a family for free." Steve, a confirmed bachelor, not only got a new bride but two children as part of the wedded bliss package—an eight-year-old boy with some pretty big challenges and an eleven-year-old daughter entering puberty. I'm sure he wondered, more than once, *What happened to my nice, quiet, predictable life?*

Steve was considered the "new boy" in our family—and my two kiddos did not cut him any slack right away! But Steve was patient in his role and understood something that many men never grasp: Steve realized much quicker than most husbands do that motherhood is not merely a role women play; for some of us it provides a 24-7 gut-wrenching, heart-splitting, pull-your-hair-out kind of joy.

Over the years Steve worked closely with me to learn what made the kids tick, and we almost always agreed on the best approach to discipline, action, motivation, and—when required from time to time—the best means of bribery. Then big trouble came our way. Before Steve and I married, I had adopted Scott. By the time he was two and a half, it was obvious that he had begun to develop several alarming personality traits. When he turned twenty, he was a nonfunctioning drug addict.

For years I worked to protect Scott. All along Steve partnered with and supported me in this heartbreaking journey. He never told me it was time to throw in the towel or asked Scott to leave. Instead, Steve allowed me to "help" (you could say "enable" at some point) Scott until I came to the conclusion, via Al-Anon, that it was time to let our son go. It was not until that very day, sitting in the parking lot after our first Al-Anon meeting, that Steve told me that for the past few years he had been waiting patiently for me to come to this realization. When I asked him how he kept quiet for so many years, he said, "I know better than to get between a momma bear and her cub." Steve knew that I more than loved my children; he understood from the get-go that I'm *in love* with them.

I know it doesn't seem fair, but there are times when a mother has to be momma bear and do all she can to care for or save her baby. She has to figure out on her own when to let go—her husband can't tell her.

> *But those who won't care for their relatives, especially those in their own household, have denied the true faith. Such people are worse than unbelievers.*
> (1 TIMOTHY 5:8)

Today, our marriage is just about us—not the kids. They're grown and gone. But because of Steve and his patience, I have complete peace; I can say I know I did everything I could do, was supposed to do, and wanted to do for Scott, because Steve allowed me to be the momma bear.

Gggrrrwww.

OUR SECRET SAUCE, HIS RECIPE
Be Afraid

I AM A BIT of an adventurer; Steve is not. I enjoy travel and the "surprises" that sometimes accompany an excursion to a new place; Steve, not so much. I enjoy meeting people and getting to know total strangers whom I will never see again; Steve, not so much.

So off I went on an adventure to India with fourteen strangers. The unknown aspects of where I was going, who I was going with, and who I would meet once I was there were a total thrill to me.

Before I took off on my twenty-four-hour journey to the other side of the world, Steve and his mom met for lunch. Harriett, a loving mother to us both, asked Steve, "Aren't you afraid for her to go?" Steve replied, "I would be more afraid to ask her to stay."

My husband not only understands our differences, he embraces them. Rather than try to mold me, bribe me, or chastise me into being someone other than who I am, Steve encourages me, even though sometimes he has to look the other way. Was he worried for my safety? Absolutely. But would he have put his worry and fear ahead of my yearning and desire for new learning experiences? Not in a million years.

You and your spouse might be different from one another; in fact, I can almost bet that you two are very different. There's no doubt in my mind that opposites do attract. Can you embrace this truth rather than trying to change it?

I can speak only from my own personal experience. Nothing makes me feel more loved than when Steve is afraid of changing me from who God created me to be.

Love each other with genuine affection, and take delight in honoring each other.
(ROMANS 12:10)

Be afraid . . . not of the growth or separation that might result from your development but of stifling the maturation that will make both of you more complete human beings—separately and together.

OUR SECRET SAUCE, HIS RECIPE
Compliment the Beauty Queen

I WAS MY DADDY'S favorite. No, really. I was. Each of my half sisters claims he loved her most, but I know for a fact that Daddy favored me. There was never a day in my life when I did not feel valued by my father. And most days, I felt like a beauty queen.

My father was generous with compliments, whether admiring my new hairstyle, a good grade on my report card, or a new outfit. He would sometimes whistle if I came out of my bedroom especially dolled up. I would twirl around as he gushed.

In her heart, every little girl longs to be the apple of her father's eye and the only woman her husband really sees. She longs for the beauty queen days of her youth. Steve gets that.

I don't know if he's ever gone a day in our marriage without complimenting me. One day it might be my outfit; another day it might be the way I handled a difficult situation with a client. Whether he tells me that I look cute or that I'm an asset to our company, I know that I am valuable to him. I know, without a doubt, that I am his beauty queen.

She dresses in fine linen and purple gowns. (PROVERBS 31:22)

Dressed in fine linen or faded jeans, this plain Jane is Steve's beauty queen.

Do I believe he has eyes *only* for me? Oh, I know Steve must look sometimes, but he's so discreet, I never catch him. It's just another way he honors the woman sitting at his side (and preserves his own life).

OUR SECRET SAUCE, HIS RECIPE
I'm Number Two

AS STEVE AND I approach our twentieth wedding anniversary, I know that he adores and treasures me as much as he did on our wedding day. But I am neither adorable nor a treat. In reality, I am one high-maintenance woman. So how is it Steve honors me when I am so imperfect?

Steve's priorities are different than most men's, and I know without a doubt that I am number two on his list.

Whatever is of greatest concern to our husbands is what their hearts and minds will focus on. If a man's priorities are set on making money, improving his golf game, or achieving some other goal, it's likely that his family, *especially his wife*, has been or will be moved to a distant third or fourth on the list. And this is why many marriages only exist rather than flourish. If we really, I mean *really*, want our secret sauce to *cook*, we must take a look at those things that occupy our hearts and minds and consider resetting our priorities.

So what's Steve's number one priority? Steve loves God.

But hang with me here. He's not a deacon, a leader, a teacher, or an elder in the church. Nope, he's just an average Joe. As a matter of fact, my husband could be a lot like some of the husbands reading this entry. Steve loves rock 'n' roll—especially turned up loud. Although I have complete disdain for motorcycles, the only thing he enjoys more than riding his 1972 Norton Commando is tinkering with its parts. And he loves to hug the curves of Texas country roads as I hold my breath and brace myself against the dashboard of whatever five-speed transmission he's driving at the time. But my fun-loving, bass-thumping, fast-driving husband is a man of deep faith and commitment. He loves his Lord and goes to him for direction.

I can't tell you why, but there is something powerful about a man who humbles himself before God. There is something comforting about a man who has huge faith. Even though I am Ms. Independent, I know that when *life* happens, Steve, with his faith and strength, leads our family. And there is something just downright sexy about this man who cherishes me *because of* his love for God. His faith and his wife are his priorities.

As for me and my house, we will serve the LORD. (JOSHUA 24:15, NASB)

Of all the riches my husband could leave our children, he models this instruction especially well: love the Lord first, and everything else will fall in line.

OUR SECRET SAUCE, HIS RECIPE

AT THE END of this section, I invite you to do something a bit different. If you're married, you might ask your husband to read the entries on Steve's contributions to our secret sauce and then pray about how God might have him love his family even better. Of course, it wouldn't hurt to let him know that you are praying that God will help you love and honor him better too.

Father God, may I come before you today asking that you bless my marriage by helping me to

- [ ] support and celebrate my wife's success, not only in our home but in her professional life;

- [ ] remember to help with the dishes. I understand, God, that great sex usually starts outside the bedroom and, Lord, I really do want to be helpful;

- [ ] understand that, as the momma bear, my wife may go to extremes to help or save our children;

- [ ] embrace our differences, rather than try to change her into someone else;

- [ ] remember to look at her, value her, and compliment her with kind words;

- [ ] prioritize my relationship with you above all else.

ACTIONS I WILL TAKE:

Example: I will take over kitchen duty on Monday and Friday nights, and Wednesday nights will be my night to help the kids with their homework.

1. _____

2. _____

3. _____

Father, I thank you today for my wife. You have given me a precious gift, and I praise you for allowing me to spend my life with her. Take control of my will, Lord, that I might be the husband to her that you want me to be. Give me patience, determination, and, Lord, enable me to be what she most needs me to be. Amen.

STICKS AND STONES

Today I bent the truth to be kind, and I have no regret, for I am far surer of what is kind than I am of what is true. ROBERT BRAULT

"STICKS AND STONES may break my bones, but words can never hurt me."

Oh, good grief! We need to stop propagating this lie.

Whoever made up this little ditty of a saying either had no experience, no heart, or no enemies. Words not only hurt—they can destroy. The wrong words, used at the wrong time, can destroy someone's self-esteem; they can destroy both new and old friendships; and they can destroy the ties that bind families together. It doesn't matter if you're six or sixty, words can either heal or harm. And the healing, if it does occur, usually takes a lifetime.

We try desperately to move beyond those things told to us as children, sometimes by the very people whose job it was to build our self-confidence. We work hard to forgive and forget cutting words yelled, or worse, quietly released at us by the man we promised to have and to hold. And many of us try to shake off arrows that were slung our way in last week's business meeting by our trusted colleagues. Yes, we know how words hurt *us.* But rarely do we consider our own role when it comes to word choices. Living in our "all about me" world, I'm afraid we ignore the effect of the syllables *we* hurl.

> *Don't use foul or abusive language. Let everything you say be good and helpful, so that your words will be an encouragement to those who hear them.*
> (EPHESIANS 4:29)

I think we could all use a reminder that our words—both the things said and those things not said—have the power and energy to make people whole or to tear them down.

Will you choose your words wisely today? And when you do speak the truth, will you also be kind?

STICKS AND STONES
When the Truth Hurts

LET'S FACE IT. Many of us would rather eat June bugs than confront someone. We long for peace and unity, so we stuff the truth because it's easier to sit quiet than deal with the fallout. But girlfriends, there's nothing harmonious about living out a lie and nothing more hurtful than when you learn your relationship is a scam.

We skirt issues with our spouse, deny there are problems with our children, and even avoid people at work to keep that knot in our stomach at bay. We struggle with speaking the truth when we know it's going to hurt. But I have a news flash for you—it's going to hurt them *more* when they realize that you've been hiding what you really feel; and you know as well as I do that sooner or later the truth *always* comes out.

At some point you're going to have to tell that person that

- "I'm resentful."
- "I'm restless."
- "I'm disappointed."
- "I'm lonely."
- "I'm hurt."
- "I'm embarrassed."
- "I made the wrong decision."

To soften the sting when addressing someone else's actions, take responsibility for your own feelings. I had to do this at work recently. Even though it was difficult, we both felt better once the cards were on the table—faceup.

Approaching someone in humility makes it much more likely that he or she will listen. "If you fail to confront, you will lose," says noted psychologist Dr. Henry Cloud. "But, if you confront poorly, you will also lose. So, you must confront, but confront well. That means that the truth-telling side of your character must be integrated with the loving and caring side of your character. When you show up to deal with a problem, you must bring both of them together. Confront the problem, but in a way that preserves the relationship and the person."[31]

Don't wait until you're exhausted, frustrated, and have checked out of the relationship. Be sincere. Be direct. Be kind. And be responsible for your feelings.

Then we will no longer be immature like children. We won't be tossed and blown about by every wind of new teaching. We will not be influenced when people try to trick us with lies so clever they sound like the truth. Instead, we will speak the truth in love, growing in every way more and more like Christ, who is the head of his body, the church. (EPHESIANS 4:14-15)

Learning to confront well takes courage and practice. Begin today.

STICKS AND STONES
Words *Not* Said

TO WHOM DO you owe an apology?

Whom should you have thanked last week?

Whom do you appreciate that you still haven't told?

We live in a world that moves at warp speed, but it takes only seconds to say thank you to someone who has done something nice for you. Aren't you hurt when others fail to express their appreciation for a sacrifice you've made or a service you've bestowed? Guess what—I guarantee, regardless of how good we all think we are at saying thank you . . . we fail to acknowledge people in our lives every day. Don't believe me? When's the last time you thanked your husband for his support, for working so hard to take care of you financially and/or emotionally, for loving you? See? . . .

And it happens at our workplaces, too. We work in a macho-professional, dog-eat-dog environment where it's *expected* that people give 150 percent. But aren't you disappointed when others don't comment on your contribution to a project? Of course you are. But guess what—I guarantee, regardless of how good we think we are, we, too, fail to acknowledge the contributions of others, from our team members to our bosses. Don't believe me? Walk down the aisle of cubes and ask yourself, *When was the last time I congratulated someone for their great work?* See? . . .

We express our disapproval verbally and physically (you should see the hand gestures used on Central Expressway in Dallas by irate commuters) every day but often fail to share words of encouragement or appreciation. We make excuses that we either don't have the time or that we don't know what words to use. It takes only thirty seconds, and you don't have to be a poet to say

- *Thank you.* I know this was a sacrifice for you to invest your resources—both time and money—on my behalf.
- *I appreciate you.* You have really gone out of your way to support me and my projects, and you have been such an important contributor to the outcome of this endeavor.
- *I apologize.* I sometimes get too busy and caught up in my own affairs to really consider others. I'm sorry.

Do not withhold good from those who deserve it
when it's in your power to help them. (PROVERBS 3:27)

Life is short, and we have a limited number of days to say important words. So often, it is the words that go unsaid that hurt the most.

STICKS AND STONES
Baby Talk

IN OUR ATTEMPTS to make casual conversation we often ask innocent questions:

- How are things at work?
- What book are you reading?
- Have you seen any good movies lately?

Here are a few questions that might seem innocent to us but can be deadly posed to the wrong person:

- Are you thinking about having children?
- Are you pregnant yet?
- When are you going to give me a grandbaby?
- Why didn't you have kids?

Girlfriends, for many women these questions break hearts, threaten peace, or sound like judgment being sent down from heaven above.

For my young girlfriends (and their husbands) who are in your childbearing years, I apologize for all of us who ask without considering that you may be trying, unsuccessfully, to get pregnant. I cannot begin to imagine how frustrating it must be to try and try, only for the blessing not to come—when it seems to come so easily for others. How heartbreaking it must be for you to try to answer these difficult questions.

For my girlfriends (and their husbands) whose parents pressure you to carry on the family name and gene pool, I apologize for all of us who fail to realize that, for reasons your parents might not understand, having children is not right for you, whether now or in the foreseeable future. What a peace stealer it must be when you're made to feel that the only valuable contribution you could make to your family would be to produce a grandchild.

For my girlfriends (and their husbands) who have chosen not to be parents, I apologize for all of us who ask—*when it's none of our business*—if or why you elected not to have children. You should never be made to feel that you must justify your decision to have or not to have one (or a household of) kiddo(s).

Death and life are in the power of the tongue. (PROVERBS 18:21, NASB)

When it comes to baby talk, perhaps it's best to let a woman bring up the topic of motherhood—on her terms.

STICKS AND STONES
At a Loss for Words

ABOUT TWENTY YEARS AGO, one of my girlfriends lost her second-grade son; he was killed while driving a go-cart. I, a very young mother myself, went to her the morning of the funeral as she sat so small and still on the foot of her bed. I was at a loss for words.

After another girlfriend had waged a fierce battle against brain cancer, her doctor told her that her time was very limited—she had less than six months. I asked her, "What can I do?" She said, "Throw me a going-away party." I was at a loss for words.

Sitting on the living room sofa holding hands with our then fourteen-year-old son, Scott, Steve and I listened as our son told us, "I'm gay." We were not surprised; we knew before he did and that this day was coming, but still—I was at a loss for words.

We've all been there, haven't we? When there just are no words that are even close to being able to express our grief, our concern, our heartbreak, our disbelief, or our desire to make things different.

In each of these situations, my mind raced for the right words: words of comfort, words of wisdom, words of hope. In every situation, I sent up an express-o-gram prayer, "Oh, Father God, give me words." Not empty words—like "I know how you feel" (because I didn't) or "I'm sorry this has happened" (how does that help?). I prayed for his direction to use only words that would matter.

If I could speak all the languages of earth and of angels, but didn't love others, I would only be a noisy gong or a clanging cymbal. (1 CORINTHIANS 13:1)

In each of the three instances, as I caught my breath and recovered, the Lord provided me these three important words: I love you.

Sometimes when it comes to words, less is more.

STICKS AND STONES
Kindness and Fondness Are Mutually Exclusive

Kindness is in our power, even when fondness is not. SAMUEL JOHNSON

OH, PLEASE. This quote drives me crazy because it always seems to come to mind when I so want to be rude. Let me give you an example.

I have this huge pet peeve about how the airline industry treats their customers. I could fill an entire chapter with true and bizarre stories of the most hateful, rude "customer service" experiences I've both endured and witnessed. But that doesn't give me a pass on being kind.

When I walk up to the gate and am glared at by a cynical, burned-out ticket agent, I smile my biggest, brightest eight-tooth smile. Sometimes I get an eight-tooth reflection. Usually I get no eye contact and a request for my ID. It doesn't matter. My job is to be kind in this situation, even though fondness for this person evades me.

When I step on the plane and the flight attendants look like they'd rather be anywhere in the world than on that plane, in that airport, I greet them with a heartfelt "good morning," or "good afternoon." Sometimes I get a warm response, but mostly they pretend they didn't hear me. It doesn't matter. In the absence of fondness for these folks, it is still my responsibility to be kind.

When I leave the plane and the captain is standing at the door, arms folded and eyes cast to the back of the plane just waiting for these poky passengers (in other industries we're called customers) to get off the plane, I always thank him or her. Only about twenty times in my last fifteen years of flying (and I have flown well over 2 million miles) have I had a pilot respond while making eye contact. Scary that this is how airlines often treat their customers. But it doesn't matter. My role in this relationship is to be kind.

Since God chose you to be the holy people he loves, you must clothe yourselves with tenderhearted mercy, kindness, humility, gentleness, and patience. Make allowance for each other's faults, and forgive anyone who offends you. Remember, the Lord forgave you, so you must forgive others. (COLOSSIANS 3:12-13)

So often we feel that we are not obligated to be polite when others mistreat us, but that's not true. As Mr. Johnson said, "Kindness is in our power, even when fondness is not." Oh, please.

STICKS AND STONES
The Last Word

It is very easy to forgive others their mistakes; it takes more grit and gumption to forgive them for having witnessed your own.   JESSAMYN WEST

I'M PRETTY FAST on my feet when it comes to talking. Especially in a heated debate. I can usually articulate my position with the precision of a sharpshooter. And I can usually get in the last word.

I regret the way I've ended some conversations, however. Intent on strategizing my next verbal move in order to defend my position and honor, I believe I often failed to hear what the other person was thinking or the motivation behind their defense.

I know I did this with my mother. Anticipating what she was going to say, I was like a boxer in a ring, bouncing on my toes, mentally begging for her to "bring it on." I was ready with my last word before I picked up the phone.

I did this when the kids were teenagers. Knowing that I was about to be lied to, I would let my zinger rip before they got to part two of their never-ending tale of deception. Failing to learn the motivation behind the lie, I was prepared with my last word before they drove in the driveway.

And I know I did this at work. My mind racing as I multitasked, I could end a meeting before everyone got settled in their chairs. Reading the sales reports in advance and completing my research, I was prepared with my closing line before my coworkers got their first cup of coffee.

Some of us feel the need to have the last word when competition is fierce, pride is king, and we're afraid. And when people are afraid—especially afraid of being wrong or irrelevant—retorts that smart get hurled in an attempt to save face, save jobs, or save budgets.

But never will a zinger spewed bring you peace, even if you have all your facts and have them right.

I have found that while I may temporarily feel better for having responded with a quick quip, 99 percent of the time my euphoria turned to regret—about the time I was trying to fall asleep.

Let your conversation be gracious and attractive so that you will have the right response for everyone. (COLOSSIANS 4:6)

For those of us who have been given the gift of oration, it is our duty to have the last word. Let's just plan for that word to be kind.

STICKS AND STONES

FATHER GOD, you have spoken to me and I have learned that I need to

- ☐ confront others and share my position respectfully, truthfully, and kindly;

- ☐ share words of encouragement or appreciation more often;

- ☐ be sensitive to those who may be struggling to have or have chosen not to have children;

- ☐ say I love you to _____;

- ☐ remember that even when I'm not fond of someone, I don't have an excuse to be unkind;

- ☐ make sure my last word to someone is always kind.

ACTIONS I WILL TAKE:

Example: I will spend more time thinking how I might confront _____ in a loving, truthful way that protects her dignity and also my own.

1. _____

2. _____

3. _____

Heavenly Father, I know that my words can serve as a cup of water to those who are hurting or can cut as sharply as a knife when used inconsiderately. Give me discernment and bless me with kindness so that every word I say might be a blessing to you and to others. Amen.

CATCHING MY SECOND WIND

I DON'T COMPETE in races—shoot, I don't even consider myself a runner. But I do jog my three miles in 33 minutes and 15 seconds every Monday, Wednesday, and Friday. Sweating like a Texas sow in June, I do fine right up until I'm about 2.25 miles into the run. But then I hit a wall. My legs become heavy, my breathing is more labored, and I convince myself I can't go on. *This is stupid. Who am I trying to kid? I'm too old for this nonsense.*

For the next quarter mile, I doubt my ability to finish. For the next three minutes, I lose all confidence in myself; I dwell on my shortcomings; I focus not on what I've accomplished but on what's left to be done; and I become discouraged.

But I travel on. I continue to put one foot in front of the other because I know at about my 2.5-mile mark, I will catch my second wind and have just the energy I need to carry me to my goal (and breakfast).

According to *Wikipedia*, there are several theories behind this phenomenon of catching one's second wind. One is that the second wind is the result of the body finding the proper balance of oxygen to counteract the buildup of lactic acid in our muscles; another theory is that the second wind is the result of an increase in endorphin production (endorphins are a type of hormone that reduces the sensation of pain and affects emotion); the final theory is that there are no physiological changes in the body at all, but that the second wind is purely psychological, the by-product of the confidence and pride one gains by passing one's supposed limitations.

Some gals hit the wall in their midforties; others find they lack the stamina, interest, or even the desire to run a meaningful life race in their fifties or sixties. No matter the decade, I think it happens to a lot of us, including the guys. Finishing the race becomes a challenge, and finishing it well becomes pure fantasy.

Therefore, since we are surrounded by such a huge crowd of witnesses to the life of faith, let us strip off every weight that slows us down, especially the sin that so easily trips us up. And let us run with endurance the race God has set before us. (HEBREWS 12:1)

As I lace up my sneakers, I consider instead going to the kitchen and having a Danish. But is that the legacy I want to leave—a legacy of giving up just as I hit my stride?

I've yet to find a Bible verse that instructs us to retire; to quit; to be complacent. I think God intends for us to make a difference until the day we die. If you agree, will you join me as we catch our second wind?

CATCHING MY SECOND WIND
Confidence and Pride

A thousand words will not leave so deep an impression as one deed. HENRIK IBSEN

I'M INTERESTED in what you did in your twenties and thirties.

How many of you were PTA moms who could organize and run the Halloween carnival better than P. T. Barnum himself?

How many of you were office managers, delegating, motivating, and negotiating better than the most experienced politician on Capitol Hill?

How many of you were sales reps, representing your company's products or services and fixing problems as smoothly as a magician pulls a rabbit out of a hat?

Do you remember those days when you commanded a room? When you were proud of the service you delivered to your children; your employer; your customers? Remember when you were *really* confident in your abilities? Remember that feeling of pride that you had for a job well done?

Draped in confidence, a woman named Pearl knocked on my front door. I was a teenage mom who had just moved away from my family and the only home I'd ever known to a suburb of Dallas. Since I had no family to support me, Ms. Pearl, about fifty years old at the time, waltzed into my home (after a bit of sleuthing on my part to determine if this woman was for *real*) and shared her wisdom with me and her lap with Shauna. This woman literally saved my sanity (and probably Shauna's life—I hadn't a clue what I was doing). When I asked her a couple of years later how I could ever repay her, she said, "Sometime in your future, you will come across a mother who needs you. Make sure *you* share with her what you've learned and be available."

Pearl didn't invest twenty hours a week in a mother/child development course; she volunteered her mothering and grandmothering services to Shauna and me for about two hours a week. For 120 luxurious minutes she took Shauna or sat with her in our home, giving me the only two-hour break this very young, very poor, very inexperienced mom would get all week.

Here's one of only about a hundred things I learned from watching Ms. Pearl: She recognized a need and she took action. She wasn't timid. She had caught her second wind and realized that her second-half contribution to society would be one mother and one baby at a time. Don't think that sounds life-changing? It was to me.

Just as the body is dead without breath, so also faith is dead without good works.
(JAMES 2:26)

Whether you volunteer your managerial services to a nonprofit, share your gifts of event planning with your church, or lend a lap to a neighbor's child, catch your second wind. People need you. Your second wind will fuel you with confidence and pride when you step out and realize you really are making a difference.

CATCHING MY SECOND WIND
Finding the Proper Balance

ARE YOU DEPRESSED? Wow! I just put it out there in black-and-white, didn't I?

I think a lot of women wake up at their midlife mark feeling tired; burned out by work or family, or both. Some feel lost and alone; the kids are grown and gone while hubby still has his work. Others have told me they feel irrelevant; the world just seems to be passing them by. After a while, the more we think about it, the deeper we tumble into our despondency.

We all know that depression can be caused by hormonal imbalances or brought on by a trauma or crisis. But depression can also be triggered when we fail to balance our self-centered obsessions (yes, I know this is a strong word, but let's be honest and call a spade a spade) with thoughts or actions invested on behalf of others.

My girlfriend Dina told me a great story about her mom, Patricia. Pat had been a little "down in the dumps" with too much time on her seventy-three-year-old hands. Through Dina's sister, Pat learned about a woman with terminal cancer who needed someone to drive her to her chemotherapy treatments. Not thinking much of it, Pat volunteered to drive her one week. Then she volunteered to drive her the next week, and the next, and the week after that. Dina said that her mom's attitude changed overnight due to this young mother's spirit of gratitude for every day of life she was given to spend with her three children, the youngest only four years old.

Pat's new sense of balance between self-concern and other-concern gave her a second wind. But here's something else important that happened: Pat, at seventy-three years, is *still* role modeling, providing yet another example of living an authentic, purposeful life for her grown daughters and granddaughters.

Dina is so proud of her mom that she was beaming through the phone as she told me the story. Knowing that her mother is providing a wonderful service for this young dying mother, Dina could hardly get the story out fast enough. She said, "Mom's not investing a lot of time or money, but for three hours a week, she's making a huge difference in this woman's life. And this woman is such a great influence for my mom. I couldn't be more proud of her for stepping up and saying, 'I'll take her.'"

Girlfriend, are you spending too much time in your "oh, woe is me" world? If you're not careful, your self-centered focus may blind you to the needs of others, causing your wee problems to loom much larger than they really are. Worrying about yourself and concentrating on the needs of others cannot cohabitate in the same mind, at the same time.

Wise words bring many benefits, and hard work brings rewards.
(PROVERBS 12:14)

Move out of the darkness and into the light by turning your depression into action. Someone needs you.

CATCHING MY SECOND WIND
The Downhill Stretch

WHEN ASKED HOW long she and her husband, Bill, have been married, my girlfriend Kathy says, "We've been married for thirty-four years; twenty-nine of those happily." This just cracks me up.

Growing pains are a given in a young marriage. While one partner is learning to understand and appreciate the finer details of what it means to *need* a new "outfit" (how can he not know what it means to accessorize?), the other spouse is gaining insight about the *need* for new speakers and a subwoofer (I quickly learned that music—especially the bass—can *never* be loud enough).

About the time you get the basics ironed out, careers take off and kids arrive on the scene. Life becomes a never-ending relay between round-the-clock work, soccer games, orthodontist appointments, house renovations, moves from coast to coast, and the occasional family vacation. But then, almost without warning, the kids leave home or the job is over. And the silence is deafening.

It is at this time that many couples roll over in bed and look at their mates for the first time in twenty years and ask (if only to themselves), *Who in the world are you and what could we possibly have in common?*

My first marriage ended after ten years, so I know the agony that goes with saying the *d* word. But when I hear of a thirty-year marriage that's come to a slow, unbearable end, my heart just stops. Could this marriage that's seen the good, the bad, and the ugly have made it if one or both partners had caught their second wind?

Marriage can be hard work—so hard, in fact, that we become fatigued in our fight to save it. And if you're the only one battling the invisible foe of separation, it's a weary, lonely, exhausting struggle.

Then the LORD God formed the man from the dust of the ground. He breathed the breath of life into the man's nostrils, and the man became a living person.
(GENESIS 2:7)

Is it time for some mouth-to-mouth resuscitation in your marriage?

CATCHING MY SECOND WIND
The Downhill Stretch (Part Deux)

IF FIFTY IS THE NEW thirty and sixty is the new forty, we shouldn't be surprised that divorce among men and women ages forty to seventy-nine is rising—not just in the United States but worldwide. This phenomenon has been dubbed "gray divorce," but I think it should be called "dismayed divorce." Or at least I was dismayed when my father announced, as I was planning my parents' silver wedding anniversary, that there wouldn't be one. As a totally self-centered seventeen-year-old, the first words out of my mouth were, "Can't you guys just wait until one of you dies?" (Oh, how mature of me.) I didn't know then what I know now—that only about 55 percent of all newlyweds will dance to the oldies at their twenty-fifth anniversary celebration.[32]

I have two theories on why people wait thirty years before divorcing, and neither hypothesis involves children. My first theory is this: they think it will get better.

Even though they have moved through their marriage more as siblings than as lovers, they think that one day the old libido is just going to magically correct itself. It will not. Ladies, your box springs need to get the same pounding as your treadmill. And like your exercise routine, this takes discipline. Not a very sexy term, but, girlfriends, you need to get back into the routine of making love to your husband, and he must get into the discipline of making love to you (though this never seems too hard for them).

I also think that couples believe that their friendship will rekindle. Just like bodies need to be fed daily, so do marriages. You can't go twenty-five years stifling rich conversation, failing to develop mutual interests, and forgetting how to dream together. Your relationship will die of starvation.

You want what you don't have, so you scheme and kill to get it. You are jealous of what others have, but you can't get it, so you fight and wage war to take it away from them. Yet you don't have what you want because you don't ask God for it. (JAMES 4:2)

Are you on the downhill stretch, thinking it will get better? Maybe it will—ask God to show you how to make it to number fifty.

CATCHING MY SECOND WIND
The Downhill Stretch (Part Trois)

The important thing is this: to be able at any moment to sacrifice what we are for what we could become. CHARLES DUBOIS

THERE ARE HUNDREDS of theories, reasons, and conditions that lead to marital breakups, just one of which is that the couple grew apart, thinking that one day it would get better. But I have a theory that growing apart is not the only issue; *not growing* is where I think many relationships become unhinged.

If you or your mate fails to invest in your own development, education, hobbies, work, or volunteerism, you may become a relationship defeatist by hyperfocusing on and overanalyzing every little piddly thing the other person does. If either of you has nothing to focus on other than your children or your career, there's a good chance that when the kids are gone or the job ends, you're going to feel lost. And neither of you—not in a million doggone years—can fill this void in the other. It's up to *you* to find new interests.

When one of my girlfriends sent her last chickadee off to college, she lamented that she and her husband had become total strangers. The last twenty-five years had been all about the kids and their work—both of which were coming to a close. She asked me one evening, "What do we do?"

I didn't know the answer to her question. But I do know this. When you choose to invest in your own development you will be fulfilled; when you are fulfilled you will be more confident; when you're more confident you will be happier; and when you're happier—you'll be a lot more fun and interesting to be around. And being a fun, interesting person can only improve your relationship, not hinder it. Now, if both of you will invest in your interests, those you pursue together and alone, imagine how the sparks might fly!

And we know that God causes everything to work together for the good of those who love God and are called according to his purpose for them.
(ROMANS 8:28)

Girlfriends, you're on the downhill stretch. Catch your second wind. It might save that twenty-five-year commitment. Look toward the future and think how glorious it will be to hear you both say, "We've been married forty-five years and the last twenty *totally rocked*." Leave a legacy of a marriage that didn't just endure, but matured.

CATCHING MY SECOND WIND

FATHER GOD, I am tired, but I recognize that

- [ ] you have gifted me with talents to fill real needs on this earth;
- [ ] I often spend too much time thinking about my circumstances when I could be serving others;
- [ ] in order for my husband and me to have a marriage that matures gracefully, we must rekindle our flame;
- [ ] personal development is my obligation to myself and to the betterment of my marriage.

ACTIONS I WILL TAKE:

Example: I will stop procrastinating and sign up for Spanish lessons.

1. _____

2. _____

3. _____

Father, blow the winds of your Holy Spirit into my sails. Open my eyes to the needs that I can fill. Refocus my attention from my own circumstances so I may see those whom I can serve. Thank you, Lord, for giving me the gift of my husband. Take my mind, heart, and body, and help me to rekindle the flames of passion with him. And let my continued personal growth be a blessing to my family and to you as I live out my last days in the middle of your will. Amen.

GETTING A DO-OVER

I BELIEVE THAT, regardless of our age, we need mentors in our lives. We need successful men or women who have walked ahead—who can lend us valuable insight and objectivity when we're caught up in the turmoil of life rather than thoughtfully, purposefully *living* our lives.

My mentor is my girlfriend Elaine. She is older; she is wiser; and she is honest (sometimes brutally, as I'm not the easiest person to direct). If I have doubts about where I'm going, what I'm doing, or how I'm going to get there, I often call Elaine. Now I know not everyone has an Elaine. Shoot! She didn't even show up in my life until 1997, but when she did, I realized I had been missing a crystal-clear "voice of experience" (that wasn't my mother's).

One thing a mentor can lend you is her "been there, done that" story. I call these do-overs. In case you don't have such a great role model in your life, I thought I'd collect and share with you a few do-overs from some of my girl-friends. Their do-overs are experiences to which, had they had a mentor, they might have acted or reacted differently—*even though they wouldn't change their lives today*. These gals range in age from forty plus to sixty plus; some are single, some are married; some have stayed home with kids, others have juggled mother-hood while racing around the professional track. But all of them live lives of uncommon joy.

Because our do-overs are personal (mine will be included), all of my friends, their precise ages, where they live, and their original hair color will remain anony-mous. I will paint for you, however, a picture of these women's personalities in the hope that you will be able to relate to them and their experiences. I think you'll benefit from their hindsight too.

> *The heartfelt counsel of a friend*
> *is as sweet as perfume and incense.* (PROVERBS 27:9)

There's no doubt—we're all going to make our own mistakes. We don't always choose wisely. But my desire is that the wisdom, insight, and experiences of others will give you something to ponder so you can minimize the frustration, pain, and disappointment that sometimes come when we're caught up in the whirlwind of life.

GETTING A DO-OVER
I Would Live Rather Than Perform

LIVING RATHER than performing. How many of us can relate to this do-over? I imagine about 80 percent of the girlfriends reading this book, but it was my girlfriend Caren* who brought to my attention this life lesson of learning to focus on my life, rather than my performance.

I have to tell you, I was a little surprised. Caren is a highly degreed professional who has it all together. She has the gift of discernment unlike anyone else I've seen; she "hears" when others only listen; and she can remove herself from the trappings of this world better than any other person I know. She is true to herself, her convictions, and her goals. So again—I was a little surprised that Caren said she would have lived more intently for herself. She said if she could do a few things over she would:

- Never have put herself through the grind and pressure to make straight A's in graduate school. Who cares today? Caren explained that she missed out on life and the building of important friendships due to her self-imposed pressure to make perfect grades.
- Never work sixty-hour workweeks again. Who cares today? The self-imposed, as well as the management-imposed, pressure to have everything done right and perfectly took the joy right out of her profession. She left a career in which she was truly gifted because of burnout.
- Never succumb to the world's standard for success. Who cares today? Working ridiculous hours and dealing with ulcer-inducing stress is not living. In fact, performing to meet a standard works against the beauty of life, peace, and happiness.

I can relate to Caren because I'm a performer too. I am hardwired to do the best I can, even when it flies in the face of my sense of balance.

For in many dreams and in many words there is emptiness. Rather, fear God.
(ECCLESIASTES 5:7, NASB)

Thank you, Caren, for bringing those of us who are perfectionists back to center. I'm learning to let it go.

---

*Caren is not her real name, but she is my favorite person to talk to because she knows my heart.

GETTING A DO-OVER
I Would Stop the Abuse

WHEN I VISITED with my girlfriends on their do-overs, several of them said they learned important lessons at work.

My girlfriend Carrie* told me an amazing story, especially in light of her personality. Carrie has built a very successful company based on her intelligence, wit, and creativity. She's a lot like glitter—she sparkles, and you can't miss this woman when she walks into a room. In addition, Carrie is strong-willed, highly charged, and very competitive. So it came as a shock to me that Carrie said her do-over would be to have "stopped that woman from abusing me."

When Carrie was in her midtwenties, she worked for a female boss who left her with knots in her stomach every day. One day, Carrie was the best thing on the planet; the next day, without warning, her boss would attack her verbally. The inconsistency and ultimately the verbal abuse caused Carrie to have health problems—due in part to the many evenings when she drove home in tears. Carrie's boss, who took issue with Carrie's religious beliefs, had managed to degrade her and so negatively affect her self-confidence that Carrie began to believe what her boss said. Over time, Carrie lost faith in herself.

So what would Carrie have done differently?

- She would have focused on identifying the difference between constructive criticism and abuse, and left the position earlier, before her self-esteem took a beating.
- She would have reported the religious discrimination she experienced to human resources. (Carrie thought she was taking the high road, but now wonders how many other people this "Christian" woman abused.)
- Although the next job was a great springboard for her and actually a good step, she said she should have never accepted that job only to get away from a bad situation. By doing so, she said, she gave away her control.

This I declare about the LORD:
He alone is my refuge, my place of safety;
*   he is my God, and I trust him.* (PSALM 91:2)

Girlfriends, you don't have to give up control to stop the abuse but you do have to take control. Ask God to guide you and provide you with the discernment you need to see the situation as it is.

*Carrie is not her real name, but she *is* a lot like glitter.

GETTING A DO-OVER
I Would Stop the Abuse (Part Deux)

YOU KNOW, Carrie was so shocked to find herself in a verbally abusive situation that she wasn't sure that what she was experiencing was real.

Girlfriends, do you recognize verbal abuse when it happens to you?

This has been my experience: the first time it happened to me (and there were many because this went on for over ten years), I was shocked that a person I respected and cared for could use such hurtful words toward me. I dismissed the individual's tone and disapproval as stress induced.

The second time it happened, the familiarity offset the shock, and I felt only the pain of the words. But I dismissed those feelings because I believed, as I had been told, I was overly sensitive.

Every time the abuse occurred after that, I began to think that I must deserve what this person was dishing out. If you love someone or consider them an authoritative figure in your life, after a while you begin to believe them because they seem so sure and so confident in their accusations and assessment of you.

Can you relate to this? If you're in this type of situation, share your experience with a friend who can help you be objective and who can help bolster your self-esteem. No one in the world has the right to use words, tones, or threats that undermine your self-confidence.

> *The LORD is for me, so I will have no fear.*
> *What can mere people do to me?*
> *Yes, the LORD is for me; he will help me.*
> *I will look in triumph at those who hate me.*
> *It is better to take refuge in the LORD*
> *than to trust in people.* (PSALM 118:6-8)

You have the right and the power to choose to stop the abuse. What are you waiting for?

GETTING A DO-OVER
I Wouldn't Flirt with Him

SOMETIMES OUR do-overs in life are small; other times they are huge. Just absolutely huge. Girlfriends, this was a really hard do-over for my girlfriend Marilyn* to share with me, and I hope you will read every word of this. And then read it again.

Although we have not known each other for long, Marilyn and I have been friends forever. I think we were born friends; we're a bit like soul mates. When we first met, she would say something, and I would just immediately think, *Me too!* And with her, more than anyone else in the world, I laugh. I mean big ole Texas-style belly laughs.

Marilyn works in a profession that few women dare attempt and has reached the pinnacle of her field while raising a family; but there's no attitude with this gal. Marilyn is the most approachable, easygoing person I know. She has a laugh that just cracks me up, and her eyes . . . girlfriends, they twinkle. Literally. She always looks like she's up to something. Anyway, I wrote Marilyn and asked her, "So, girlfriend, what's *your* do-over?"

A few days later the phone rang; it was Marilyn. She said, "Ellen, I wouldn't have flirted with him." I held my breath. I had no idea.

Marilyn had married young, and in the process of working on an advanced degree, managing an extremely demanding workload, and having kids, her marriage became strained. The promise and excitement she and her husband had once enjoyed were replaced by obligations and frustration. There was nothing about her husband she found stimulating; their careers and interests were taking them in two very different directions. And it wasn't just her; he always seemed aggravated and on edge with everything she did or didn't do. They just weren't connecting.

Anger gives a foothold to the devil. (EPHESIANS 4:27)

But there was someone at work who wasn't frustrated with her, someone she found most enchanting. Their relationship was very professional at first. But she realized after a few months that it had turned into something else—and it wasn't friendship. Marilyn found herself anticipating the possibility of seeing this coworker in the hall or working with him on a project; she went out of her way to make sure they had "encounters." She knew she was headed down a slippery slope when she began to flirt.

Girlfriend, this is a do-over that sometimes can't be undone. Don't give a foothold to the dark one.

---

*Marilyn is not her real name, but her eyes *do* twinkle.

GETTING A DO-OVER
I Wouldn't Flirt with Him (Part Deux)

ONCE YOU OPEN the door to flirtation, things can get out of hand. Fast. So what advice does Marilyn have to share?

- For you single, young girlfriends: don't marry young. Marrying young has several disadvantages, but here's the biggest one: as you mature and your personality continues to form, you will begin to wonder if you married the man who was really perfect for you. Doubt opens the door for reckless thinking.
- For the rest of us: guard your heart, especially when your marriage is not at its strongest. Giving in to temptation is way too easy and comforting when you're not feeling appreciated. But that comfort won't last and will be replaced by a self-loathing that will eat at you from the inside out. The resulting conviction and guilt you'll feel is something that will be hard to shake.
- Be careful with your feminine lure. Flirting can seem harmless to you, but it's jet fuel to a guy, and he may turn on his charms in ways you're not prepared for. Just don't go there.
- Lastly, most marriages ebb and flow. Wait. Wait. Wait. Work. Work. Work. When you see trouble brewing, seek the best marriage counselor you can find and don't give up.

Marilyn's a really smart gal, and she knew that the affair must come to an end or she could well lose her family. Marilyn said to me, "You know, no one in the world knows about this affair, but it has haunted me all my life. Even though I asked God to forgive me, I can't forgive myself. This ugly, painful knot in my stomach resurfaces regularly. I think I'll feel convicted about this mistake for the rest of my life."

The temptations in your life are no different from what others experience. And God is faithful. He will not allow the temptation to be more than you can stand. When you are tempted, he will show you a way out so that you can endure.
(1 CORINTHIANS 10:13)

Marilyn put her own advice into action, and work, work, work she and her husband did. She invested herself emotionally in her marriage again. The couple will celebrate their thirty-seventh wedding anniversary this year.

GETTING A DO-OVER
I Should Have Quit before I Got Fired

HAVE YOU EVER struggled to be successful in a job or with a company that just wasn't right for you?

My girlfriend Sophie* is a very successful professional. She holds a doctorate, but she's more than smart—Sophie is incredibly *wise* (there is a big difference, right?).

When she opens her mouth to speak and share her thoughts, every ear turns her way. In addition, Sophie has a calming effect on people; she's as cool as a cucumber, and that confidence is comforting when you're being led by her. So what's her do-over? Sophie said, "I should have known. I should have quit before I got fired."

Sophie explained to me that she had ended up in a job, just a few years ago, that wasn't a good fit for her. Ignoring the numerous indications, both internal and external, that the position wasn't a perfect fit, Sophie thought she could overcome the obstacles with hard work. The fact that she was talented and eager to please probably clouded her judgment a bit too.

Intrigued by her story, I asked Sophie what nuggets she could share with my girlfriends who might also be in a position or with a company that is not right for them. This is what she said:

- Don't allow the external voices telling you about who you are or should be to become louder than your own internal voice. If you do, you may quickly find yourself off track and lost.
- Listen to the signals around you. If it doesn't feel like a good fit, if things just aren't working for you (and they always have before)—pay attention. Sophie said she knew three months before she was invited to leave that it was time to go. She said she was simply too pigheaded to listen; she was sure if she worked hard enough, she could turn it around.

I believe in your commands;
now teach me good judgment and knowledge. (PSALM 119:66)

Do you allow the voice and opinion of others to trump your own? How often we fail to give our own internal voice the same weight and respect we give to the words of others.

---

*Sophie is not her real name, but she *is* as cool as a cucumber.

GETTING A DO-OVER
I Should Have Quit before I Got Fired (Part Deux)

AS SOPHIE told me her story, I flashed back to the faces of people I have fired over the past twenty years. From young, promising kids with MBAs to men with twenty years' experience in their field—it didn't matter how old they were or what had gone wrong—letting someone go is always gut wrenching. The firing itself was usually the first step in their personal recovery. The hard part was watching their self-confidence evaporate before my eyes as they tried, flailed, and failed. When I met with them to deliver the news, I would tell them, "This is not about you; it's about the job," but that truth never seemed to sink in right then.

So I asked Sophie what advice she has for other women who might suffer from bruised and beaten self-esteem due to a job description that doesn't fit them well. She shared these two important tips:

- You can't work hard enough, long enough, or pretzel yourself into weird enough positions to please everyone. Trying to do so is the surest road to career (and life) disaster—not to mention high blood pressure, weight gain, and "victim" thinking.
- Don't confuse organizational fit with personal worth. Whether or not you're right for a given organization has nothing to do with your value as a human being—despite what others might tell you.

God is our refuge and strength,
  always ready to help in times of trouble.
So we will not fear when earthquakes come
  and the mountains crumble into the sea. (PSALM 46:1-2)

Girlfriends, you are not your job. You are wonderfully made by Christ himself. He may simply not have made you for this job!

GETTING A DO-OVER
I Should Have Quit before I Got Fired (Part Trois)

I HAVE HAD some rich discussions with the folks whom I have reprimanded (or had to terminate) over the years. We sometimes talked about aligning our God-given talents with other forms of work; we sometimes talked about taking the initiative to create change (rather than have the change happen to us); and we sometimes talked about admitting to ourselves that we play the starring role in our success and failure. Rarely is something done to you without your active involvement.

I asked Sophie what she thought about these topics and how she would direct someone who is facing the reality that a job change is imminent. Here are her thoughts:

- Following your life purpose will disappoint someone in your life, perhaps even many someones. Not following it will disappoint you and dishonor why you are here.
- God always challenges us in one of three ways—by pulling us (*It will be fun and exciting to go there*), pushing us (*I'm not having fun here anymore*), or kicking us in the rear (*I'm seriously ill;* or *I have been let go*). If we don't listen to the pushes, we will eventually get that kick.
- Being kicked is painful but not fatal if you realize that 1) you've learned some valuable lessons; 2) you created, or at least in some way contributed to, the situation in some way; and 3) redemption (something better or knowledge that will help you or others) is always an outcome if you allow it to be. That means letting go of the "what-ifs," resentments, and desire to see yourself as the victim.

But by the grace of God I am what I am, and His grace toward me did not prove vain; but I labored even more than all of them, yet not I, but the grace of God with me. (1 CORINTHIANS 15:10, NASB)

Choose to be true to yourself. Keep your chin up. You'll find the right fit.

GETTING A DO-OVER
I Would Look for God

I WISH YOU knew my girlfriend Marcie.* She is one of my favorite people in the world. Marcie was a vice president for a global company prior to opening her own company. She is incredibly generous with her time and energy, and is so much fun to hang out with because she's always in a great mood. In addition, she is a gifted artist. Did I mention she looks like Barbie? Sickening, isn't it?

When I asked Marcie if she had anything that she would do over, she immediately answered, "Yes. I wish I had made my spiritual life a priority when I was younger. I would have looked for God."

Marcie explained that a personal relationship with Christ was a pretty foreign concept until she began dating and later married a devoted follower of Christ. Attending church every Sunday, participating in Bible studies, and engaging in deep conversations about the unconditional love of Christ motivated Marcie to rethink her understanding of all things spiritual. During the past several years, as she focused more on her spiritual maturation, she began to realize how much of life she had really missed out on. Instead of her faith restricting her, Marcie said her spiritual growth has liberated her. Through learning and discussing Scripture in a small-group Bible study and spending time in daily prayer, she now operates with a new faith and a deeper belief system than ever before.

I think about my own spiritual maturation and wonder, *Is it experience that strengthens my faith or faith that lends me the confidence to seek new experiences?* Either way, I know I am safe in my willingness to explore and question those topics for which there is no definitive answer and where others might unknowingly lead me astray.

> O LORD, you have examined my heart
>   and know everything about me.
> You know when I sit down or stand up.
>   You know my thoughts even when I'm far away. . . .
> You know what I am going to say
>   even before I say it, LORD. (PSALM 139:1-2, 4)

Are you secure enough in your salvation to ask the hard questions, and confident enough to accept that you might not get a clear answer? Since God already knows the questions in your heart, maybe it's time to come clean.

---

*Marcie is not her real name, but she *does* look like Barbie.

GETTING A DO-OVER
I Would Look for God (Part Deux)

MARCIE'S DO-OVER made me think about my own spiritual journey—specifi-cally as it relates to my role in the church. One of the challenges I wrestle with is feeling . . . well . . . "less than." Since returning to work full-time in the late 80s, I never have felt that I truly "belonged" because there are few opportunities for an everyday working gal like me to contribute to the operation and development of the church. Let's just call it like it is. I'm not a "church lady."

I wish I were. Church ladies are fun. I think if we were to commission a study we'd find that they laugh more than the typical woman. They're smart too. Church ladies are in perpetual learning mode, gaining insight from fabu-lous teachers and one another. On Thursday mornings, while I'm studying data and consumer reports, they're digging into the Word of God. And they're sweet. Really sweet. They care about their church family like it was their own. They can fire up a prayer chain to pray for our healing before we even know that our sniffle has blossomed into a full-blown cold. And cook! These women can do things with a casserole dish we didn't even know possible.

The other thing that works against me is that I'm not chatty. I know this seems strange in light of the fact that I love the girlfriends whom I write and speak to; I can get down to business with you one-to-many on all matters of the heart. But I don't do this one-on-one very well. I don't care to talk about what Sarah wore to Sally's wedding. I don't meet for coffee on Tuesday morning—unless it's with clients.

The church lady and I live very different lives. I'm not sure you can tell from my writing, but I don't do casseroles; I have never participated in a prayer chain unless it is for someone I knew personally; and my Bible study would be totally stunted if it weren't for my girlfriend Kathryn who opens her home every Monday evening to make sure the working women of Dallas don't become total heathens.

So where it concerns the church, the body of Christ, where do I fit it in?

Through Christ Jesus, God has blessed the Gentiles with the same blessing he promised to Abraham, so that we who are believers might receive the promised Holy Spirit through faith. (GALATIANS 3:14)

Although I aspire to be, I doubt I will ever achieve full church lady status. You too?

Well then, let's just get over the fact that we're different and embrace who we are, being all Christ called us to be. Let's continue to remind ourselves and one another that we are important and relevant to the work of the church when we remain true to ourselves as high-heeled, briefcase-carrying gals who love their God.

GETTING A DO-OVER
I Would Look for God (Part Trois)

God brings men into deep waters not to drown them, but to cleanse them.
JAMES H. AUGHEY

I THINK ABOUT my girlfriend Marcie and how differently we were raised. While she had little guidance regarding spiritual matters, I experienced just the opposite.

I joined my Sunday school class when I was six weeks old and stayed with the same classmates until I left home at the age of sixteen. Throughout my childhood, my faith was the focus of my week: Sunday school and church; Sunday evening choir practice (and church again); Wednesday evening Sunbeams and Girls Auxiliary (and church *again*—in case your cup wasn't running over from the services three days before). There was also vacation Bible school, church camp, and choir tours. I was constantly and consistently fed a spiritual diet as I moved forward in my spiritual maturation and understanding.

My faith journey wouldn't begin to stall until I got older and found more sinful things that I enjoyed. I knew I was constantly conflicted, keeping one eye on God and one eye on the world, and not making strides with either. Disgusted that I couldn't do better, I finally realized that living the Christian life is something like dancing the Texas two-step—in this case, two steps forward, one step back.

Eventually you get around the dance floor, but it might take you the entire length of a country-and-western song, depending on the tempo! And I think our spiritual maturation is also like this during different stages of our lives. We desire to do the right thing, but we also allow circumstances to take us off course. The good news: God is the DJ and will change that next song to a waltz.

Forward one, two, three . . . one, two, three . . .

> *Even there your hand will guide me,*
> *and your strength will support me.* (PSALM 139:10)

Are you two-stepping or just out of step? Ask God to change the song—but this time, let him lead.

GETTING A DO-OVER
I Would Look for God (Part Quatre)

I am perfectly happy to be nobody, even to God.   MOTHER TERESA

AS I VISITED with Marcie, she mentioned that one thing that surprised her was how little she had to give up to follow Christ. Marcie had always seen the Christian walk as a sacrifice to living the good life. Oh, little did she know!

I think a lot of us get caught up with pulling out the scales to weigh what we think we might have to sacrifice (an exciting run of fun, fame, and fortune) versus what we might gain (a boring existence of joy, peace, and contentment). So many nonbelievers or new believers seem to have difficulty grasping that their lives are his, either way they go. And boring is the last thing he wants for them.

Several years ago, I was visiting with a young woman who had lost her baby to sudden infant death syndrome (SIDS). Her grief burdened my heart. As she struggled in despair even years after her child's death, I asked her if she was willing to give her life—and the grief of losing her child—to Christ. Her answer was immediate and flat: "No. I'm not about to give control of my life to someone else. Not even God." Although her marriage had dissolved, her depression had taken her to rock bottom, and she functioned less every day, she thought she was doing a better job than he could.

Grief can do this to us. So can stubborn pride. As can ego. We so desire to live the big life, to be somebody, that we really don't want to let go and give it all to God. But, girlfriends, giving up control of our lives is not sacrificial, it's empowering. Once we hand over the keys of our heart to him, he can better align our will with the outcome he desires for us.

But the person who loves God is the one whom God recognizes.
(I CORINTHIANS 8:3)

And there's no place in the world more exciting, more fun, or more satisfying than being smack-dab in the middle of his will.

GETTING A DO-OVER
I Would Look for God (Part Cinq)

MARCIE'S FAMILY were not churchgoing people. Having traveled across the pond when Marcie was a baby, they were members of the Church of England. Marcie had a "book-knowledge" understanding of Christ, but she didn't have that close encounter many of us have been blessed with. She just hadn't been exposed to very many views on theology.

I have made my rounds with the churches—I have worshiped as a Baptist, a Methodist, an evangelical, and a Presbyterian. (If you don't belong to one of these affiliations, don't feel left out—it just means I haven't gotten to yours yet.) And here's why I have made a number of moves: I really struggle with one-size-fits-all organized religion. I'm not convinced that any one of them has it all figured out.

I realized that my own spiritual maturation was being thwarted because I was getting hung up trying to sort through all the theology, politics, and views. Once I understood that my problem wasn't my spiritual journey but the round holes I was trying to fit my square peg into, I finally began to grow. But this was scary.

To look beyond the faith or doctrine we were raised with as a means to grow in our personal walk seems counterintuitive. But for me, the questioning, prayer, and revelation have made me a stronger believer.

Marcie said that she now realizes that happiness, peace, wisdom, and thankfulness don't come from experience or age but rather from finding truth. And that truth brings her uncommon joy.

And you will know the truth, and the truth will set you free. (JOHN 8:32)

Have you chosen to discern the truth?

GETTING A DO-OVER
I Would Focus on the People—Not the Paper

The first thing in all progress is to leave something behind.   GEORGE MACDONALD

MY GIRLFRIEND DeAnn* is quite a package. Beautiful (model beautiful), intelligent (street smart *and* book smart), and warm (you know she loves you—she loves everybody). She's a successful entrepreneur, mother of two, adoring wife, and loyal friend to the end (how many of those do you know?). She is so charismatic that the room literally comes to life when she walks in. Trust me, we all want to be DeAnn when we grow up.

When I asked DeAnn what she would do over professionally, she said she would like to go back and focus less on the tactics of doing a job and more on the relationships that are required to get the job done. I was simultaneously intrigued and convicted.

DeAnn explained that prior to opening her own business, she worked in a corporate environment that was highly charged and deadline driven. (Sound familiar to anyone?) Now that she's left behind the excitement and demands of that career, she realizes she had been investing her energy in the wrong things. DeAnn noted that she would never have gotten through all the piles of paperwork, endless meetings, to-do lists, and daily e-mails in her corporate job. The more she focused on the paper, the phone calls, and the e-mails, the more they seemed to multiply.

Well, DeAnn had me hooked. As I mentioned, I was convicted by this conversation with her because I know that investing in the development of relationships at work is not my strong suit. I'm a results-oriented person, so I typically put my head down and get to work and don't look up until it's time to go home. So I needed pointers.

What was DeAnn's first piece of advice?

Spend less time working on stuff and more time talking with people. Spend a minimum of 20 percent of each day dialoguing with individuals within your company, as well as with individuals outside your four walls.

Twenty percent? Are you kidding me? I know for a fact that I don't spend 10 percent of my day in dialogue unless I'm putting out fires or answering direct questions.

To focus on the people, not the paper, I knew I would need divine intervention.

I replied by sending this message to them: "I am engaged in a great work, so I can't come. Why should I stop working to come and meet with you?" Four times they sent the same message, and each time I gave the same reply. (NEHEMIAH 6:3-4)

Are you doing a great work with people? Don't get distracted.

---

*DeAnn is not her real name, but she is one of my most favorite people in all the world.

GETTING A DO-OVER
I Would Focus on the People—Not the Paper (Part Deux)

Great opportunities to help others seldom come, but small ones surround us every day.
SALLY KOCH

AS I BEGAN to consider DeAnn's challenge, I knew that I would have to give up some of my "maximizer" tendencies. Doing a job is one thing, but I am driven to maximize my opportunities. Of course, this is a great attribute when you're building a new business model, selling your services, or developing a product. But this same talent becomes a hindrance when you need to shift your attention and priorities to people rather than concepts.

I told DeAnn my struggle, and she gave me some great advice. She said, "Focus your attention and time on people you admire. Identify those who are trustworthy and wise—people you aspire to emulate. By spending time with these individuals, you will forge both professional and personal bonds that could be important to you for the rest of your life."

Then she added this kicker: "Ellen, people admire you and want to learn from you. Because they know they can trust you to be honest and forthright with them regarding their careers, they want to engage with you."

Uh-oh. Now, this is getting tricky. I certainly know men and women in my industry whom I respect, and I always enjoy our exchanges. I learn so much about our marketplace, as well as the challenges and solutions others are implementing. But someone wants to gain insight from me?

Girlfriends, you may be like me and not see clearly the important role you could play in others' lives if you'd just be willing to have an occasional lunch or break with them. We all need mentors—in life and at work.

Instead, you must worship Christ as Lord of your life. And if someone asks about your Christian hope, always be ready to explain it. (1 PETER 3:15)

As you look for a mentor for yourself, consider the fact that you could be one to someone else.

GETTING A DO-OVER
I Would Focus on the People—Not the Paper (Part Trois)

AS A BUSINESS OWNER, I have always been deeply interested in ensuring we provide excellent service to our clients, that we operate efficiently as an organization, and that we provide a culture in which individuals can succeed. It seems like a simple concept: a team that works reputably, efficiently, and positively. It's an easy philosophy to grasp but a difficult one to implement. Why? Because people are involved!

So often we fail to embrace the motivations of the individuals, focusing instead only on the desired outcome.

One thing DeAnn said she wishes she would have done on the job is spend more time networking within her own company. If she had interfaced with members of other departments, she would have learned what motivated them. This knowledge would have made it easier for them to work together to develop solutions, eliminating interdepartmental stress and territorial issues. This is a great insight.

In the book *First, Break All the Rules*, Marcus Buckingham and Curt Coffman give great advice for CEOs and mothers alike:

> Remember the Golden Rule? Treat people as you would like to be treated. The best managers break the Golden Rule every day. This presupposes that everyone breathes the same psychological oxygen as you. . . . So the best managers reject the Golden Rule. Instead, they say, treat each person as *he* would like to be treated, bearing in mind who he is. Of course, each employee must adhere to certain standards of behavior, certain rules. But within those rules, treat each one differently, each according to his needs.[33]

There will be no mercy for those who have not shown mercy to others. But if you have been merciful, God will be merciful when he judges you. (JAMES 2:13)

As you prepare to go into the office (or the kitchen), reconsider what's behind the bad attitude, sloppy work habits, or territorial protection. Maybe spending more time problem solving together will eliminate that knot in your stomach.

GETTING A DO-OVER
I Would Focus on the People—Not the Paper (Part Quatre)

THE LAST PIECE of advice from DeAnn helped me as I shifted my focus from paper to people. It's likely something you already have down pat. But for me, this last tip required extreme focus and discipline. DeAnn advised me to "share lunch or maybe just five minutes having a hallway chat with a fellow worker." I thought, *No, not that!*

My problem: I'm not chatty.

Yes, I can carry on for hours with my girlfriends over dinner, but start up casual conversations with coworkers I barely know? This is not in my DNA. But I realized that is no excuse. Over time, I have learned to occasionally invest a few minutes for a bit of small talk, and I have seen the rewards. I was once viewed as disinterested or unapproachable; now my coworkers know that I am interested in what's going on with them both professionally and personally.

When I finally pulled myself out from behind my desk and looked up from my computer, I realized that only people really matter.

Are you like me—too often focused on results and missing the most important part of our work: other people?

DeAnn decided to retire from her corporate position to take time to raise a young family and start a new business. She said that when her job was over and she moved on, she took only the relationships with people with her. She left the paper behind.

As iron sharpens iron,
so a friend sharpens a friend. (PROVERBS 27:17)

Choose people over paper. They're way more interesting.

GETTING A DO-OVER
I Can, I Should, or I Want

I HAVE ONE REALLY cerebral girlfriend I'll call Jennifer.* Not only is Jennifer a great thinker and a great strategist, she is a person who loves: she loves her fellow human beings, loves her girlfriends, loves her customers, and loves to contribute. She enjoys making a difference in the lives of others and has even applied this life lesson do-over in a program to help other women.

Jennifer spent much of her successful career trying to make herself love positions she held because she knew she could do them (she had the skills) and she should do them (the positions paid well and were highly respected). But for her, these were energy-sapping tasks, not energy-filling careers. After a nudge she says came from God, Jennifer finally answered the nagging call to make a change—both in her work and her attitude. The result: she landed a job she wanted, a job that uses her God-given talents.

So what advice does this virtual mentor send you?

- Recognize whether you're doing a job because you can, you should, or you want to. Work chosen because you can or you should is often less fulfilling.
- Be willing to make the life changes (sometimes financial ones) required for you to do the work you want to do and were meant to do. It won't feel like a sacrifice when you're doing what you love to do every day.
- Determine if you're using your talents. If you're not sure, read *Now, Discover Your Strengths* by Marcus Buckingham and Dr. Donald O. Clifton.
- Follow your heart—sometimes it's the vehicle God uses to direct you best.

Jennifer's do-over hit me between the eyes. I think it was the first time I ever considered that even though I *could* do a job, I wasn't *obligated* to do it. Yes, that is a liberating view of life work!

We can make our plans,
but the LORD determines our steps. (PROVERBS 16:9)

Choose "I want," and let the Lord direct you.

---

*Jennifer is not her real name, but she does make a difference in everyone's life—especially mine!

GETTING A DO-OVER
I Would Invest in Myself

IT IS MY HONOR to introduce you to my girlfriend Melissa.* I have been in awe of Melissa for many years. She navigated an incredibly successful professional career as an executive of a Fortune 100 company, has been married to her husband for forty years, and has "reinvented" herself in her retirement. Melissa is one of the smartest women I have ever met, so I'm always a bit intimidated and tongue-tied when I talk with her. Can you imagine? Me, tongue-tied? Yes—when I'm with Melissa or talking with her on the phone, I just want to listen.

So listen is what I did when Melissa told me her do-over would trace back to her first few years of marriage. Melissa explained that she had had some "strange thoughts" about what a good wife and mother should be.

Melissa said she believed her husband was responsible for taking care of things—everything from providing for them financially to ensuring that his little family was happy and content. It was not until years later—after they had made huge sacrifices financially so he could return to school full-time and after they returned to what Melissa believed would be their "normal" life—that she realized that she had cheated herself out of her own growth and development in order to support him during his years of higher learning.

Melissa's do-over would be to not deprive herself on behalf of her husband and child, but to invest as earnestly in her own well-being as she did in theirs. I asked Melissa what she would pass on to other young wives and mothers. She said:

- You will be a better wife and mom when you are growing and are fulfilled. Don't play the role of martyr—invest in your own intellectual and emotional development.
- Establish your identity and interests apart from your husband and children. Don't blame them if you wake up one morning to realize your life is only and totally about them.
- Take responsibility when it comes to the future financial welfare of your family. Don't expect your husband to bear the burden, alone, forever.

She is energetic and strong, a hard worker. She makes sure her dealings are profitable; her lamp burns late into the night. (PROVERBS 31:17-18)

Melissa said she's still head over heels in love with her husband of forty years and believes their marriage is strong because they're not the same people they were when they married. She attributes their successful marriage to being able to grow, adapt, and develop—individually and together.

When you choose to invest in yourself, others will also benefit from the return.

*Melissa is not her real name, but I do get tongue-tied when I talk to her!

GETTING A DO-OVER
I Would Have Embraced the Adventure

MY GIRLFRIEND Ashley* is a self-made superstar who exudes confidence; she is calm and precise, with never a hair out of place. This gal walks the talk of a well-balanced life that comes from making wise, carefully considered choices. So needless to say I couldn't wait to hear her do-over! Would she even have one?

I connected immediately with Ashley's do-over. She said, "If I could do one thing over, I would have stopped and taken in the wonderful sights on my business travels rather than just focusing on getting my job done." Because Ashley enjoyed a twenty-year career with a major entertainment company, she had the opportunity to visit many wonderful cities. Rather than really visit them, however, she blew through town. Why? Because she was focused on "doing the right thing" for the client or her company—always preparing for the next meeting or coordinating the next event, rather than just experiencing sixty minutes in a new destination and enjoying a new adventure. What would Ashley recommend to you girlfriends who are flitting about the country for business?

- Arrive with the mind-set of a tourist. Many business travelers have the opportunity to stay in wonderful hotels. Stand in the lobby and drink in the sight of the people coming and going; smell the bouquet from the flower arrangement that is bigger than your house; sit by the window and watch the pedestrians pass by on the street. Don't just rush up to the registration desk and check in—you're in a new place that you may never return to. Live it.
- Give yourself a thirty-minute power tour, especially if you're in a wonderful downtown city like San Francisco, Chicago, New York, or Seattle. There is nothing like walking these sidewalks to feel the energy of that city's people and culture. Arrive early or stay late, but don't miss out on the opportunity to enjoy the ambience of the place.

Those of us who are results driven and working in competitive marketplaces often cheat ourselves of wonderful adventures and sights.

How pleasant to see a new day dawning. . . . Young people, it's wonderful to be young! Enjoy every minute of it. Do everything you want to do; take it all in. But remember that you must give an account to God for everything you do.
(ECCLESIASTES 11:7, 9)

Are you working to live or living to work? Maybe you need rescuing from your overtaxed mind.

---

*Ashley is not her real name, but she is my role model for what confidence really looks like!

GETTING A DO-OVER
I Would Have Embraced the Adventure (Part Deux)

We don't stop playing because we grow old; we grow old because we stop playing.
GEORGE BERNARD SHAW

THE LAST THING that Ashley said she would do over was to invest more time in her own well-being. She said she took sick days when she was very ill, and most of her personal days off were taken to tend to her mother or other family members.

When's the last time you took a day off just for you? If your schedule is anything like mine, this might be a stretch, but if you choose to, you *can* find a few hours or a day to take in a museum, sit in a park, go to a play, or see some other sight. Really. When you think about it, in the grand scheme of our life, what's a few hours to create this memory or adventure? What's a few hours to energize your heart and mind?

When I was younger and traveling on business, many of my friends would "ooh and ahh" over my opportunities to visit new cities. They soon became bored and disenchanted with my travel tales because I could describe only the layout of the airport or the cleanliness of the taxi.

Even so, I have noticed one thing, at least, that is good. It is good for people to eat, drink, and enjoy their work under the sun during the short life God has given them, and to accept their lot in life. And it is a good thing to receive wealth from God and the good health to enjoy it. To enjoy your work and accept your lot in life—this is indeed a gift from God. (ECCLESIASTES 5:18-19)

I'm with Ashley. I wish I had taken a couple of hours and gone to the play. What about you? Will you invest in yourself next time you're on the road?

GETTING A DO-OVER
I Would Have Had More Babies

I THOUGHT I knew my girlfriend Sarah* pretty well; goodness, we've been girl buddies for nearly fifteen years. But I laughed out loud when she wrote me that her do-over would have been to have had more kids. I literally cracked up! This is the most professionally driven woman I know. Focused and direct, she's a take-no-prisoners kind of gal, and even though she's a terrific mother, I just couldn't believe that this do-over was the one coming out of her mouth!

So I had to call her, and Sarah said, "No, really. If I could do one thing over, I would have had one or maybe even two more children."

Sarah explained that having children when she was in her twenties and while she and her husband were building their careers seemed overwhelming. Even though she hails from a family of five children and her husband from a family of six, managing two kiddos while juggling two demanding careers seemed insane at the time. So talk of a third or fourth was out of the question. Not that they don't love children—they do—it's just that the timing to procreate seemed to collide with ten-hour workdays.

Now that her babies are in their midtwenties, what does Sarah know today that she didn't know when she was younger?

First, she said it was too easy to coddle her children. Kids from smaller families struggle more with sharing with other kids and fail to embrace the concept of delayed gratification.

Second, it was too easy to play to their impatience. Children from smaller families often have fewer experiences dealing with children of different ages or with larger groups of kids.

Sarah also sees now that it was too easy to let them off the hook. When Sarah observes families with four or more children in public, she sees kids who seem more well behaved, helpful to their siblings, and willing to entertain themselves.

Finally, she says she found it too easy to "assist" her children. Sarah recalls that during her childhood, her parents couldn't help every child with homework, practice, and other responsibilities the way she could help her two kids with the same challenges. By necessity, children from larger families had to do more things for themselves and, even more importantly, for others.

Devote yourselves to prayer with an alert mind and a thankful heart.
(COLOSSIANS 4:2)

Are you on the fence about adding to your crew? You have to admit, Sarah makes some good points. But before moving ahead, I'd pray for guidance (and a whole lot of patience)!

*Sarah is not her real name, but she is megasuccessful in both her professional and personal life.

GETTING A DO-OVER
I Would Have Had More Babies (Part Deux)

I ASKED SARAH if she had any important insights she could offer about how she and her husband raised the two awesome kids they have. Here's her advice:

Make sure, she said, that regardless of the number of children you have, you teach them to be helpful, patient, and nurturing. Our children have to be reminded daily that they are not the center of the universe—just an important part of it.

Make sure that you are teaching them independence. They must learn how to work, including how to cook and clean and how to manage their finances. Kids must learn how to succeed on their own without too much "help" from Mom and Dad.

Make sure that you invest in family night. Playing games, reading novels together, having daily devotions, or going to sporting or performance events are all very important to building a family unit and developing happy, healthy, self-sufficient, and caring adults.

Make sure that you provide for your children a calm, relaxed environment, even if it is only for a few days a week. Our house was generally hectic for many years, as all four of us had to be out the door by 7:30 a.m. with a reverse process at 5:00 or 6:00 around dinnertime. Everyone was stressed, including the kids!

Make sure that you keep your priorities clear. Career is important, but don't let it take away from your most important job: raising your children. Despite what they say, kids are not as aware that they're missing "things" or their own bedroom, as they are aware if you are not there with them. So live below your means as necessary to have the right work/family balance. There will be plenty of time to concentrate on building your career and making more money when the kids are grown. Time flies by, and before you know it, they are out of the nest.

Sarah told me how extremely blessed she is to have a wonderful husband, children, lifestyle, and career, and she thanks God for his many blessings. Be happy with your kids and your choices—your life is what it is. Looking back does not change that, but starting today, consider the big picture when you're making important decisions.

> *Give thanks to the LORD, for he is good!*
> *His faithful love endures forever.* (PSALM 136:1)

Of course, now that Sarah's over fifty, she thinks it would be nice to have a few more kids come visit her and to have lots of grandchildren to look after her when she's older. I told you she was intensely focused, and her two kids will be wishing they had more siblings, too, as this girl ages. I have no doubt this one will live to see one hundred!

GETTING A DO-OVER
I Would Have Pedaled Slower

WANT TO KNOW my do-over? To choose just one is difficult. Not that I agonize over the past; I don't. But I fully recognize that I made decisions and did things that often were not good for me or for those I love.

As a young mother, I was always so busy trying to "do good" and "be good" that, when I look back now, I see that I missed so many things that *were* good. I wish I had not been afraid to slow my pace. I wish I would have pedaled slower.

I didn't make the connection between my productivity, my creativity, and my happiness until my kids had moved away from home. I'm a type A, over-achieving, need-to-do-it-perfectly type of person, so it never once occurred to me that if I would just slow down, I would truly come into my own. I regret the fact that I learned this late and missed out on many opportunities to be present with my husband, my children, my coworkers, and most importantly, myself. Even today I have to remind myself that my best work, my best *me*, happens not when I work harder and longer, but when I slow down.

I try not to give unsolicited advice to my daughter, Shauna, but as I watch her holding her precious baby, Ava, I tell her often to slow down and relish this time. Although she's overwhelmed with the things to do and the things to learn that accompany motherhood, I want her to know that she will never pass this precious place again with this child.

When it comes to pedaling slower, I would like to go back and read books to my kids again. If I could do this over I would read to them until they were big enough to hold me. Yes, I read to the kids when they were little, but when they were old enough to read for themselves, they read their own books.

Oh, how we missed out on taking wonderful adventures together when they were twelve and fourteen years old! Can you imagine the lessons we could have learned together and the rich conversations we would have shared by reading The Chronicles of Narnia books, *Anne Frank: The Diary of a Young Girl*, or *The Adventures of Huckleberry Finn* as a family?

But we were all pedaling so fast.

Turn away from evil and do good.
  Search for peace, and work to maintain it. (PSALM 34:14)

I wonder if the world would have stopped turning if our family had reserved one night a week to journey together through a classic? I wish I would have pedaled slower on Thursday nights.

GETTING A DO-OVER
I Would Have Pedaled Slower (Part Deux)

BESIDES THURSDAY NIGHTS, do you know when else I wish I had pedaled slower? On Sunday mornings. If I could do it over, we would have skipped church. *What!* you say.

Yes, this Bible-totin', sittin'-in-the-pew-every-Sunday-morning mother would have reserved one Sunday a month for nothing more than pancakes and snuggles. I can watch a television commercial for pancake syrup and feel such pangs of regret—it's been known to bring me to tears. Now, who in their right mind cries over an Aunt Jemima commercial? Hallmark cards, yes, but Aunt Jemima? Well, I do.

There is something magical and, of course, sacred, about Sunday mornings. Everything seems to move at a little slower pace; the sun shines sweetly through the windows, and everything is at peace. Unless you're getting the teenagers up for church.

Then, the yelling starts—"You've got to get up or we're going to be late"; "Scott, for heaven's sake, you can't wear that, we're going to church, not a garage sale. Go change"; "Shauna, go back in the house and get your Bible." Everything moves at a slower pace on Sunday mornings all right (especially the kids), but *peace* wasn't the word we would have used to describe our household at 8:55 every Sunday morning as we tried to hit the 9:30 service.

Compare this scene to the Aunt Jemima commercial where the mom, dad, and kids hustle around the kitchen laughing. Sunlight streams into the kitchen. The kids are talking. The parents are listening. It's sacred. And I turn gray with regret.

Just as it is sacred for us to take one day a week to take the time to thank God and worship him, I think he'd be so pleased and blessed to watch us take this sacred day, one day a month, to focus on our families. To talk about our questions and our faith. To listen to the kids' hopes and dreams. And to rest in their precious company.

Remember to observe the Sabbath day by keeping it holy. (EXODUS 20:8)

Yes, we sometimes had our family breakfast on Saturday, but it wasn't a sacred time. I wish I had pedaled slower on Sunday mornings.

GETTING A DO-OVER
I Would Have Pedaled Slower (Part Trois)

All work is spiritual work. All work has meaning beyond the surface realities of a job, a production schedule, a product, or a paycheck. All work concerns spirit and soul and involves our ability to connect them with surface realities.[34] DICK RICHARDS

I STOLE FROM my employers. And I have stolen from my clients. And I'm ashamed. If I could do it over, once a quarter I would have pedaled slower on a Friday.

When we fail to invest in our own mental wellness, we rob those we work for and those we work with. Our employers and our customers need us at our best, but we often neglect the feeding and clearing of our mind because we feel we can't afford to take the time off. But we need a new perspective on this topic: taking time off is not a luxury—it's an investment in your productivity for the rest of the quarter!

Climbing the corporate ladder, I didn't take all my vacation days because I felt I couldn't afford to be out of the office. There was always so much work to do, and taking time off for anything other than family vacations or the kids' sick days was, in my mind, not what professionals do to get ahead. Looking back, I realize I cheated my employer and myself from my best work.

Regardless of our roles—from moms, to CEOs, to line workers—creativity is a basic requirement. Problem solving, working with employees, and improving processes all require some level of creativity. But we're not creative when our minds have become dead weight from physical, emotional, and mental stressors.

Only in the last few years have I learned that it takes energy, enthusiasm, and time away from the office to be creative in the office. Not once in all these years of writing has an idea for my Truth Nuggets come to me while I was sitting in my office or at my computer. Instead, my creative juices have been stimulated while riding a bicycle, running, driving my car, listening to music, or playing with my family. You're never going to have your best ideas when you're constantly staring at a computer screen or sitting in a gray cube.

> *He renews my strength.*
> *He guides me along right paths,*
>   *bringing honor to his name.* (PSALM 23:3)

I wish I had pedaled slower on one Friday per quarter to melt my brain freeze and renew my mind and spirit. You need a day off too.

GETTING A DO-OVER
I Would Have Pedaled Slower (Part Quatre)

EVERY MINUTE of every day, choose to enjoy who you are and where you are.

I was plagued by a strange (yet, to many women, familiar) condition for almost twenty years. Regardless of where I was, I always felt guilty, sensing I was in the wrong place. If I was at work and it was 4:30 p.m., I felt like I should be at home with the kids. If I was home when the kids were sick, I felt guilty that I wasn't at work (this was before the days of the Internet and home offices).

If Steve and I went out as a couple, I felt we should have the kids with us (*What a terrible mother I am*). When the kids were with us, I felt like Steve and I needed more couple time (*What an inconsiderate wife I am*). Shoot! I couldn't win for losing.

I was pedaling too fast in every aspect of my life. If I could do it over, I would pedal slower in my head! My panic that I should be somewhere else robbed me of glorious experiences because I often wasn't present in the moment. It was panic that I wasn't fulfilling every obligation 100 percent that robbed me of glorious experiences by not being present with the person in front of me.

During those years, I didn't have a mentor. No one was there to tell me it was okay (much less desirable) to jump off the hamster wheel every now and then. No one to explain that you and those you care for and serve will actually *benefit* from your slower pace. Our culture demands all of us to do more. Couple that with this crazy techno-world we live in, which is connected 24-7, and it's no wonder we're missing the moment. Our most glorious moments.

> *Don't be afraid, for I am with you.*
> *Don't be discouraged, for I am your God.*
> *I will strengthen you and help you.*
> *I will hold you up with my victorious right hand.* (ISAIAH 41:10)

Girlfriends, technology will continue to rev up, and our culture is not going to change. It's up to you to determine how fast you will pedal. Be courageous. Go slow.

GETTING A DO-OVER
I Would Have Apologized Less

AS I MENTIONED BEFORE, I would do lots of things differently. I love my life and have few regrets, but I think it's imperative that we reflect on those philosophies we once had or the things we once did to congratulate ourselves for "passing over" to maturity; for embracing our experiences and hard-gained wisdom. So I'll close this chapter with one more of my do-overs:

I would have been a more honest person. I would have apologized less.

As a young woman, I literally railroaded myself trying to please everyone and keep peace. I apologized for things I couldn't control; I apologized for things that others accused me of that I didn't do or didn't know I did; I apologized for introducing an issue or concern that needed to be addressed. And worst of all, I apologized for telling the truth. And in every one of those instances, I lied.

I admire the young women in my life who approach difficult situations with confidence, integrity, and authenticity. I watch them navigate difficult conversations and am in awe of their ability to express their voice, unapologetically and with honesty. I am clearly a late bloomer.

Only in the past few years have I come to the place where I can express my opinion with self-assurance—without the need for disingenuous blabber. If I could have this as a do-over, I believe my credibility as a woman, a professional, a mother, and a friend would be much stronger today.

"Run up and down every street in Jerusalem," says the LORD. "Look high and low; search throughout the city! If you can find even one just and honest person, I will not destroy the city." (JEREMIAH 5:1)

Quick survey: what did you apologize for yesterday that was outside your control? See?

GETTING A DO-OVER
I Would Have Apologized Less (Part Deux)

MAYBE YOU CAN relate to my youthful, dishonest self. My sentences, either in business, at the family dinner table, or with a group of friends, would frequently begin with "I'm sorry, but . . ." I wish I had used different phraseology.

The young me, apologizing for a situation another person had caused, would say, "I'm sorry that we can't hit your deadline, but the information came in late."

Why was I apologizing? This wasn't something for me to regret. My business peer or customer was the one who failed. Today, I say something like: "Unfortunately, due to the missed deadlines last week, your proofs will arrive to you on Thursday rather than Monday."

The young me often apologized for miscommunication: "I'm sorry I didn't bring a cake, but I had no idea you expected me to provide dessert."

I often apologized for other people's lack of clarification. Communication is a 50/50 proposition; it's not successful unless both parties *know the other* is clear on what he or she means. Today I say, "I guess we'll save the calories tonight—I didn't understand I was to bring a dessert!"

When I was younger, I regularly apologized for failing to meet someone's expectations due to circumstances outside my control. I would say, "Honey, I'm so sorry that dinner isn't ready yet, but both kids are coming down with something."

Most people live in their "me-centric" world and have no idea what your world is like. Today I would explain, "We're having takeout; the kids are barfing up their toenails and won't be joining us. I'm turning them over to you while I soak in the tub."

I once tolerated toxic people in my life who made me feel like I needed to apologize even for taking up space on this earth. I was constantly apologizing: "I'm so sorry I have disappointed you again, but I promise I'm trying to be the person you expect me to be."

Girlfriends, you're only supposed to be who God called you to be. No one has the right to berate you and make you feel unworthy. Today I would say with a smile, "That's an interesting observation you lend. Perhaps I'll take it into consideration at a later date."

It took me several years to perfect this, but I think I've got it down now. I finally realized that 99 percent of the things I apologized for weren't in my control or weren't my fault. And, of course, I finally learned I should never apologize for who I am.

> Bring all who claim me as their God,
>   for I have made them for my glory.
>   It was I who created them. (ISAIAH 43:7)

Honesty can be kind. And unapologetic.

GETTING A DO-OVER

FATHER GOD, I thank you for second chances; you have spoken to me and I am convicted that I

- ☐ often perform for the praise of others rather than living a more balanced life with uncommon joy;
- ☐ have allowed others to abuse me;
- ☐ have put my marriage at risk by participating in risky, flirtatious behavior;
- ☐ often listen to the voice of others before the voice of the Holy Spirit;
- ☐ have allowed my spiritual maturation to stall;
- ☐ am trying to run my life without you and outside of your will;
- ☐ need to study your Word at a much deeper level;
- ☐ focus more of my attention on action items and tasks than I do on people;
- ☐ have confused "I can," "I should," and "I want";
- ☐ am not investing in my own personal development;
- ☐ am missing precious opportunities with my children, my husband, and in my work because I am preoccupied and pedaling too fast;
- ☐ have allowed self-imposed obligations to rob me of uncommon joy;
- ☐ hear the call of God to have more babies;
- ☐ often apologize for other people's failings or for things outside of my control.

ACTIONS I WILL TAKE:

Example: We will make Thursday night family pizza and game night.

1. _____
2. _____
3. _____

My gracious Father, I thank you for giving me a do-over. I thank you for women who will share their insight and wisdom to help me be the woman you have called me to be. I ask that you will strengthen me, guide me, and help me to learn from my own do-overs and to share willingly with other women as we create your Kingdom on earth, one that is pleasing to you. Amen.

MOVING THROUGH THE FOG

A FEW YEARS AGO, Steve and I took a road trip to Santa Fe, New Mexico. We spent five glorious days just reconnecting. We shopped for art, ate great food, and cozied up by the fireplace at night. October in the Southwest—the weather was picture perfect.

But on our way out of town, as we journeyed through the mountains toward home, we were hit by a wall of fog. Not just a smattering of fog; this was an extreme weather condition we met without warning, and when I say it was dense—well, think of trying to look through a cotton ball.

Steve continued to slow down until we found ourselves moving about 2 to 3 mph. Unable to see more than a few inches in front of the car, we had no idea whether there were automobiles in front of us or coming at us. To complicate the situation, we had no idea where we were because we couldn't see any landmarks; we were all but paralyzed. We certainly couldn't turn back. We could only creep forward.

Disappointments can be like a fog. They come on when we least expect them, and even though we have a life plan—we know where we want to go—the setback often causes us to stop dead in our tracks.

When you have invested significant time and emotion in a dream that goes sideways, it's easy to become cynical and hardened. But is that the way you want to spend your life? Like moving through the fog, you choose whether to stay in your bitterness or to move forward, if only at 2 to 3 mph.

As different as we may be from one another, this is one area in our lives that we *all* have in common. Every person you know has had a serious setback. That means every person you know could have an attitude of defeat—but they don't, do they? No, many people have elected not to be defined by their trials.

For I can do everything through Christ, who gives me strength.
(PHILIPPIANS 4:13)

Perhaps today is the day to choose to move through the fog. Let God guide you safely to the other side.

MOVING THROUGH THE FOG
Put Regret in the Closet

WHILE I WAS in Chicago on business, one of my business associates asked me to join her in some "hat shopping" one Saturday afternoon. The boutiques in a given area of town were having a "Mad Hatters" event, displaying all styles, sizes, and colors of headwear options.

We laughed our way through literally hundreds of hats—floppies, straws, velvets, pill boxes, you name it—we tried it on. But the longer we shopped and modeled for one another, the more *maw-ve-lous* we believed we became. Six hours later, after losing all objectivity, we purchased our hats. I wore mine only once: Steve kept referring to me as Raisa (as in Gorbachev's wife), so I haven't dared don it again. But I keep it. In my closet. In a box, high on a shelf. I don't open it, but I know it's there. It offers me an important reminder: hats aren't for me.

We all have regrets. Whether it stems from a poor fashion choice or a moral failure, regret is one thing we have in common. Our differences surface in the manner we choose to deal with our mistakes.

Coming to grips with a disappointment, some of us appropriately mourn the loss but then make the mistake of wallowing in the regret. This rumination on our past failings only thwarts the forward momentum to recovery. You can't throw your mistake away—as much as you might like to sometimes—because it is part of the fabric of who you are. But like I did with my hat, you can shelve it. Because you might need to call on the experience again (in order not to repeat the mistake), regret should not be so far from your recall that you can't benefit from your previous intimacy with the associated heartache. But your disappointment should never become your "life theme."

Consider how psychologist Albert Bandura explains the effects of a downward spiral in Marcus Buckingham's book *The One Thing You Need to Know*: "Memories of negative events increase despondency, and despondency lowers self-efficacy beliefs; the lowered beliefs, in turn, weaken motivation and spawn poor performance, breeding an even deeper despondency in a downward cycle. So if you really want to ruin your chances of sustained success, ponder your weaknesses, ruminate on your past failings, chew on your flaws."[35]

> The LORD is my shepherd,
>   I shall not want.
> He makes me lie down in green pastures;
>   He leads me beside quiet waters.
>   He restores my soul. (PSALM 23:1-3, NASB)

God wants you to live a full and meaningful life—even if you did buy a stupid-looking hat. Put it in a box.

MOVING THROUGH THE FOG
Put Regret in the Closet (Part Deux)

IT'S NOT THAT my hat was *that* expensive. But it did cost money, and well, it looked so good on me in Chicago! I had a hard time letting it go.

We do that with our mistakes. And until we do let go, we can't really move through the fog.

So stop talking about it. Stop obsessing over it. We can't let our failures affect our spirit, determination, and drive for a better life, a better tomorrow. We have to find the strength and our feisty inner child to overcome our disappointments. I come from a good gene pool of spirited women. When my aunt broke one of those five-and-dime Ping-Pong paddles on the backside of her ten-year-old daughter, my cousin defiantly announced, "That didn't hurt!" I'll tell you what doesn't hurt—having a fighting spirit.

My determination to overcome hurt came in handy ten years later. Born an entrepreneur, I opened my first business when I was twenty, but it failed. I had borrowed $30,000—which might as well have been $3 million to me in those days. The financial debt and blow to my self-esteem were overwhelming. The failure could have paralyzed me, but I kept creeping forward . . . at 2 to 3 mph. I paid off my debt in full by selling Oldsmobiles. There I was, one of the first three women in the state of Texas selling cars—at the age of twenty-two. What was I thinking? I was thinking I had to right my wrong. The lessons I learned from that brief stint of rebuilding my self-esteem truly made me who I am today. I refocused myself to begin the slow, steady progress toward reaching my goal of owning my own business. Fifteen years later, I finally had the experience, education, determination, and contacts I needed to try my wings again. I did not let my past disappointment, failure, and regret define my future. And this time, my experience and drive worked like a charm.

Such things were written in the Scriptures long ago to teach us. And the Scriptures give us hope and encouragement as we wait patiently for God's promises to be fulfilled. (ROMANS 15:4)

Put those regrets on the top shelf in the closet of your mind. Learn from your past, but don't let it control your destiny. Out of sight, out of mind—unless you open the hatbox.

MOVING THROUGH THE FOG
You Can't Do a Swan Dive in Shallow Water

THINK ABOUT this truth: you can't do a swan dive in shallow water.

Sometimes our disappointments are self-inflicted. Have you ever made the exact same mistake twice? Urrggghh . . . I hate when I do that! How is it that we don't see the makings of disaster the second time around? I believe it's because we fail to invest the time required to analyze how we ended up in the situation. And I think this lack of reflection causes some people to try to do a swan dive in shallow water . . . again, even though their heads still hurt from the last time they tried it!

> *As a dog returns to its vomit,*
>   *so a fool repeats his foolishness.* (PROVERBS 26:11)

King Solomon wasn't joking when he said wisdom is clearly the key to a happy life. My dictionary defines it as the ability to *apply* knowledge, experience, understanding, or common sense and insight. But before we can apply the knowledge gained from a downfall, we must first identify what was at the root of it. So what are the basic questions we should ask ourselves when we find ourselves in a mess?

- What in the world just happened?
- Has this ever happened before? (If yes, this is the reason you better analyze the situation now!)
- Why did it happen?
- What role did I play? Did I cause it or enable it? Could I have prevented it?
- Can I fix it?
- If I can, when and how will I?
- What precautions can I take to ensure this same scenario doesn't happen again?
- What are the warning bells I should identify now to alert me that I'm heading toward trouble again?

Girlfriends, when you identify exactly what happened and why, you're much better prepared to see the warning signs if you're faced with a similar situation in the future. And as strange as it is, you most likely will find yourself back at the top of the *same* platform looking down at the *same* shallow, muddy water! Be prepared.

MOVING THROUGH THE FOG
You Can't Do a Swan Dive in Shallow Water (Part Deux)

ANALYZING THE SITUATION is our first step toward ensuring we don't make the same mistake twice, but I think there's another important step in applying the wisdom gained from a painful situation. Ask yourself:

- What's the lesson learned? There's always a takeaway.
- How am I better for the experience? There's always growth of some kind.
- How can I turn this disappointment into a springboard to greater accomplishments? Your losses will build character and provide meaningful lessons for your next endeavor.

To seriously analyze a situation, sometimes it helps to talk to an objective outsider—perhaps someone you know who has had a similar experience, or even a professional counselor. Friends or family may not be helpful; sometimes, they're just too close to you or the situation. They're likely either to be brutally honest with you and tick you off—resulting in no wisdom gained, only hurt feelings—or they will tell you what you want to hear, which is no help whatsoever.

An outsider might also be better equipped to challenge you to rise above the downfall; he or she won't allow you to wallow in a pity puddle too long and will also help you put things into perspective so you can forgive yourself.

It's during the rough times in life that we find out what we're made of. Self-inflicted disappointments can be very ugly, but often you'll come out on the other side a deeper, more interesting, more thoughtful, and more purposeful person.

Job stood up and tore his robe in grief. Then he shaved his head and fell to the ground to worship. He said, "I came naked from my mother's womb, and I will be naked when I leave. The LORD gave me what I had, and the LORD has taken it away. Praise the name of the LORD!" In all of this, Job did not sin by blaming God. (JOB 1:20-22)

Girlfriends, you can't do a swan dive in shallow water. It's only when the water is *very deep* that your beautiful soul is truly revealed. Rejoice through the pain and allow God to turn your belly flop into something beautiful.

MOVING THROUGH THE FOG
Mourn, Baby, Mourn

ONCE WE RECOGNIZE our defeat (and that of course is a big step in itself, as many of us stay in denial a bit too long), I think our first step in overcoming the downfall is this: mourn, baby, mourn.

Some of us are hardwired to circumvent grieving; I personally avoid it at all costs because it ruins my mascara. Except when I watch Aunt Jemima commercials or sing praise songs, I'm fairly dry eyed. But I don't think this has served me well when I have moved through my personal fogs and disappointments. I think my pride thwarted my recovery. Then there's another issue some of us face. I'm not sure we all know how to grieve.

I think a lot of us prefer to put on our masks of happiness and pretend that we're fine. Of course, this will work for a while, but when the mask begins to bind and get itchy, we peel it off—exposing our vulnerabilities. Those of us who are by nature incredibly optimistic are probably the worst offenders of this. I know I was. When I was younger, I tried to bypass the tears to "get on with it." I would pull myself up by my bootstraps and keep going. I tried to ignore pain to make it go away. But it didn't, and failing to meet the grief head-on just prolonged my recovery.

There are some excellent books and Web sites that define the stages of grief. Five stages are commonly given, though some authorities feel there are as many as twelve. I once studied the topic and really like the following acronym I came across:

T—To accept the reality of the loss (the analysis phase)
E—Experience the pain of the loss
A—Adjust to the new environment without the lost person or subject
R—Reinvest in the new reality

A time to cry and a time to laugh.
A time to grieve and a time to dance. (ECCLESIASTES 3:4)

Have you properly grieved your loss, or is your mask getting uncomfortable too?

MOVING THROUGH THE FOG
Mourn, Baby, Mourn (Part Deux)

MY AFRICAN AMERICAN girlfriends . . . now *they* know how to experience the pain; so I took a lesson from them.

We all grieve in our own way and in our own time, but after I moved on from my mask phase, I found that for me, falling prostrate, forehead-to-the-floor, tears flowing like the Colorado River after a big rain, worked best. Now, if you think this will work for you, I recommend you do this when you're alone—it may be disturbing to others.

I can say that I'm old enough and have lived enough to have fallen to the floor sobbing a few times. Each time, it was a vital step in healing my hurt. In that excruciating moment of pain I realized two very, very important truths: first, that *I was very much alive* and second, that *I would survive.* And although I was furious with God for not rescuing me from my disappointment, I knew he would carry me through to a new day.

> *I have called you by name; you are mine.*
> *When you go through deep waters,*
> *I will be with you.*
> *When you go through rivers of difficulty,*
> *you will not drown.*
> *When you walk through the fire of oppression,*
> *you will not be burned up;*
> *the flames will not consume you.*
> *For I am the LORD, your God,*
> *the Holy One of Israel, your Savior.* (ISAIAH 43:1-3)

But there is one other thing I learned about mourning my losses that came as a total surprise: even though I might have grieved something "correctly," the pain would sometimes return when I least expected it. It hit me like a tornado in the middle of the supermarket. One minute, I was acting totally normal while strolling along the chip aisle; the next, I was sobbing while staring at rows of Campbell soup. Those of you who have grieved the loss of something or someone very precious probably have experienced this too. Fortunately, this public outpouring didn't happen often, and I was never "escorted" from the grocery store!

To move through the fog, you have to allow yourself the space and place to mourn. It's a vital step in moving forward . . . even at 2 to 3 mph.

MOVING THROUGH THE FOG
Shave Your Legs and Paint Your Toenails

IF YOU HAVEN'T had a major disappointment, it's because you're either smarter than the rest of us, you're younger than the rest of us, or you're fibbing! For those of you who *have* experienced a setback, I welcome you to the club of *WHEW!*

Women who
Have
Experienced
Washout!

But there's one more critical step you must take to move through the fog: shave your legs, paint your toenails, and get back out there.

Baby, life goes on. Very few of life's 10-on-the-Richter-scale disappointments can be fixed. It's time to start anew . . . and that beginning starts with a new attitude.

Heartbreaks due to a failed love affair may be one of the hardest disappointments for women to move through. After my first marriage ended, I felt unworthy of another love. Even though I was young, I determined that I would not remarry. I had failed in my marriage, and unfortunately I allowed that failure to define me and my future.

But this guy named Steve (a confirmed bachelor until our first date) had other ideas. For nearly twenty years now I have lived and loved in a fairy-tale marriage. Moving a little faster than 2 to 3 mph, I managed to get through the fog and see the light! And the light was handsome, smart, funny, and now brings me a cup of coffee every morning.

Oh, yes! I'm *so happy* I shaved my legs!

You have turned my mourning into joyful dancing.
You have taken away my clothes of mourning
and clothed me with joy,
that I might sing praises to you and not be silent.
O LORD my God, I will give you thanks forever! (PSALM 30:11-12)

We must be resilient. We must be open to learning. We must be open to making new mistakes. It's not the failure that will get you in the end—it's the decision to allow it to limit your future.

What color can I get for you? I'm painting my toenails pink.

MOVING THROUGH THE FOG
When You're Not in the Driver's Seat

OKAY. Let's say that you've dealt with your disappointment. You've grieved like my sisters at the Bethel Baptist Church. And you've moved on. What's your role when it's one of your best girlfriends who is stuck in the fog?

For those of us who like forward progress, it can be gut wrenching and painful to watch a friend who cannot move forward. We want to take the wheel and floor it—let's get through this darkness! But that's not our role.

Our role with our girlfriends is to ride shotgun. Allowing her to stop and start. Allowing her to swerve every now and then. And sometimes we have to sit quietly as she puts her forward motion in reverse. Biting our tongue. Putting aside our personal need for our "old friend" to come back to us. Our personal aggravation with the situation has to be just that. Our own problem.

I have walked beside girlfriends working through profound grief and have found my friendship, my patience, and my own self-care put at risk as I rode in the passenger seat. When my self-absorption just couldn't take it another day, I remembered that it was not my car. I could step out for a while, stretch my legs, and then climb back in, ready to sit a little longer with her as she continued to journey on.

Encourage those who are timid. Take tender care of those who are weak. Be patient with everyone. (1 THESSALONIANS 5:14)

As hard as it is, sit quietly with your grieving sister. Don't try to take the wheel. And whatever you do, remember to get out at the rest stop; the journey might be long.

MOVING THROUGH THE FOG

FATHER GOD, I am operating in a fog and I know that

- [ ] you will give me the strength to move through it;
- [ ] I need to put my regret in the closet;
- [ ] I have allowed my past mistakes to define my future;
- [ ] I am repeating past mistakes and must analyze the "why" behind my destructive behavior;
- [ ] I need to mourn _____;
- [ ] it's time to shave my legs and paint my toenails;
- [ ] I need patience with my girlfriend as I sit shotgun while she drives through her fog.

ACTIONS I WILL TAKE:

Example: I will decide today to no longer allow my mistake of yesterday to define my tomorrow.

1. _____

2. _____

3. _____

Kind Father, I thank you not only for your forgiveness but for your forgetfulness for my mistakes and sins. Guide me as I heal from my past in order to fully enjoy every day on earth and every minute in your presence. Give me a tender heart and a patient spirit to minister to my girlfriends as they deal with their life blows and tragedies. Amen.

A DIFFERENT PERSPECTIVE

STEVE AND I are art nuts. We particularly enjoy and appreciate contemporary art. A favorite Saturday pastime of ours is visiting some of the galleries in Dallas. While kicking around a few weeks ago, Steve and I stumbled upon two fascinating works of art. As we stood in the gallery and studied the paintings, we smiled; they were breathtaking. Because we were not sure if the massive canvases would hang perfectly in the areas we had in mind for them, the gallery owner had the art delivered to us the following Monday on approval. This is the art dealers' version of a test drive.

They didn't work out as we had planned—neither of these pieces would fit well or complement the spaces we had in mind for them. However, each work began to come alive, taking on a whole new personality, after hanging in our home for just a few hours. We moved the art from room to room, changing the spotlights, stepping back from the subject, and then moving in close. For forty-eight hours, we worked and worked and worked to find the perfect resting place and the perfect lighting for each piece. Only by considering options and looking at the paintings from many different perspectives did we gain a whole new appreciation for the artist and his gift.

Over the next seven days, I'd like for us to do the same by considering a few topics, each from a very different perspective. Some subjects will require us to move in close—looking at the subject brushstroke by brushstroke. Others will require us to stand back and take in the big picture. And sometimes we'll even need to shine a new light on the subject to ensure we see the part of the painting that captures its deepest meaning. There is so much we have yet to learn.

Then God said, "Let there be light," and there was light. (GENESIS 1:3)

One thing is for sure—we're all a part of a masterpiece; sometimes we're just a bit too close to the subject to fully appreciate our role in the creation!

A DIFFERENT PERSPECTIVE
Stepping Back from the Canvas

ON SEPTEMBER 16, 1986, my life took an abrupt left-hand turn. All of my dreams for my young family and my hopeful teaching career came to a screeching halt at 6:20 p.m. on that seemingly normal fall day. By nightfall, I had my doubts that things would ever be good or right again. Nothing would be as I had dreamed—for any of us.

Now, over twenty years later, I can look back on that day and see that a wonderful story—my new life story—was actually just beginning. I can see, by stepping back from the canvas, that all things, even the very bad things, *have* worked together for good.

Have you recently faced a crisis that you feel you may not emerge from? Can you step back from your tragedy? Can you shine a different light on your situation? Are you far enough away from the event now that you can see—from standing back here—that while one dream didn't come true, other, even more beautiful *realities* (that you had never allowed yourself to conceive of) have been gifted you?

No, I didn't get to finish my degree and become a teacher. Instead, I embarked on a career in the technology industry that would eventually lead me to business ownership. No, I wasn't able to hold my marriage and family together the way I had dreamed. Instead, a man would later enter my world and love me, and my children, in a way that I didn't know was even possible.

Would I have believed this new life story was actually being birthed on that long-ago September day? No. Girlfriend, I was standing in the middle of the canvas, crying buckets—watching all my brushstrokes run together.

Those who trust in the LORD will find new strength.
They will soar high on wings like eagles.
They will run and not grow weary.
They will walk and not faint. (ISAIAH 40:31)

If you're in the middle of a crisis, I know you can't see clearly either. It's hard when you're smack-dab in the middle of it. But tomorrow you won't be. You'll be looking at your masterpiece from a new perspective and you'll be absolutely amazed at your new life story and the difference a bit of distance can make. Hang on.

A DIFFERENT PERSPECTIVE
Successing Our Kids to Failure
or Failing Our Kids to Success?

WE FAIL our children when we don't allow them to fail.

You can quote me on that. I know this like I know my hair is turning gray. I think when it comes to our kids, we all need to stand back from the artwork and turn off the light. Now don't get all huffy and close the book. Hang with me for a minute.

Like you, when I was a child, my parents did not get involved in my school-work; my homework was just that—*my* homework and *my* responsibility. With the exception of open house in the fall, they did not meet with my teachers; those were *my* teachers and I had to deal with them—the good, the bad, and the ugly. (Most of them were terrific; a few of them were frightening.) My parents did not go to the principal to argue on my behalf to ensure I had special teachers or special classes; that was for me to navigate based on my class performance. Nor were my parents hovering and nagging me to fill out college applications; if I wanted to go, I would need to take the initiative and pick up a pen; oh—and I had to figure out how to pay for it too.

My parents worried about me when my feelings were hurt, but they did not rescue me from my spats with friends; they were good, empathetic listeners, but they were not going to intervene by calling someone's mom. They did not make excuses for me when I made bad decisions; more than once I lived with the ramifications of poor choices.

Were my parents bad parents? No, I think I had *excellent* parents. When it came to helping you define yourself and gain independence, your parents probably were pretty good too. They prepared you for the real world—where work is hard, managers are unreasonable, and life isn't fair.

For you know that when your faith is tested, your endurance has a chance to grow. So let it grow, for when your endurance is fully developed, you will be perfect and complete, needing nothing. (JAMES 1:3-4)

Will you allow the paint to be smeared, smudged, and messy as your children learn to navigate their own problems, find their own answers, and call upon their inner strength? Don't circumvent the building of *their* faith.

A DIFFERENT PERSPECTIVE
Successing Our Kids to Failure
or Failing Our Kids to Success? (Part Deux)

I CAN LOOK at this topic more objectively today than I could even a few years ago—both as a mother of grown children and as an employer. I know that as a generation of parents, we have failed and are failing our children by getting overly involved in their lives, which deprives them of vital experience in navigating life when things get tough.

I have mentored, interviewed, hired, and fired numerous young adults over the past fifteen years. The one thing they all had in common: they were overly successed by their parents. These kids were not allowed to be average and had never been told that they were anything other than excellent at everything. So you can imagine the shock for these young adults at their first job review—who were *at best* average in the workplace. Based on my experience, I'd say less than 2 percent of all employees are exceptional, and typically not until they have five to ten years of experience in their field!

Because many of these kids were not given the freedom to make their own choices (good or bad), when faced with major decision-making challenges in the workplace, they have a meltdown and cry in the restroom—or worse, lose their cool in front of a client! As children and teens, they were awarded trophies and put into honors classes when in fact they were no more distinctive than their fellow teammates or classmates. How does this affect them in the workplace when they're twenty-four years old? They glide in with a sense of entitlement that's embarrassing.

Do you wonder why my generation never had this attitude? We learned humility when we had to sit on the bench, when we didn't win the trophy, and by watching those who truly were gifted excel.

Haughtiness goes before destruction;
humility precedes honor. (PROVERBS 18:12)

Lay your heavy burden down. Moms, they're going to be closer to perfect after experiencing a little bit of failure and humility.

A DIFFERENT PERSPECTIVE
Moving My Art Around

The kind of beauty I want most is the hard-to-get kind that comes from within—strength, courage, dignity.   RUBY DEE

SOME PEOPLE rearrange their furniture. Steve and I rearrange our art. Moving the pieces around from room to room helps us determine where each looks its most glorious, and we enjoy viewing the art from a new perspective. I think when it comes to our perspective on aging, we could all consider rearranging our opinions and priorities.

This morning I found three, count 'em three, significant lip wrinkles—I call these my Mother Puckers (I think they are the result of all the kissing I did on my babies). But these little devils were not a welcome sight. I gasped right out loud . . . and then laughed at myself. This represents a new life stage for me—one where I know that my physical youth and attractiveness have left the building just as my inward beauty *begins* to mature and evolve. For me, it means I need to move my art to another room—from my face to my heart. But to do this I will need a different perspective when it comes to beauty. Maybe you do too.

We will need to view beauty as something that has nothing to do with the reflection in the mirror but has everything to do with the reflection of our character, our mind, and our spirit. Rather than pine for a face without crevices, we will learn to take pride in the fact that we have become women of substance; women focused far more on the condition of the world than on the crow's-feet that extend into our hairline. Rather than long for the muscle tone of our twenties, we will delight in our hard-won grace, dignity, and confidence as we walk into a room filled with strangers. Rather than compare our aging process and progress to that of our girlfriends, we will instead focus on the legacy of joy, inspiration, and adventure that we will individually and collectively leave to every little girl and young woman whose lives we touch.

> *Charm is deceptive, and beauty does not last;*
> *but a woman who fears the LORD will be greatly praised.* (PROVERBS 31:30)

Girlfriends—*if we want to*—we could be the generation of women that moves our culture away from this obsession with beauty. We could be the generation of women our granddaughters talk about one day—the one that taught them and lived for them the art of *being* beautiful.

A DIFFERENT PERSPECTIVE
Are We All Unique or Uniquely Alike?

STEVE AND I LOVE to entertain and often invite guests to our home. As we walk them through the house, they take in our contemporary art. Some of them say, "I don't get it."

We're never offended. We understand completely. We often go to art shows and are baffled by a work or a particular artist—unsure where the artist is coming from, going to, or if he or she was just on drugs while painting.

But we always turn on the art lights and allow our company to spend time with the paintings. After a while, some of them say, "You know what? This stuff is growing on me; I think I'm beginning to actually like it!" Did the art change? No, the visitors merely allowed themselves to be exposed to something different and *looked* for the things in the art that spoke to them.

I think if we were all to turn on the light and spend a little time with those who are different from us, our attitudes might change too. We might find we can connect with people even if we don't understand or agree with all their choices. We might begin to appreciate and even like those who, *at first*, seem so different from us.

My Truth Nugget subscribers have very different life stories. They hail from places as large and far away as Hong Kong and as small and nearby as my little hometown of Bells, Texas. They are distinctive in their lifestyles, their political and religious affiliations, and their life stages. But they all have one thing in common. See if you can guess what it is.

- A forty-six-year-old Baptist woman who lives on a white rock road in rural Texas; contrast her with a forty-one-year-old Jewish woman who lives in a high-rise in New York. They have one thing in common.
- A fifty-two-year-old president of a women's league living in the Midwest, recently separated from her husband of twenty-two years; compare her to a thirty-two-year-old president of a gay business association living in the Northwest, recently separated from her partner of ten years. They have one thing in common.
- A red-state, suburban thirty-year-old mother trying to balance the budget, the shopping, the career, and the kids; then look at the blue-state forty-year-old single woman, living downtown while trying to balance the budget, the shopping, the career, and dating. They have one thing in common.

Nothing . . . will ever be able to separate us from the love of God that is revealed in Christ Jesus. (ROMANS 8:39)

Can you guess what these women, so seemingly different, have in common?

A DIFFERENT PERSPECTIVE
Are We All Unique or Uniquely Alike?
(Part Deux)

If you judge people, you have no time to love them. MOTHER TERESA

GIRLFRIENDS, as different as the Baptist woman in Texas is from the Jewish lady in New York, as different as the president of a women's league in the Midwest is from the president of a gay business association in the Northwest, and as unique as the thirty-year-old suburban mom is from the forty-year-old urban single, they, like all women, have the same *heart.*

- We all long to love deeply.
- We all need to be loved unconditionally.
- We all have been hurt badly.
- We all wrestle with how to forgive completely.

How do I know this? I have learned a bit about my "girlfriends" over the past few years as they reply to my e-mails and participate on my blog. It's so interesting how I often get an identical response from women who are very different from one another; women I've never even met. And that response? "How did you know what was in my heart?"

> *This is real love—not that we have loved God, but that he loved us and sent his Son as a sacrifice to take away our sins. Dear friends, since God loved us that much, we surely ought to love each other. But if we love each other, God lives in us, and his love is brought to full expression in us.* (1 JOHN 4:10-12)

Too often we subconsciously play out our prejudices based on things like status, level of education, race, and even lifestyle (e.g., some moms choose to work; others choose to stay home). But here's the kicker: we are in fact much more alike than any of us think. It is only our limited exposure to people who walk a different road that prevents us from forging not just friendships, but basic human compassion for one another. Just as Steve and I do for our art-perusing houseguests, I think we need to turn on the light and *look* for those things that speak to us in another human being.

A DIFFERENT PERSPECTIVE

FATHER GOD, I want to consider a new perspective, and I realize that I need your help to

☐ look beyond my crisis of today in order to see your promise and hope for tomorrow;

☐ allow my children to learn important lessons through the experience of failure;

☐ move my focus from my outward beauty to the beauty of my character;

☐ remember that other women, although they may be from very different backgrounds, religions, or of different political leanings, are really not that different from me—we all long to love and to be loved.

ACTIONS I WILL TAKE:

Example: I will let my kids do their own homework and fight their own battles this week!

1. _____

2. _____

3. _____

Father, I realize that I am sometimes narrow in my views, living in your beautifully created world with my blinders on. Convict me when my focus is turned inward rather than on others. Strengthen me as I let go of the grasp of perfection for my children—remind me to allow them to make mistakes. Thank you for your promise of tomorrow. Amen.

DANCING WITH LAZARUS

OVER THE YEARS I've watched on television and read numerous articles about people who have physically died but have been resuscitated. In almost every instance, these people said they have a new outlook on life, a renewed sense of purpose, and a healthy perspective on what's really important.

Thank God I didn't have to die for him to get my attention, but he did give me quite a health scare. Several years ago, as a result of a day surgery gone south, I began to have a very strange numbing and tingling sensation throughout my body. Visiting with the surgeon on this new condition, he rather bluntly and emphatically said, "Those are the symptoms of MS. You have multiple sclerosis." For seven days, as I had a number of appointments and tests and then waited for the final diagnosis, I asked myself, *What if this is it? What if my life as I know it today is over? What would I do differently?*

For my girlfriends of other faiths or for those of you who are not Bible-thumpers, let me introduce you to a guy named Lazarus who has a similar story.

Lazarus, who was a good buddy to Jesus, had fallen ill. Because Jesus was out of town doing his Jesus thing, Lazarus died. When Jesus returned to Lazarus's home, he was told that Lazarus was dead (which was no surprise, of course, to Jesus).

Unfortunately, Jesus couldn't use the paddles. Lazarus was really a goner—he had been dead for four days. Now Lazarus's sisters, Mary and Martha, must have been really ticked off with their best friend, Jesus, for not coming in time to save their dear brother. Can you imagine? It's as if your best friend was the world's most famous heart surgeon and refused to perform surgery on your brother! But do you think these women gave up their Lazarus without a fight?

Of course not. And this is what we love about women. We will do whatever is within our power to help those we love. For Martha, that meant giving Jesus a piece of her mind. For Mary, that meant an outpouring of her grief before the feet of Jesus.

> *When Jesus saw her weeping and saw the other people wailing with her, a deep anger welled up within him, and he was deeply troubled. "Where have you put him?" he asked them.* (JOHN 11:33-34)

Do not for a minute believe that your anger, your grief, and your pain doesn't affect your Lord. He's weeping for you. He longs for you to move out of your darkness in order to dance again.

DANCING WITH LAZARUS
Peeling Off the Wrapping

JESUS DECIDED to show Mary and Martha a whopper of a miracle: he raised Lazarus from the dead. Jesus said, "Lazarus, come out!" and he then instructed the witnesses to "unwrap him and let him go!" Lazarus, bound head to toe in his funeral wrappings, was probably more than a bit anxious to get out of his gauze. (I can relate—you should see me stripping out of panty hose after an eight-hour sentence.)

This story contains numerous teachings and subplots that are pretty awesome (you can read all about it in John chapter 11), but it's the statement "Unwrap him and let him go" that speaks loudest to me. Not until my brush with a life-altering disease did I begin to understand God's desire to remove us from our bindings and free us from the trappings of this world; free us from our negative self-talk; free us of our twisted thinking toward our families and fellow man.

Are you dead and wrapped up spiritually?
Are you dead and wrapped up emotionally?
Are you dead and wrapped up in your own self-oppression?

I can only imagine that Mary, Martha, and Lazarus had a pretty rich conversation around the dinner table that evening. Like me, I'm sure Lazarus saw his brief time on earth through new lenses too.

So go ahead. Eat your food with joy, and drink your wine with a happy heart, for God approves of this! (ECCLESIASTES 9:7)

Once he was rehydrated, I bet ole Lazarus was dancing to beat the band! So with that, I have decided to dance in my new body too . . . the polka, the fox-trot, the rumba . . . it doesn't matter to me. I have a new perspective on the steps I'm to take.

DANCING WITH LAZARUS
The Jitterbug or *Swan Lake*?

We can't take any credit for our talents. It's how we use them that counts.
MADELEINE L'ENGLE

DURING MY SEVEN-DAY wait for a CAT scan, I conducted a rather in-depth self-analysis. For the first time in my over four decades on this earth, I asked myself, *Am I living the life I was called to live? Is this who I'm supposed to be?* Rather than plan some of the important aspects of my life, it seemed I had just allowed them to "happen."

Oh, don't get me wrong. I lived a charmed life. But the nagging question in my heart and in my head was, *Am I fulfilling the purpose for which I was uniquely made?* Something in my gut told me that I was neither tapping into my full potential nor investing the energy required to live the life I was called to live. But figuring out the "what" was the hard part. So I waited and watched—while praying for direction. Would God direct me to dance the jitterbug or *Swan Lake*? I was open to either but needed some guidance!

> *This is why I remind you to fan into flames the spiritual gift God gave you when I laid my hands on you.* (2 TIMOTHY 1:6)

Not too long after my health scare, the book *Now, Discover Your Strengths* hit the market. With its help, I began to fully grasp not only how I was uniquely wired but which of my talents I had purposely ignored, stuffed, and many days even denied. By taking the tests in the book, I could articulate what my unique skills are. Now it was up to me to step out in faith and put my gifts to work to become the person I was created to be.

- Would this mean change? Yes.
- Would this require some discomfort? Yes.
- Would this involve taking risks? Absolutely.

Yes, this transformation has been a ride, but I can tell you this. Without a shadow of doubt, I know now that I was called to be your girlfriend, someone who will walk part of your journey with you.

DANCING WITH LAZARUS
The Fear of Simon

YOU KNOW the TV show *American Idol*, right? And Simon? The judge? Oh, my. I so respect the contestants as they audition and perform. I could never face the harsh critique of Simon (whether I could sing or not—which I cannot). When I was younger, my problem was that I always placed too much value on what others thought of me. Thus, my performance was far too important. I finally realized that this was undermining my ability to live my life to the fullest for God.

Some of us fall prey to the critical comments of an authority. But that authority (anyone you give credence to) may or may not have the expertise to properly critique your life performance. Others of us are drawn, like a moth to a lightbulb, by the roar of the audience applause. Both are equally dangerous, as either can undermine your ability to objectively consider your options and take the risks needed to answer your calling.

In Alexandra Stoddard's book *You Are Your Choices*, she shares this anecdote: "After his first audition, Fred Astaire received the following assessment from an MGM executive: 'Can't act. Slightly bald. Can dance a little.'"[36]

Girlfriends, what if Fred Astaire had listened to his "Simon"?

> *When I am afraid,*
> *I will put my trust in you.*
> *I praise God for what he has promised.*
> *I trust in God, so why should I be afraid?*
> *What can mere mortals do to me?* (PSALM 56:3-4)

I had to get over the "judge"—and for me, that was what others thought. Neither their critique nor their applause should affect my calling. You see, I have a safety net. The only judge who matters has choreographed my performance.

Get behind me, Simon!

DANCING WITH LAZARUS
Dancing with the Stars

I'D SEEN THE TEASER commercial for a TV show called *Dancing with the Stars*, and I knew I had to check it out.

I've daydreamed all my life about being a graceful ballroom dancer, gliding across the floor in a white chiffon gown. In this dream, I'm five foot ten. Yes, it's pure fantasy. I can do Chubby Checker's Twist on one foot, but that's about it. So I cozied up in front of the television (alone—this is not my husband Steve's idea of evening entertainment; it's not likely I'll get him to an Arthur Murray Dance Studio in our lifetime) for what I hoped would be an opportunity to see what I was missing.

But I was quickly disappointed. The beautiful gowns had been replaced with . . . well . . . not much. Those girls were nearly naked! And the suave, sophisticated leads have been replaced by guys who dribble on basketball courts or who speed skate! Yes, it's impressive that they can move across the dance floor, but is this really dancing at its finest? No, of course not—this is about risk taking! These "stars" are putting themselves on the line.

As I considered what changes were required for me to live intentionally, I knew that risk taking would be involved. Being an entrepreneur, I'm pretty schooled on the importance of taking business risks—but personal risks? Oh, no.

I think timidity gets in the way of our living the big life—we've become a bunch of fraidy-cats.

- Loving? No. We can't love deeply; we could get hurt if we aren't loved back.
- Forgiving? No. We won't forgive; where's the justice in that?
- Advancing? No way. We'll make a mistake; and mistakes result in embarrassment.

Girlfriends, if Emmitt Smith, three-time Super Bowl champion, can masquerade as Gene Kelly, risking the ridicule and teasing of the entire NFL, surely we can put ourselves on the line too—especially if the payoff is a life lived authentically.

The LORD directs the steps of the godly.
He delights in every detail of their lives.
Though they stumble, they will never fall,
for the LORD holds them by the hand. (PSALM 37:23-24)

Stop being a chicken. Put on your dancing shoes and hit the floor. I'm heading out to shop for that white chiffon gown.

DANCING WITH LAZARUS

FATHER GOD, I want to reclaim the joy of life, and I realize that I

☐ am wrapped up and bound in negativity and self-oppression;

☐ often take life itself for granted;

☐ am not fully utilizing my strengths and talents for your glory;

☐ have allowed my fear to trump your direction.

ACTIONS I WILL TAKE:

Example: I will stop being afraid of failure and will utilize my talent of _____ _____ for God's glory.

1. _____

2. _____

3. _____

Father, the maker of miracles, the giver of life, I praise you for my every breath. I pray that you will fortify my spirit with courage and bold determination to put my strengths and talents to the test, that they may bring you joy and honor. I ask that you unwrap me from my negative thoughts and bless me with a spirit to live a meaningful life. Amen.

CROSSROADS

SITTING AT THE INTERSECTION, I was as lost as a goose in a new world. For the life of me, I couldn't get my bearings. I was so turned around I couldn't tell if I was heading north or south, and the rain only compounded my confusion.

I had flown into San Jose early that morning, and after a full day of client meetings, it was time to head to the hotel. But somehow I got turned around on one of the "loops," and along the way I got lost. To make matters worse, I was starving; low blood sugar significantly heightens my level of frustration.

I was finally able to exit the freeway, and as I sat at the light, I knew that to continue on my current path was a mistake; I also knew that the direction I had come from would not lead me to a plate of fried rice and a cozy bed. But which way to turn? I had neither enough information nor experience in this part of town to make a good decision, so I did what any intelligent human being (at least female) would do—I stopped at the nearest convenience store and asked for directions from the man behind the counter. Ahmed became my navigational confidant.

Regardless of age or life stage, we all come to a crossroads from time to time—in our marriage; with our work; in our relationships with family members; in our personal development. So where is "Ahmed" when we're dazed and confused, not knowing which way to turn?

Actually, God has placed "Ahmeds" all around us, and for me, they show up in the form of girlfriends. I'm surrounded by women who are rich in character, spunky in spirit, and successful, not only in their careers, but in living meaningful lives. I invited some of them to share an experience they had while sitting at an intersection and decisions they made that would change their lives forever.

The LORD keeps watch over you as you come and go,
  both now and forever. (PSALM 121:8)

If you're sitting at a crossroads today, I hope their stories will inspire you. Unlike my friend Ahmed in San Jose, they can't tell you which way to go, but I hope they will give you confidence as you turn on your blinker.

CROSSROADS
At the Intersection of Resentment and Forgiveness

I WANT TO LOOK and act like my friend Connie when I'm seventy years old. Energy and enthusiasm follow her like an orb as she zips through her daily three-mile walk around our neighborhood. One word sums her up: light. She's pure light.

So, intrigued by this beautiful woman who is chronologically old enough to be my mom but young enough in spirit to be my baby sister, I invited Connie to lunch. I wanted to know about the important decisions she had made in her life and how they had shaped her. I knew there was much to learn from this feisty character.

Connie said, "One of the biggest choices I had to make throughout my life was whether to extend forgiveness or to hold on to resentment. I took the wrong road. I chose to harbor my hurt."

Connie was birthed to a seventeen-year-old mom and an absentee father. Connie's mother, being both a glamorous and fun-loving woman, lacked the emotional maturity to be the mom Connie longed for. For twelve years, while her mom dated, Connie's grandmother, who lived with them, provided her care and direction. But at last her mother did settle down with a fabulous father figure for Connie, and she looked to establish the mother-daughter bond that Connie had longed for, for so many years. But it was too late.

In those short but formative first twelve years, Connie had learned to revel in resentment toward her mother. As her mother tried harder and harder to reach her, Connie realized that she had something to hold over her mom, and Connie found that she enjoyed the power. Connie told me, "I fed my hurt."

Connie would continue to find herself at this same intersection over and over, as her mom sought to soothe the pain she had caused her then-young daughter. But Connie would always turn onto the road of resentment instead of forgiveness, looking for justice.

> He will not crush the weakest reed
>   or put out a flickering candle.
>   He will bring justice to all who have been wronged. (ISAIAH 42:3)

Withholding forgiveness can be a power trip for some people; they know they hold the keys to hurt and pain and the keys to peace. Which set dangles from your key chain?

CROSSROADS
At the Intersection of Resentment and Forgiveness (Part Deux)

The bitterest tears shed over graves are for words left unsaid and deeds left undone.
HARRIET BEECHER STOWE

AS CONNIE CONTINUED to withhold forgiveness through the years, her own kids were amazed that their mom—so giving and so forgiving of others—held on to bitterness with both hands when it came to their grandmother.

But as Alzheimer's besieged her once-healthy mom, Connie's heart began to soften. Her mom, who still recognized Connie, was comforted by having her only child be her caregiver. Still, the important words had not been said. Finally, Connie found herself sitting at the corner of resentment and forgiveness for the last time.

As her mother lay on her deathbed in a deep comatose state, Connie sent her family from her mother's room. She laid her head upon her mother's pillow and whispered softly in her mother's ear, "Will you forgive me?" Against all odds, Connie's mom, never opening her eyes, squeezed her daughter's hand.

Isn't it interesting that for sixty-five years, Connie's mom sought her forgiveness, but in the end it was Connie who asked for hers? Connie realized that she had sacrificed years of incredible joys and celebrations in order to harbor her hurt, feed her pain, and try to right a wrong from so long ago.

Connie mourned her mother's death, but her tears were not bitter—she had made peace with her mom, and herself. But as this wise and precious woman sat across from me at our table in the restaurant, her tears flowed with regret for the years wasted.

Are there words you need to say? Is there forgiveness you need to extend . . . or to request?

So we have stopped evaluating others from a human point of view. At one time we thought of Christ merely from a human point of view. How differently we know him now! This means that anyone who belongs to Christ has become a new person. The old life is gone; a new life has begun!
(2 CORINTHIANS 5:16-17)

Girlfriends, turn on your blinker. Stop feeding your pain and extend grace. Don't waste the last precious years you have with someone by clutching your hurt like it's a priceless treasure. The treasure you lose will be all that you might have enjoyed together.

CROSSROADS
Another's Child or Empty Arms

THIS CROSSROADS experience does not belong to a friend but is another topic I have grappled with over the years. I was twenty-one years old when I fell in love with a short, fat, bald guy. He smiled sweetly at me from a two-by-three-inch photo, and I knew I had to have him.

Scott's adoption was a private affair. His teenage mom had tried to keep him but found the stress and responsibility of caring for an infant to be more than she could handle at the tender age of fifteen. In her absence, Scott's extended family determined that a private adoption to a loving family would provide him with the stability and love he deserved. And I was game.

Excited to add another little person to our family and provide a little brother for Shauna, I called my parents to share the incredible news with them. Knowing how much my dad loved children, I dialed him first, sure he would be thrilled. After I told him, Dad sat quietly on the other end of the phone. Finally, he spoke: "That child will break your heart."

What did you say? My father told me, diplomatically, lovingly, but emphatically, that he thought I was making a huge mistake. He went on to explain his view of nurture versus nature and wanted to be sure I knew what I was signing up for. Shocked, miffed, and even a bit hurt, I told him I was going through with this adoption because this baby needed me.

When Scott was doing drugs and living on the streets, sometimes disappearing for years at a time, my friends asked me if I had known what was coming, would I have so eagerly taken on the child who did indeed break my heart. This question still surprises me.

Although a few of my friends have had a biological child completely destroy their peace, finances, and family tranquility, I've never thought to question if they regretted having that child.

If you're planning either to bear your children or adopt them, I believe there are a few things you must prepare yourself to accept, in advance of the stork's arrival. And one of those things is that all the nurture in the world can't undo the hardwiring of Mother Nature.

So you have not received a spirit that makes you fearful slaves. Instead, you received God's Spirit when he adopted you as his own children. Now we call him, "Abba, Father." For his Spirit joins with our spirit to affirm that we are God's children. (ROMANS 8:15-16)

God adopted us, and in spite of our sinful nature, he hasn't given us back.

CROSSROADS
Another's Child or Empty Arms (Part Deux)

MY IDEALISTIC HOPE for a perfect little family unit quickly unwound after Scott's arrival. We knew before this little guy was talking that we were in for a ride. But my love for this cutie-pie, my can-fix-anything mother mentality, and my desire to hang with Scott no matter what never waned. Well, that's not exactly true. When he ran away for the fourth time and disappeared from our lives for over three years, I have to admit that at times I didn't think I could go on.

Children are a wonderful blessing, yet I urge you to become a parent with your eyes wide open. I offer you these few pieces of advice:

- Accept that this child might be a stranger to you and your family. Despite our incredibly close ties, Steve, Shauna, and I laugh, along with Scott, at his uniqueness. He eats different foods. His interests and taste in music are different. He even walks at a different pace than that of the rest of the family. In many ways he is a stranger in his own land. To make it work, you have to embrace this child's individuality, seeing him or her as a blessing to your otherwise "boring" family. Acceptance trumps conformity.
- Know that there could be profound challenges with this child. Addictions. Learning difficulties. Anger. Not all kids are type A overachievers. To make it work, you have to eagerly accept that your purpose may be providing counsel or care—for a lifetime. Commitment trumps condition.
- Approach the adoption or addition to your family from a position of what you're giving, not getting. Realizing the importance of this was a transformational moment for me. Once I remembered that I adopted this baby because he needed me (not the other way around), my love became much less conditional. My nurture trumped his nature.
- Know that this child could add immense joy to your family with his or her quirks, personality, and sense of humor. As a toddler and young boy, Scott brought us joy through his enthusiasm, energy, and affectionate ways. He still does. Joy trumps pain.

Whether the birth certificate is signed at the hospital or the courthouse, raising babies ain't easy. But this mom can tell you that, of all the things I've done, having Shauna and adopting Scott are the two things that have brought me the deepest sense of living in the middle of God's will.

He will feed his flock like a shepherd.
He will carry the lambs in his arms,
holding them close to his heart.
He will gently lead the mother sheep with their young. (ISAIAH 40:11)

And even when it's hard, God's love trumps everything else.

CROSSROADS
At the Intersection of Making Money or Making a Life

INTELLIGENT, ARTICULATE, discerning, thoughtful, loving, and more fun than a barrel of monkeys are the words that describe my best friend, Paula. Focused and ambitious are two other words that describe this beautiful woman. Like many of us, she discovered that her quest for professional success created a distraction as she arrived at a crucial junction in her marriage.

Nine years into their marriage, Paula was at the pinnacle of her career and was handsomely rewarded for her contributions to her organization. But thanks to a boss whose management style was—well, let's say unpredictable—Paula had developed a love-hate relationship with her job. Relishing the sound of her high heels clicking across the manufacturing floor and the pride that accompanied building an efficient, productive team, Paula precariously balanced the enjoyment of her work with popping Tums whenever the president entered her office doorway.

In the meantime, her husband, Mark, was also concentrating his energies and attention on his career, traveling around the world and dealing with the pressure of the fast-paced world of sales. He was no more physically or emotionally available to Paula than she was to him.

Days turned into weeks, which turned into months, as the two slowly drifted apart, rarely engaging in meaningful conversation. While her husband turned to coworkers to unwind after an intense day, Paula relied on evenings out with her girlfriends as a form of stress management. Traveling in the same direction but in different cars, they found themselves at an interesting intersection one Friday evening when Paula stated unapologetically and unemotionally, "I'm not happy."

As her husband passionately probed, Paula's tears finally fell as she expressed her frustration and stress with work. Although knowing intellectually that "it wasn't personal," her weariness from managing the pressure of an unreasonable boss had finally taken its toll. Interestingly to Paula, the work—not the crisis in her marriage—brought her to tears. The two now had a decision to make as they sat at the crossroads of making money or making a life.

No one can serve two masters. For you will hate one and love the other; you will be devoted to one and despise the other. You cannot serve both God and money. (MATTHEW 6:24)

So which master are you devoted to today—making money or making a life?

CROSSROADS
At the Intersection of Making Money or Making a Life (Part Deux)

I've learned that making a "living" is not the same as making a "life."
MAYA ANGELOU

ONCE THEY'D EXHAUSTED their conversation, Mark and Paula continued to sit on the back deck watching the ducks swim on the pond as the sun sank behind the trees. When they finally made their way into the house, Paula wasn't sure which way things would go.

But within twenty-four hours, Paula made the decision to put her professional calling on hold. Then she began building their life with the same gusto she had invested in building a successful career. Paula shifted her focus to the nuances of creating a nurturing, fun home life; she learned to cook and entertain. In addition, she focused her attention on learning how to be more emotionally supportive to her husband as he built his career. And success—in her husband's work life and in their marriage—quickly followed. Mark returned the favor several years later, taking early retirement while Paula went about building a new, rewarding professional life, one where her talents and gifts benefit the team she manages—for me. Paula runs my marketing agency.

Paula told me, "Looking back, I can see that we only knew how to make money; we had absolutely no concept of what it took to build a life or to connect in a meaningful way with our family. But because we chose life, I became a more balanced person, richly blessed by these 'prizes'—husband, family, and friends."

If making money is contributing to the diminishing return on the quality of your life, maybe it's time to consider the road less taken. Choosing the greater mission—to make a life—takes sacrifice, conviction, and commitment. As Paula and her husband approach their silver anniversary this fall, they know they chose the right road for them.

Light is sweet; how pleasant to see a new day dawning. (ECCLESIASTES 11:7)

Another note: Paula is my closest friend, and you can bet that I count her among *my* prizes.

CROSSROADS
At the Intersection of Yesterday and Tomorrow

I HAVE A NEW FRIEND in my life; her name is Terri. I just love this quick-witted gal who entered my world via one of my best guy friends (it appears he does, after all, have good taste in women). During dinner one evening with the boys, Terri shared a story with me about a very recent crossroads in her life. This one might have you, like me, turning on your blinker.

During her senior year in high school, Terri returned to the United States from Brazil when her father's work assignment ended. What could have been an awkward, lonely time was instead fifty-two weeks of teenage bliss. This charismatic kid was quickly adopted by her fellow classmates in her suburban Michigan school. She formed an especially close friendship with a girl named Marny.

Terri and Marny became inseparable, and the term *opposites attract* clearly applied to this odd couple. Spirited, adventurous Terri taught Marny how to have fun (and not get caught); in return, the studious Marny introduced Terri to "the word of the week," hoping to expand Terri's vocabulary and heighten her interest in her schoolwork. I can just picture this "Oscar and Felix" team watching the boys from the bleachers (they did have that in common).

After graduation they went to their respective colleges, keeping in touch and visiting each other often. Then on one visit Terri got her feelings hurt. Fueled by jealousy, Terri allowed her immature reaction to an innocent mistake override their deep and dear friendship. Because she never revealed or honestly discussed the situation with Marny, Marny was left in the dark as to what had come between her and her best friend. Marny finally gave up and withdrew after Terri became unpredictable and irresponsible, often canceling plans with Marny at the last minute. Knowing she was being immature and hurtful, Terri said she still allowed her ego to trump truthfulness, never admitting that her feelings had been hurt or that she harbored a grudge.

Deceit fills hearts that are plotting evil;
joy fills hearts that are planning peace! (PROVERBS 12:20)

Girlfriends, are you holding a hurt in your heart without even being honest with the person against whom you're holding the grudge? Consider speaking the truth in love or letting it go.

CROSSROADS
At the Intersection of Yesterday and Tomorrow (Part Deux)

We read that we ought to forgive our enemies; but we do not read that we ought to forgive our friends.   SIR FRANCIS BACON

TIME HEALS all wounds? Well, yes . . . maybe. But how much time?

A few years later, still estranged, Terri and Marny met at a friend's wedding, but the two wouldn't even speak to one another. Their old high-school friends were shocked and confused that the two chums were no longer close. And at their ten-year reunion this dynamic duo, once as thick as flies, could be seen having only a cool, cordial conversation in passing. They each sat at the intersection of the hurt feelings of yesterday and the hopes of reconciliation for tomorrow. Both turned to the wounds of yesterday. Neither would allow the healing of their scraped knees.

But when we allow it, time can work its magic, and hearts do soften—especially when we finally grow up and realize how few tomorrows we really have.

Preparing for her twenty-year reunion, Terri realized it was past time to turn on her blinker. Holding her breath as she clicked the send button, Terri resolutely reached out to her buddy from so long ago. I asked Terri, "Were you afraid you'd be rejected?" She answered, "I didn't think about that. I just knew that reaching out to Marny was the right thing to do."

Sitting under a tree on their high school lawn, the best friends reunited and began the journey toward reconciliation. Catching up on two decades of joys, disappointments, successes, and failures, Terri said all she could think was, *What a loss.*

> *The seeds of good deeds become a tree of life;*
> *a wise person wins friends.* (PROVERBS 11:30)

Girlfriends, there's a good chance that most of us either have or will have to sit at this intersection with an old friend. Are you still turning toward yesterday, refusing to let your scraped knee heal? Take a chance and take a right onto tomorrow; I have heard that reconciliation might be in the next block.

CROSSROADS
At the Intersection of Prestige and Fulfillment

AT THE INTERSECTION of Prestige and Fulfillment, you'll often find an accident caused by a professional woman who either sat at the light too long or turned before the light changed green. When your financial livelihood and emotional well-being are at stake, making a successful turn onto Fulfillment is all about timing. Two important women in my life, like me, left prestigious positions in corporate America (think Rodeo Drive) for the scary, bumpy road of "something more" (which, from a distance, can look like Freddy Krueger Drive).

My friend Terry was truly at the top of her game, serving as the senior vice president of sales and technical services for a Fortune 100 company. Her position personified the three Ps of corporate success: Prestige. Power. *And private jets.* But the aggravations that accompany the corporate arena finally began to take their toll, and at fifty-seven, Terry bailed.

Terry said she never looked back: "To be self-directed is the most fulfilling thing I've ever done. I am living, rather than just working." And she began living just in the nick of time. Three years into retirement, Terry took on a battle with breast cancer that would have exhausted the most bullish CEO. Having the fortitude to deal with it appropriately, Terry elected for an aggressive form of treatment. Today Terry is a successful career- and life-coach. Her timing was perfect.

Debbie was the vice president of merchandising for a major retailer and a visionary in computer retailing; her influence and reputation commanded respect and delivered some pretty cool perks. A world traveler while raising teenagers, Debbie had no flexibility, no time to invest in her physical well-being, and no time to pursue her own interests. But in 1995, Debbie took a huge risk to join an unknown, start-up consulting group in an attempt to find balance. Today, she works when she wants, as much as she wants, and from where she wants. Debbie told me, "Having the space to pursue my interests, while enjoying a rewarding career, has made me a much more balanced person." Her timing was perfect.

My story is similar to Terry's and Debbie's. Of the three of us, I was the first to walk out of my corner office and across a dark parking garage, arms loaded with boxes—scared out of my mind. But like Debbie and Terry, I knew in my heart that if I didn't trade the prestige and security of my position for a more sane workload, I would eventually forfeit my mind and body (and some days, I swear, they were after my soul). Facing this crossroads and then choosing just the right time to open my own marketing company was among the five best decisions I have made in my life. My timing was perfect.

Let all that I am wait quietly before God, for my hope is in him. (PSALM 62:5)

Are you sitting at a similar intersection? Ask that your timing be God's timing. He won't steer you wrong.

CROSSROADS
At the Intersection of Prestige and Fulfillment (Part Deux)

I HAVE LOTS of young girlfriends who tell me they love their pressure-packed jobs despite the stress it puts on them and their marriages. And that's not all bad. It's important that you embrace every life stage and each experience. I'm not advising my young girlfriends to put their professional drive in neutral. If you're on the way up the corporate ladder, my suggestion is that you *enjoy* the climb.

But when you arrive, if the view is not all it was cracked up to be and you decide to turn around—before you shimmy back down, let me share this with you:

Even though Terry, Debbie, and I found success after leaving the corporate world, many women regret leaving their security for a new adventure. When I speak to professional women, the topic of this crossroads often surfaces, and women ask for my counsel. These are the first five questions I tell them to answer before turning onto Fulfillment:

1. Do you have savings or another source of income to float you for twelve months? (It's harder, and usually takes longer than you ever forecast, to spin up a new business venture.)
2. Do you have a large network in which you are highly regarded? (The bigger and stronger your professional network, the better your chances for success.)
3. Are you leaving at the top of your game? (Here's where timing is critical. If you plan to continue working in your same industry, you must leave your current employer on an extremely high note.)
4. Are you determined you will not fail? (This probably doesn't need explanation, but determination and grit are keys to success.)
5. Will you be content if you earn less than you do today? (Not always, but sometimes, fulfillment comes with a price tag.)

As for me, I look to the LORD for help. I wait confidently for God to save me, and my God will certainly hear me. (MICAH 7:7)

If you can answer yes to all five questions, the lights might be timed about right; only then, with a sound business plan in hand, should you proceed to Fulfillment—with eyes wide open and two hands on the wheel.

CROSSROADS
At the Intersection of Insecurity and Confidence

REMEMBER MY GIRLFRIEND Connie, who sat at the intersection of Resentment and Forgiveness as she hung on to resentment toward her mom? Well, during our lunchtime conversation several weeks back, Connie also told me about the season in her life when she sat paralyzed at the intersection of Insecurity and Confidence. I am happy to share another profound lesson from this very wise woman.

A mother of four, Connie stayed home with her children while her husband built a successful career. Socializing and networking were critical to his advancement, but the circles in which her husband worked included people who were both incredibly creative and highly educated. Connie felt like an outcast around these interesting characters. Because she stayed home with the kiddos, she believed she added little to no value to the conversations. Over time, her confidence plummeted; her sense of self-worth cratered.

Having dropped out of college to have children, Connie's insecurity ultimately led to jealousy, and her jealousy led to accusations. The accusations led to an ongoing argument with her husband that poisoned the atmosphere of their home and the future of their marriage.

For nearly twenty years, Connie came to this same intersection, always turning onto Insecurity rather than taking a proactive approach to address her issues. But that all changed when she elected to take a part-time job at a community college. Working in the counselors' office exposed Connie to course work and degree plans, and this new information inspired Connie to return to the classroom. Over a period of ten years, taking one course at a time, Connie earned her bachelor's degree . . . and found her voice. Her maturity and life experience made her the teacher's pet and, along with her good grades, gave her a newfound confidence that she did have something important to share with the rest of the world.

On a roll, Connie went on to complete her master's degree. Attending classes on Saturdays and grinding through evening courses, Connie was an example of grit and determination as she studied side by side with her teenage children. Connie's self-assurance fueled her and reignited her marriage; she and her husband will celebrate their fiftieth wedding anniversary this June (oh, they are the cutest couple you've ever seen!).

I took my troubles to the LORD;
I cried out to him, and he answered my prayer. (PSALM 120:1)

Are you sick of driving around and around Insecurity Circle? Perhaps it's time to change that one thing that keeps you from being the person you were destined to be. Perhaps it's time to let go of self-doubt in favor of the pride in accomplishment. Perhaps it's time to boost the low self-esteem that not only threatens the quality of your life, but the quality of life for those you love.

CROSSROADS
At the Intersection of Missouri and Costa Rica

MY GIRLFRIEND DINA is one adventuresome gal! Given the option of financial assistance to pay for a car or a summer spent as an exchange student in Costa Rica, Dina opted for the road less traveled by the average American teenager. Speaking not a word of Spanish, this towheaded seventeen-year-old left her hometown on the outskirts of Branson, Missouri, for Costa Rica—a trip that would alter the course of her life.

Dina's eyes were quickly opened to the rest of the world when she arrived at the home of the family that she would live with. In Costa Rica, the "middle-class" host family lived in conditions nothing like the home she left in Missouri. They lived in a small dwelling located to the rear of the family's retail storefront. Their tiny home had no running hot water and only one bathroom for a family of five. Dina wasn't fazed; she was in heaven. Dina had found "home" in this warm, welcoming family and community.

Dina was a painfully shy teenager when she left home in May, but she returned a confident young woman, enlightened to a world much bigger than her graduating class of one hundred. Today, twenty-five years later, she radiates the excitement and enthusiasm from her youth.

Turning onto the road of adventure set Dina's life on a course destined for success and fulfillment. This one trip ignited a passion for foreign language and travel, and it opened Dina's mind and heart to accept people and cultures very different from her own. Dina said, "I can point back to this one decision, made at the age of seventeen, as the thing that has most influenced the person I am today."

I will praise you, LORD, with all my heart;
I will tell of all the marvelous things you have done. (PSALM 9:1)

Are you sitting at an intersection where you think you would benefit from an "out-of-this-country" experience? You're not getting any younger. Turn on your blinker.

CROSSROADS
At the Intersection of Cynicism and Trust

A cynic is a man who knows the price of everything and the value of nothing.
OSCAR WILDE

I MET A WOMAN named Petey under the strangest of circumstances. She and I call it a "God wink," after a book written by Squire Rushnell. His theory is that some coincidences and chance meetings are just too bizarre not to be divinely appointed.

Steve and I met Petey and her husband, Jim, while we were shopping for a condo in downtown Dallas. We had been on the hunt for a while and had finally decided to take the plunge. We were ready to place our deposit on a unit in a soon-to-be state-of-the-art commercial and residential building on the east end of downtown. While waiting for our sales representative, we introduced ourselves to another couple (Jim and Petey) who were excitedly fidgeting with a tape measure.

"Yes!" Petey replied to my question if they were considering purchasing. "We'll be neighbors! Which unit did you buy?" she asked. I took her to the scaled model, flipped on the light in the dollhouse-sized building, and she blinked. "That's our unit," she said. Hmmm. . . . Clearly, the sales team had made an error. We walked away without the unit but kept Jim and Petey as very dear friends.

Jim and Petey are like peas and carrots. Just as Steve balances me, so Jim provides the sea of calm to Petey's hyperactive mind and body. Their interests and values are perfectly aligned. I had assumed they had been married for thirty years. But you know what they say about assumptions. . . .

As Petey shared with me her story of true love, I learned that Petey almost missed the turn onto the road of marriage bliss. Her first young marriage failed when her husband revealed he was gay. Union number two dissolved when she refused to succumb to any more verbal and mental abuse. Number three—yes, that's three, count 'em—failed when her husband refused to treat his mental disorder. So you can see why Petey might not have wanted to turn onto the road of trust. Cynicism could have been a much easier right-hand turn for this intelligent, self-made, beautiful woman.

But testing this love (and Jim) through a five-year courtship resulted in a marriage made in heaven. Petey's wise discernment was coupled with a trusting heart.

> *O LORD, listen to my cry;*
>   *give me the discerning mind you promised.* (PSALM 119:169)

Have you been burned by a bad relationship? Are you afraid to trust again? I was a lot like Petey, and my Steve had a lot of convincing to do for me, too. But in the end, like Petey, I had to turn on the blinker. Thank God for the gift of a discerning mind.

CROSSROADS
At the Intersection of Heart and Head

The will of God will not take you where the grace of God cannot keep you. ANONYMOUS

DR. KATHRYN WALDREP is one of the most precious women to walk the face of this earth. A faithful believer who opens her house every week to sixty professional women to study God's Word, she is the most authentic, caring, and honest person I have ever met in my life.

In addition to being *really* real, Kathryn is a doctor. One of the first female ob/gyns in Dallas, she opened her practice with her partner in 1983 and has been voted one of the best ob/gyns by her peers for *D* magazine for eight consecutive years. Her gift of compassionate Christian care to her patients is renowned.

So I was shocked when Kathryn told me she almost didn't become a doctor. "Not a doctor? Then what were you going to be?" I asked. Kathryn, a brilliant young woman, had been granted a full academic scholarship to Southern Methodist University's school of engineering. *Engineering?* "You were going to be an engineer?" I laughed out loud.

As Kathryn sat in class her freshman year, she realized circuits and schematics bored her to tears. However, chemistry and the sciences had become her passion. But what to do about the scholarship?

A nineteen-year-old hailing from a small Texas community, Kathryn didn't know how she was going to manage her tuition, books, and living expenses without her scholarship. Kathryn's mother insisted Kathryn do the logical thing and graduate with her engineering degree. But Kathryn sat at the crossroads, knowing that if she didn't follow her heart now—she might never have the chance again.

How easy it is to make decisions based on logic—especially when we're scared, broke, and without the emotional support of others.

Teach me to do your will,
 for you are my God.
May your gracious Spirit lead me forward
 on a firm footing. (PSALM 143:10)

Kathryn is hands down the strongest Christian and the greatest prayer warrior I have ever met. And she gets what few of us are willing to learn: God will put in our heart what he wants us to do. It's up to us to have the courage to follow.

CROSSROADS
At the Intersection of Gratitude and Discontent

I've learned from experience that the greater part of our happiness or misery depends on our dispositions and not on our circumstances.   MARTHA WASHINGTON

TO CLOSE OUT this chapter on crossroads, I would like you to pause at the intersection you're sitting at right now. Regardless of your life stage, your socioeconomic condition, your political leanings, or your spiritual understanding, you sit at the intersection of Gratitude and Discontent—with every other woman—every morning and at the end of every day and several times in between.

It is so easy for us to turn onto Discontent when people hurt us, when business is hard, when our expectations are not met, and when the brightness of tomorrow seems to never materialize. It's easy to whine, complain, and demand more out of everything from our relationships to our hotel stay (a source of my discontent last week—don't get me started). But to turn onto Discontent is a choice. And it's a choice that does us absolutely no good; a choice that is not just a "zero" in its effect on our state of contentment, but a negative. Turning onto Discontent only robs us of embracing those marvelous things we do have, usually in abundance.

So regardless of where you are today or what you're doing, I hope you will stop right now and start a blessings checklist. Every time you encounter another frustration or disappointment, I hope you will consider its opposite benefit—the blessing you either have already received or will receive in the future. And for every gift that doesn't cost you a thing—those people in your life whom you love and who love you, nature in all her splendor, and your next heartbeat—I hope you will consider those things, too, as you drive down Gratitude Way.

I will thank the LORD because he is just;
  I will sing praise to the name of the LORD Most High. (PSALM 7:17)

You know, now that I really think about it, I'm just grateful that I had a bed to sleep in at that hotel last week.

CROSSROADS

FATHER GOD, I pray for your direction. You know that

- ☐ I am sitting at a crossroads, paralyzed, not knowing which way to turn;
- ☐ I am struggling to forgive _____;
- ☐ I am miserable sitting in this place of resentment;
- ☐ I need to invest in making a life;
- ☐ I need to reach out and attempt to reconcile my friendship with _____;
- ☐ I am struggling in making important decisions that will affect my fulfillment at work;
- ☐ my insecurities are threatening my most important relationships;
- ☐ I need a new experience that will stretch me, teach me, and inspire me;
- ☐ my heart needs to learn to trust again;
- ☐ my passion and my logic are locked in a raging battle; show me your will;
- ☐ my discontent is robbing me of the uncommon joy that can be realized through a spirit of gratitude.

ACTIONS I WILL TAKE:

Example: I will decide today to put my resentment away. It's time to forgive and move on.

1. _____

2. _____

3. _____

Father of light, I thank you for revealing to me your desire that I live a life of peace and joy. I am comforted by the fact that you know I struggle and am often confused when sitting at these crossroads, but I thank you for convicting me to turn the right direction. I lift up my need to forgive, my insecurities, and my discontent, and ask that you send the Holy Spirit to fill me with a new attitude and a spirit of peace. Amen.

WHAT DOES IT LOOK LIKE?

WHAT ARE THE SECRETS to living an honorable life? The advice is endless. You can read about them in books or in magazines. You can watch the discussions on *Oprah*. You can go to a psychologist, hire a coach, or learn about them online. You can even chime in on the topic on blogs like mine. But have you ever seen what the attributes of an honorable life look like?

On December 7, 2007, I fell in love for the first time in almost twenty years, and I fell hard. Tears flooded my eyes and my mind raced as I looked upon the precious face of my first grandchild, Ava, and considered all she would behold in her lifetime and the important lessons she would learn. My role as her grandmother (I'm coaching her to call me Sugar) seemed a daunting one as I considered all my grandmother had been to me: my teacher, my playmate, my confidant, my spiritual advisor, my role model. How would I compare to the greatest Mammaw of all time? (But don't call me Mammaw—I'm way too hip.)

For the first several weeks after Ava's birth, I kept a list of the things that I hoped she would see in her lifetime. Although the list is long, it doesn't include Disney World, Miley Cyrus, or the shoe department at Neiman's. No. My list includes intangibles; intangibles that due to a change in our social fabric, our busy family lifestyles, or our lack of mindfulness or creativity, we fail to model for our children and grandchildren. And, unfortunately, since many of us were raised in not-so-perfect households, some of these same intangibles were not modeled for us.

So what are some of the things on my list that I want Ava to see?

- timeless honor
- selfless devotion
- genuine respect
- work/life balance
- considerate inclusion
- family traditions
- mindful appreciation
- working friendships
- marriage partnerships
- successful divorce

Successful divorce? Yep. There's a lesson here for all of us.

Let each generation tell its children of your mighty acts;
let them proclaim your power. (PSALM 145:4)

Because children are always watching (and because teenagers never listen), we know for a fact that our actions speak louder than words. So let's begin the important discussion as to how we, as sisters, aunts, godmothers, mothers, grandmothers, and great-grandmothers, can model an honorable life for the next generation.

WHAT DOES IT LOOK LIKE?
Timeless Honor

LYING BY OMISSION. Skirting the rules. Shirking our responsibilities. Failing to admit fault. These are just a few of the more benign characteristics of a disgraceful life we have seen modeled for us. Disgrace—yes, we've seen it. But honor? *Do we know what it looks like?*

I once heard General Colin Powell speak about his concern for our country and our role on the world stage. As he discussed this topic and other societal issues, he said that bringing dishonor to his family was not an option. He and his cousins were raised with the concept that disgrace is not a personal thing; it's a family matter. That got me thinking: how do you instill the concept of honor in a child?

You've read about the struggles we've experienced with our son, Scott. I can be honest after twenty-eight years of denial. Disgrace pretty much summed up the situation. Today, he's working hard to right his course, but as for the concept of honor, until just recently, I don't think he had a clue.

On the flip side, our daughter, Shauna, was born a truth-teller. I would just crack up at the things she would volunteer; at the innocent age of three, she would "fess up" just to get those *sins* off her chest! She was born a person of integrity; I didn't teach her that, any more than I taught Scott to lie. I can no more take credit for the honorable life and high moral standards our daughter lives by than I can shoulder the blame for our son's failure to live by a code of ethics. But did I miss something in my own personal modeling and explanations of *expectation* when it comes to honor? I think maybe I did.

You see, I know exactly what honor looks like. Honor sat at the dining room table with me celebrating his eightieth birthday last month. There, in flesh and blood, was a man of profound integrity. My second cousin Jerry and his wife of fifty-six years have lived a life of such dignity that I was literally bursting with pride at the mere thought of being related to them. And let me tell you, *their* example of a life without compromise has worked—you should meet their two sons, their spouses, and their grandchildren; they are absolutely amazing people of character. But this isn't an anomaly; the two preceding generations of the Wilson family lived equally honorable lives. I think that we should turn the whole clan into a lab test so we can study them in order to repeat this success of *generations* of exceptional human beings. Do you know a family like this? If so, you know what I'm talking about. This is not the rule in our society today but the rare exception.

> *Then the way you live will always honor and please the Lord, and your lives will produce every kind of good fruit. All the while, you will grow as you learn to know God better and better.* (COLOSSIANS 1:10)

My question for all of us is this: how can we create honorable families?

WHAT DOES IT LOOK LIKE?
Timeless Honor (Part Deux)

SO . . . BACK to the rest of us. How do those of us, whose parents did not model honorable lives or who have made grievous mistakes, right the wrongs for our next generation? I would like to propose an equal balance of family pride and shame. Let's start with the unpopular topic of shame.

Some generations of our society have no concept of shame. This word is so ugly we have purged it from our vocabulary. It's a tool in building a life of character that we've buried for the sake of building our children's self-esteem. Sure, you can shame someone to the point of damaging his or her self-confidence or psyche. But have we gone overboard? Have we failed to define and explain honor because the opposite—the teaching tool of shame—is out of vogue?

In lieu of shame, my parents indulged me with a benign version of vague scolding so as not to damage my self-esteem. I, along with millions of other mothers of my generation, followed their example with my own children: forfeiting any mention of shame—which they might inflict on themselves or our family—out of concern that it might shake their confidence. But by eliminating the concept of shame, I failed to introduce her counterpart—pride.

Family pride, that is. And this is what I believe my cousins Jerry and Betty have modeled and taught. They teach their kids that they have an obligation to their family and out of that obligation comes a *desire* to be a person of distinction, a person who lives above the fray.

So as I think about my granddaughter, Ava, and what I want her to see, I realize I want her to see what honor looks like. I can't right my past wrongs, but I can be mindful of my examples and teachings today. I will assist her parents as they balance the teaching of shame with stories of generations of honorable ancestors. We will model for her that *a life of honor is developed one important decision at a time.* And following Jerry and Betty's example, Steve and I hope that Ava will feel the same sense of family pride as she one day looks across the dining room table at us.

> *For the LORD grants wisdom!*
> *From his mouth come knowledge and understanding.* (PROVERBS 2:6)

I'm praying that together we can revive an old-fashioned trait. Will you join me and lead a discussion with your family on the concept of family honor?

WHAT DOES IT LOOK LIKE?
Selfless Devotion

NOT LONG AGO my sleep-deprived daughter, sporting spit-up on her blouse, looked me straight in the eye and said, "No one told me it was going to be this hard." I just looked at her and blinked. The "no one" she was referring to was me. Uh-oh.

After she left, I basked in self-pride. I must have made motherhood look so easy. But then I became confused. Wait . . . how could she not know this is sometimes very hard? Had she not seen selfless devotion for these past thirty years?

Well, of course she had; but like most of us, she didn't know what she was looking at.

Our recognition of selfless devotion is like our relationship with the sun: it comes up every morning without our doing a single thing. We take it for granted, enjoying its light and relishing its warmth. But even though it's a constant in our lives, we rarely really "see" it. Only the occasional spectacular sunrise or sunset gets our attention. And we certainly don't appreciate what's going on in the background. Few of us understand the way our solar system hangs together. No, we give little thought to what it takes for Mr. Sunshine to smile on us every day. It's the same with selfless devotion.

My friend BJ didn't know what it looked like either; not because she took it for granted, but because she had never laid eyes on it. Ever.

When she was a baby, BJ's biological mom gave her away to a woman who worked in a bar, who—when BJ was only fifteen—left BJ alone to raise herself. And somehow, by the grace of God, she did it.

Fast-forward to BJ at the age of forty-six. Prior to a major surgery, BJ began looking for someone to hire to take care of her as she recuperated at home. But a precious friend, who had invited BJ into her family, volunteered her mom, Genny, for the job, insisting that this was the solution to BJ's convalescence needs. Little did BJ know that this would be a close encounter of the selfless kind.

But the Holy Spirit produces this kind of fruit in our lives: love, joy, peace, patience, kindness, goodness, faithfulness, gentleness, and self-control. There is no law against these things! (GALATIANS 5:22-23)

Do you remember the day you realized that you were looking selfless devotion in the eye?

WHAT DOES IT LOOK LIKE?
Selfless Devotion (Part Deux)

MOST CLOSE ENCOUNTERS of the third kind happen at night. BJ's did too.

Late one evening, after BJ got up to go to the restroom, she returned to her bed—but the bed was not as she had left it. BJ held her breath; she was in awe. While BJ was up, Genny had quietly crept into her room to straighten her sheets and blankets . . . and Genny had *fluffed her pillow.* In all her life, BJ had never had anyone fluff her pillow. As BJ told me the story, I could just see this precious little woman padding across the floor to deliver selfless devotion under the cover of night. But unlike the rest of us who have had our pillows fluffed since the day we were born, BJ knew what she was looking at. It was like she was looking at the sun for the very first time.

I know that many of you, my girlfriends, are young mothers who are just learning the ropes—and I'm sure there are days when you're overwhelmed (as we all were). As you sacrifice your physical, material, and emotional needs for those of your child, I hope you will take time to think about and thank your own mom. As imperfect as she might have been, she also sacrificed for you—even if you didn't notice all that was going on in her solar system, behind her eyes . . . and in her heart. There were sacrifices I'm sure she made, even if you didn't know what you were seeing. And you, too, will sacrifice for your child.

And I am praying that you will put into action the generosity that comes from your faith as you understand and experience all the good things we have in Christ. (PHILEMON 1:6)

Shauna will make mothering look easy; so much so that Ava probably won't know it's selfless devotion that she's looking at either. And one day, thirty years from now, Shauna can think of her own good answer when Ava says, "No one told me it was going to be this hard."

WHAT DOES IT LOOK LIKE?
Genuine Respect

"DON'T USE THAT tone with me, young lady." If there's a female child in your life and she's old enough to talk, there's a good chance you've had the opportunity to use this line. If you haven't—well, clearly she has not yet entered puberty.

Respect. Most of us expect our children to respect us. But can they define it? Do our children know what it means because we've shown them? Or do we simply demand it of them?

I define respect as an attitude of gratitude and the discipline of self-control. With the exception of a couple of hormonal outbursts when she was a preteen, our daughter, Shauna, has always been respectful. And now it's my turn to return the favor. You see, genuine respect is a two-way street, and the respect I want Ava to see is the attitude of gratitude I have toward her parents. I had a good role model for this one; I know what it looks like because my Mammaw showed me.

As I've shared with you in previous Truth Nuggets, my mom struggled with substance abuse as the result of mental illness. As a child I idolized her, but as I grew older, her *issues* became a source of embarrassment for me. By the age of fifteen, my respect-o-meter had hit an all-time low.

Taking my grievances to my grandmother, I ranted and raved. But not once, *not once*, in all my years of Mom-bashing would Mammaw join in. My beautiful gray-haired grandmother would quietly listen and then remind me how much my mother loved me as she gently turned the conversation to a more positive topic. Mammaw modeled for me that respect is not only something a mother hopes to receive from her child but is something a mother also returns.

Let's face it. We're a critical bunch. Even if those in our family are highly honorable people, we still find fault with them. And, worse, we voice that displeasure in front of our wee ones.

> Then keep your tongue from speaking evil
>   and your lips from telling lies!
> Turn away from evil and do good.
>   Search for peace, and work to maintain it. (PSALM 34:13-14)

Consider your words carefully. Do not use them to tear others down.

WHAT DOES IT LOOK LIKE?
Genuine Respect (Part Deux)

I KNOW THAT this topic cuts close to the bone for those of you who have been on the receiving end of negative comments from a parent or an in-law. You know firsthand the pain this inflicts, not only on you, but on your child. You've sat with your little one on your lap trying to explain why Grandma said those "mean words" about you. It's hard. And confusing.

When anyone uses harsh or hurtful words toward you, particularly about the way you parent, you're likely to be confused about your role and how you are to react. Negative talk about any family member completely undermines the philosophy of respect. Because some of you were hurt, you understand this intangible of genuine respect at a gut level, and most likely you model it well for the children you influence.

Every word out of our mouths has an impact on our children's lives. Snide comments, hurtful teasing, and unreasonable criticism can destroy their respect for us as well. I heard a story not long ago from a lady who told me that her grown daughter had asked her teenage daughter why she was so angry toward her paternal grandmother. The teenager, even as a child, had always been distant and reserved with her grandmother, and the mother was hoping to inspire her to be more respectful. But the teenager came clean: "Mom, when I was little, Grandma would say the meanest things about you. I told her once, 'Stop talking bad about my mommy.'"

Try spinning the philosophy of genuine respect to a teenager when something like this happened ten years ago. The teenager refused to discuss the topic of respecting her grandmother.

> Those who control their tongue will have a long life;
>   opening your mouth can ruin everything. (PROVERBS 13:3)

Every word, every tone is either positive or negative. Nothing is neutral.

WHAT DOES IT LOOK LIKE?
Genuine Respect (Part Trois)

ALTHOUGH AVA is only seven months old as I write this, we have begun to model genuine respect for her.

At the *Sugar Pop* (which is wherever *Sugar* and *Pop* live at the moment), we tell Ava stories as we rock her: we tell her the story of handsome King Adam who found his beautiful Queen Shauna at the Kingdom of Texas Tech in the land of Lubbock, and how on his black Mustang (Ford), he carried her away to build a wonderful castle. And in this castle they lived and laughed and loved—and then were blessed with Princess Ava.

Cinderella and Prince Charming will have nothing on King Adam and Queen Shauna's love story.

As we feed her and rock her and play with her, we tell Ava about the many charming characteristics of King Adam and Queen Shauna—their goodness, their generosity, their kindness, their faith, and their strong work ethic.

Snow White and the Seven Dwarfs will not compare to the wonderful attributes of the Archer Kingdom.

Yes, Ava only hears my babble today, but over the days to come, she will learn this one cold: she's blessed to have these two awesome human beings as her parents. When she gets fed up with them when she's a teenager, she will know that there will be no Mom- or Dad-bashing at our house.

Give respect and honor to those who are in authority. (ROMANS 13:7)

Learning the ropes of parenting an adult child is not much different from parenting a newborn; it's all trial and error. We make it up as we go along, sometimes without thinking of the greater consequences of our actions. But today I am thinking. And I'm thinking that what I say or don't say will have a lasting impact on Ava Lynn's understanding of genuine respect. And because I have something good to say, I'm going to take the time to say it.

WHAT DOES IT LOOK LIKE?
Work/Life Balance

AS I WRITE this morning, I am completely overwhelmed. Standing in the middle of my three-ring circus of family, work, and personal pursuits, I have moved from my favorite role of ringmaster (I love being in charge) to the lady riding bareback on the white pony (preparing for a huge client presentation) . . . while performing a courageous act with the tigers (completing the manuscript for my book) . . . in my clown suit (while babysitting Ava). Before noon today I will have performed every role in my personal crazy circus. *And I love it.*

Loving the fact that I'm overwhelmed probably seems counterintuitive—or just sick. But for those of us who have learned what work/life balance is, it makes perfect sense. And this is what I want Ava to see: that work/life balance doesn't mean sacrificing things as much as it means loving the acts we're allowed to play. Work/life balance is not something you do or don't do; it's about the enthusiasm with which you greet your roles.

Shauna was six and her brother, Scott, was three when I worked two part-time jobs and took sixteen-hour semester loads in college. Complicating the situation was the terms of my academic scholarship, which allowed me only one B per year. I was focused, driven, and super-organized.

My schedule was as perfectly timed as the finest trapeze artist's—up at 5:00 a.m. and to bed at midnight. In between my two jobs we carpooled, did homework and housework, and because money was very tight, cooked all meals from scratch. For early-evening fun, we often jumped on our trampoline—until I pinched a nerve in my back doing a flip. Yes, I was a walking, talking lunatic.

But I wouldn't trade one minute of that exhausting life stage. Why? *Because I had something to be enthusiastic about.* I loved my role as mother. I loved my role as student. And I loved my roles as teacher's aide and piano teacher. Were those days hard? Yes, of course. But I softened my mental load by spending more time celebrating my life at that moment than I did lamenting about how hard tomorrow would be.

And it is a good thing to receive wealth from God and the good health to enjoy it. To enjoy your work and accept your lot in life—this is indeed a gift from God. God keeps such people so busy enjoying life that they take no time to brood over the past. (ECCLESIASTES 5:19-20)

Work/life balance? My enthusiasm made me immune to the concept.

WHAT DOES IT LOOK LIKE?
Work/Life Balance (Part Deux)

We act as though comfort and luxury were the chief requirements in life, when all that we need to make us really happy is something to be enthusiastic about.
CHARLES KINGSLEY

BUT A DAY was coming when I would be plagued by the conflict of work/life balance.

Fast-forward eleven years. Balancing a long commute with two teenagers and a demanding career in a Fortune 500 company wasn't that hard either—until I lost my wonder for it all.

Spending nearly three hours in the car every day, becoming less important to my children, and realizing that the top rung of the ladder was not where I wanted to be caused my excitement for all things from work to family to wane. And with waning comes complaining.

It's not that my circus performance was any more difficult than it was in my young-mom days, because it wasn't harder—just different. My conflict began to occur because I failed to be entertained by any of my own acts.

Work/life balance? I grappled with the topic for about six months and then realized that I seriously needed an attitude adjustment. I realized that for me, work/life balance was more about what was in my head than what was on my to-do list.

As Ava grows, she'll watch her Sugar run a marketing company (she comes to the office with me on Mondays). She'll sit with me as I craft Truth Nuggets and blog to my girlfriends all over the world. She will watch me as I write books, and I will send her pictures as I travel to faraway countries. She will watch me balance my priorities as I love her Pop and invest time to play with her each Monday. And although there are lots of acts going on in my circus, I will show her that work/life balance is not as much about the number of rings in our circus as it is about the pure rush of climbing on that pony.

You thrill me, LORD, with all you have done for me!
I sing for joy because of what you have done. (PSALM 92:4)

Could you use more excitement in your circus?

WHAT DOES IT LOOK LIKE?
Considerate Inclusion

We may have all come on different ships, but we're in the same boat now.
MARTIN LUTHER KING JR.

EVERY SATURDAY MORNING, Steve and I hop on our bikes for our ten-mile ride around White Rock Lake. The small city lake and park are a Dallas treasure. It's a fabulous place. Lots of trees, picnic areas, running and biking trails, squirrels, ducks, sailboats, and people. Lots of people.

People in cars. People on foot. People with strollers. People on bikes. People on skates. Alone. Together. Sometimes with kids. Sometimes with dogs. Sometimes with dogs and kids and on skates. It's a fabulous place.

Everyone is accepted—people in good moods and people who are fussy. The friendly people take the hateful ones in stride, and the cranky people (usually on fast bikes) somehow manage to pull every ounce of patience together in order to get around the lake without running over anyone.

I hear people speaking languages I've never heard, walking along in brightly colored sarongs and plastic flip-flops. The women are laughing. I don't get the joke, but I get the joy. We smile at one another.

I smell fajitas being grilled as people celebrate the weekend with their families. They're cheering, in Spanish, as a little fellow finally takes off on his two-wheeler for the first time. I remember the jubilation.

Although our native tongues and clothes are different, we're not so far apart in what we value. A good joke. Laughing with our girlfriends. Encouraging our children. A sizzling fajita!

If you love only those who love you, what reward is there for that? Even corrupt tax collectors do that much. (MATTHEW 5:46)

I want Ava to see that considerate inclusion is forgetting about what makes us different and remembering those things we have in common. And learning to love those who may not love us first.

WHAT DOES IT LOOK LIKE?
Considerate Inclusion (Part Deux)

AS WE CONTINUE our ride around the lake, I watch twentysomething women in teensy-weensy shorts and halter tops jogging (without sweating) as they look for tonight's date. They laugh together at something a young hunk-of-a-man just said in passing. I remember flirting.

I marvel at the seventysomething people, lean and tan, looking like they've run a thousand miles. They laugh at everything because they know something we don't. I remember that laugh from my grandmother.

I barely see the Lance Armstrong wannabes as they whiz by on their bikes like a bullet train. They're not *all* high strung. As they pass me on my left, I hear them laugh as they share a story about something that happened at the office. I think of *my* office mates and smile.

People of all ages—newborn to nearly dead. People of all ethnicities—plain white to midnight and every shade in between. People of all sizes—short, tall, thin, very thin, heavy, very heavy. It's a fabulous place.

And this is what I want Ava to see. A world where *everyone* is welcome to laugh, to love, and to be loved.

I want Ava to see that considerate inclusion is the opposite of isolation; considerate inclusion means meeting people on common ground where we *all* experience life. It's learning to belong to the human race by engaging in life alongside others—even if we're not involved in their conversation. It's learning, through the expression of respectful interest, about those whose cultures and religions are different from our own; and it's learning to be respectful of one another, even when our value systems don't perfectly align.

So now, come back to your God. Act with love and justice, and always depend on him. (HOSEA 12:6)

In Dallas, as in most towns and cities across the country, we still usually localize and live among our own. But on Saturday mornings at White Rock Lake, we come together. Everyone is welcome. And I can't wait to take Ava. It's a fabulous place.

WHAT DOES IT LOOK LIKE?
Considerate Inclusion (Part Trois)

Life is not measured by the number of breaths we take, but by the moments that take our breath away. ANONYMOUS

RECENTLY OUR REGULARLY scheduled weekend routine was interrupted by life, so we missed our weekend bike ride. To get back on track with our exercise routine, Steve and I opted for an early morning ride around White Rock Lake that Monday. But it was a totally different scene from Saturday mornings.

At the crack of dawn on Monday morning there were no people! Just Steve, me, and an occasional biker or runner. But still there were the trees and water and swans and ducks and squirrels and clouds and . . . a sunrise. Yes, just as on Saturdays with all of its hustle and bustle, the park is still a fabulous place on Monday mornings.

As I rode that early morn through God's creation, I was reminded ever so gently how he has considerately included me in his world.

On that morning, the holy Creator, who blew the thin, wispy white clouds over the rising sun to make a miraculous sunrise, considerately placed me on the west side of the lake to behold his artistic design.

A few miles down the biking path, the holy Creator, who placed the glorious bald cypress tree near the bank of the water, considerately drew my attention to it to take in its majesty. I had passed that tree a hundred times but had never taken the time to realize that I was included among its admirers.

Around the bend, the holy Creator, who designed the black prissy duck that walked flirtatiously onto the running trail, considerately placed me three feet away so that I could be entertained and tickled pink by her. That morning, God included me in the front row of her audience.

And as I was nearing the end of my ride, the holy Creator, the God of the universe with his crazy sense of humor who created this goofy little creature we call a squirrel, motivated that little dickens to dart out in front of me while I was pedaling my bike at 20 mph. He placed that squirrel in my path to remind me that I'm not in charge. I thank him for the reminder and for considerately including an excellent braking mechanism on my bike.

For ever since the world was created, people have seen the earth and sky. Through everything God made, they can clearly see his invisible qualities—his eternal power and divine nature. So they have no excuse for not knowing God.
(ROMANS 1:20)

So what do I want Ava to see as it relates to considerate inclusion? I want her to know that we are to be examples of considerate inclusion because our Maker has so considerately included us in his creation.

SEPTEMBER 23

WHAT DOES IT LOOK LIKE?
Considerate Inclusion (Part Quatre)

Patience is something you admire in the driver behind you, but not in one ahead.
BILL MCGLASHEN

I WAS SO CONVICTED this week when I realized how inconsiderate I often am with others. How easily I exclude those who are s . . . l . . . o . . . w.

I'm always in a hurry. As hard as I try to slow down, I just can't. I walk fast. I talk fast. I drive fast. I ride my bicycle fast. But I'm terribly slow when it comes to learning important lessons about patience. I have no problem with patience when it comes to things or circumstances—just people. I now realize that this is actually a form of inconsiderate exclusion. Considerate inclusion must be extended to those who think and operate at a slower rate than we do. And this is where I sometimes act like a jerk.

It started one Saturday morning—on my bicycle. Steve and I were pedaling pretty fast when we came upon five people, walking together slowly, on the path around the lake. The problem was—they took up the whole doggone lane! As our brakes locked and tires squealed, I managed to yell "On your left!" in such a rude tone that I embarrassed myself.

On Wednesday, the Lord blessed with me another opportunity to show considerate inclusion to a waitress who was slow, whose computer system was down, and who was not exactly a Winston Churchill–type communicator. I failed the test, as I mumbled through gritted teeth, "Give me the check, here's the cash, keep the change." I got out of the restaurant, but I can't say I was satisfied—especially with my personal lack of considerate inclusion for this young woman who was slow.

But if nothing else, the Lord is persistent! On Sunday, Steve and I, running a bit late for church, were walking briskly in the 100-degree heat from the parking lot (me in heels). As we got to the steps, we had to slow to a crawl as we followed a homeless man, shuffling in his flip-flops, into our church foyer. As I watched the faces of our congregation and church leaders smile at the man and welcome him—dirty clothes, tangled hair, and all—I can't tell you how blessed I was to be walking slowly behind him. Seeing the considerate inclusion of this poor soul by our well-heeled congregation made me so proud of who we are as Christians.

May God, who gives this patience and encouragement, help you live in complete harmony with each other, as is fitting for followers of Christ Jesus.
(ROMANS 15:5)

It took three tries and a whole week, but God finally got my attention: there is a blessing in the patience and in the considerate inclusion we extend to those who move at a slower pace. Sometimes we just need to walk behind them.

SEPTEMBER 24

WHAT DOES IT LOOK LIKE?
Family Traditions

I knew I belonged to the public and to the world, not because I was talented or even beautiful, but because I had never belonged to anything or anyone else.
MARILYN MONROE

BELONGING. Some of us read that word and feel connected and safe. We know we are a member of a tribe—either a family or community (for some folks, their friends *are* their family)—and our participation in traditions comes naturally. But for others of us, the word *belonging* conjures up nothing but feelings of aloneness and vulnerability. Wouldn't it be great to break the cycle and establish family traditions for our future generations?

I'll be the first to admit that when it came to developing family traditions, I wasn't the most creative cat in the barn. What few traditions we established when the kids were young mostly centered around food: tamales and chili on Christmas Eve (after church), Saturday morning McMillers (our much-improved family version of the Egg McMuffin), sausage balls on Thanksgiving morning (Shauna has picked up this torch and carries it nicely), and herb-crusted beef tenderloin on Christmas Day (you can count on it). But as I think about our family traditions and about creating a haven for Ava where she knows she belongs, I know in my heart that food alone will not sustain her.

In order for our society to create an environment where our children thrive as part of a greater family unit, grandparents are essential. While Mammaw created traditions for me that provided me with a firm sense of belonging, my children, because their grandmothers were not active participants in their upbringing, didn't enjoy that same sense of inclusion in a larger family unit.

Together, we are his house, built on the foundation of the apostles and the prophets. And the cornerstone is Christ Jesus himself. (EPHESIANS 2:20)

Our mobile culture, with families on the move and the shallow disagreements with extended family, is robbing our children of the one thing they need more than anything else: to belong.

267

WHAT DOES IT LOOK LIKE?
Family Traditions (Part Deux)

I HAVE LEARNED about the deeper meaning of family traditions from my Jewish friends.

By participating in their celebration of the bar mitzvah and bat mitzvah, I realized that many of us fail to use traditions as an important teaching tool to pass on our family's social values, our sense of family identity, historical understanding of our family heritage, and spiritual values—both personally and historically.

My friends Gary and Linda invited Steve and me to attend their son Alex's bar mitzvah a few years ago. We were in total awe at the poise and grace this gangly thirteen-year-old demonstrated as he led his congregation through the service, speaking and singing *in Hebrew*. I didn't understand a word of what he said, but I sure understood the significance at the end: Alex knew he belonged to something much greater than just Alex. Oh, to teach that critical lesson to all our children!

I visited with Stephen, a friend of mine, a few weeks ago on the topic of his sons' bar mitzvahs. I wanted to better understand the meaning, commitment, investment, and preparation required behind this religious, cultural, and family tradition. He said, "At the core, we want our children to understand what it means to be Jewish and to recognize their responsibilities to the faith, their rich history, and the culture." As he shared the story of his younger son's struggle during his study, his eyes welled with tears of pride when he said, "But his presentation and d'rash [interpretation] were perfect. It made me almost want to have another kid." Now, when your thirteen-year-old son makes you so proud you want to start over, that's saying something!

Which led me to ask myself, *What family traditions do we have that challenge our children to think, to learn, to lead, and to reflect?* What experiences do we share with them to explore our family heritage and the connection to our belief system?

I want Ava to have that same sense of confidence and security in her faith, her family, and her culture that my Jewish friends have passed on to their children. In addition to sharing vacations as an extended family and eating an occasional McMiller with her, I want to invest the time and mental energy to create other family traditions that I hope will help Ava better understand who we are, where we came from, what we believe in, and *why*. All with the hope that one day she will know that she is connected to something much greater than just herself.

So it is with Christ's body. We are many parts of one body, and we all belong to each other. (ROMANS 12:5)

So what do I want Ava to see? That without a doubt, she belongs to our tribe.

WHAT DOES IT LOOK LIKE?
Family Traditions (Part Trois)

I figure all any kid needs is hope and the feeling he or she belongs. ELVIS PRESLEY

I KNOW I'M NOT ALONE in this. Surely other mothers and grandmothers out there are curious about how to create family traditions that provide our children and grandchildren a sense of belonging and, so importantly, a sense of who they are.

As I mentioned, when my children were younger, we didn't create many significant traditions to teach our family history, social values, or connection to our faith. As a young working mother, just getting the turkey on the table was a challenge! But I'm older now, with a lot less on my mind, which has given me time to create and plan traditions that I hope will cement Ava's sense of belonging.

Ava was three weeks old on her first Christmas Eve when she received the first installment of a new family tradition—a membership to the Sugar and Ava Book Club. In this book club, Ava will receive from me, every birthday and every Christmas, a book that was significant to me when I was her age. We will read this book together, sharing the valuable lessons experienced by the characters. Can you imagine the fun we will have doing this when Ava is ten years old? And when she's thirty, do you not think she will still enjoy the sharing of a wonderful story with her grandmother? And by the time Ava turns fifty, I imagine it will be Ava who will be gifting the books to her grandchild.

In the beginning God created the heavens and the earth. (GENESIS 1:1)

Yes, Ava will know that she belongs and what value systems we share through the reading of our books. What are you reading with your grandchildren?

WHAT DOES IT LOOK LIKE?
Family Traditions (Part Quatre)

BUT BOOKS ARE NOT the only trick in my family tradition bag.

Ava will receive her next family tradition on her first birthday. I began a project for my godson in 2006 that I plan to continue for Ava Lynn. Taking well-known Bible stories from both the Old and New Testament, I have written what I call biblical Truth Nuggets. Essentially, I personalize the teachings for the children by explaining the stories in plain terms. I discuss how their faith will be tested at school, how their witness will be a positive or a negative influence for their friends, and how their every decision is a reflection of their character. Ava's Truth Nuggets will make Bible stories not only understandable but *personally* relevant. Ava will know that she belongs, and she will know what spiritual insights we share through the learning of our faith.

The most recent tradition I created was delivered to Shauna on her first Mother's Day. This gift, which I call our family heritage album, is to be handed down to every daughter or son when he or she becomes a parent on his or her first Mother's or Father's Day. I wrote a short story, introducing our future generations to their ancestors, beginning with Martha Jane Anne Dishner Sanford, my great-grandmother. Accompanying her story are a number of pictures, including one of her on her wedding day when she was eighteen years old and another taken a few months before her death at the age of ninety-six. I did the same for my grandmother and my mother and then inserted pictures of me. My story is blank—to be written by Shauna upon my death. And so on, and so on. Ava and her grandchildren will be able to see five or more generations of women—women whose same blood runs through their veins.

But I lavish unfailing love for a thousand generations on those who love me and obey my commands. (EXODUS 20:6)

Yep, Ava will know that she belongs and maybe even where she got her sense of humor or chubby thighs as she flips through her Blessings of Generations family album.

WHAT DOES IT LOOK LIKE?
Mindful Appreciation

Who and what we love defines us. ALEXANDRA STODDARD

THE ECONOMY STINKS; grocery prices are up; stock values are down.

The world is at war; children are starving; our ice caps are melting. Things have gotten so bad I feel like I need to take an antidepressant before I turn on the news.

But I don't want Ava to see me negatively influenced by what's wrong in the world. When it comes to mindful appreciation, I want Ava to see that the things we should be most grateful for, the things that bring us the most joy—are things that have nothing to do with the economy, our jobs, crime, or even the weather. I was reminded of this lesson last year by two little sweethearts in California.

While I was visiting with my girlfriend Stacie and her husband, Lewis, we sat down for a beautifully prepared dinner. The children sat patiently waiting for their dad to come to the table and ask the discussion question of the evening. That night's question was, "Girls, what are you most thankful for today?" Caroline, age six, and Samantha, age four, both exclaimed that they were most thankful that Aunt E had come to visit them. As they went on to ask the blessing for the food, they extended mindful appreciation for the people, not the things, in their lives.

From "out of the mouth of babes" I was reminded that we can't buy happiness—we can't even rent it. So why do we allow the negativity of the world or work or life situations to rob us of appreciation for the things that really do bring us personal joy? Inspired by those two giggly cherubs, I started my personal joy list on the plane ride home:

1. Listening to music
2. Sitting outside (when it's not 106 degrees)
3. Crocheting a gift
4. Laughing with my friends
5. Watching the sun set

And the list goes on . . . Because there is so much in our world that's not right, I believe we must be extra diligent to observe all the things in our lives that *are* right. We must acknowledge those things and people that bring us true joy.

> *Let all that I am praise the LORD;*
>   *with my whole heart, I will praise his holy name.*
> *Let all that I am praise the LORD;*
>   *may I never forget the good things he does for me.* (PSALM 103:1-2)

So what will mindful appreciation look like to Ava? A long list of blessings that Sugar adds to every day. And what do you think my blessing number 199 is? Holding Ava while she sleeps.

WHAT DOES IT LOOK LIKE?
Mindful Appreciation (Part Deux)

GROWING UP, I had no concept of economic classes. I knew some folks had some things I didn't, and I knew that it was because we didn't have enough money to purchase them. I had no idea, however, that we were poor!

Fast-forward to the days when my kids were in high school. One year we remodeled our home. That same year we bought a new car (we usually bought used), *and* we went on a family vacation. One afternoon, Scott mentioned a video game he wanted, and I gave the pat mother answer, "We'll see."

Then he asked, "Why can't we get it now? We're rich."

Really? I knew that financially things were easier for us than my family growing up, but I had no idea we were rich!

Though my family's financial position today is more secure than in my childhood when material things were few and far between, nothing has really changed for me when it comes to mindful appreciation. I credit my parents and grandmother for this attitude.

During the Great Depression, my dad and his former wife raised three kids. During that difficult time, my mother, not yet a teenager, watched her family struggle. Both my parents experienced extreme hardships during this era, but neither were bitter. Like everyone, they buckled down and did without. When they did receive the basics like a small job or meat to go with their dinner, they were grateful. And I've seen this same scenario play out over the past year.

As a volunteer at our local homeless center, I work in the assembly line filling plates. I have never seen people more grateful for food. Hungry people have mindful appreciation for a cup of fruit cocktail.

When I drop off our household items and clothing at LifeNet, I know I have never seen people more grateful for my castoffs. Poor people have mindful appreciation for a warm coat and cookie sheets.

And as I walk beside my girlfriend Karen, who is grieving the loss of her young husband, I realize I have never seen a person more grateful for the people in her life. Those who have lost much have mindful appreciation for what they still have.

> *I give thanks, O LORD, with all my heart;*
> *I will sing your praises before the gods.*
> *I bow before your holy Temple as I worship.*
> *I praise your name for your unfailing love and faithfulness;*
> *for your promises are backed by all the honor of your name.* (PSALM 138:1-2)

Do I want Ava to be poor or to lose someone she loves? Of course not. But I didn't live through the Depression, and Steve is still alive and well. So it will be up to our family to show Ava mindful appreciation, just as the grieving and poor model it for us.

WHAT DOES IT LOOK LIKE?
Mindful Appreciation (Part Trois)

Envy comes from people's ignorance of, or lack of belief in, their own gifts.
JEAN VANIER

YEARS AGO, right after Christmas, I went in to see my hairdresser and asked her how her holidays went. She was beside herself! With her scissors flying across the top of my head, she animatedly explained the frustration she felt when every gift that she gave seemed unappreciated by the recipient. Even though she had invested substantial time and money in thinking about and purchasing the gifts, she watched as her gifts were quickly cast aside.

"No, you shouldn't have!" We've all heard someone squeal this as he or she opens our gift. It's a toss-up whether the person is sincere. Does he or she mean, *I love it, but you really shouldn't have gone to this great expense on my behalf?* Or is he or she really thinking, *No, you really shouldn't have bothered at all; I hate this present.* I wonder if we sometimes toss aside our Creator's gifts to us as well.

So often, the talents we've been blessed with are ignored, discarded, or allowed to atrophy as we envy the beauty, the brains, the financial means, or the personality of someone else. Indirectly we are telling God, "No, you shouldn't have. I don't want this gift. I want the ones you gave [fill in the blank]."

I want Ava to mindfully appreciate the gifts her Creator has given her. I want her to see clearly that her talents are unique to God's will for her and her calling as she fulfills her purpose for him.

> *You are the light of the world—like a city on a hilltop that cannot be hidden.*
> (MATTHEW 5:14)

What do I want Ava to see? That mindful appreciation is not just about saying thank you for presents or services; it's about saying thank you for the things that didn't cost her or anyone else a dime.

WHAT DOES IT LOOK LIKE?
Working Friendships

I look forward to being older, when looks become less of an issue and what you are is the point. SUSAN SARANDON

FOR OVER TWENTY-FIVE YEARS, my grandmother and eight other silver-haired women gathered at one another's homes every other Saturday night for an evening of Forty-Two. This domino game is played much like a card game and includes winning bids and tricks. Only an occasional ice storm every three to five years would deter the gathering of the Forty-Two Club.

From my childhood through my teenage years, I was called upon every ninth week to help Mammaw serve finger sandwiches, Fritos and onion dip, Creek Water iced tea, and homemade lemon icebox pie. This role helped hone my hostess skills, but more importantly, it allowed me to observe what it takes to build lasting friendships.

Mammaw and the gals demonstrated that in order for the game of friendship to work, you had to be willing to play both sides of the table. Otherwise the friendship would become superficial and lack the necessary depth. Mammaw and her girlfriends showed me that to have a network that works you must be willing to invest a generous portion of give-and-take.

I think most of us are pretty good at playing the hand in friendship that is all take—where our problems trump everyone else's and everyone else must fold to placate our moods.

But we all know that all take and no give is not a long-term winning strategy. We might feel better because we won one hand, but what about the game—twenty-five years from now?

So whatever you say or whatever you do, remember that you will be judged by the law that sets you free. (JAMES 2:12)

Do you have a long-term friendship strategy, or are you playing only for today?

WHAT DOES IT LOOK LIKE?
Working Friendships (Part Deux)

EVERY TWO MONTHS, I heard the sidesplitting laughter during those Forty-Two matches when one of the gals told a joke. Even if it wasn't funny or they had just heard it two weeks before, they roared with laughter. I saw the twinkle in their eyes as they ribbed a partner who had made a bad play, but I don't remember ever hearing anything that resembled sarcasm or ridicule.

I remember hearing them celebrate for one another, and their families, at a simple life win. There wasn't a self-centered one in the bunch; each of these women expressed great interest in the lives of others.

And you can imagine that nine women meeting together twenty-six times a year for twenty-five years (including the years they were going through menopause) had to do a whole lot of forgiving and forgetting.

I watched them age—the salt and pepper turning all salt; the buttermilk skin slowly becoming etched with beautiful laugh lines. But it didn't matter to the Forty-Two Club. What they looked like was never the issue, because who they were was the point.

Over the years, canes and walkers became their companions to the event. As I grew older, I saw them comfort one another as they attended funerals together; first husbands, then—one by one—the members of the Forty-Two Club themselves. They are all gone now, but their legacy lives on.

My girlfriends and I don't play Forty-Two (although if one of them has her way, we're *going* to have game night!), and if we're gray, you'll never know it. As long as Avalon Salon is open, most of us will die blonde. But we will be women of purpose and character; we will be women who laugh, celebrate, banter, and mourn with one another. And like the Forty-Two Club, we will forgive and move on. And we will age. Together.

There is no greater love than to lay down one's life for one's friends.
(JOHN 15:13)

And that's what I want Ava to see: a network of girlfriends—that works. And how to make a lemon icebox pie.

WHAT DOES IT LOOK LIKE?
Marriage Partnership

MY FRIENDS often ask me where my inspiration for my series comes from. Most of the time, I'm either running or biking and a thought comes to me. But often someone will say something or ask me a question that makes me catch my breath. The title of this series, "What Does It Look Like?" came from a brief encounter with a total stranger.

A woman in her early forties took the seat next to mine for a flight from Dallas to Orange County, California. She was on her mobile phone as she walked up the aisle, and she stayed on it until we took off. Once in the air, as I was digging into my work, she pointed to my left hand and, without introduction, said, "I like your ring. I used to have one of those." I glanced at her naked left hand and knew that, for whatever reason, she needed to talk. To me.

I asked her about her lost love, and she shared the sad tale. As she concluded, she asked about my marriage. "How is it going?" When I told her I was married to my best friend and that I was still on my honeymoon after eighteen years, she said, "I don't know what that looks like."

My seatmate went on to tell me that her parents were married, miserably, for over forty years. Distant bitterness, manipulation, and verbal abuse seemed to be the primary themes of her parents' marriage. She had never seen a healthy relationship.

As I took in her story and looked into her sad eyes, my heart wept for this perfect stranger . . . and for all of us. So many of us muddle through our lives without the knowledge and example of what a marriage can be and should be: a fabulous union.

Now may the God of peace—who brought up from the dead our Lord Jesus, the great Shepherd of the sheep, and ratified an eternal covenant with his blood— may he equip you with all you need for doing his will. (HEBREWS 13:20-21)

Did you have good role models? More importantly for your children and grandchildren, are you and your spouse good role models?

WHAT DOES IT LOOK LIKE?
Marriage Partnership (Part Deux)

AFTER MY NEW CONFIDANTE shared her story, my mind raced. With thirty-nine minutes left in the flight, I was unsure if I could paint a picture of a healthy marriage for her. However, I knew she was a successful business executive, so I tried to give her a picture of something I thought she could relate to.

A good marriage, I told her, moves to a great marriage when each person *agrees* to an equal partnership. There should be no Alpha Dog or victim in a marriage partnership. Virginia Satir, in *The New Peoplemaking*, says it best: "For each person to flourish, each needs psychological permission to be him- or herself, to develop these interests and parts that especially fit. Furthermore, each partner willingly and knowledgeably supports the other in this regard and, in turn, is supported. Each is respected by the other, each is autonomous, and each is unique."[37] Both parties must agree that their opinions are equal in value—and deserve to be heard.

As in a strong business partnership, each person brings his or her own gifts and talents to complement and augment the other. My personal theory is that successful relationships, in work or marriage, occur when a "how" person teams up with a "what" person. In our marriage and in our business, I'm the "what" person; I come up with the ideas. Steve is better at operations than me—a "how" person, he figures out (a) if the "what" can be done and (b) importantly, how to do it. Two "whats" or two "hows" often struggle in business or love.

A business will not thrive if one person is left to carry the workload—physically, mentally, or emotionally. Sometimes one of the business partners will be "off his or her game," so the other partner picks up the slack until the distracted partner gets his or her second wind. It's never a 50/50 workload, in business or in marriage. Sometimes you carry the load; sometimes you *are* the load.

An enthusiastic business partner with a vision for the future makes it stronger. So it is in marriage. Each person should appreciate the other's vision and dreams, knowing that a highly engaged partner makes the business (or marriage, in this case) stronger. Without growth and enthusiasm for goals, partnerships atrophy.

In healthy business environments, teammates dignify their partners with their tone of speech and attitude of respect. Barking orders, ridiculing, and giving the silent treatment are not condoned (at least not in my workplace). A marriage partnership might survive under these circumstances, but it will never flourish.

A wise woman builds her home,
but a foolish woman tears it down with her own hands. (PROVERBS 14:1)

When I finished speaking, my new girlfriend looked at me skeptically. I'm not sure if she got the picture or not. But Ava will. Because at thirty thousand feet, a total stranger pointed out to me that children must see our philosophies and value system in action in order to believe them.

WHAT DOES IT LOOK LIKE?
Marriage Partnership (Part Trois)

I've learned that people will forget what you said, people will forget what you did, but people will never forget how you made them feel. MAYA ANGELOU

AS I VISITED with my traveling companion, she admitted that, not only had her husband degraded her, she had not so kindly returned the favor.

My question for you is, how do you make your husband feel by the tone of your voice, the content of your words, and your day-to-day interactions with him?

Do you bark commands—"Close the door!"—making him feel like a child?
Do you give him the cold shoulder, making him feel that he's not loved?
Do you make decisions without his input, making him feel like a second-rate citizen of the family?
Do you repeatedly cut him off—"Shut up!"—making him feel that his opinion or comments are not valued?
Do you withhold sex, making him feel that he is loved and cared for only conditionally?
Do you mock him, correct him, or ridicule him in front of others, making him feel embarrassed?

Now on the flip side: based on his tone, words, and day-to-day interactions with you, how do you allow him to make *you* feel?

When he gives you the silent treatment, do you feel unloved, or do you turn on your favorite rock 'n' roll to reset a good vibe in the house?
When he is rude to your sister, do you seethe, or do you provide him with the scenario of how he would feel if you treated his family the same way?
When he makes decisions without your input, do you get your feelings hurt, or do you immediately take the opportunity to weigh in on the decision?
When he tells you to "shut up"—do you? Or do you explain that you are his marriage partner and refuse to be spoken to that way and in that tone?
When he withholds sex . . . never mind, that will never happen.
When he mocks or corrects you, do you wallow in the hurt, or do you calmly confront the issue?

A servant of the Lord must not quarrel but must be kind to everyone, be able to teach, and be patient with difficult people. (2 TIMOTHY 2:24)

How do you make your husband feel? And how do you allow him to make you feel? When one of you has passed on, all the things said and done will fade away. All you will remember is how the other person made you feel.

WHAT DOES IT LOOK LIKE?
Marriage Partnership (Part Quartre)

Love at first sight is easy to understand; it's when two people have been looking at each other for a lifetime that it becomes a miracle. AMY BLOOM

A GENTLEMAN SAT with me in a conference room waiting for his peers and staff to join us for a meeting. As we exchanged pleasantries, he mentioned he was going on vacation the next week. Knowing he had a family, I inquired if he and his wife were going alone or were taking the children. This was a family vacation, he said.

But then something flashed across his face and he added, "Maybe my wife and I should schedule something alone. It's like we've become roommates."

About five years into a marriage, the perfect storm arises: our schedules get busy, our lives become complicated, and our libidos diminish. Day-to-day survival is all we can manage, and we fall into a rut—two ships passing in the driveway. The romance dissolves.

While the kids were growing up, Steve and I allowed ourselves four days, every other year, to vacation. Alone.

Our time away always included a romantic dinner; an adventure; new discoveries; and a time to talk—uninterrupted. As a result, we fell more deeply in love.

Ava is eight months old as I write this, and her parents are planning their first four-day rekindling vacation. The stresses of caring for a firstborn and managing challenging careers and hectic schedules will be left in Dallas. While on their Portland rendezvous, Shauna and Adam will look at each other with new eyes—and fall in love all over again.

I ask you again, does God give you the Holy Spirit and work miracles among you because you obey the law? Of course not! It is because you believe the message you heard about Christ. (GALATIANS 3:5)

Although Ava won't know what she's looking at this year, she will in years to come: she'll witness the miracle of rekindled love.

WHAT DOES IT LOOK LIKE?
Successful Divorce

We can't fall off the face of the earth or destroy or get away from all we had yesterday.
We need to include and integrate the things that belong to yesterday.   VIRGINIA SATIR

AS I CLOSE this series on those things I want Ava to see, my heart is full because of the beautiful examples others have lived out for me. The intangibles that contribute to living intentionally are not mystic philosophies; most have been modeled for me with brilliance. I have even seen a "successful" divorce.

Now hear me out: I'm not saying that divorce is a good thing. But I believe that, depending on how two former spouses interact, they can model a "successful" divorce.

My husband, Steve, was raised by two of the most exceptional human beings I have ever met. I am among the most blessed to have in-laws who are not only highly honorable individuals, but who truly consider me their own daughter. You'll never hear an ugly in-law joke from me; I couldn't be more loved or accepted.

What's truly remarkable about them is that Harriett and Al have not lived together for many years. They divorced when Steve was thirteen years old. The separation could have ended the family unit, and for a while, it did. But Harriett and Al realized something few parents get: even though they had separated from each other, they understood that neither should punish Steve by separating from him. For two decades, I have watched Harriett and Al unfailingly treat one another with respect around our dining room table.

At every holiday I set places for Al, Harriett, and Harriett's husband, Dean. Harriett and Al, always kind, thoughtful, and respectful, converse and "rib" one another like old friends. Steve's stepfather, Dean, is equally gracious as the three of them stroll down memory lane. No tension. No judgment. No passive-aggressive behavior. Just joy for the here and now and a respectful remembrance of yesterday. Time does heal—if we will just *allow* it.

Harriett and Al, with remarkable class and style, have taught me that parts of yesterday really do belong to today. And that couples who divorce from everything in the past cheat their child. They've shown me that, for the sake of our children and grandchildren, maturity and selflessness must trump past hurts and disappointments.

And Nehemiah continued, "Go and celebrate with a feast of rich foods and sweet drinks, and share gifts of food with people who have nothing prepared. This is a sacred day before our Lord. Don't be dejected and sad, for the joy of the LORD is your strength!" (NEHEMIAH 8:10)

And this is what I want Ava to see as *her* grandparents (all six of us) gather at her dining room table: Maturity. Selflessness. Respect. And joy for the here and now.

WHAT DOES IT LOOK LIKE?

FATHER GOD, I desire to pass on your truths. I ask that you bless me to be a woman who

- [ ] is an example to others of an honorable life;
- [ ] makes good decisions, one decision at a time;
- [ ] learns to use appropriate shame to instill a sense of family pride;
- [ ] delivers selfless devotion under the cover of night;
- [ ] chooses her words wisely in order to model genuine respect;
- [ ] embraces each life stage with enthusiasm;
- [ ] engages in life alongside others—regardless of our differences;
- [ ] remembers that you have considerately included us within your creation;
- [ ] extends patience and inclusion to those who might move at a slower pace;
- [ ] establishes a sense of belonging for my friends and family;
- [ ] appreciates the material things in life, the way poor people do;
- [ ] is mindful of the people and things that bring us the *real* joy;
- [ ] remembers that my talents are gifts from you;
- [ ] is a blessing to my girlfriends;
- [ ] glorifies you in the way I treat my husband;
- [ ] lives in the joy of here and now.

ACTIONS I WILL TAKE:

Example: When disciplining the children, I will carefully teach and tactfully balance the concepts of shame and family pride.

1. _____

2. _____

3. _____

Father, each and every blessing is sent from you above. Thank you for your goodness and love. Thank you for helping me to be the woman you desire me to be—a woman who is a blessing to future generations. Amen.

DIGGING IN THE DIRT

ALTHOUGH I'M A CITY GIRL today, I wasn't always. My roots run three generations deep in a small Texas town of 777 souls where every house had a front porch; where most every man, woman, and child knew a funny story about my grandmother; and where every family living along our country road had their very own personal vegetable garden. Now, I'm not talking about one of these *sissy* gardens that city folks have, where they grow tomatoes in terra cotta pots. No—I'm talkin' 'bout a *real* garden with *rows and rows and rows* of fresh vegetables.

My dad loved his garden, not just for the bountiful harvest it produced for his family, but for the pleasure he gained in tending something from a tiny seed and working intimately with nature. Although I whined incessantly about picking okra in the 100-degree heat, I loved his garden, too, because it was an activity I could share with him. Little did I know that decades later I would realize another benefit from digging in the dirt: in the garden I gleaned important business principles by walking the rows, planting by the moon, and learning to share our abundance.

> *Abide in Me, and I in you. As the branch cannot bear fruit of itself unless it abides in the vine, so neither can you unless you abide in Me.*
> (JOHN 15:4, NASB)

The cicadas are humming, the tomatoes are ripening, and the green onions are calling out to be pulled. So pull on your garden shoes and come with me to the garden. And bring a grocery sack. It's picking time—and we have business to tend to.

DIGGING IN THE DIRT
Walking the Rows

EVERY EVENING during the summer, just after dinner, my dad would head out to the garden. He'd often invite me to keep him company on his journey as he walked the rows. After years of such meandering, I finally asked him why we toured the garden on such a regular basis. He said, "We can't see the weeds from the kitchen window."

It's the same in our work, is it not? Whether we work in an office—where we're divided by rank, department, or business unit—or at home, where we're usually outnumbered two or three to one, we work independently and sometimes even at cross-purposes to one another. Unintentionally we close ourselves off from others in the name of productivity. We're focused on getting our work done. In reality, our most important contribution might be walking the rows and actually having a conversation. Texting and e-mail are often counterproductive to solving problems.

Regardless of one's job title or experience, walking the rows is critical to identifying weeds. You may have heard of the business concept of "management by walking around." While this is a sound leadership principle, I don't think it should be reserved only for managers. I think we all, regardless of our title or responsibility, should walk the rows and talk to find new ways to solve an age-old problem: effective communication. People don't wake up every morning and go to work with the intention of making your life miserable (although sometimes they're so good at it you swear they must have a graduate degree in the study). Nor do your kids' teachers or your fellow moms in the car pool line spend time plotting a way to get under your skin. No, they're just in the same preservation mode as you.

If you're perplexed by someone's behavior, visit with him or her to learn what is driving that person's decision making. It might give you the fresh insight you need to address problems that everyone else has long given up on. The most successful workers are the ones who are willing to adopt and solve problems that are not necessarily their own or of their own making.

Yes, the body has many different parts, not just one part.
(1 CORINTHIANS 12:14)

When is the last time you stepped out of your cube or your front door and walked the rows?

DIGGING IN THE DIRT
Walking the Rows (Part Deux)

IF YOU ARE a manager, either of a home or a workplace, walking your rows is critical to solving short-term and long-term challenges. You must understand intimately and care deeply about the issues your team faces and be the first to celebrate their victories.

But walking the rows also offers a key benefit to *you*: you will determine who your "what" people are and who your "how" people are. Let me explain. I realized a few years ago that every person is either a "what" person or a "how" person. The "what" people at my company are those who easily identify *what* we need to do for our customers, our firm, and our suppliers. By spending just one day a year strategizing with this team, I discover three to five new services we can offer.

Two weeks after the "what" team meets, it presents its ideas to my *how* team, which is made up of excellent operators. It is the *how* team's job to brainstorm and determine how we will implement the plan, when it can be launched, and what resources (people and budget) it will require to pull off. Most importantly, the people who are doing the work and dealing with the problems are developing the solutions . . . not me. This simple shift in our strategizing has made a huge difference in revenue, profit, productivity, and morale.

The same principle applies at home. The *what* people are the idea generators. Let's say you are a "what" person who points out to your husband that you're not staying as connected with your college-aged children as you'd like. Perhaps your husband is gifted at figuring out the *how*. After consulting with you, he might take the initiative in setting up a family Facebook page, teaching you to "text" on your phone, or arranging to spend a weekend at a hotel near your child's dorm.

But our bodies have many parts, and God has put each part just where he wants it. (1 CORINTHIANS 12:18)

To do this well, either in your home or business, you must recognize who are your "what" people and who are your "how" people. And you do this by walking your rows.

DIGGING IN THE DIRT
Walking the Rows (Part Trois)

REGARDLESS OF OUR INDUSTRY or business type, some issues plague all of us. And one in particular seems to exist everywhere. The average American worker is stressed beyond belief because he or she is burdened by unrealistic expectations from management.

The most effective executives understand that never-ending, excessive expectations demoralize employees and that they'll never get the greatest return from their people if they destroy their self-confidence. The best "coaches" win in their marketplace because they get this concept, whereas their competitors don't. I've seen this occur in both large and small enterprises, but it is particularly the case in publicly held companies where the pressure to make the number each quarter becomes a weed that chokes the creative life out of employees. Wall Street is not going to change, but *how* you communicate with your employees can.

Execs, I challenge you to walk the rows. See your employees' faces; look into their eyes. These are real people who may be giving their all to your organization—even as they're burning out fast. Give them a reason, *besides a paycheck*, to continue to invest their hearts, minds, and bodies in your enterprise. It took me years to get brave enough to do this, but it works: you will win them faster by sharing your own struggle in the fight. It's okay to let them know you're tired, too, but that you continue because you believe in them. Trust me; they'll respond to your honesty and vulnerability, coupled with confidence and leadership, much faster than another disheartening critique.

Of course, the same is true at home. Sure, you may be exasperated because you've noticed your children can hear an ice cream truck six blocks away but never respond to your requests, made from the doorway, to come set the table. Maybe your husband never finds time to repaint the shutters but refuses to miss a televised Sunday afternoon football game. While you have the right to expect family members to contribute to the running of your household, they're likely to respond better to firm but loving requests than to commands yelled from the next room.

For God is working in you, giving you the desire and the power to do what pleases him. (PHILIPPIANS 2:13)

Yes, I know it's hot out there. And, yes, I know you have a lot of work to do in your own office and at home. But you can't see the weeds from there. Come on. It's time we get out from behind our desks (or our kitchens) and walk the rows.

DIGGING IN THE DIRT
Hoeing the Weeds

ONE REQUIREMENT of successful gardening is hoeing the weeds. Regardless of how much I loved to be around my father, I dreaded this aspect of gardening.

But I do remember a time when I was small, maybe six years old, when there was this "hoeing party" at my grandmother's garden. Now, it wasn't a real celebration (no one was laughing and carrying on but us kids), but because my grandmother, parents, aunt, and cousins were all there, it seemed like a party to me. Looking back, I can only surmise that when my grandmother needed help the reinforcements were called in.

Great companies recognize their reinforcements as their suppliers, vendor partners, and service organizations. And great companies use them to their advantage. Because my marketing firm falls into the category of all three, I have had the opportunity to learn the advantages of calling in reinforcements.

Our best clients communicate their vision and their mission succinctly to us and their other business partners. The best suppliers *always* have a choice whom to support with their best talent and resources—you or your competition. Because top talent is a limited resource in any organization, those clients who share their vision with their business partners usually get their suppliers' best employees assigned to their accounts. Often I have heard of marketing organizations utilizing the A team to get the business and assigning their B team to manage the company's day-to-day business. Sometimes this is a sales strategy, similar to a bait and switch. But often companies do this when they no longer feel they can make a strategic contribution to a client's forward plans or growth.

Do you want to get more than your fair share of your service organizations' allocation of product or talent? Be clear. Be consistent. Be timely.

Don't look out only for your own interests, but take an interest in others, too.
(PHILIPPIANS 2:4)

Don't keep your partners in the dark; they'll do a better job if there's a little daylight to hoe by.

DIGGING IN THE DIRT
Hoeing the Weeds (Part Deux)

GREAT COMPANIES know that when they treat service organizations with respect and consideration for their business model—(how they make a profit)—their best suppliers will watch their back. Because my company is a service organization, I have a soft spot for other businesses that sell services too. Our company works hard to ensure that our best suppliers know that we understand and respect *their* business model. In return, these suppliers take good care of us—like an awesome printer partner we do business with.

For a variety of reasons, we recently had some files go out that were less than perfect. Because of our printer's excellent service attitude, we didn't eat thousands of dollars in printing costs. He was watching our back. That's an example of good reinforcement if ever there was one. Your suppliers will hoe the weeds like there's no tomorrow when you show them that you respect their business model and appreciate their service.

Companies that are proficient at long-range planning excel because they intimately understand the business and economic factors that their partners are anticipating. Would you like to improve your forecasting? Do you want to hedge a soft economy? Would you like to develop new strategies or service and product offerings? Spend time with your vendor partners in *their* garden. The insights you gain from others will make your own vision much more clear.

Then make me truly happy by agreeing wholeheartedly with each other, loving one another, and working together with one mind and purpose. Don't be selfish; don't try to impress others. Be humble, thinking of others as better than yourselves. (PHILIPPIANS 2:2-3)

This garden work is tedious, and the best gardeners overlook nothing. Hoe the weeds with your suppliers to ensure you have the resources and goods you need in order to produce an awesome crop. Depend on your reinforcements.

DIGGING IN THE DIRT
Feeding the Customer

MY DAD WOULD occasionally vary what he grew in his garden, but we could always count on beets, cucumbers, green beans, tomatoes, onions, black-eyed peas, okra, and squash. You see, my dad was in tune with his customers—his family. He knew what we liked and worked hard to meet our expectations, delivering only those items that were yummy to us.

This seems like such an obvious approach to customer satisfaction, but it's long been lost on most corporations. Why? Because it requires someone from an enterprise actually *talking* with customers about their needs and wants. It involves getting to know each client, understanding its future expectations as well as what drives those expectations and the disappointments it has experienced with your company in the past.

You'll never know what your patrons really expect from your organization unless you listen to them, and you won't learn what services and products they're hungry for just by reading online surveys. But it also requires accepting the information and guidance your customers are trying to give. So often companies invest in gathering information only to challenge or dismiss a customer's opinion. Is this crazy or what?

If you build your business model, products, and services around your customers' desires, rather than just your own agenda, there's a good chance you're going to benefit. You'll gain not only stronger sales, but you'll also enjoy a greater sense of accomplishment and pleasure. There's nothing more gratifying than customers who say they *enjoy* doing business with you and your organization.

Don't forget to show hospitality to strangers, for some who have done this have entertained angels without realizing it! (HEBREWS 13:2)

When you're planning your next garden, call your customers to the table and ask them what they like. If they say tomatoes, give them tomatoes; if you grow okra instead, get out the cornmeal—there's a good chance you'll be eating it by yourself. Do you need to set a place for your customers?

DIGGING IN THE DIRT
A Bumper Crop

IN ADDITION to our garden, my dad had a small peach orchard. Some years the peaches were sweet, juicy, and fragrant. Other years they were wormy—literally. But one year, due to perfect growing conditions, we had an excessive crop of peaches. The fruit seemed to be running out our ears!

We ate them whole, sitting on the picnic table in the backyard. We ate them on cereal. We ate them on ice cream. We made homemade preserves. We made pies and cobblers. And when we couldn't stand to eat one more peach, my parents sliced them and stored them away in the deep freezer for use in the fall and winter.

But those crazy peach trees kept producing, as did the green beans, the squash, and the tomatoes . . .

So my dad and I gathered up our excess bounty and filled the trunk of our blue Ford Custom 500 with grocery sacks full of loot. Then we drove door-to-door in our little town to give away our bumper crop. We took them to elderly neighbors, too frail to garden, and to neighbors with smaller yards than our own. After we provided fruit to these folks, we traveled on to our neighbors who also had gardens; those were the ones who sent us away with some of their own excess: fresh watermelons, cantaloupe, and corn. Wow! What a treat . . . we weren't expecting more food in return—especially my favorite, watermelon!

There is a talent, character trait, or specific knowledge that you have in abundance that someone else can benefit from. Experience. Encouragement. Specific knowledge in a trade or industry. A network of contacts. Expertise in some area of running the home. You possess something that, if you'd be willing to share it, would bring you so much more in return.

> So let's not get tired of doing what is good. At just the right time we will reap a harvest of blessing if we don't give up. Therefore, whenever we have the opportunity, we should do good to everyone—especially to those in the family of faith. (GALATIANS 6:9-10)

I find it interesting that some of the most successful, powerful people are also the most gracious. Gracious with their time, with their network, and with their counsel. What do you think came first—their success or their willingness to share their abundance?

DIGGING IN THE DIRT
Risky Business

WHEN YOU THINK about the business of gardening realistically, it's amazing that anyone ever attempts to sow a single bean! Consider the top five reasons not to even try:

1. You could spend days behind a tiller turning up the soil, only to learn months later that the earth has been robbed of its nutrients.
2. You could invest hours planting those tiny seeds and covering them ever so carefully by hand, and then have a hard spring rain come the next day and wash them out in an hour.
3. You could pull the weeds, keep the bugs at bay, and pick at the optimum times, only to have the sun bake the new growth on the vine; there's always a drought sometime in the growing season.
4. You could seed, weed, and pick vegetables all summer, only to find out that all of the conditions were just *slightly* less than favorable. Your crop—while it produces—will not sustain you. Man cannot live on green beans alone.
5. You could have a bumper crop and then be burdened with bags full of vegetables rotting on your back porch.

Oh, good grief! There are just too many things that could go wrong. Let's forget about this garden business and just pick up some Del Monte at the Piggly Wiggly.

There are always reasons not to go into a business or invest in your existing trade. You can always find more negative scenarios to worry you than positive facts to comfort you. But thank heaven for the risk takers—or we'd be starving for fresh ideas and innovative concepts (not to mention green beans, corn, and tomatoes).

Gardening is about carefully calculating your risk and forecasting the worst-case scenario—and then being willing to live with it. This type of risk taking is also required to succeed in any business venture. But like the gardener, at some point you're going to have to walk on faith . . . or be content to eat canned spinach. Yuck.

He who watches the wind will not sow and he who looks at the clouds will not reap. (ECCLESIASTES 11:4, NASB)

Research and assess the possible downside or risk to starting a new business. Forecast what you're willing to lose if a hard rain comes. Then be willing to accept it if the worst happens. But for goodness' sake—at least walk around back and *consider* the bounty you could be enjoying!

DIGGING IN THE DIRT
Planting by the Moon

PATIENCE IS NOT one of my strong suits. Let me just say that now is *never* soon enough for me. So I was totally frustrated, at the age of about twenty-six, when my father all but forbade me to plant my garden on a given weekend (at the time I was living in the suburbs, so this was a *semi-sissy* garden).

With his Native American heritage, my dad believed in planting the garden by the moon. He carefully explained to me that even though that weekend might be convenient for me, planting then would not produce a bountiful crop. He insisted I wait until the second half of the first period when the moon would begin to wax toward the half-moon phase. Good grief! Are you kidding? I didn't want to wait around for the moon to wax—I wanted to plant the garden now! The ground had been tilled; the seeds had been purchased; and the kids had been "farmed out" for the day (pun intended).

I was sure my dad was wrong. Just a few weeks after sowing them, the plants took off. I called my dad every few days to gloat about my gardening success and insisted that his *planting by the moon* was some old Indian wives' tale that he needed to give up. Being the kind and patient father he was, he just replied, "We'll see." Days came and went. The plants shot up—deep leafy green. They blossomed—the squash were beautiful. And then, after a very short production cycle, they *died.* They had grown too quickly, never putting down the healthy, deep roots they needed to sustain them through the hot Texas summer.

Something similar happens in business and in our homes every day. We're so excited to see results . . . to do something . . . to take action . . . that we pull the trigger on our plan before the timing is perfect. Even though the plan is right, the timing may not be.

> *For everything there is a season,*
> *a time for every activity under heaven.* (ECCLESIASTES 3:1)

This is where an experienced mentor can be so helpful. Look for a sage advisor who can direct you and problem solve with you and remain objective about your performance. And don't be so quick to dismiss those who have gone before you . . . they may know something about the moon that could increase your bounty. Are you a believer?

DIGGING IN THE DIRT
We're Either Growing or Dying

THERE'S NO SUCH THING as maintenance mode when you're a garden plant. Plants are either on their way up or on their way down: seed, sprout, stalk, leaf, bloom, produce, produce like crazy, stop producing, die. Never in its life cycle does a garden plant "just exist."

Companies and individuals are the same way; we either grow or die. Maintaining is often the first step toward death. So how can we ensure we're always producing?

Put down roots. I think it's important for our growth that we fully adopt the company we work for as our own. I understand that you might be skittish of such an idea—especially if you've been mistreated by a previous employer. I get that. But it's like learning to love again after having your heart broken. To fully engage in your career, you'll need to put your whole heart into it. And like your new love, you should also recognize it's not perfect, and never will be. But you're going to have to put down deep roots to be able to survive the heat. And, girlfriends, regardless of where you work, we know it's going to get hot.

Reach for the sun. You probably do your best work when you're challenged with a clear set of objectives. When you have a stated set of responsibilities and a clearly articulated goal, and when you're learning something new, you're likely to remain invigorated. Unfortunately, managers often fail to give folks well-defined goals, instead expecting them to motivate themselves to reach new heights. If you've not been given a set of goals, create them for yourself or expect to wither on the vine.

Stand up to the rain. Every organization includes at least one person who likes to rain on someone else's parade. These people will beat you down like a six-week planting hit by a gully-washer. Personality conflicts can really challenge your growth if you let them. But here's the key: you're in charge of how much you allow other people to affect your attitude, your thought process, and your willingness to take risk.

> *I am certain that God, who began the good work within you, will continue his work until it is finally finished on the day when Christ Jesus returns. . . . I pray that your love will overflow more and more, and that you will keep on growing in knowledge and understanding.* (PHILIPPIANS 1:6, 9)

If a three-inch bean plant is determined enough to withstand a torrential downpour (and it can), you can determine not to allow the naysayer to wash you out either.

DIGGING IN THE DIRT
Bloom Where You're Planted

NOW THAT STEVE and I live in the city, the closest I get to a veggie garden is the farmer's market in downtown Dallas. But every spring I still get the fever to dig in the dirt.

In our first house in Dallas, our lot was small and the vegetation was very mature. Actually, it was a little too mature in a few spots, so we decided to do a bit of updating to the beds. This, of course, required Steve to dig up four-foot plants and prepare them to be transplanted into our daughter's yard.

The work was going well. Steve was digging, and I was "coaching" (you can imagine how much he loves it when I do that). We safely bagged and transported the plants to the kids' house—except for one. When Steve dug up a camellia bush, he laid it behind a divider wall in our yard and forgot about it. From the house, you couldn't see the abandoned plant.

The next weekend, we discovered our camellia, lying on the ground, roots bare to the world, and *blooming* up a storm. Never mind that the camellia blooms in February; this one was putting on a brand-new red, roselike show for us in May—lying on its side.

What a lesson. If we could all just learn to bloom where we're planted . . . to produce our best work, to be our loveliest, and to thrive, regardless of the conditions or circumstances we have been given.

Remember this—a farmer who plants only a few seeds will get a small crop. But the one who plants generously will get a generous crop. You must each decide in your heart how much to give. And don't give reluctantly or in response to pressure. "For God loves a person who gives cheerfully." (2 CORINTHIANS 9:6-7)

At times we are all less than enchanted, either by our work itself or by the companies we serve. If we, like that camellia bush, just remember that our work and our talents are both from God and for God . . . oh, yes, we would humbly give it our all and bloom where we're planted.

DIGGING IN THE DIRT

FATHER GOD, please open my eyes and remind me to

- [ ] walk the rows to improve my communication with others;
- [ ] walk the rows to better learn the strengths of my coworkers;
- [ ] walk the rows to encourage my coworkers and family;
- [ ] hoe my weeds and communicate my mission and vision to my business partners;
- [ ] feed my customers with the food they enjoy;
- [ ] share my bumper crop of talents and resources with others;
- [ ] boldly and wisely engage in risk by walking in faith;
- [ ] learn to seek wise counsel, being willing to plant by the moon;
- [ ] remember I'm either growing or dying—help me focus on growth;
- [ ] bloom where I'm planted.

ACTIONS I WILL TAKE:

Example: Today, I will recommit myself to bloom where God's planted me and approach my day with a positive attitude!

1. _____

2. _____

3. _____

Father, I praise you for the bountiful garden you provide for me. I thank you for my many opportunities and pray that you will guide me to use my gifts abundantly that you might be honored with my work and my life. Please allow me to flourish— to bloom where you have planted me even when the conditions are not the most favorable to this camellia bush. Amen.

DWINDLING RESOURCES

MY FATHER WAS A QUIET, gentle man—in every way a gentleman, and wise. Born in 1904 and raised on a dusty farm in northwest Texas, Daddy left school to help support the family when he was fourteen.

Twenty-five years later, Daddy found himself working to feed a family of five during the Great Depression. He watched both world wars from home; he was too young to serve in World War I and too old to serve in World War II. But he participated in the sacrifices that were required by all Americans. During this time he learned how to make good decisions, and he learned how to conserve resources.

In the 1970s, when a gallon of milk soared 88 percent to $2.16 a gallon, Daddy said, "You haven't seen anything yet" and then encouraged me to drink the last drop. "You pour it; you drink it" was the motto in our house. There was no wasting even a drop of milk.

I'm not sure what we paid per kilowatt, but clearly it was expensive to cool and light our 1,100 square-foot home because every month he claimed "highway robbery" as he opened the electricity bill. I wouldn't even make it to the doorway before he'd turn the lights out behind me.

By 1980, as America was still reeling from our first energy crisis and gas had just soared above one dollar a gallon for the first time in history, Daddy told me, "This is only the beginning." He encouraged me to drive slower and "coast to the stop sign."

Daddy didn't retire on a pension but relied solely on Social Security. For thirty-two years, he added to his little nest egg while living a full life on that small income.

But more importantly than encouraging me to conserve our tangible resources, Daddy taught me something about conserving our most precious intangible resources—friendship, personal energy, hope, love, and wonder.

Keep putting into practice all you learned and received from me—everything you heard from me and saw me doing. Then the God of peace will be with you.
(PHILIPPIANS 4:9)

I'm still learning from the old man.

DWINDLING RESOURCES
Friendship

What you leave behind is not what is engraved in stone monuments, but what is woven into the lives of others. PERICLES

OUR SENSE of well-being is threatened by the loss of three major resources: money, time, . . . and one few of us think about until it's too late . . . friends.

Although we invest the greater part of our waking days thinking about it, making it, investing it, and spending it, money is the one mind-consuming resource that can bring us material comfort—but no consolation. No sooner do we score the big sale or close the deal than we're out looking for the next big win. No sooner do we hang the Trina Turk in the closet or place the new sofa in the family room than we begin to assemble the next shopping list.

Time has always seemed a fleeting resource to me. I feel there's just not enough time in the day to check off my personal to-do's, my professional obligations, and my family commitments. I'm racing the clock like an Olympic sprinter . . . but I always seem to be pulling up the rear. As I approach my mid-century mark, my race with time has moved beyond the twenty-four-hour clock to one with a final alarm. Am I doing those things I was destined to accomplish?

While we're busy making and spending our money and playing chase with Father Time, I think women often fail to consider one of the most important contributors to living a life of uncommon joy—the keeping and rekindling of friendships. Money will not sit at your side as you face heartbreak, nor will time celebrate with you the joys of retirement and the birth of grandchildren. Running out of both time and money in his early nineties, my dad buried his coworkers, fellow church congregants, and all but one running buddy. He did not mourn for more experiences or things, but grieved the loss of his most valuable resource—his friends.

Finally, all of you should be of one mind. Sympathize with each other. Love each other as brothers and sisters. Be tenderhearted, and keep a humble attitude. Don't repay evil for evil. Don't retaliate with insults when people insult you. Instead, pay them back with a blessing. That is what God has called you to do, and he will bless you for it. (1 PETER 3:8-9)

In our final days, accomplishments and wealth will play no role in our sense of belonging. In our final days, time will just move faster and there will be no peace with it. In our final days, there will be one lasting resource that will bring laughter, contentment, meaning, and belonging. Friendships, new and old, will be the resource that brings us uncommon joy.

OCTOBER 24

DWINDLING RESOURCES
Energy

Some cause happiness wherever they go; others, whenever they go.   OSCAR WILDE

I THINK MOST of us are in the middle of a major energy crisis—and I don't mean oil.

If I were to ask you how your energy level is today, how would you answer? Are your engines revved and raring to go . . . or as Daddy would say, are you "*too pooped to pop*"?

I work hard to channel my energy, but sometimes I make bad choices emotionally, physically, and mentally. I expend way too much energy trying to reason with unreasonable people; I push myself unnecessarily trying to be healthy; and I fry my brain cells working hard, rather than smart.

Case in point: rather than walking away from a fight *I knew I wouldn't win*, I battled with the new owner of the dry cleaners we had used for four years. The previous owner was an honorable man who had once promptly replaced my sweater when an employee shrunk it.

But the new owner must have missed customer-service day when he was getting his business training. The cleaners washed, rather than dry-cleaned, my brand-new white slacks. I took them back the next day, pointing out that the fabric was damaged and that they had shrunk. He said he could "fix it." Hoping to get my new summer pants in my closet, I agreed to let him try. But, of course, they weren't right. He tried again. And then again. Finally, I told him, "Clearly this is not working. Would you please refund the replacement cost of these pants?" No. He said I must have gained weight and that's why they no longer fit.

Oh, talk about spoiling for a fight—not only had the cleaners ruined my brand-new clothes, the owner had insisted I gained weight! For ten days I returned to his business, arguing, pleading, and even trying on the pants, all to prove he was wrong. I expelled tremendous emotional energy trying to get him to right his wrong. What a waste of my emotional energy!

The godly are rescued from trouble,
and it falls on the wicked instead.
With their words, the godless destroy their friends,
but knowledge will rescue the righteous. (PROVERBS 11:8-9)

Why do we try to reason with unreasonable people?

Some of us do this with significant others and family members. We wear ourselves out trying to instill reason to their whacked-out thinking when we really should apply some of that reasonable thinking to our own approach: *Give. It. Up.*

DWINDLING RESOURCES
Energy (Part Deux)

A FEW WEEKS AGO I began to "hit a wall" with my daily workout. Looking for a way to maximize my exercise routine, I researched and found out that for the past year I had actually been overexerting myself. I had been working my body too hard with absolutely no benefit to me physically. What a waste of both time and energy! Why do we think that running faster is always better?

I had this same twisted mentality when it came to my mental workouts too. While trying to balance my work at the office with writing this book, I suffered a total mental meltdown—unable to perform at my peak at either. Bouncing from task to task, I left the office every day mentally whipped with nothing tangible to show for it. Getting nowhere fast, I finally stopped trying to multitask every day. Instead I decided to compartmentalize my life until my manuscript was complete. Taking a day off from work and a day off from my family on the weekend reenergized me for both the writing and the creative problem solving I need to do at the office. When we know that working hard is not always working smart, why do we continue to do it?

To conserve our available power, we must accept that there are positive energy forces in our lives that fuel us and negative energy forces in our lives that deplete us. But we must also remember that we're the only ones responsible for how much we allow each of them to affect us.

As the keepers of our energy source, we alone must choose the rate of our energy expenditure and determine our own acceptable level of exertion. We must be careful about the battles we fight, the physical energy we expend, and the mental exercises we participate in. Because at the end of the day, we should have mental, emotional, and physical reserves still available for *ourselves*.

A cheerful heart is good medicine,
  but a broken spirit saps a person's strength. (PROVERBS 17:22)

If you find yourself having an energy crisis, remember first and foremost that God *designed* us to require rest. Then, *after your nap*, when you're thinking clearly, consider who you're exerting your effort on, what you're investing your energy in, and how your return on investment is working for you. It might be time to turn off the lights to conserve your energy.

DWINDLING RESOURCES
Authenticity

AT A RECENT GATHERING of some very high profile chicks, I watched the women cautiously enter the room. It didn't matter that many of them were actually very famous, well-recognized gals; they still came to the party in costume, complete with masks.

Their masks didn't come in a cardboard box with a cellophane window, nor were they the flamboyant kind one would wear to a masquerade party; no, these were invisible masks of protection worn because of fear of rejection.

I have found that regardless of social status, income, or race, many women have difficulty revealing their true selves. Big, beautiful personalities are consciously squelched for fear of stealing the spotlight; brilliant, insightful minds are dumbed down in order not to intimidate; perfection is painted on in order to cover up our dysfunction; and wealth or success is demonstrated in order to compensate for who we are not. That is until the woman hits her late fifties or early sixties. That's when I think women begin reading Dr. Seuss again.

Be who you are and say what you feel, because those who mind don't matter and those who matter don't mind. DR. SEUSS

Some of the women I enjoy the most have adopted Dr. Seuss's philosophy. They are comfortable demonstrating to those of us who are younger that authenticity equals confidence. My girlfriends have shown me that being who we are supposed to be, rather than who we think people want us to be, is the way to exude grace and confidence.

I know from my older girlfriends that authenticity equals honesty. Honest people don't play games and won't pretend to be something or someone that they're not.

Watching these gals move around at a party, I realize that authenticity equals respect for others. Because my girlfriends think so highly of others, they expose their real selves. When I'm with these girlfriends, I'm included; I belong.

Last, I know from being with these women that authenticity equals acceptance. Because my girlfriends are not going to judge me, they know I'm not going to judge them. I know I am accepted, just as I am, when I'm with them.

To acquire wisdom is to love oneself;
people who cherish understanding will prosper. (PROVERBS 19:8)

Grace. Confidence. Honesty. Trust. Inclusion. Belonging. Acceptance. Want some? Get real and come with me. Let's peel off the masks.

DWINDLING RESOURCES
Wonder

There are only two ways to live your life. One is as though nothing is a miracle. The other is as though everything is a miracle. ALBERT EINSTEIN

I WAS DRIVING on autopilot while traveling home from south Texas. Since I know Interstate 35 so well, I set my cruise control and pointed the car due north. Over two hours later, I looked out the window and suddenly realized I had no idea where I was! Everything was flat (it was Texas after all), and one small town looked like the next (every town with a population less than five thousand has a Dairy Queen on the frontage road). I obliviously had been cruising along, missing signs of danger, but more importantly, signs of wonders, along the way.

If we're not careful, we just might cruise through life this same way. Zoned out with our routine, mesmerized by safety, and dulled to the miracles all around us, it's easy to live on autopilot—unless you have a young child in your life.

Watching my granddaughter reach out and wrap those chubby little fingers around a toy, I celebrate with her the miracle of our hands. Isn't it amazing that we can think about it, reach for it, and *put it in our mouth* in a matter of seconds? Or better yet, isn't learning new tricks at any age, a miracle? Girlfriends, let's make a commitment to awaken our minds to the wonder of things yet to learn.

When Ava was crawling, I followed her around our apartment as we crawled on all fours, moving from room to room exploring Sugar and Pop's new digs. I celebrated with her the miracle of arms and legs. Isn't it amazing that we can desire to move to another location and our arms and legs go there with little effort? Or better yet, isn't the spirit of adventure, at any age, a miracle? Girlfriends, let's make a commitment to awaken our souls to the wonder of exploration.

Sitting nearby as Ava pulled up to the coffee table, I watched as she let go in a desire to walk to the window. I celebrate with her the miracle of free will. Isn't it amazing that we can desire something that defies logic, go after it anyway, and fall down only to get up and try it again and again and again? Or better yet, isn't focused determination at any age, a miracle? Girlfriends, let's make a commitment to awaken our hearts to the wonder of the rewards of risk.

Let us not grow old to experiencing knowledge—imagine what we could do with these minds now coupled with maturity! Let us not become bored with adventure—imagine what things we might see with these eyes that are now wise. And let us never become complacent—satisfied only with holding on to the coffee table.

Then God said, "Let lights appear in the sky to separate the day from the night. Let them be signs to mark the seasons, days, and years. Let these lights in the sky shine down on the earth." (GENESIS 1:14-15)

Let's never stop wondering at the wonder of it all.

DWINDLING RESOURCES
Optimism

No pessimist ever discovered the secret of the stars, or sailed to an unchartered land, or opened a new doorway to the human spirit. HELEN KELLER

I AM OPTIMISTIC. I am positive. I can always see a brighter tomorrow. Well, almost always.

When you're a leader, the *almost always* can be a big problem. And regardless of our titles, we're all leaders; someone somewhere is indirectly watching us or purposefully looks to us for direction, inspiration, and hope. That can be a hard role to fill when times are tough.

As the economy slid into recession in 2001, my optimism slid with it. As one employee told me years later, "Ellen, it was written on your face." While I don't think that "faking it" or painting an artificially rosy picture is appropriate, I do believe that I could have created a more hopeful environment during those difficult times. Because pessimism is a viral contagion with ugly symptoms and dire consequences, it is critical that we protect against it.

One way to preserve hope is to be purposeful in our thoughts. The energy invested in thinking and talking about all the things that aren't right robs us from focusing our resources and talents on the things that are right. Learning from my mistakes in 2001, I have reengineered my thinking to better lead my organization through the economic thunderstorm that began in 2008.

Another key to protecting this valuable resource is to know when to shoulder the blame. Optimists rarely blame others for mistakes made by themselves, their team members, or their families. They know that "the buck stops here" and that laying blame erodes morale. I have seen leaders turn teams around by knowing the difference between holding someone accountable and holding someone hostage.

Finally, optimists by nature know they must stay motivated in their work, their hobbies, and their goals. Optimists get up every morning aware that they can't make a positive impact for others without a strong sense of belief in the future. There are few hard-and-fast rules in this world but here's one optimists know well: pessimists inspire no one.

If your resource of optimism is dwindling, look to shore it up. Surround yourself with people who talk positive, think affirmative, and live with a sense of hope.

Let the message about Christ, in all its richness, fill your lives. Teach and counsel each other with all the wisdom he gives. Sing psalms and hymns and spiritual songs to God with thankful hearts. (COLOSSIANS 3:16)

We have stars to discover, seas to sail, and—more important—we have the responsibility to unlock the human spirit. Girlfriends, believe with me that you can be the catalyst for hope.

DWINDLING RESOURCES
Grace

I do not at all understand the mystery of grace—only that it meets us where we are but does not leave us where it found us.[38] ANNE LAMOTT

GRACE. A word that has all but disappeared from our vocabulary. A concept that rarely crosses our preoccupied minds. An asset few of us enjoy—either as the giver or as the recipient.

Of all the dwindling resources, grace is the asset I most often find myself struggling to preserve; the one I must learn to store up in the warehouse of my heart. Fierce competition, expectation, the daily whirl of my hectic schedule, independence, and my egocentric thinking all challenge my capability to extend or receive grace. I excel at neither.

Receiving grace is difficult for me because my pride gets in the way. I want to look like I have it all together; thus I become embarrassed when someone wants to extend to me a gift of service. Then there's the issue that sometimes I'm suspicious. I always wonder, *What's behind this? What does this person expect of me in return? What are her motivations for doing this?* I run through these mental gymnastics because, in my past, my extended favors were conditional. I was expecting something in return.

So four years ago when my new friend Donna showed up at my door with food, a card, or a hug, I was stumped! It took me almost a year to learn how to receive her grace without strings. Undeserving of her warm gestures of kindness and care, I had to learn to accept freely (and without the conviction that I must return the favor) the thoughtful service and warmth of this young woman. I intuitively understood that not to accept would be the equivalent of shunning grace in the flesh.

If your gift is to encourage others, be encouraging. If it is giving, give generously. If God has given you leadership ability, take the responsibility seriously. And if you have a gift for showing kindness to others, do it gladly. (ROMANS 12:8)

And if you have been gifted with such a person as Donna in your life, respond to his or her grace—graciously.

DWINDLING RESOURCES
Grace (Part Deux)

GIVING GRACE is only slightly less difficult for me than receiving it.

My impatience, expectation, judgment, and desire for excellence often go toe-to-toe for a three-second match in the boxing ring of my mind. Extending grace to my family is easy—I love them! And actually, extending grace to total strangers (in the elevator, sitting in traffic, etc.) is not so hard either. It is for "everyone else" in my life that my resource of grace runs out. Friends and employees don't always receive their fair share of my grace.

But I'm learning from, interestingly enough, my sarcastic husband. Steve, one of the finest grace givers of all time, is my role model. He has shown me how to give someone a pass; he has encouraged me to occasionally let issues or challenges resolve themselves (without confrontation); and his generous spirit has taught me how to do for others what they can't do for themselves. It has all become graciously seductive. The rush of goodwill racing through my veins was about as foreign as a hit of cocaine.

I've heard it reported that it takes twenty-one days to form a new habit. I wonder to myself if I can keep up what I'm learning in order to become a grace giver like Donna and Steve.

Because I have seen grace in the flesh, I know she is elegant. Her beauty comes from a place deep in the heart. Her gestures flow with ease. Her poise communicates confidence. And her humility of service is stunning.

A gracious woman gains respect,
but ruthless men gain only wealth.
Your kindness will reward you,
but your cruelty will destroy you. (PROVERBS 11:16-17)

Yes, this is an asset I will continue to work to store up as I watch the beauty of grace all around me.

DWINDLING RESOURCES
Moxie

ARE YOU RUNNING LOW on moxie? Lost your nerve? When you look in the mirror, do you see Dorothy's Cowardly Lion looking back at you?

I'm afraid . . . afraid that as we age, we lose our courage and passion to be change agents.

Before there was Rosa Parks, there were three other important young women in the civil rights movement. If you're not a student of African American history you might not be familiar with Irene Morgan, who at twenty-seven was thrown in jail, eleven years before Ms. Parks's history-making arrest. Perhaps you've never heard of Claudette Colvin, who at the tender age of fifteen also stayed seated as she stood up for her civil rights and was arrested nine months before Ms. Parks. Eighteen-year-old Mary Louise Smith took the same step just forty days before Rosa Parks; like them, she was arrested.

Where did *these girls* get their moxie? And where can we get some?

As I think about all the women throughout history who have taken a courageous stand, I wonder about us and our generation. What are we doing to improve the racial, social, and family conditions that exist today? How can we mobilize our moxie? I say we start by following Irene, Claudette, and Mary Louise's lead:

We must have an opinion and know that the foundation of our opinion is firm. We must be convicted. Each of these three women clung to her belief and hope for a positive outcome. Like these young women, we must be passionate, knowing that if we fight the good fight, we may impact future generations.

All three of these young women wrestled daily with the issues of racial discrimination, but they didn't work alone. These women knew the power of consensus and were part of a base of strength.

And they endured. They knew they would be arrested. They knew there would be fines to pay. They knew they would suffer physical and emotional duress. And each one knew she would likely lose her individual battle, but she stayed in the fight to win the war.

None of these women had status. None had money. There was not an Ivy Leaguer in the bunch.

They just had moxie.

Without oxen a stable stays clean,
but you need a strong ox for a large harvest. (PROVERBS 14:4)

What are you passionate about? What can we change together? How can we impact the world with our actions, rather than our continuous complaints? Maybe it's time we stink up the stall.

DWINDLING RESOURCES

FATHER GOD, you have fired a desire in my heart to

☐ recover my dwindling resource of friends;

☐ stop investing my personal, positive energy in unreasonable people;

☐ conserve my physical energy and spend it wisely;

☐ work smart, not just hard;

☐ remove my masks in order to expose my real self;

☐ live each day knowing that everything is a miracle;

☐ think purposeful thoughts directed toward a future of hope;

☐ learn how to both give and accept grace, gracefully;

☐ become a woman of moxie and be a woman of change.

ACTIONS I WILL TAKE:

Example: I will stop dwelling on that negative exchange with _____
and focus my energy on positive people and experiences.

1. _____

2. _____

3. _____

Father, I praise you for all the rich resources you have given me and ask that you will make me ever mindful of each and every opportunity to do your will as I consider my responsibility with the resources of friendship, energy, authenticity, wonder, hope, grace, and courage. In the name of the Father, Son, and Holy Spirit, I pray. Amen.

A CITY VIEW

We are not what we know but what we are willing to learn.   MARY CATHERINE BATESON

LIKE SOME OTHER WOMEN, I often have to share my husband's attention with another. Luckily for us both, Steve's mistress is a new project. Occasionally the new venture is a sexy piece of metal with an engine that purrs, but usually she sports "good bones" and lots of windows.

It all begins with simple infatuation. While reading the sensual description of marvelous homes in the paper's real estate section, Steve will often mutter "mmm" under his breath. The serious flirting continues at the bookstore, where he'll pick up architectural magazines and books, studying their centerfolds with lust. I recognize the affair is escalating when we head to an open house. It's out of control when he requests a personal introduction to the beauty by her agent.

By now, I know this dance well. Yet this affair took on a whole new meaning when we decided to move from our single-family home on "Leave It to Beaver Lane" to a multifamily dwelling in the city. Move number seven is scheduled to occur in just six months, when we move into our new high-rise condo in the heart of downtown Dallas.

While our condo is being constructed, we've made a high-rise apartment in the Uptown section of Dallas our temporary home. Perched 120 feet in the air, we look out into the night sky of twinkling lights and artfully lit high-rise buildings that reflect perfect Indian-summer sunsets.

Coinciding with this move, my friend Gretchen invited Steve and me to volunteer with her and some of her other friends at the Dallas homeless shelter known as The Bridge. Less than three miles away from our home, the shelter offers a strikingly different city view. Standing less than twelve inches away from poverty, I see things I've never seen before. The lights are on here too. And this view also takes my breath away and makes my heart pound.

Nothing is as I would have thought.

God blesses those who hunger and thirst for justice,
  for they will be satisfied. (MATTHEW 5:6)

Over the next several pages I will take you along on my city-living adventure. I want to share with you the view I now see with new eyes. And I'll also share the message of hope that twinkles here—if we'll just spend the time to take in the view.

A CITY VIEW
The Invisible People

"I DIDN'T THINK you saw me."

I caught my breath, fighting for composure as my eyes welled with tears. "Yes, sir," I answered the bearded homeless man sitting alone at the table. "I see you clearly. Are you ready for your lunch?" As I placed the tray before the crippled man, he looked up at me. His eyes twinkled with the same intensity as my Dallas downtown skyline view on a Saturday night. He knew he wasn't invisible. And I knew for a moment—*that moment*—I wasn't either.

During the next ninety minutes, my fellow volunteers and I served food and filled water glasses for over seven hundred men and women. My city view was eyeball to eyeball, our hands often touching as we passed the glasses back and forth. I could feel them, I could smell them, and most importantly I could see them—and I knew they could see me. Each person connected with me and I with him or her as we exchanged pleasantries in the crowded dining hall. When I spilled water on the floor, we locked eyes and laughed together about my poor waitressing skills. At the end of my shift, my heart raced, my spirit was buoyed, and my soul sang. I was connected to the human race.

I needed this.

God blesses those who are poor and realize their need for him, for the Kingdom of Heaven is theirs. (MATTHEW 5:3)

I love community. I love neighbors. I love the energy that is created by lots of people in a given space. So needless to say, when we moved temporarily into an apartment building, I looked forward to connecting with a community—if only in the elevator. But I quickly found out that the city is not the place to make friends.

A CITY VIEW
The Invisible People (Part Deux)

Our greatest strength as a human race is our ability to acknowledge our differences, our greatest weakness is our failure to embrace them. JUDITH HENDERSON

WHEN WE FIRST moved into our apartment, we noticed that our young neighbors would get on the elevator with their heads down, texting on their phones. They never looked up; I swear, I thought I was invisible! They'd enter the downstairs gym in a dazed state of sleep deprivation, connected to their iPods as if they were permanent appendages. Even when I was on the treadmill, I was invisible. I watched them come and go through the lobby, always talking on the phone—they were verbally connected to one another, but not to me. Does this generation know what it means to look into a stranger's eyes, to connect with that person as a fellow human being? Or must they have my mobile phone number in order for me to be a part of their world?

I was greatly amused and surprised to recognize that it was Dallas's homeless citizens, more than the young, urban professionals I saw daily, who made me feel alive during my first months of living in the city. It was the homeless folks who energized me. It was those without a home who made me feel like a welcome addition to this great city. And it was those who make their beds on concrete sidewalks who awakened me to the concept of invisibility and the importance of connecting with our eyes . . . if only for a moment.

So I made it my mission to see my high-rise neighbors and for them to see me. They were probably confused and amused by my extroverted greetings in the halls, in the parking garage, in the elevator—and I'm sure I seemed absolutely obnoxious at 6:30 a.m. in the gym. But after several weeks, I saw a change. Giving them the "twinkle eye," I made it a point to reach out and welcome them to my world. And, yes, I even made a couple of friends (who probably think I'm a nut job).

God blesses those who work for peace, for they will be called the children of God. (MATTHEW 5:9)

I wanted to be sure my neighbors knew that *they* were not invisible to *me*, so I extended to them the same welcoming spirit my homeless friends extended to me. I welcome them to my world. We are, together, part of the human race.

A CITY VIEW
Beautiful People

I'M NOT SURE how we qualified for the apartment; Steve and I were neither young enough nor pretty enough to live in that building. The fire alarm went off one night, and we all gathered downstairs in the lobby, spilling out into the circle drive. Never in my life had I seen such a concentration of so many physically gorgeous men and women (except in Newport Beach, California)! Dressed to the nines in designer duds, they should have been living inside the pages of *Vogue*. But they're not all beautiful people.

My perception of beautiful people changed drastically after our move.

While I'm an ardent believer of "pretty is as pretty does," I guess I hadn't seen it played out with much contrast until we moved downtown. Like many young people today, my neighbors rarely said please, thank you, or pardon me. They drop their candy wrappers in the hall; they leave their cups by the pool; and oblivious to those around them, they stand and stall in the hallways, expecting others to move around them. Contrast these well-heeled, well-educated young adults with our city's homeless.

Of the seven hundred people we serve during lunch, I estimate that only a handful have not repeatedly said thank you and please and then extended another note of appreciation for our volunteer service. As I watch nearly a quarter of them bow their heads to say their own personal thanks for the tuna sandwich sitting before them, I am as starstruck by these beautiful homeless people as I am dumbfounded by our so-called beautiful society.

Don't be concerned about the outward beauty of fancy hairstyles, expensive jewelry, or beautiful clothes. You should clothe yourselves instead with the beauty that comes from within, the unfading beauty of a gentle and quiet spirit, which is so precious to God. (1 PETER 3:3-4)

How can we teach gratitude when we have had so much?
How can we teach grace when we rarely extend it ourselves?
How can we teach the power of an apology when we're never wrong?
How can we teach the concept of beauty when, in reality, we have forgotten what it looks like?

A CITY VIEW
Beautiful People (Part Deux)

If you get to thinking you're a person of some influence, try ordering somebody else's dog around. WILL ROGERS

I THINK ABOUT all the beautiful people I have encountered over the past eight weeks. What do I remember about the six-foot-tall beauty on the elevator? That she was carrying a Stanley Korshak bag with three pairs of designer shoes (*three!*) and never looked up from her BlackBerry. I think she might have been blonde—but other than that, I can't tell you a thing about her.

On the other hand, I remember fondly the frail little seventysomething woman who dined with us two months ago at The Bridge. She wore a hand-me-down suit and nylons, and I remember that she smelled like rose water. I remember that she was drop-dead gorgeous as she bowed her head to pray. And that later she winked at me when she thanked me sweetly for pouring her another glass of water—all with the voice of an angel and the grace of Jackie O.

When you think of the beautiful people you've encountered over the past few weeks, what do you remember? And what do you think others remember about you? Do they experience beauty in your presence?

This past Sunday, as I reached for a gentleman's glass, I asked him, "How are you today?" It was 26 degrees outside, he wore a thin coat, and his worldly belongings sat in a grocery bag at his feet, but he answered me with a smile the size of Texas and the enthusiasm of a cheerleader, "Ma'am, I'm blessed!"

May others be blessed by the beauty that resonates from *your* grace and gratitude. And may God bless us all with truly beautiful people to keep us humble.

God blesses those whose hearts are pure, for they will see God. (MATTHEW 5:8)

I don't know about you, but I think I'll head on down to the shelter for my beauty tips.

A CITY VIEW
Scary People

Do one thing every day that scares you. ELEANOR ROOSEVELT

I'LL BE HONEST with you. My first day volunteering at The Bridge, I was happy to be assigned to the salad bowl. Standing on the other side of the serving line put me at a safe distance from my new "customers" (and within a few feet of the back door if an incident broke out). But within thirty minutes I regretted getting this assignment; I wanted to be out front where the action was. As they greeted those of us who were filling their trays and thanked us for volunteering, my homeless customers began to look downright neighborly. These folks, despite some negative press in the local paper, weren't scary; they were just hungry.

You see, I know about scary now that I live in a high-rise.

Scary was the woman who was in the elevator with Steve and me one Friday. Yelling profanity into her phone, the late-twentysomething, model-like beauty scared the fool out of me. It appeared from the one-sided version of the conversation (which I had no choice but to overhear) that her roommate had "borrowed" a pair of her shoes, broken one heel, and then returned the shoes to her closet. *Can you believe it?*

Don't mess with a young woman whose designer shoes have been damaged. The gal was beside herself—and like many of the beautiful ladies who live here, she was angry. Steve made the observation early on that many of the women in our building seemed to live in a constant state of aggravation. Which made me wonder—with their nearly six-figure incomes, trendy clothes, and high-rise living, are their lives really all that bad? Or is it the absence of *real* hardship that causes them to live in a state of disillusionment? Maybe if they realized their purpose was something greater than landing a date for Saturday night, they would be more content.

> *And now, dear brothers and sisters, one final thing. Fix your thoughts on what is true, and honorable, and right, and pure, and lovely, and admirable. Think about things that are excellent and worthy of praise.* (PHILIPPIANS 4:8)

When you consider that the "they" I'm writing about might be "us," it's downright frightening. Scary people aren't the homeless people at The Bridge; scary people are those of us who get all stewed up over a whole lot of nothing.

A CITY VIEW
Scary People (Part Deux)

THERE ARE OTHER THINGS to fear in our high-rise elevator rides. Scary was the man who got on one morning with a *pit bull*.

Do you know anyone who has been bitten three times by a dog? Well, you do now. Yes, dogs just aren't that into me. So can you imagine how terrified I was when a man got on the elevator with me at 8 a.m. with a pit bull? I stood quietly, holding my breath (praying that on this day I *would* be invisible). When we stopped at another floor, a man got on with two, count 'em two, schnauzers. *Unleashed.* Yes. You see where this story is going. By the time we made it to the ground floor, we had six adults and three growling dogs penned in a four-by-four-foot space. My blood pressure didn't come down for two hours.

I'm not sure if these guys had a clue that they could be putting themselves, their pets, or other residents at risk that morning—or if they just didn't care. I imagine that in their minds, they were just two average guys going about their average day to walk what they felt were their very average dogs. To some of us, pit bulls aren't average canines, but then dogs running off leash, regardless of how small or cute they are, aren't allowed in the city of Dallas either. Scary is self-absorption coupled with self-rule. And terrifying is when our own self-absorption and self-rule create emotional (or physical) risk to others.

I love the LORD, because He hears
  My voice and my supplications.
Because He has inclined His ear to me,
  Therefore I shall call upon Him as long as I live. (PSALM 116:1-2, NASB)

My city view, now up close and personal, has changed my perception of fear—the guys and gals standing on the corner of Young and Harwood aren't scary, but riding my elevator is. From now on, I'm taking the stairs.

A CITY VIEW
Charitable People

IF YOU'VE WATCHED *Law and Order* anytime over the past eighteen years, you've seen at least one episode in which homeless people take things from one another; they steal. I'm sure this scene is rooted in reality. There are always those among any social group (yours and mine included) who take advantage of and outright steal from their neighbors, coworkers, or shareholders.

I know people who steal directly, and I know people who steal indirectly by withholding from others. People who, regardless of their income or net worth, do not share. They hoard their money and protect their own interests, leaving those less fortunate to fend for themselves. This type of stealing is not usually depicted on any nighttime TV show, nor is the deep well of generosity that dwells in the hearts of many homeless folks. It just doesn't make for sensational TV viewing.

I have watched in awe as those with not a penny to their name share their food and hope with one another. I have watched as they have given 50 percent of their entire net worth (which is represented by the food on the tray in front of them) to their neighbor. Our son, Scott, who was once homeless, has this same charitable attribute. He eagerly and lavishly gives to those in need. Could you give 50 percent of all you own? I couldn't. Compared to these people, I am a stingy person.

The square footage of our apartment is about 70 percent smaller than that of our previous home. Some of our belongings are in storage, including my baby grand. Some of our treasures are crammed in closets (I refused to store my shoes though). But others are boxed, stacked floor to ceiling in the second bedroom of our apartment, which we call "the garage." In these boxes are knickknacks, books, linens, dishes, cookware, vases, photos, and art pieces. All out of sight. All out of mind. All excess to living a life of uncommon joy.

Every morning as I look at my city view, with the sun rising in the east, I am reminded how blessed I am and how much I have to offer. And that makes me happy. But I'm also sad. Not just because our city's population of homeless is rising but because as members of the human race we don't do anything about it. I know in my heart that I'm a part of the "we."

Charitable people give time. Charitable people give food. Charitable people give money. Charitable people give hope. Let us follow the model of selfless giving that our homeless brothers and sisters have so beautifully portrayed before us.

God blesses those who are merciful, for they will be shown mercy.
(MATTHEW 5:7)

Let's put our money toward something that won't be stored in a box.

A CITY VIEW

FATHER GOD, open my eyes and my heart to view my fellow man as you do. Help me to

- [ ] extend grace to those who are in need;
- [ ] remember to be the person who ensures that others do not feel invisible;
- [ ] see the hurt, anger, and aggravation of my fellow human beings and love them, not judge them;
- [ ] reassess what a beautiful person really looks like;
- [ ] give generously to all those in need.

ACTIONS I WILL TAKE:

Example: Today, I will look into the eyes of strangers and smile as I greet them.

1. _____

2. _____

3. _____

Father, I am a richly blessed person. Thank you for my home, my family, my physical and mental health, and for providing me with food and clothing. Convict me to see with your eyes those less fortunate. Be with me as I take action to help the oppressed. In the name of your Son, Jesus, who showed us best how to love the loveless. Amen.

YOUR MARKETING STRATEGY

"Finding oneself" is a misconception. A self is not discovered but formed by deliberate contemplation and action. JACQUES BARZUN

AT A RECENT CHARITY EVENT, Steve and I, along with two of our friends, dined like royalty. Celebrity chefs from all over the country had come to one of our favorite Dallas restaurants. As we gorged ourselves on each of the eight courses served, a rock-star chef would take the microphone, briefly mentioning the unique ingredients and explaining how each savory dish had been prepared.

With great efficiency, the chefs told us about each recipe. But what they failed to tell us—and what all the foodies in the room wanted to know—was the philosophy behind the fabulous eating establishments each of them ran. These guys and gals had a captive audience that longed for the "meat" of their stories (pun intended) so we could better understand how these everyday cooks became celebrity chefs. But they never elaborated on their restaurants, missing a great opportunity. I wonder how often we do the same.

Directly or indirectly we communicate something about ourselves, our dreams, our insecurities, our gifts—the list goes on—every day. Body language, tone of voice, word choice, our appearance . . . we're definitely communicating, but what kind of message are we sending? Are we expressing what we really want others to remember about us? Or, like the audience at the charity event, do people want to know something other than what we're superficially saying? Most importantly, can we clearly articulate who we are and what we bring to the party?

I think in order to communicate who we are, we must be deliberate about the words we use and the other nonverbal ways we express ourselves.

If you didn't take marketing in school, or if you did and could use a refresher course, I hope you're willing to head back to class with me, back to Marketing 101. But this time our marketing project or case study won't revolve around a product or service. Instead we're going to explore how to effectively market ourselves by reconsidering how to

write and communicate our positioning statement,
promote our features and benefits,
create packaging that sells, and then
deliver the goods.

You made all the delicate, inner parts of my body
and knit me together in my mother's womb.
Thank you for making me so wonderfully complex!
Your workmanship is marvelous—how well I know it. (PSALM 139:13-14)

Ladies, get out your pen and paper—our lesson begins tomorrow.

YOUR MARKETING STRATEGY
Your Positioning Statement

Imagination was given to man to compensate him for what he is not, and a sense of humor to console him for what he is.   SIR FRANCIS BACON

AT A RECENT PARTY, a woman asked me what I did. I assumed she meant professionally, so I told her that I am a marketer. She looked at me blankly. As I went into my "pitch" to explain my company's differentiator and value proposition, I could see that my marketing spiel was working: in about two minutes she appeared to understand my company's value in the marketplace.

Later on that evening, a friend of mine approached me and my new acquaintance and asked me about my upcoming trip to India (which you'll read more about later) and how my book was coming along. The other woman turned to me and began firing questions: how did my being in a documentary in India, and writing a book for women coexist with running a marketing company?

Because I hadn't worked out my positioning statement for the more personal and purposeful aspects of my life, it took me a good ten minutes of babbling and fumbling with my words to explain to her what I did (when I wasn't working). When I finished, she still looked confused.

Do you know who you are? If you're over the age of thirty, I imagine you do. But what if your life, like mine, is multidimensional? Can you clearly articulate what you contribute to and the value of that contribution? And can you do it confidently? I believe if we give our personal positioning statement some thought, we will subconsciously exude confidence. However, if we fail to be clear with others, we might come across as lost or less self-assured than we are.

You saw me before I was born.
Every day of my life was recorded in your book.
Every moment was laid out
before a single day had passed. (PSALM 139:16)

To begin, ask yourself what makes you unique and what value you bring to your organization and family. And then ask yourself, *What does* God *value about me?*

YOUR MARKETING STRATEGY
Your Positioning Statement (Part Deux)

ONCE YOU DETERMINE what makes you special, it's time to write your positioning statement.

So what exactly is a positioning statement? In business, it is a fact-based statement used internally by a product or service organization to focus the employees on the product or service's key differentiator. In your personal life, crafting such a statement may help you bring clarity and confidence to your roles in life.

The fill-in-the-blank exercise looks like this:

_____ PROVIDES _____
(product's name)   (what the product delivers)

BECAUSE OF _____ _____.
                    (product's name)   (key differentiator)

To clarify and articulate our value as individuals, try this exercise so that it applies to you:

I PROVIDE _____
(what you bring to your relationships or marketplace)

BECAUSE OF MY _____.
(your experience or value system)

I've included my three positioning statements below as examples:

My professional positioning statement: I provide marketing strategies and creative solutions to my clients because of my proven twenty-year success in selling goods and services in the consumer marketplace.

My personal positioning statement: I provide my husband, grown children, and granddaughter both the time and attention they deserve because of my devoted love to them and my desire to leave a meaningful legacy to my family.

My purpose positioning statement: I provide biweekly e-mails to my girlfriends to encourage them to live a life of uncommon joy because I think we all take on too many projects, which messes with our minds. Heh, heh, heh . . .

> *How precious are your thoughts about me, O God.*
> *They cannot be numbered!* (PSALM 139:17)

Actually, my real purpose positioning statement is to encourage my girlfriends to live intentionally with uncommon joy, but I think it's also important to have fun with this exercise. As you write, I hope you will learn to really love who you are and *why* you are. There's nothing better for self-assurance than a little self-love.

YOUR MARKETING STRATEGY
Communicating Features and Benefits

People who throw kisses are hopelessly lazy. BOB HOPE

I DEFINE MARKETING as a craft that is 60 percent art and 40 percent science. Beautiful pictures and carefully chosen words are merged to entice a specific marketplace (determined by reams of data) to buy a product. The pictures and words are meaningless unless they resonate with those who will want or need the product we're marketing. The science part of the equation determines who makes up a market for a product and how large the market is. The art form is represented in pictures and words designed specifically for that target market. One message doesn't fit all people any better than a one-size-fits-all T-shirt does.

One-size-fits-all messaging doesn't work for us as individuals either, because we must always be mindful of our audience, and what words, tones, and expressions will resonate with them. And we must always be careful to communicate our benefits, as well as our features.

As an example, I offer clients insight gained from experience, the ability to communicate a focused message, and the skill to present an idea to a large group of people. These features might interest some people, but unless I communicate a specific benefit to a target audience, they are only that—somewhat interesting.

However, if I customize my benefit statement for a prospective client, the message is much more favorably received. Leveraging my insight gained from experience, I can communicate that the client can be confident in my counsel because it is based on my twenty years of consumer marketing experience.

But the insights I've gained serve not only companies looking to market products but also women who are looking to embrace life. So the same benefit I offer my clients—insight gained from experience—is available to my girlfriends, for whom I've customized my benefit statement in the following way: share inspiration and encouragement to women who, like me, have lived the first chapters of a less-than-perfect life but seek to live the next chapters intentionally and with uncommon joy.

When you understand the benefits you bring to your relationships, your workplace, and your family, you're not only focused and able to maximize your features, but those who work and live with you will never mistake what you bring to the party.

> LORD, *you alone are my inheritance, my cup of blessing.*
>   *You guard all that is mine.*
> *The land you have given me is a pleasant land.*
>   *What a wonderful inheritance!* (PSALM 16:5-6)

Don't throw your kisses; who knows where they'll land. Be purposeful and target your audience. Then plant a big one—right on the smoocher.

YOUR MARKETING STRATEGY
Packaging Sells

A woman "is well dressed if people say, 'She looked heavenly but I can't remember what she had on.'"[39] JACKIE KENNEDY ONASSIS

MY MOTHER WAS a 1964 fashion plate. Her blonde hair was teased high and shellacked with hairspray, and her foundation garments were always securely in place. She usually added three inches to her height by donning stilettos. We didn't have much money, but my mom still looked like a million dollars every morning as she headed off to work.

On Saturdays, she'd doll herself up for our weekly trip to the Piggly Wiggly for groceries. By the way she dressed, you'd think President Johnson himself was handing out samples! I don't remember a single outing when my mother wasn't appropriately attired.

By the time I was a teenager, I had taken her Mary Kay look for granted—secretly believing that her vanity had the best of her—until she stopped me one day on my way out the door for a date: "You're not going out like that." I ran to her bedroom to take in my full view in the mirror but was confused. I was modestly dressed, albeit sloppily.

"*What?*" I asked.

She said, "Other people have to look at you—be respectful."

Oh. At sixteen years of age, the light came on and I realized that my attire and how I looked was not only a sign of self-respect, it was also a sign of respect for others. Someone else had to look at me.

Product packaging, like fashion, can be subjective. What is compelling to one person may be atrocious to another. However, liking or not liking a package design rarely hinders sales completely. Unless it is distasteful or offensive. And there lies the rub in our "packaging" today.

Many current fashion trends are inappropriate for young women; inappropriate for the workplace; and, yes—inappropriate for church.

> *I can hardly believe the report about the sexual immorality going on among you—something that even pagans don't do.* (1 CORINTHIANS 5:1)

Call me old fashioned if you want, but, girlfriends, we have to have a conversation about our packaging and what exactly we're selling.

YOUR MARKETING STRATEGY
Packaging Sells (Part Deux)

I KEEP A FEW package design rules at the front of my mind when I am assessing product packaging or working with our creative team on a new design. As I reflected on the rules recently, I realized these guidelines apply to us personally too!

Begin with the objective to enhance the brand, not detract from it. Girlfriends, do you look as smart as you are? Others will take you seriously when you take yourself seriously—and that starts at 6:30 a.m. in your closet.

Use design elements that appeal to the target customer. Girlfriends, are you considering how your packaging choices make others feel? You may be communicating a lack of respect for the audience or the situation.

Consider what the design will subconsciously communicate. Girlfriends, are you subconsciously communicating *I'm cheap* or *I'm valuable?* Every day you're sending a message from the time you walk out of the house.

Avoid unnecessary embellishments. Clean designs are classic. Girlfriends, do your accessories compete with the twinkle in your eye? Don't allow your bling to overpower those beautiful eyes.

Avoid using materials that can quickly become shopworn. Honey! How old is that suit? I don't care if it's your "lucky outfit." For heaven's sake, toss it before it unravels!

Ensure the package size that has been designed will fit on the retail shelves. Darlin'! Did you look in the mirror before you left the house? If you can see the cellulite—they're too tight; if you can see cleavage—he can too.

Casual workplace. Casual church service. Casual dining. Our casual world is a far cry from the pillbox hats and white gloves of 1964. And since I try to stay with the general trend, I'm a pretty casual girl. Mom would have a cow if she saw me scooting around town in my jeans.

> *Search me, O God, and know my heart;*
> *test me and know my anxious thoughts.*
> *Point out anything in me that offends you,*
> *and lead me along the path of everlasting life.* (PSALM 139:23-24)

But I think she'd approve that no one would remember what I had on. (And that I had on my makeup *and* my high heels.)

YOUR MARKETING STRATEGY
Delivering the Goods

There are three constants in life . . . change, choice and principles.   STEPHEN R. COVEY

WHERE'S THE BEEF?

As a marketing firm, my organization is sometimes asked to market products that . . . well . . . honestly, they're meatless. They sound good, but in reality, they don't deliver much in the way of substance. It's all sizzle and no steak.

At the end of the day the product has to be at least as good as the messages promise. As Debbie, our executive vice president of retail strategies, says, "Products rule." What she means is that as a marketing firm we can do our research, develop strong plans, design great packaging, and develop innovative campaigns, but if the product doesn't deliver to the consumers' expectations, the best marketing in the world can't save it. The experience users have with the product trumps marketing. And, of course, the same goes with us.

As we close this series on developing our marketing strategies, I would be remiss if I didn't mention that, in the end, we have to deliver the goods too. In other words, we'd better be consistently living out the traits we tout in our value statement. I have lived long enough to have blown this more than once. When we fail to deliver on the expectations we have worked so hard to establish, I can tell you from experience that we will tarnish our reputations.

Envy, gossip, negativity, prejudice, grudges, flirting, cursing, cheating, lying, manipulating, blaming, denying, backstabbing, and judging are just a few of the ways we undermine our brand and unravel our personal marketing strategies.

If you have a strong brand, choose to stand firm in order to protect it. If your brand has been weakened, it is within your power to change it. Because in the end it is only the principles by which we choose to live that fuel our ability to deliver the goods.

Let me hear of your unfailing love each morning,
  for I am trusting you.
Show me where to walk,
  for I give myself to you. (PSALM 143:8)

I don't know about you, but I'm going to ensure that there is meat with my sizzle.

YOUR MARKETING STRATEGY

FATHER GOD, I want to be a better communicator. Help me to

- ☐ better understand my value and key differentiators in my professional and personal life;

- ☐ clarify those benefits I bring to my work, my family, my church, and my friends;

- ☐ discern appropriate packaging and dress in a manner that is pleasing to you;

- ☐ deliver my value daily and not undermine my reputation or Christian witness.

ACTIONS I WILL TAKE:

Example: I will write a positioning statement.

1. _____

2. _____

3. _____

Father, thank you for making me who I am. Guide me as I better define my abilities and the tremendous benefit I bring to those I love. Allow me to see myself as you see me: beautifully and wonderfully made. In the name of your Son, Jesus. Amen.

TONGUE-TIED

In prayer it is better to have a heart without words, than words without heart.[40]
JOHN BUNYAN

I'M ASHAMED to admit this. For a woman who is never without words, I sometimes get a bit tongue-tied when it comes to my prayers—especially when my spiritual walk has morphed into a spiritual crawl. Oh, I'm down on all fours all right, but I'm not exactly in a prayerful state of mind.

When I'm strolling with Jesus, it's as if he is walking at my side. My conversation with him flows with all the focus and passion and clarity of a woman in love. I am in tune with him and can feel that he is also with me.

But let there be a change to my schedule, an upheaval to my world, or stresses due to imposed deadlines, and my conversations with God become clipped and abbreviated spiritual babble. This challenge to my prayer time has a negative effect on my spiritual growth. I lose focus on his will. I lose passion for our relationship. And I lose clarity in my ability to communicate clearly.

I try to pray, but I find myself tongue-tied. The perfect words to dialogue with the almighty God don't surface. The wellspring of passion is depleted. I can hear the crickets chirping. Of course, this couldn't come at a worse time. This is when I need his direction and guidance more than ever. And when he most lovingly longs to hear from me.

> *Therefore, let all the godly pray to you while there is still time,*
> *that they may not drown in the floodwaters of judgment.*
> *For you are my hiding place;*
> *you protect me from trouble.*
> *You surround me with songs of victory.* (PSALM 32:6-7)

So rather than sit in silence when these dry spells come, I return to the prayers of my childhood. But this time I give them a big-girl spin.

TONGUE-TIED
As I Lay Me Down to Sleep

As I lay me down to sleep,
I pray the Lord my soul to keep.
Guard me, Jesus, through the night
And wake me with the morning light. Amen.

I'M NOT SURE how old I was when my parents taught me this bedtime prayer. I must have been very young, because I don't remember a night when I didn't recite it. Only after I accepted Christ at the age of ten did I begin to augment my rote prayer with more personal requests, notes of thanksgiving, and specific prayers for my friends, family, and world peace—I longed for the Vietnam War to end.

I am a communicator, especially with my family. I love to talk, but when it comes to my kids, I really love to listen. Just as I love to communicate with them, I also long for my quality visits with God. Most of the time, I'm in constant communication with him. The concept of praying without ceasing is part of who I am. But when I get distracted with life and stressed with work or family, I often find myself having superficial rather than meaningful conversations with him.

When these seasons visit, I turn back to my precious bedtime prayer. My big-girl version goes like this:

> Father, I lie in this bed in need of a restful night, but I know that even as I drift off, I will most likely awaken at 3:00 a.m.
>
> I am worried. Are you there?
>
> Stay with me tonight and protect me from my own negative thoughts. Provide me direction and the wisdom to discern your will over my own.
>
> Tomorrow will be a new day, with both new challenges and new blessings. Remind me not to take either the lessons you strive to teach me or the gifts you have given me for granted.
>
> Thank you for the promise of tomorrow and your direction. In the name of your Son, Christ Jesus. Amen.

I will bless the LORD who guides me;
even at night my heart instructs me.
I know the LORD is always with me.
I will not be shaken, for he is right beside me. (PSALM 16:7-8)

As I lay me down to sleep . . .

TONGUE-TIED
God Is Great

God is great.
God is good.
Let us thank him for our food.
By his hand we must be fed.
Thank you, Lord, for our daily bread. Amen.

WHAT CHILD has not recited this prayer in a sing-songy, sweet, little squeaky voice? Most of us who were raised in Christian homes learned this one long before we learned our ABCs. A prerequisite to being served the first course (which we all knew we had to muddle through to get to the important part of the meal—*dessert*), this prayer provides the ultimate foundation for any of us when we get tongue-tied.

My grown-up version goes like this:

Father, I praise you for who you are: the almighty God.

Father, I praise you for all you do: the holy Creator.

Father, I know that all gifts are provided by you; forgive me when I become proud or haughty or self-reliant. I know I can do nothing without you.

Father, I thank you for everything I have in my life.

My relationships—thank you for giving me people to love and people to love me.

My home—thank you for providing me safe shelter.

My work—thank you for providing me with a place to contribute my talents.

My food—thank you for my full belly.

My clothes—thank you for my full closet.

My health—thank you for this breath.

You have provided for all my needs today; forgive me when I test you and worry about tomorrow. In the name of my Savior, Christ Jesus. Amen.

Shout joyful praises to God, all the earth!
Sing about the glory of his name!
Tell the world how glorious he is.
Say to God, "How awesome are your deeds!" (PSALM 66:1-3)

God is great. . . .

TONGUE-TIED
God, Hear My Prayer

God in heaven, hear my prayer,
Keep me in thy loving care.
Be my guide in all I do.
Bless all those who love me too. Amen.

I BELONG to a women's Bible study where we share our prayer requests with a small group. There is only one rule: the request or praise has to specifically relate to our immediate family; our spiritual walk; our challenges with a sin; or our well-being. In other words, we can't offer up a vague prayer request for God to solve world hunger or to cure our sister's coworker's brother of cancer.

Every week we go around our circle, spilling our guts (all held in strict confidence, of course). We each make cryptic notes. We pray. And then I sometimes forget.

"Please pray for me" is a common plea among the Christian sisterhood. "I will" is the common, dishonest response. Oh, we all mean well. We don't lie on purpose. We intend to pray for others, but in all honesty, when we finally get around to our bedtime or morning prayer, we've long forgotten about anyone else's problems.

I'm afraid we often approach our prayers in the same self-absorbed manner as we approach everything else. "I have ten minutes to talk to God and twenty minutes of problems to unload. I don't have the prayer bandwidth for other people's problems today." However, I've found that when my spiritual walk has come to a standstill, it's sometimes the best time for me to refocus my prayer time on others.

🍃 My Father God, I pray that you will hear your servant today; I pray that you will guide me in all I do and that it will be pleasing to you.

I lift up my dear friend _____, and I pray that you will provide her with wisdom and direction.

I ask that, if it be your will, you give her the desires of her heart.

I praise you for covering her in peace, and I praise you for loving her. Let her feel your presence today.

In the name of my Father, who has blessed me with such sweet Christian sisters. Amen.

In times of trouble, may the LORD answer your cry. May the name of the God of Jacob keep you safe from all harm. May he send you help from his sanctuary and strengthen you from Jerusalem. May he remember all your gifts and look favorably on your burnt offerings. (PSALM 20:1-3)

Bless all those who love me. . . .

TONGUE-TIED
A Child's Prayer for Morning

Now, before I run and play,
Let me not forget to pray.
To God who kept me through the night
And waked me with the morning light.
Help me, Lord, to love thee more
Than ever I have loved before.
In my work and in my play,
Be thou with me through the day. Amen.

LIFE IS HARD. Sometimes stupid hard. So why do we try to take it on alone?

I wish I had a nickel for every time I ran out the door for work, stressed out
with the problems of yesterday following me into my workday today.
I wish I had a nickel for every time I drove to the grocery store, mind racing
with more to-do's than any person could humanly accomplish in one day.
I wish I had a nickel for every time I sat at my keyboard, vapor-locked as
to what words or thoughts would be meaningful to my readers.

I wish I had a C-note for every time I stopped putting on my makeup
to approach God to help me manage my stress.
I wish I had a C-note for every time I stopped making my to-do list and
replaced it with a thankful list.
I wish I had a C-note for every time I bowed my head, asking that God
provide divine wisdom and for the words I speak not to be mine, but his.

But instead, I will replace my wishes with a prayer:

&. Father, I ask your blessing on my mind to keep my thoughts clear.

I ask that you bless my heart to keep my motives pure.

May my thoughts be your thoughts; may I only desire to do your will;
and may you bless me this day with your mercy.

In the name of your Son, Jesus Christ, Amen.

I love you LORD; you are my strength. The LORD is my rock, my fortress, and my
savior; my God is my rock, in whom I find protection. He is my shield, the power
that saves me, and my place of safety. (PSALM 18:1-2)

Be thou with me through the day. . . .

TONGUE-TIED
A Child's Evening Hymn

I hear no voice, I feel no touch,
I see no glory bright;
But yet I know that God is near,
In darkness as in light.
God watches ever by my side,
And hears my whispered prayer;
A God of love for a little child
Both night and day does care. Amen.

TIME-OUT was a disciplinary measure that I found mildly effective with my children. Although they carried on like their solitary confinement was some form of cruel and unusual punishment, I actually found it quite relieving—five to ten minutes of peaceful bliss from their arguing, whining, and general "naughtiness."

After they ran out of "one more chance," I'd place their little fannies in a chair in their room. They were not to get up and play, nor could they come into the room where I would go to enjoy some precious quiet.

Of my two children, Shauna especially dreaded "the hole." She would wail as if I had beaten her with a stick. But it was Scott who, at the age of about two and a half, walked quietly to where I was standing in the kitchen with his hands covering his eyes. In his little thirty-month-old mind, I guess he thought if he couldn't see me, well, then most certainly I couldn't see him!

There are times when I have longed to feel the breath of God. Times when I thought for sure he had abandoned me. No voice. No touch. No nothing. Just an empty place where he once filled my heart. Are you sitting in time-out too?

🎵 Father, are you there? I can't feel you. I can't hear you.

I'm desperately alone; only you can fill this void in my soul.

Father, are you there? I know you love me. I know you will never forsake me.

Whisper your love to me, Father God.

He's there . . . just peep through your hands.

O God, do not be silent!
Do not be deaf.
Do not be quiet, O God. (PSALM 83:1)

A God of love for a little child. . . .

TONGUE-TIED

FATHER GOD, when my spiritual walk has slowed to a crawl, help me to

- [ ] remember that you alone are my hiding place;
- [ ] remember that you are my source of calm at 3 a.m.;
- [ ] praise you for providing all my daily needs;
- [ ] be less self-focused and fervently pray for my friends and family;
- [ ] slow down and pray before I start my day without you;
- [ ] remember that you have not abandoned me; you're just taking a rest from my whining!

ACTIONS I WILL TAKE:

Example: I will pray specifically for my friend _____.

1. _____

2. _____

3. _____

Father, what a privilege to be able to come to you as your child and talk with you. Thank you for providing peace in my storm and calm to my craziness, and for caring enough for me to provide for my every need. Remove my self-centeredness, Lord, and remind me to pray earnestly for my friends and family, lifting their needs and causes before you. Thank you for your constant love. In the name of your Son, Jesus, I pray. Amen.

I HEARD IT ON THE RADIO

WHEN YOU'RE TIRED, just absolutely worn out with the world, where do you go for your "Gatorade"? How do you nourish yourself to move on when life's challenges just won't stop chasing you?

When you're confused and you can't see the forest for the trees, what source of truth clears your vision? How do you gain a new perspective so you can look at the situation holistically rather than microscopically?

And last, when your bucket has a hole in it and your self-confidence is leaking out all over the kitchen floor, where do you get the goo of encouragement to plug the leak? How do you mend your broken spirit?

Like some of you, I often turn to books to provide new perspective and insight; we are fortunate to have at our disposal hundreds if not thousands of authors and motivational writers who can help us see old circumstances with new eyes.

Like many of you, I also turn to God for guidance and wisdom. My Christian faith and wise clergy provide me not only with the direction I need when I'm confused, but with peace and hope to carry on when I've convinced myself I can't.

And, like you, I often look to my girlfriends to provide me with direction and encouragement (which usually comes with a reality check and a "thump upside my head").

But sometimes I turn on the radio.

From Sinatra classics to rock 'n' roll, this next series will take us through thirteen important truths we should all remember. Inspiration, perspective, and encouragement with a 4/4 beat and a thumping bass. What a way to learn!

I will sing of the LORD's unfailing love forever!
Young and old will hear of your faithfulness. (PSALM 89:1)

Turn it up—I love this song!

I HEARD IT ON THE RADIO
"You're Gonna Miss This"

THE ROAD BETWEEN Dallas and Austin is flat as a pancake. In the summer, regardless of the time of day you travel, the sun beats you silly. The two-hundred-mile drive can get a bit monotonous as well.

One day while driving to the state capital for business, I got tired of my satellite radio and switched to my FM band. I was between major cities, so the radio scanned for a minute before tuning in to—what else in Texas?—a country station.

A strong baritone voice, smooth as butter, sang to me: "You're gonna miss this. . . . You're gonna wish these days hadn't gone by so fast."[41] This ballad begins with Trace Adkins singing about a teen who tells her mother she can't wait to turn eighteen. Her mom, while understanding, tells her someday she'll miss life as it is now.

Friday night football, giggling with girlfriends, and free food. Life at seventeen is something to savor, isn't it? If only we had the ability to see our lives from a perspective of thirty-five years in the future . . . *we might start savoring the moment and the life stage we're in rather than yearning or rushing for the next one.*

The song fast-forwards a few years in the girl's life. Now a new bride, she tells her daddy she plans to have babies and buy a house right away. Her dad, too, advises her to take it slow because she'll miss these days before long.

Late-night movies, furniture bought at garage sales, and cheap rent. Our early married years are something to savor. If only we had the ability to see our lives from thirty years in the future . . . *we might start savoring the moment and the life stage we're in rather than yearning or rushing for the next one.*

The story picks up five years later when the young wife has become a young mother. As the dogs bark and her kids scream, she apologizes to the plumber (who's working on her broken water heater—how many of us remember those days?) for the commotion. The plumber sweetly tells her not to worry. The kids don't bother him; he had two babies of his own—one's now thirty-six; the other is twenty-three. He, too, tells her that someday she'll miss these days.

Pitter-pattering feet, bedtime kisses, and free child labor. Raising babies is something to savor. If only we could see our lives from twenty years in the future . . . *we might start savoring the moment rather than yearning for the next one.*

> *My heart is confident in you, O God;*
> *my heart is confident.*
> *No wonder I can sing your praises!* (PSALM 57:7)

Our challenge each day is to stop rushing down the road we're on in order to take in the scenery of the life stage we're passing through. We won't be back this way again, and trust me, my young girlfriends—you're gonna miss this. It's hard to believe . . . one of my babies is thirty-one; the other is twenty-eight.

I HEARD IT ON THE RADIO
"Up to the Mountain"

AS I WRITE THIS, I feel like I'm sitting in a pressure cooker with two hundred pounds of steam. Something's gonna blow. I am racing the clock to complete my manuscript before I jump on a plane to India.

Running my business. Being a wife, mom, and grandmother. Writing Truth Nuggets. Publishing this book. Participating in a documentary filmed halfway around the world. None of these things are optional—they are my callings. I dare not drop one of them because I know it is my purpose to see them all through.

The same goes for my girlfriend Karen. After losing her husband, Kelly, on Mount Hood in December 2006, she answered the call to write her husband's story. She knew there was much for us to learn from her mountain-man hero and his destiny on the mountaintop. But answering the call is not always easy, especially when it forces one to relive love and romance—now lost but to memories; to replay a traumatic rescue attempt—now a nightmare; and to look into the face of the future—without him.

Patty Griffin sings one of the most beautiful, soulful songs ever recorded. She based the lyrics of "Up to the Mountain"[42] on Dr. Martin Luther King's 1968 speech entitled "I've Been to the Mountaintop." If you, like my friend Karen, are struggling to fulfill a difficult mission or purpose you know you're "called" to fill, you might relate to the song's opening: "I went up to the mountain because you asked me to."

After a lot of hard work and tears on the keyboard, Karen completed her manuscript. Kelly's story would be told. On November 11, 2008, *Holding Fast: The Untold Story of the Mount Hood Tragedy* was released. No, it wasn't easy; yet the book's publication has brought Karen the peace that comes from knowing she's in the middle of God's will.

We also pray that you will be strengthened with all his glorious power so you will have all the endurance and patience you need. May you be filled with joy.
(COLOSSIANS 1:11)

If you're facing insurmountable odds in the fulfillment of your purpose, listen to that sweet voice. And keep going.

I HEARD IT ON THE RADIO
"Stand Back Up"

WITH THE SOULFUL DEPTH of a woman twice her age, Jennifer Nettles of the duo-band Sugarland sings truth in this country song of determination and restoration: "Go ahead and take your best shot."[43]

I have had numerous conversations over the years with young women who have told me they are afraid of the future—not because anything bad has happened to them or their families but because nothing bad *has* ever happened; life has been wonderful, sometimes, just too good to be true. They're wise enough to know the first shoe will drop—they just don't know how or when or where.

For those of us who have already crossed the River Despair, there's only a slight liberty from this fear. It doesn't haunt us like it did before our first disappointment, but it still wakes us up at night. The difference is that our past experience proved to us that we possess the grit, determination, and power to move through the hurt. We can sing along with Nettles as she promises, "I will stand back up."

Jobs evaporate. Children err. Marriages disintegrate. Friendships flounder. Sometimes we fail. But we also learn. We learn to harness the failure for our future success.

If life is wonderful and carefree for you today, I celebrate with you! Enjoy this time and drink it in. You can file this page away for future reference.

If you are a seasoned veteran of troubled waters who's been on the floor before, congratulate yourself today for turning that fight into your own victory.

And if this entry finds you in a place where for the first time in your adult life your self-confidence has been shaken, beaten, and bruised, let me give you this one promise to hang on to: you *will* stand back up.

We give great honor to those who endure under suffering. For instance, you know about Job, a man of great endurance. You can see how the Lord was kind to him at the end, for the Lord is full of tenderness and mercy. (JAMES 5:11)

Hang in there, girlfriend.

I HEARD IT ON THE RADIO
"Wild Women Do"

OVER THE PAST ten years, the women's magazines that haven't led with a cover story about sex are few and far between. The other day I picked one up in the nail salon, and as I read the article, I know my face must have matched the "passionately pink" on my toes!

So if there's so much written, *so graphically*, on the topic, why does it appear that sex *in marriage* has died? Are we preoccupied with work? exhausted from the kids? aggravated with our husband? Is it that we feel unattractive?

Let's start with work. I know that when I'm under pressure from clients, financial obligations, or challenges with employees, a romp in the hay is not exactly on my list of priorities. But if I place more value on the quality of my marriage than on the quality of my work, sex with my husband will move to the top of my to-do list.

Kids? Well, at least we know you had sex once. But have you had it since? Climbing into bed with Mommy and Daddy, those little toots really have a way of draining the romance out of a marriage. But if I place more value on the intimacy of my marriage than the immediate comfort of my children, I will march the little munchkins right back to their own beds.

He got home late from the office (again) and didn't help with the kids' homework (again). This kind of stuff is a definite mood breaker for us, gals. But if I place more value on the tenure of my marriage than on my displeasure with him tonight, I will fall asleep in his arms rather than with my face to the wall.

And then there's the issue that we just don't feel sexy anymore. We gain weight. Our muscle tone sags. Cellulite invades. Age can do a real number on a woman's psyche when it comes to sex. But if I place more value on my marriage rather than the idol worship of my body, I will be moved that he's *still* moved by me.

"Wild women do, and they don't regret it."[44] So goes the song—and so should we, with our husbands.

Wives, submit to your husbands, as is fitting for those who belong to the Lord. Husbands, love your wives and never treat them harshly.
(COLOSSIANS 3:18-19)

Ladies, sex is a critical component of a high-quality, long, and intimate marriage. Make your marriage bed an honor unto God. Get wild.

I HEARD IT ON THE RADIO
"Come Blow Your Horn"

I LOVE THE CLASSICS. Tony Bennett, Frank Sinatra, and Ella Fitzgerald. The elegance, the clarity, and the beauty of the instrumentals played by big bands are such a refreshing reprieve from today's modern scores. That's why I often tune in to the Sinatra Channel on my satellite radio. Yes, there is something for everyone on the airwaves these days.

"Come Blow Your Horn,"[45] originally recorded by Sinatra, was written to embolden an audience of young men. But this fun song provides a critical message for women of all ages today: "Make like a little lamb, and wham you're shorn; I tell ya chum, it's time to come blow your horn."

There was a time in my life when I thought "blowing one's horn" was unattractive, because I believed it implied bragging. But now I understand the value of networking, both in business and personal pursuits. I see that many of us were never taught the difference between boasting and horn blowing via self-confidence, self-assurance, self-promotion, and self-awareness.

Self-confidence allows us to operate with a feeling of abundance. The most self-confident people I know never feel cheated or like they must win. You'll recognize self-confident people—they are the ones who walk away from an unnecessary fight.

Self-assurance allows others to disagree with us. The most self-assured people I know are never cocky and are always respectful of others' opinions. You'll recognize self-assured people—they've not only found their voices, they know how to use them respectfully.

Self-promotion allows our actions to speak louder than words. You'll recognize accomplished self-promoters—they never talk about their personal success without attributing it to the skills, talents, and efforts of their team.

Self-awareness allows us to conduct ourselves appropriately by reading the conditions and needs of those around us. The most self-aware people I know are never called flakes or airheads. You'll recognize self-aware people—they know everything about *you*.

Because so many of us were taught that meekness means being a doormat or that expressing one's opinion will stir up unnecessary debate, many women are just now allowing themselves to express their thoughts.

Sing a new song to the LORD,
for he has done wonderful deeds. (PSALM 98:1)

Some of us have sat silently for so long that we're having a hard time finding our voices. It might be a little squeaky at first, but the more you use it, the better it will get. Pick up your horn and pucker up.

I HEARD IT ON THE RADIO
"Even Trade"

WHAT DO YOU THINK you're worth?

I realized *my* monetary value on a schoolyard at the tender age of six.

My best friend, Casey, a boy who, if I'd understood the concept of a boyfriend would have been my "steady," traded me during recess to a classmate for a pocketknife. Sam, the recipient of his new prize (me), proudly announced the trade to the entire class as we lined up to go back to our studies. *I was furious.*

With hands on my hips and pigtails waving madly, I caused quite a stir as I set both boys straight—I was not to be traded! It came as a shock to the young lads that I didn't belong to either of them. They could work it out between themselves as to who was now the rightful owner of that stupid pocketknife. But under no condition did I consider this an even trade. Not only did I believe I was worth more than a trinket bought at the five-and-dime, I believed I deserved a seat at the bargaining table.

In his song "Even Trade,"[46] songwriter and poet Terence Martin sings of a few things that we indirectly trade, like a string of cloudless days for a refreshing rain shower or sundown for the promise of another day. "You can call it an even trade," he sings.

As I consider the trade my heavenly Father made for my soul, I am humbled. Not a rusty old pocketknife for an innocent pigtailed girl, but the life of his only Son for a woman who sins.

> *For God loved the world so much that he gave his one and only Son, so that everyone who believes in him will not perish but have eternal life.*
> (JOHN 3:16)

I guess I knew from the get-go that I was adored, treasured, and wanted. But not until today did I realize my value and true worth.

I HEARD IT ON THE RADIO
"Do What You Do"

I LAUGHED OUT LOUD in 1999 when I heard Martina McBride belt out this message of self-confident independence with a peppy tempo and a smile in her voice: "Hey, don't give 'em what they think they want, 'cause they don't have a clue."[47]

For the first twenty-nine years of my life, I woke up every day with one goal in mind: to please every person I came into contact with.

I thought if I could give my first husband what he wanted, all would be good. I wouldn't learn until later that he didn't have a clue as to what he wanted—for himself or from me.

I also strove to please those I worked for—until the pivotal age of thirty. Thinking that they knew better than me what I should do and how I should do it, I forfeited my ability to discern and reason for myself. I wouldn't learn until later that executives are sometimes just as clueless, and sometimes more so, than those who deal with the customers and employees every day in the trenches.

Girlfriends, I didn't come into my own until I turned thirty, and I didn't have a clear identity as to who I was, or what I had to offer the world, until I was forty. I spent most of the first half of my life patiently trying to be what others expected or wanted me to be—trying to be someone I was not.

Arise, shine; for your light has come,
And the glory of the LORD has risen upon you. (ISAIAH 60:1, NASB)

I have learned that to live a life of uncommon joy, baby, you must do what you do. And that begins with trusting yourself.

I HEARD IT ON THE RADIO
"Life Is Just a Bowl of Cherries"

THE YEAR IS 1931.

Finding a job is nearly impossible as U.S. unemployment tops 8 million.

What little money people had put aside for a rainy day has evaporated. Another 2,300 banks have failed this year, on top of the more than one thousand banks that closed in 1930.

And food is scarce; the Dust Bowl era enters year two, forcing thousands of farmers to abandon their homes and livelihood.

People are out of work. Out of money. Out of food. And most are running out of hope.

But on the radio, listeners can let a peppy little tune penned by Buddy DeSylva and Lew Brown cheer them, at least for a moment. The songwriting duo remind their listeners to keep their financial losses and material possessions in perspective: despite all our work and worry, we won't take our stuff with us in the end. "Life is just a bowl of cherries," they sing, so "live and laugh at it all."[48]

Good advice even today, more than seventy-five years later! Although prices are up, the dollar is down, and our retirement fund is shrinking, we live in a time of great economic prosperity compared to our parents and grandparents. I wonder: If the financial bottom were to fall out from under us, as it did them, would we demonstrate the same character and determination they did? Would we be able to live and laugh at everything?

I don't know, but what a good reminder for those of us who get caught up in the acquisition and laying up of wealth. Let's all remember that we're not even renting our stuff on earth—it was God's before we got here and it will be his when we're gone.

Do not store up for yourselves treasures on earth, where moth and rust destroy, and where thieves break in and steal. (MATTHEW 6:19, NASB)

Because I know they're not mine in the first place, I think I'll borrow another bowl of cherries—and spit out the pits.

I HEARD IT ON THE RADIO
"Everyday"

WHAT KEEPS YOU going during tough times? How about these three things: love—having a friend or partner to weather the storm with you; time—the invisible healer and consummate miracle worker; and hope—a belief system that sustains you when the resolution to your problems is nowhere in sight. That's just what the rock band BoDeans sings about in their recording of "Everyday."[49]

Steve told me a story last week about a time, over twenty years ago, when a friend of his got caught up in a "force reduction." Cutbacks in payroll cut him out of a job. The guy worked the job circuit and his networks like a pro, but job leads never materialized into an opportunity.

After he finally landed a job, he told Steve, "Man, I got so desperate, I even started praying." The BoDeans can relate to that. They sing: "Well, I've never been one to pray, but I think I might try today."

We often take the hard road, trying to solve our problems ourselves or worse, relying on others to fix things for us. Love can only go so far—our friends or partners can only keep our self-confidence afloat for so long. Things most always work out in time, but what's harder than waiting? And if Father Time is being difficult, our belief system, regardless of how strong it once was, will begin to deteriorate unless we pray.

I'm not sure why folks consider prayer the last resort instead of the first. I guess some people think they're bothering God with their tiny troubles. Others probably feel a bit embarrassed, since they show up for a conversation only when things get tough. Some don't believe; some are stubborn; and I guess some just don't know where to start.

And that's what I love so much about this song: the guy understands that he has to try; he has to say something from the heart; and he realizes that he's helpless without the great Helper.

As I consider my challenges, I know I am blessed. I have love; I couldn't have a better life partner or sweeter friends. I have time; at least until God says "time's up." And I have hope; well, until I'm 150 days into a life challenge. Then my hope begins to wane.

Ask, and it will be given to you; seek, and you will find; knock, and it will be opened to you. For everyone who asks receives, and he who seeks finds, and to him who knocks it will be opened. (MATTHEW 7:7-8, NASB)

But what I have that sustains me is help from a really great Helper. As long as I remember—pray first, act second.

I HEARD IT ON THE RADIO
"Brand New Day"

AT THE BOTTOM of each Truth Nugget, I give my subscribers the option to click to my Web site, forward the post to a friend, or unsubscribe. I don't often have girlfriends opt out of my biweekly ramblings—unless I write about forgiveness.

I've found that my audience can be touchy about this topic. By a margin of nearly ten to one, it's the most unpopular subject among my girlfriends. Knowing what's coming, some of you might even wish you could click the "get me out of this" button right now. Why? I have no earthly idea.

When my girlfriends opt out, I want to ask them: Why don't you want to explore the freedom that forgiveness will bring you? Why do you continue to punish yourself by holding on to a hurt caused by someone else? Why don't you want to try to live with joy today, without the pain of yesterday? And why don't you want to wake up without that ball and chain of resentment?

In his song "Brand New Day,"[50] Van Morrison sings of the heartaches many of us have experienced: betrayal, victimization, abandonment, abuse, isolation. But then he reminds us that, with the right perspective, bitterness does not need to rob us of the promise of a day fully lived: "And it seems like yes it feels like, a brand new day."

Moving on into a new day begins with forgiving the people who have wronged you. You don't need to confront them; you don't need to notify them; you don't necessarily need to invite them back into your life.

If you forgive those who sin against you, your heavenly Father will forgive you. But if you refuse to forgive others, your Father will not forgive your sins. (MATTHEW 6:14-15)

You just need to let it go to wake up to a brand-new day. Wake up and look at the sun. Forgiveness is a powerful thing—for you.

I HEARD IT ON THE RADIO
"Get Over It"

BEFORE THERE WAS Dr. Phil, with his plain-talk psychology and simple answers, there were the Eagles. Back in the early 1990s, with the song "Get Over It,"[51] they were already lamenting the people they saw on TV feeling sorry for themselves and blaming other people for their problems.

Agh, victim thinking. Most of us probably know people who have allowed themselves to become victims of their past. In fact, some of us might even be the victim thinkers! I know from experience that there's nothing quite like the wake-up call that comes when a good friend (or mother) points out that it's really time to deal with the past and move on. This refreshing perspective may not be immediately welcomed, but it will eventually calm the raging mind.

We need to recognize when we have allowed ourselves to be locked in a victim mentality—or maybe have even begun to make victimization our life theme.

Some of us latch onto the injustice of yesterday to define who we are today, leaving us friendless and lonely. Our friends, as much as they long to help, usually get worn out with those of us who wear the tiara of pain. The most helpful words they could share with us might come straight out of the Eagles' song: "All this whinin' and cryin' and pitchin' a fit, get over it." (Okay, so perhaps they could phrase it a bit more kindly than these rockers did.)

The troubles of my heart are enlarged;
bring me out of my distresses. (PSALM 25:17, NASB)

If you're stuck in negative thinking, seek counsel. Talk to your clergy. Find a good psychologist. Or download this song at iTunes for 99 cents. But for heaven's sake—move on and get over it.

I HEARD IT ON THE RADIO
"Rumbleseat"

WHEN IT COMES to putting things into perspective and offering a fresh point of view, there's probably not a better storyteller and vocalist than John Mellencamp.

In his folk-rock song "Rumbleseat,"[52] John takes us to a place where many of us have been before—*Loserville*. Do you remember a time when you felt like a second-class citizen? Do you remember an incident that crushed your spirit, when your self-confidence took a beating? Do you remember how easy it was to physically and emotionally withdraw and to lose all objectivity?

In a three-minute song, John reminds us that our station in life today is not indicative of where we might be tomorrow. We can choose to look at what we lost yesterday or to find hope in the promise of tomorrow. We can choose to belittle ourselves or to better ourselves. In the end, sitting in the rumble seat is more about our mental perspective than our physical destination: "I'll be ridin' high/ with my feet kicked up in the rumbleseat."

So which rumble seat are you sitting in today: the one where you feel a failure or the one where you're "ridin' high" because of the lessons and insight you've gained?

> *But God released him from the horrors of death and raised him back to life, for death could not keep him in its grip. King David said this about him: "I see that the LORD is always with me. I will not be shaken, for he is right beside me. No wonder my heart is glad, and my tongue shouts his praises! My body rests in hope."* (ACTS 2:24-26)

Tomorrow is a new day. A gift. Open it with anticipation—and a new outlook.

I HEARD IT ON THE RADIO
"How You Live"

I CLOSE THIS SERIES with what I wish could be every woman's theme song. You know . . . like the one Mary Tyler Moore had on her sitcom in the seventies.

Recorded by the female Christian vocal group Point of Grace, it's not necessarily a spiritual song but rather a positive score on the importance of living a quality life. In three stanzas and a chorus, the secret to living with uncommon joy is laid out for us: just by celebrating life—whether by taking a moment to feel the sun's warmth on our faces or by getting out the fine china for tonight's ordinary dinner—we will find the simple but satisfying path to a joy most of the world never finds.

I love this song because it encourages us to do one very important thing. It's the one thing we usually forget: we're supposed to *live.*

And the girls encourage us, in four-part harmony and with the voices of angels (and a great string section), to "turn up the music." In the end, they remind each of us, it's not the people you knew or what you did that counts; "it's how you live."[53]

How many times in the past week did you get caught up in *stuff*? Stuff that drained your life energy rather than restored or embellished it? Things like schedules, restrictions, limitations, expectations, judgment, jealousy, envy, competition, and resentment. Point of Grace reminds us that one day we will look back. And when we do, we will have to live with the decisions we made today: to stuff our BlackBerry's database with contact information that reads like a who's who; to get a million to-do items scratched off our pad—or to strive for a life well lived.

I really hope you download this song. Play it every morning on your way to work, as you drive the kids to car pool, or as you take off for a day of shopping. And when you do . . . turn it up loud.

I am the light of the world. If you follow me, you won't have to walk in darkness, because you will have the light that leads to life. (JOHN 8:12)

P. S. Wow. In a four-minute-and-twenty-eight-second song, songwriter Cindy Morgan said everything I've written over the past three years. Now that's a gifted writer.

I HEARD IT ON THE RADIO

FATHER GOD, you opened my ears to understand that

- ☐ I am failing to embrace my current life stage and today's blessings;

- ☐ when I struggle to fulfill your purpose for me, your strength will help me prevail;

- ☐ my self-confidence is drained, but with your help, I will stand back up;

- ☐ I have placed the priority of work, children, or self above that of developing a healthy sexual relationship with my husband;

- ☐ I need to learn to blow my horn through the modeling of self-confidence, self-assurance, self-promotion, and self-awareness;

- ☐ I have spent too much time and energy trying to please others instead of being true to the person you created;

- ☐ you consider my soul an even trade for your Son's life;

- ☐ I need to move beyond resentment so I can experience your glory;

- ☐ I need to pray first and act second;

- ☐ what I considered my stuff is really your stuff;

- ☐ it's time to get over it and stop wearing the tiara of pain;

- ☐ it's time to gain a new perspective about where I sit in the rumble seat;

- ☐ I often get caught up in the wrong things; in the end, I will judge the quality of my life by how I lived.

ACTIONS I WILL TAKE:

Example: I will be a wild woman with my man tonight!

1. _____

2. _____

3. _____

Father, thank you for using songwriters, vocalists, and musicians to teach us important lessons on living with uncommon joy. I praise you for guiding me to live an abundant life of promise, hope, joy, and celebration, and for the lessons I've learned through despair, failure, disappointment, and grief. In your Son's name, Amen.

ON THE GROUND

Life is your current view of things. Change your view, and you change your life.
VIRGINIA SATIR

ON OCTOBER 10, 2008, I boarded a plane with fourteen strangers for a two-week adventure. But this was no Caribbean cruise we were taking. Having been selected to be part of a documentary called *Friendly Captivity*, I was one of seven women who would take part in an experience of a lifetime—in India. This team of women, with nothing in common except our willingness of spirit and love of learning, would be followed by a camera crew and producers as we were challenged to come to grips with the contradictions of India, our views on poverty and injustice, and what—if anything—we would personally do about it.

After a twenty-hour plane ride from Dallas, we landed in Mumbai, previously known as Bombay. Affectionately referred to in India as Bollywood, this would be the most cosmopolitan city of our four-city tour. As we drove out the gate of our luxury accommodations near the airport, we were immediately confronted with debris, poverty, and some of the most inhumane living conditions we had ever witnessed.

As I sat in the air-conditioned bus, I looked out the window at men so skinny you could see their ribs, sitting helplessly and hopelessly with their heads in their hands. I watched out the window as a beautiful woman, dressed in her immaculate hot pink sari, emerged from a gray lean-to slum home and gracefully walked around the human waste spilled out on the ground. But I looked away as children walked the crowded streets alone, some totally naked.

As extreme as these conditions were, they were not quite real to me as I peered through my impenetrable window. That changed, though, once we stopped and stepped out of the bus.

On the ground there was no buffer; the experience became personal. Life in India became real. Real fast.

Yes, I am the vine; you are the branches. Those who remain in me, and I in them, will produce much fruit. For apart from me you can do nothing.
(JOHN 15:5)

Are you watching life go by as you look out the bus window of your life? Once I stepped out, I was forever changed. Could God be calling you to step out too?

ON THE GROUND
Filthy Rich

I GUESS MY FAMILY was considered poor as I was growing up. Of course, the families in town that had even less than we did probably thought of us as rich.

I didn't always have lunch money to eat at the downtown diner with my friends—but I had lunch every day; I never went hungry.

I didn't live in a three-bedroom, two-bath brick home—but our small frame house, with one busy bathroom, was always clean and tidy; and it was always warm on winter days.

I didn't get a car of my own when I turned sixteen—but I did get a set of car keys; Daddy and I shared a 1966 red Ford Mustang. I had to walk to school only a time or two when I missed the bus.

I didn't have a closet full of clothes—but in addition to my few store-bought things, I had some awesome hand-me-downs sent to me by my older, *much cooler*, way-hip cousins. Diane von Furstenberg had nothing on my aunt Barbara—that woman could sew!

I didn't have a college fund set aside with my name on it—but I did have a good work ethic and a scholarship; I managed until my senior year.

As a kid, it's hard to tell how well off your family is. As an adult, it can be even harder. But regardless of how good a seat you have on the bus in the United States, you are filthy rich by India's and other third world countries' measure. I am now painfully and unforgettably aware of that fact.

> *God blesses you who are poor,*
> *for the Kingdom of God is yours.*
> *God blesses you who are hungry now,*
> *for you will be satisfied.*
> *God blesses you who weep now,*
> *for in due time you will laugh.* (LUKE 6:20-21)

To gain an honest perspective of poverty and what it really means to you, you'll have to get off your bus of limited understanding and step out onto the ground. Only then will you begin to understand the challenges of the world's poor as well as the difference you can make.

ON THE GROUND
Filthy Rich (Part Deux)

The issue of poverty is not a statistical issue. It is a human issue.
JAMES WOLFENSOHN, FORMER WORLD BANK PRESIDENT

AS WE DROVE through Mumbai, I saw makeshift homes lining the sidewalk (in front of the InterContinental Hotel, no less). These "structures" were made of four poles or sticks securing a tarp that served as an outside wall and roof. Looking through my bus window, the scene was sad. But as I stood on the ground, face-to-face with mothers begging for food to feed their babies, poverty moved from a sad scene outside my window to a personal problem. Not just a poor mother's problem, but now mine too.

As we drove on the outskirts of the city, I looked out my bus window and saw miles and miles of slums with garbage and waste floating in their canals. We left the bus to tour one slum that, with alleys paved in broken and cracked concrete, was considered more upscale than some of the others. While standing on the ground with the smell of human waste hanging in the air, I locked eyes with a smiling, impish child as she reached for me. At that moment, poverty moved from a landscape of gray slums to a warm little hand. Her challenges became my own.

Looking through my bus window in Chennai, a large city in northeastern India, I saw villages of thatched-roof huts. These were considered middle-class homes because they had concrete floors. Some residents even had toothbrushes— their prized possessions, which they often hung on a wall in a position of prominence. Once off the bus, we walked single file behind working-class village women. They delicately lifted their saris as we trekked along a path flooded with water ten inches deep. Suddenly poverty, with all the challenges it throws at these women, was no longer just another working woman's problem; it had become a personal challenge to me.

> *Give generously to the poor, not grudgingly, for the LORD your God will bless you in everything you do.* (DEUTERONOMY 15:10)

If we will all just step off the bus and into the real world—either here at home or abroad—we'll realize that, regardless of the size of our stock portfolios, our job situations, or our living conditions, we're filthy rich. If we will all just step off the bus and connect to another human being's suffering, our perspectives will change—as will our willingness to do something about it.

Are you feeling poor today? Step outside your bus. Wealth awaits you on the ground.

ON THE GROUND
What Hate Feels Like

Let my heart be broken by the things that break the heart of God.
BOB PIERCE, FOUNDER OF WORLD VISION

I HAD NEVER experienced prejudice up close and personal. Before India, I hadn't even seen it through a bus window. I was raised in a primarily white Southern town by parents and grandparents who considered the few African Americans who lived down the road part of our own family. In fact, in my early years, my parents entrusted my physical and emotional development to their care. For the first six years of my life, I probably spent more time cuddled up to the 44DD bosom of a black woman named Lerlene than I did in my own mother's lap. To put our relationship in perspective, 'Lene, as I affectionately called her, sat proudly next to Mom in the family row at my first wedding.

But just because I hadn't seen it looking out my bus window doesn't mean it didn't and doesn't still exist. My girlfriend Mary Jo has experienced prejudice since New Year's Day 1956—when she was not allowed to stay in the nursery at Gatesville Memorial Hospital simply because she was born black. Her mother, without a car or taxi, walked home with her New Year's baby in her arms. The prizes and gifts reserved for the first baby of the New Year were given to a white mother.

Of the six adventuresome women accompanying me on the trip, three were African American. As some of us marveled at our "rock star" welcome in the slums and city streets, my "sisters" commented that they knew exactly why the children desired to reach out to touch our lily-white hands. My African American girlfriends had been "on the ground" with prejudice their whole lives and knew immediately what was happening. "It's because you're white," Traci said. Not disgusted. Not hurt. Not mad. *Not anymore.* She just made a comment that laid the fact, as she understood it, on the table: whites were preferred. Of course, that statement left me confused. Traci, Froswa, and Star quietly tried to explain their lifelong front-row seat at the play of favoritism and hate. But I still couldn't relate to what they were saying until it was *me* who was on the ground and starring in an unfamiliar role.

[Love] does not rejoice about injustice but rejoices whenever the truth wins out.
(I CORINTHIANS 13:6)

Have you ever been hated just because you are whom God made you to be?

ON THE GROUND
What Hate Feels Like (Part Deux)

WHILE SHOPPING in Chennai, our merry band of Americans joined throngs of Diwali shoppers. Diwali, known as the Festival of Lights, is similar to our Christmas. So there we were, the night before Diwali—out shopping with 1.2 billion Indians who were looking for the perfect Diwali gift for their loved ones.

As we entered the open-air market, strung with lights, the excitement hung in the air like it does in Dallas's NorthPark Center mall on Christmas Eve. A display caught our collective fashion eye, and we strolled into a shop featuring beautiful *shalwar kameez* (traditional Indian ensembles). As I shopped on the south side of the corner store, I visited with the young English-speaking merchants.

Intrigued by the brightly colored merchandise, I meandered farther into the store. Then an elderly man, standing behind the counter, began speaking to me in Hindi. Animated, he motioned for me to move; I thought he wanted me to look at the clothes on another rack. But he continued to flap his hands and arms wildly and his voice grew louder. His expression turned angry. I looked around, confused, trying to understand what he wanted me to do—until a man, standing outside the shop, looked me in the eye and said, "He wants you to get out of his store."

I was shocked. Why? What had I done? It became glaringly clear.

I was hated simply because I am an American. I am white. I am Christian. I am a woman. All I could think as I walked away—embarrassed, by the way—is *I know he would like me if he would just stop hating me for a moment and give me a chance.*

It is so easy to despise people who are different:

Left. Right.
Jew. Muslim.
Gay. Straight.
Black. Hispanic.
Male. Female.
Young. Old.
Rich. Poor.

My dear brothers and sisters, how can you claim to have faith in our glorious Lord Jesus Christ if you favor some people over others? (JAMES 2:1)

Until each and every one of us has experienced the gut-wrenching feeling of being despised because of who we are—or what someone else thinks we are—we will not overthrow the kind of prejudice Jesus fought against. He loved people others loved to hate: The poor. The sick. The sinful. Those on the wrong side of the tracks or the wrong side of the rules. Feeling the sting of someone else's hatred has given me a deeper appreciation for the boundary-breaking love of Jesus—and a stronger determination to pass that love along.

ON THE GROUND
Reality Sets In

BACK IN DALLAS, I look out my car window as my son, Scott, walks briskly to the car. He looks like the picture of health. But looks are deceiving. As he folds himself into the car, I know that my strapping young son is pumped full of drugs designed to fend off AIDS. He's HIV infected.

While I was in India, I saw others infected and affected by the disease. Most were women; some had picked up their illness from their "clients"; others contracted the disease from their husbands and then were rejected by their families. Like my Scott, they are responding well to their potent cocktails of modern medicine. Through my tinted windows, the death sentence looked just like a manageable chronic disease.

Then I stepped off the bus and was on the ground at an AIDS orphanage. The reality came crashing home in the form of a slight eight-year-old child. Sitting on the floor to play with V (an initial I have chosen to protect his identity), I quickly noticed he had the wit and charm of a lad three times his age. As I lifted this forty-pound child onto my lap to read him some of his favorite stories, my past flashed before my eyes. I remembered holding and reading to Scott, just like this. Twenty years ago seems like just last week.

> Even when I walk
> through the darkest valley,
> I will not be afraid,
> for you are close beside me.
> Your rod and your staff
> protect and comfort me. (PSALM 23:4)

Looking through the bus window of my life, I am entertained and distracted by all that whirls by me: business meetings, social events, family gatherings, and obligations. I guess this is good to some extent, because on the ground, my heart breaks for us both.

ON THE GROUND
Reality Sets In (Part Deux)

NOT ONLY DID THE DEATH sting of the AIDS epidemic become personal, suddenly I could better relate to Bruce Wilkinson's description of the crisis in another part of the world.

> Across southern Africa, the AIDS epidemic has left more than thirteen million children with neither father nor mother. . . . How does a person begin to understand the reality of thirteen million orphans?
>
> Maybe like this: Put the population of Los Angeles and New York City together. Let that combined metropolis be made up of only needy children. In that whole city, let there be not one mother or father. Let there be a ramshackle home where a nine-year-old boy is the head of the household. Let his six-year-old sister leave home every morning to look for food.
>
> Now let these children be yours.[54]

V held my hand as we walked to the clinic for his daily treatment. We donned our sunglasses as we strolled under the hot Indian sun and pretended we were movie stars as the cameras rolled. Hamming it up for the camera, V, with his quirky sense of humor, made me forget he was dying—until I looked again at his frail, tiny body as we entered the clinic. The treatment is losing its effectiveness. This is not a chronic disease; it's a death sentence, especially for the children who are too weak to fight.

> *"I was naked, and you gave me clothing. I was sick, and you cared for me. I was in prison, and you visited me." Then these righteous ones will reply, "Lord, when did we ever see you hungry and feed you? . . . When did we ever see you sick or in prison and visit you?" And the King will say, "I tell you the truth, when you did it to one of the least of these my brothers and sisters, you were doing it to me!"*
> (MATTHEW 25:36-37, 39-40)

Just as I had seen my past while reading to V, now I stared into the reality of the future. When you step off the bus and get on the ground, reality sets in. And only when reality sets in can we collectively solve the problem—here at home and abroad.

ON THE GROUND
It's Harder to Judge

WHORES. They don't rank very high on our list of respectable professions, do they? Oh let's see: doctors, professors, lawyers, nurses, teachers, businesswomen, writers, social workers, clergy. Nope. Call girls just don't make the cut.

As a woman, prostitutes disgust me. As a professional, they insult me. As a Christian, I am appalled.

Before India, I had never personally met a woman of ill repute (at least that I know of). Before India, I had never walked the streets of a red-light district. Before India, I had viewed the women behind this shameful profession only through a window, where it's much easier to judge and condemn than to understand and love.

On the ground, I walked through the streets of Mumbai where women posed at the front door of their brothels. I locked eyes with their pimps and glared at these men with disdain for their business practices. But as I looked into the eyes of the women, both young and old, waiting to begin their trade—with as many as twenty men a night—my disgust quickly gave way to anguish.

As we sat in a halfway house that rescues these women, many of whom have never learned to read or write, I listened to their stories. One after another, they told how their uncle, their father, or *their mother* had sold them into the sex trade at the tender age of twelve or thirteen. This was not the exceptional story—this *is* the story. As I looked into their eyes filled with tears and shame, I was no longer insulted by their choice of work. Instead, I was enraged that they had had no choice.

Nearby, my traveling buddies and I visited an orphanage full of little girls dressed in their Sunday best. We sang and danced the "Hokey Pokey" with these fresh-faced little cherubs whose mothers had tucked them away from the ugliness of their own world. Mothers who longed for a better life for their daughters. As I sang and played with these happy, gorgeous children, I was no longer appalled by their mothers' line of work. In fact, I was awed by their courage in giving their little girls an escape from the brothels.

Looking through a window, it was easy to be judgmental. But on the ground, these women become real people. As I heard their stories, I couldn't help but wonder how often I have misjudged people in the United States as well.

So now I am giving you a new commandment: Love each other. Just as I have loved you, you should love each other. Your love for one another will prove to the world that you are my disciples. (JOHN 13:34-35)

On the ground, as a woman, a daughter, and a mother, I was heartbroken to discover my own judgmental spirit. Might there be more to the backstory of those you judge too?

ON THE GROUND
Hope: Putting a Face with the Name

It's not who we are that holds us back, it's who we think we are not.   MICHAEL NOLAN

BEFORE MY ADVENTURE to India, *hope* seemed a pretty generic, overused word. I hoped to land a new client. I hoped the kids would enjoy their vacation. I hoped Steve would rub my feet (yes, hope springs eternal).

But on the ground in India, hope took on an altogether new meaning for me.

After meeting with thirty-six women who, because of microloans, had been able to build home businesses, hope was no longer a vague noun or an overused verb; it became a face. Each of these women was in her fourth level of lending, meaning that she had been loaned—and paid back in full—three other advances. Having borrowed amounts from approximately $100 in cycle one to over $2,000 in cycle four, these women, once *starving*, now provided for their families and community.

With the confidence of a Fortune 500 president, each woman stood, one by one, and shared with us how they had started their businesses and their plans for expansion. Just a few years earlier, these Dalit women (once called the untouchables, the lowest level in India's caste system) would not even make eye contact with other humans because they believed themselves unworthy. But on this day they exuded both confidence and determination as they presented their accomplishments with their new American girlfriends. One had opened a fruit stand; another, a flower shop. One woman who had learned to sew had a thriving business as a seamstress. Another gal opened a fish hatchery; another was a basket weaver. And one was a merchant with a newly expanded assortment for her retail enterprise. These women, representing hundreds more just like them, were inventive, impressive, and inspiring.

Faith is the confidence that what we hope for will actually happen; it gives us assurance about things we cannot see. (HEBREWS 11:1)

The small audience of American women sat in total silence during the presentations. After each one, we cheered with enthusiastic pride for what these women, of all ages, had accomplished. And no doubt, more than a few of us wept inwardly for our own personal reunion with hope.

ON THE GROUND
Hope: Putting a Face with the Name (Part Deux)

Here is what we know: all people are created equal. Given the tools and incentives for success, they will succeed, no matter who they are or where they live.
PAUL O'NEIL, FORMER U.S. SECRETARY OF THE TREASURY

THE WOMEN IN CHENNAI were so proud of their accomplishments and so eager to share their new businesses with us that some invited us into their homes to observe their operations. Walking through the monsoon-ravaged alleys, we made our way to the entrance of a small home with a dirt entrance littered with kitchen utensils, pots, and pans. I was a little confused as to why the "kitchen" was strewn across the dirt lawn until I entered the home. Standing in the small, two-room, thatched-roof hut, I realized that every square inch was covered by sewing machines and fabric.

As the beaming business owner gave us a tour of her manufacturing facility, it was clear she had moved her domestic duties of cooking to the great outdoors to make room for her burgeoning business. Showing us the finished goods produced in those tiny accommodations, she proudly introduced us to her first employees—her husband and her shy teenage son.

Later, during a meeting with the microlending recipients, two beautiful little girls dressed in school uniforms peered in through the open doorway. "What about your daughters; are you teaching them business skills?" I asked the women.

"Yes," replied one woman. "They are learning our business with us."

Rejoice in our confident hope. Be patient in trouble, and keep on praying. When God's people are in need, be ready to help them. Always be eager to practice hospitality. (ROMANS 12:12-13)

The mothers said something in Hindi to their daughters, and the little girls giggled and ran away—only to return minutes later, this time in new, brightly colored short sets. It appears that the fashion show concept knows no international boundary. And neither does hope. These children can now put a face with the name *hope*—and she is also called Mom.

ON THE GROUND
Learning to Appreciate My Learning

If you educate a man, you educate an individual. If you educate a woman, you educate a nation. AFRICAN SAYING

WITH LITTLE FANFARE, I was put on a big yellow bus as a little girl and sent to a public school, along with all the other kiddos in our small country town. Just as I barely noticed the miles of grasslands we passed on the drive to school, I also took my education for granted. That all changed on another bus—this one driven through India's city streets, teeming with people.

As we drove through India, we passed pigtailed girls and handsome young boys as they walked to and from school. In their crisp uniforms, complete with ties, they looked much like the American children who head off to school wearing backpacks loaded down with books. But on the ground, getting an education for a child in India is much more difficult than it appears through the bus window.

Education is free for Indian children as long as their parents can cover the cost of a uniform and backpack—which equals about 43 percent of the average family's total annual income. Education there is a sacrificial labor of love unlike anything we see in the United States.

Among the little girls of the Dalit caste, the possibility of getting an education was only a distant hope yesterday. Few women in this lower-class caste, as well as the tribal women, know how to read or write. As these mothers walk their little girls to school, they understand that the sacrifice they are making will change everything, both for their daughters and for future generations of Indian daughters.

During a school tour, a group of fourteen-year-old boys and girls confidently shared their hopes and aspirations with us. "I want to be a teacher because I want other children to enjoy the opportunity to learn." "I want to be a software engineer because technology is important for helping us communicate." "I want to be a pilot because I love planes." Listening to these future professionals who walk to school from the jungles or are packed like sardines and bused to school from miles away, I was convicted. Why hadn't I ever viewed my own education as a privilege and a gift?

> *Intelligent people are always ready to learn.*
> *Their ears are open for knowledge.*
> *Giving a gift can open doors;*
> *it gives access to important people!* (PROVERBS 18:15-16)

Looking out my bus window, both as a kid and as a tourist first arriving in India, I never gave enough thought to the blessing of my education. But on the ground in India I learned to appreciate my learning.

ON THE GROUND
Living Intentionally

Believe that God is looking for some disturbed people. He is searching for men and women, students, and young adults who will allow him to disturb them by making them truly see the world in which we live—so disturbed that they will be compelled to do something about what they see.[55] KAY WARREN

ON OCTOBER 24, 2008, my excellent Indian adventure came to a screeching halt. Parting at the airport from my newfound girlfriends was bittersweet: it was so hard to say good-bye to those with whom we had experienced so much in the fourteen days; at the same time, it was good to know we wouldn't be pitching our tents three to a room that night!

The seven of us were an unlikely crew. Star is a manicurist; Toni is a litigator. Sue and I have each been married for nineteen years; Jayna and Star are single. Froswa and Traci are active Christians who are raising kids; Sue is fifty, Jewish, and a recent empty nester; at thirty-two, Jayna defines herself as a "quasi–New Age, unhippie, pseudointellectual with skeptical tendencies and a secret supernatural bent." Kids are not in her immediate future. We were all newbies to India while Nanci, our facilitator, was an expert.

We were women of all sizes, from skinny to full figured. We were women of all colors, from nearly translucent to luscious dark chocolate. We were women of all faiths and persuasions. At first blush you'd think we'd have nothing of importance in common. But in reality we possessed one critical, common bond.

We all knew that to live intentionally, we had to get out of the bus.

We knew that living with meaning wouldn't be accomplished by watching life roll by as we looked through a window. And we all agreed that if we were to make a difference in our world, sometimes we were going to be uncomfortable. We knew that we could not be afraid to question and debate, to find answers. We knew we had to dig even to find the best questions.

If you are wise and understand God's ways, prove it by living an honorable life, doing good works with the humility that comes from wisdom. (JAMES 3:13)

For fourteen days I lived intentionally and dreamed dramatically with six insightful, daring strangers as we became more than life spectators. I was blessed to be among the India Seven who hit the ground running.

So what about you, girlfriend? Do you find yourself thriving or just surviving? Maybe it's time for you to get off the bus too.

ON THE GROUND

FATHER GOD, I long to stop watching my life pass by the window. Bless me with

- ☐ courage to take on adventure;
- ☐ eyes to see the poor;
- ☐ determination to fight against prejudice;
- ☐ a heart for those infected by diseases such as AIDS and malaria;
- ☐ the ability to put aside my old judgments and judgmental thinking to better love people where they are;
- ☐ a fresh appreciation for the value of education—here in the States and for our sisters and their children abroad;
- ☐ a spirit of hope and a retreat from my cynical ways;
- ☐ an opportunity to get off the bus and get on the ground.

ACTIONS I WILL TAKE:

Example: Today I will stop pitying the poor and actually do something about it; I will volunteer at the food bank.

1. _____

2. _____

3. _____

My loving Father, I lift up my sisters and their children—families a world away who have so little. I pray that you will show me what I can do, how I can make a difference, how I can impact those you love. You have blessed me with so much, Father; show me how to share this blessing with those you love. In the name of Christ Jesus, I pray. Amen.

JUST A FEW WORDS

WORDS ARE WEIRD. Alone, they're not very meaningful. Take the word *love*. It's a bit hollow until you add one little word on each side of it. Then it may make your heart race: *I love you.*

I'll give you another one. *Peace*. It's a pleasant word on its own, but it takes on a deeper, personal meaning when strung with three other one-syllable words: *Peace be with you*. To really make a word work, it needs some companions.

Of course, on the flip side, some people use a long stream of words nonstop over several minutes without ever really saying a doggone thing. Same with some writers. They rattle on, stringing their words together with little thought to the plot or significance of their story. They just talk or write for sport!

Because of my affinity for words, I appreciate those who thoughtfully and painstakingly say it all with just a few words. From C. S. Lewis to the guy who penned the words of wisdom in my fortune cookie, I lift up a prayer of thanks for the truths they impart. Like this one:

It is good to shut up sometimes. MARCEL MARCEAU

While the Holy Bible will continue to be the source of my truth, in this chapter I will share with you some other words of wisdom to live by. Written by people famous, and some not so famous, I can't help but believe that these words, too, must have had some heavenly inspiration.

I have hidden your word in my heart, . . .
encourage me by your word. (PSALM 119:11, 28)

Post them on your makeup mirror. Leave them on your nightstand. Stick one to your refrigerator door. These are also words of truth.

JUST A FEW WORDS
Hypocrisy

What you do speaks so loudly I cannot hear what you say.   RALPH WALDO EMERSON

HYPOCRISY IS A TOUGH topic for those of us who get up every day with one goal: to be a walking, talking example of Christ and his love. It's an uncomfortable subject because it seems so unfair. We're the people trying so hard, yet we seem to be judged the harshest! Just let me do one little bitty thing wrong and my whole Christian witness flies out the door. *It ain't fair.* I hate being judged by a different standard than the rest of the world. But then, when you think about it, we're not the rest of the world.

Of course, I sin like everyone else. I have big sins and little sins and sins of every size in between. My medium-size sins consist of my three biggest character flaws: a lack of generosity, a lack of humility, and an overabundant need to feel significant. Any one of these can make me look like the poster child for hypocrisy. On days I fail to give spontaneously or hoard my time (my most precious commodity these days), I am convicted—even as I'm blocking out another section of my calendar! When my proud spirit or need for significance dominates a conversation, I am again so convicted. Even as the words fly out of my mouth, I hear my internal voice say, *Here you go again.*

> *When the Spirit of truth comes, he will guide you into all truth.*
> (JOHN 16:13)

In a twisted way, I love the fact that the Holy Spirit convicts me—over and over and over. He won't let me off the hook. He tells me repeatedly that my actions must align with the truths of Christ and the fruits of the Spirit. That I am called to be better and act better than that.

Are your words and actions congruent? Or are you blowing your witness too? Listen to the voice. No, it's not the ghost of Emerson; it's the Helper.

JUST A FEW WORDS
Sin

I can't help but wonder if we would take sin as lightly as we do if we had to regularly slit the throat of an animal to seek atonement for it.[56] NANCY GUTHRIE

WELL, SINCE I TOUCHED on the subject of sin, I might as well go all the way. Let's face it. We're a mess.

In sixth grade, at the height of my hormonal carnival ride, I had surgery on my big toe. A little aggressive with the toenail clippers, I had cut them too short. One ingrown toenail surgery morphed into another when the toe just wouldn't heal. The second surgery resulted in about eight to ten stitches in my toe (and one weird-looking toenail).

Post-surgery day one, it was time for the bandage to come off for my daily foot soaking and treatment in mineral salts. But I wasn't game. I liked the bandage where it was. I didn't want to look at my toe. I didn't want to deal with it. And I certainly didn't want anyone else to see it. Drama resulted. Mom and Dad won out.

I think we're this way with our sin, too. Especially the big ones. We want to be free, but we don't trust God to unwrap the dressing. So we sit, bound up tighter than our fanny in a pair of Spanx on New Year's Eve, just hoping no one else will notice our sin and that we'll never have to deal with it. All the while, we cry in our heart, our mind, and our soul, *What's wrong with me?*

> *Wash me clean from my guilt.*
> *Purify me from my sin.*
> *For I recognize my rebellion;*
> *it haunts me day and night.*
> *Against you, and you alone, have I sinned.* (PSALM 51:2-4)

Well, I tell you. You're just like me—a sinner saved by grace. But that doesn't let us off the hook. We must unbind ourselves from the recurring sins that choke the joy out of our lives. We have to look at the ugliness.

I once took my big sins a bit too lightly. Oh, yes, I felt guilty; I asked for forgiveness; and yet, just as with my big toe, I didn't want to look closely because it was sickening. Until I finally let God treat the wound.

Unbind yourself. Freedom is a prayer away.

JUST A FEW WORDS
Peace

An eye for an eye ends up making the whole world blind. MAHATMA GANDHI

THE WORLD IS AT WAR and we're losing. Yes, *we're* losing—all of us.

Just consider the words of Miguel d'Escoto Brockmann, president of the United Nations General Assembly, which he delivered in November 2008: "The bitter reality of conflicts in many countries dwarf the ability of peacekeepers to fulfill their mandates."[57]

Political agendas. Philosophies. Social injustices. Religion. Territories. Oil. Revenge. We fight and we fight and we fight. But no one ever wins. Human beings die.

And the church is often no better at keeping peace. Talk to any friend or neighbor and they can probably recount to you firsthand the conflicts that simmer— and sometimes boil over—within their congregations.

The church is at war and we're losing. Yes, *we're* losing—all of us.

Agendas. Judgment. Self-service. Infighting. Gossip. Backbiting. Capital campaigns. We fight and we fight and we fight. But no one wins. The church dissolves.

I am at war with myself as I wrestle in the middle of the night, replaying my actions and words from that day in my mind. Poor decisions. Dreadful reactions. Harsh words spoken. Like the furry creatures in the arcade "bop a mole" game, my mistakes keep popping back up in my mind. I fight and I fight and I fight. But I never win. My peace evaporates.

And sometimes, I go to war with God. I want answers, and I want them now. When quick solutions don't surface or the answers are not what I was looking for, I wrestle with God. I fight and I fight and I fight. But I don't win here either.

What is the source of the wars and the fights among you? Don't they come from the cravings that are at war within you? (JAMES 4:1, HCSB)

When James wrote to the "twelve tribes" of Jewish believers, he really nailed the source of all our wars. Cravings are in an all-out battle within us every day. The craving to be right. The craving to be heard. The craving to convince. The craving for power. The craving for forgiveness. The craving to change. The craving for the status quo.

Jesus paid the ultimate sacrifice for a world at war, for the church he loved, and for your peace. Maybe it's time for you to take solace in that love and sacrifice and give peace a chance. Because clearly no one wins otherwise.

Peace be with you.

JUST A FEW WORDS
Power

I WONDER where today's entry finds you. Are you enthusiastic about where you are, where you're headed in life, and the legacy you're writing for those you love? Or are you in a less-than-sunny place in your life right now?

Even the most optimistic of us have valleys in our lives when disappointments rain down. We all have failings and hurts—either self-imposed or caused by others. Either way, they can leave us wounded and sometimes very negative. I was in that state one evening when we ordered Chinese.

I had been hurt by someone I considered a very dear friend. Just a few days prior to placing my order with Hunan Express, a friend had said some very hurtful things to me. I don't think he really intended for them to sound so biting, but nonetheless, they did. I was angry. I was hurt. I was insulted. Did I say I was angry? I was pretty much outraged. For seventy-two hours, my stomach churned as I replayed the tape of his words in my head.

With their quick delivery, Hunan Express is a favorite of ours, but honestly I wasn't very hungry. I picked at my General Chow Chicken. I pushed my rice around. I gave my egg roll to Steve. But as I read these words of wisdom on a quarter-inch piece of paper folded inside my fortune cookie, I experienced a power shift:

Dwelling on the negative simply contributes to its power.
HUNAN EXPRESS FORTUNE COOKIE

Actually, it was more like a power surge.

So now there is no condemnation for those who belong to Christ Jesus. And because you belong to him, the power of the life-giving Spirit has freed you from the power of sin that leads to death. (ROMANS 8:1-2)

I realized at that moment that I was feeding the power of negativity by stewing over the situation, rather than addressing what I could do to turn this unfortunate exchange into a positive one. Over the course of the next few days, I researched my facts; I gained others' perspectives; I reflected on my position; I wrote it down; I committed it to heart; I practiced it; I refined it; and, I turned what I learned into a truth that I believe will serve me well for many years to come.

Have you relinquished your optimism for negativity? It's a power struggle that only you control.

JUST A FEW WORDS
Our Purpose

The place where God calls you to is the place where deep gladness and the world's deep hunger meet.[58] FREDERICK BUECHNER

FIGURING OUT what we're supposed to be doing while we're walking the face of the earth is not easy.

We're pretty sure we should be doing something that matters. But we also want to love what we're doing.

We need to be engaged. We want to be energized by our work or projects, and we want to know in our hearts that we've found our calling.

But we also want to make money so we can provide for our families. So how can we find that intersection of those things we should do for others, we need to do for our spirit, and we want materially?

Last Sunday, our pastor, Dr. Joe Clifford, spoke briefly about how we can understand what God might be calling us to do. He reminded us that at least two of three things usually occur when God is calling us to do something specific.

First, you may hear an internal voice that tells you when you are satisfied by a specific type of work or task. When you're doing it, you are fulfilled; you love it. But there is also an external influence that is important. When others recognize your talents and begin to suggest that you consider using these gifts in a significant way, you need to pay attention. External influences are important because we often need that objectivity. Finally, sometimes a providential occurrence propels one's circumstances toward clarity or change. Whether a series of seemingly coincidental happenstances or a life-altering event, what sometimes seems a disaster one minute can be fate smiling down on you sweetly the next.

> *Don't you realize that in a race everyone runs, but only one person gets the prize? So run to win! All athletes are disciplined in their training. They do it to win a prize that will fade away, but we do it for an eternal prize. So I run with purpose in every step.* (1 CORINTHIANS 9:24-26)

In Matthew 25, Jesus tells a parable about the man who entrusted his investment money to three of his servants. Two invested it wisely, returning more to their master than he had given them. The third, however, buried what he'd been given, forfeiting any potential for gain. Jesus reveals the story's moral by telling us that "to those who use well what they are given, even more will be given, and they will have an abundance. But from those who do nothing, even what little they have will be taken away" (v. 29).

Whether we're talking about talents, as in spiritual gifts, or talents, as in money, either way, we know that God is the provider—but we have to discern the call and have the courage to step out in faith.

JUST A FEW WORDS

FATHER GOD, I thank you for what you have taught me through these men and women who use words in such a wise way. Help me to

- ☐ guard against hypocrisy and make sure that what I do is not in conflict with what I say;

- ☐ unbind myself from my recurring sins;

- ☐ live at peace with all your children;

- ☐ use positive plans and direction to empower me, rather than dwelling on negativity;

- ☐ align my passions with your needs and desires;

- ☐ remember that all I have, in material goods and spiritual talents, is given and sustained by you.

ACTIONS I WILL TAKE:

Example: I will stop dwelling on my bad experience with _____ and focus on the positive things in my life.

1. _____

2. _____

3. _____

Holy Father, I praise you for those whom you have gifted with words. Thank you for the wisdom, clarity, and guidance they provide me. I pray that you will walk with me as I focus on your will and the truths that you long for me to live by. Let me be a light in your world. In the name of your Son, Christ Jesus. Amen.

LIVING YOUR JOY

WELL, IF YOU MADE it all the way through the end of this book, you're a better woman than I am! I reflect today on how often I have bought daily devotionals, with the best of intentions to read them each day, only to find that thirty days into my commitment my discipline is woefully lacking.

But you did journey with me for these 365 days, and I am humbled. But I am also delighted.

I am delighted to know, girlfriend, that you are serious about growing as a believer and are dedicated to gaining insights from others. I am thrilled that you are passionate about living intentionally and are willing to explore new avenues. And I am excited. Excited that you have made a conscious decision to live your life with uncommon joy . . . even when bad stuff happens!

> *Give thanks to the LORD, for he is good!*
> *His faithful love endures forever.* (PSALM 118:1)

So tearfully, I write this final page, praising the Almighty for who he is and for all his creation. I praise him for making such a beauty as you! And I thank him for blessing you as you live a *real* life of uncommon joy.

May the love of God fill your heart as you love others.

May the will of God fill your mind as you discern your way.

And may the peace of God cover you and yours . . . from head to toe!

SCRIPTURE INDEX

NOTES

1. Alexandra Stoddard, *You Are Your Choices: 50 Ways to Live the Good Life* (New York: Collins Living, 2006), 111.
2. *Merriam-Webster's Collegiate Dictionary*, 11th ed., s.v. "multitasking."
3. Marcus Buckingham and Donald Clifton, *Now, Discover Your Strengths* (New York: Free Press, 2001), 208.
4. Tim Sanders, *Love Is the Killer App* (New York: Three Rivers Press, 2003), 3.
5. Ibid., 81.
6. Dick Richards, *Artful Work* (San Francisco: Barrett-Koehler Publishers, 1995), 38.
7. Joel Olsteen, *Your Best Life Now* (New York: FaithWords, 2004), 163.
8. *American Heritage Dictionary*, 4th ed., s.v. "guilt."
9. Ibid.
10. *Wikipedia*, s.v. "cardiopulmonary resuscitation," http://en.wikipedia.org/wiki/Cardiopulmonary_resuscitation.
11. Barna Update, May 4, 2004, http://www.barna.org/barna-update/article/5-barna-update/140-number-of-unchurched-adults-has-nearly-doubled-since-199.
12. Rick Warren, *The Purpose Driven Life* (Grand Rapids: Zondervan/Inspirio, 2003), 11.
13. David Bach, *Smart Women Finish Rich* (New York: Broadway, 2002), 36.
14. Ellen Hoffman, "Can Women Bridge the Retirement Savings Gap?" *Business Week*, August 11, 2008, http://www.businessweek.com/investor/content/aug2008/pi2008088_307392.htm?campaign_id=rss_null.
15. Don Kuehn, "Your Money," AFT (May/June 2004), http://www.aft.org/pubs-reports/your_money/2004/0504.htm.
16. Bach, *Smart Women Finish Rich*, 26.
17. These final three statistics come from "Statistics and Aging Information," *The Senior Source*, http://www.theseniorsource.org.
18. Liz Perle, *Money, A Memoir: Women, Emotions, and Cash* (New York: Henry Holt, 2006), 40.
19. Ibid., 228.
20. Calculations found at http://www.bloomberg.com/invest/calculators/retire.html.
21. Perle, *Money, A Memoir*, 107.
22. "Girls and Body Image Tips," Common Sense Media 2003 Research, http://www.commonsensemedia.org/girls-and-body-image-tips.
23. See http://www.teenresearch.com/PRview.cfm?edit_id=152.
24. Susan Nolen-Hoeksema, *Women Who Think Too Much* (New York: Henry Holt, 2003), 153.
25. John Maxwell, *Thinking for a Change* (New York: Warner Books, 2003), 109.
26. Sanford Bennett, "In the Sweet By and By," 1868.

27. Hugh Lofting, *The Story of Dr. Doolittle* (New York: Frederick A. Stokes Co., 1920), chapter 10.

28. Dan Baker and Cathy Greenberg, *What Happy Women Know* (New York: St. Martin's Press, 2007).

29. Carolyn Custis James, *When Life and Beliefs Collide* (Grand Rapids, MI: Zondervan, 2001), 82.

30. Patricia Raybon, *I Told the Mountain to Move* (Carol Stream, IL: Tyndale House, 2005), 128.

31. Henry Cloud, *Integrity: The Courage to Meet the Demands of Reality* (New York: HarperCollins, 2006), 191–192.

32. Alison Clarke-Stewart and Cornelia Brentano, *Divorce: Causes and Consequences* (New Haven, CT: Yale University Press, 2006), 16.

33. Marcus Buckingham and Curt Coffman, *First, Break All the Rules* (New York: Simon & Schuster, 1999), 152–153.

34. Dick Richards, *Artful Work*, 56.

35. Marcus Buckingham, *The One Thing You Need to Know* (New York: Simon & Schuster, 2005), 189.

36. Alexandra Stoddard, *You Are Your Choices* (New York: HarperCollins, 2006), 209.

37. Virginia Satir, *The New Peoplemaking* (Mountainview, CA: Science and Behavior Books, 1988), 325–326.

38. Anne Lamott, *Traveling Mercies* (New York: Random House, 1999), 143.

39. Shelly Branch and Sue Callaway, *What Would Jackie Do?* (New York: Gotham, 2005), 47.

40. John Bunyan, *The Pilgrim's Progress* (London: J. M. Dent and Sons, 1929).

41. Lee Thomas Miller and Ashley Gorley, "You're Gonna Miss This," © EMI Blackwood Music, Inc., 2007.

42. Patty Griffin, "Up to the Mountain," © Almo Music Corporation and One Big Love Music, 2006.

43. Jennifer Nettles, Kristen Hall, and Kristian Bush, "Stand Back Up," © Greater Good Songs and Dirtpit Music, 2003.

44. "Wild Women Do," © CBS Music Inc., Chalk Hill Music, No Ears Music, and Geffen Music, 1990.

45. Sammy Cahn and James Van Heusen, "Come Blow Your Horn," © Maraville Music Corp., 1963.

46. Terence Martin, "Even Trade," © Terence Martin, 2008.

47. Georgia and Angelo Middleman, "Do What You Do," © PolyGram International Publishing, Inc. and On My Mind Music, 1999.

48. Lew Brown and Buddy G. DeSylva, "Life Is Just a Bowl of Cherries," 1931.

49. BoDeans, "Everyday," from the album *Still*, © He and He Records, 2008.

50. Van Morrison, "Brand New Day," © Van Morrison, 1969.

51. Don Henley and Glenn Frey, "Get Over It," © Woody Creek Music and Red Cloud Music, 1994.

52. John Mellencamp, "Rumbleseat," © John Mellencamp, 1985.

53. Cindy Morgan, "How You Live," © Word Music, 2007.

54. Bruce Wilkinson, *The Dream Giver* (Sisters, OR: Multnomah, 2003), 7–8.

55. Kay Warren, *Dangerous Surrender* (Grand Rapids, MI: Zondervan, 2007), 356.

56. Nancy Guthrie, *Hoping for Something Better* (Carol Stream, IL: Tyndale, 2007), 101.

57. See http://www.un.org/ga/president/63/statements/peaceanniversary071108.shtml.

58. Frederick Buechner, *Wishful Thinking* (New York: Harper One, 1973), 119.

ABOUT THE AUTHOR

ELLEN MILLER is passionate about life balance. Why? Because she knows first-hand the miserable feeling we have when we're "off our game" and the joy we can find in everyday life when we're hitting on all cylinders. Her motto is: "You can have it all—just not *every* day."

Professionally, Ellen is a working gal. She served as a corporate officer for a Fortune 500 company while raising a family. She founded and now serves as the visionary for Insider Marketing, a technology marketing firm. Since 1994, Insider has had the pleasure of marketing some of the biggest brands in the technology marketplace.

But Ellen believes that her profession describes only a third of who she really is. Personally, Ellen shares her life with her husband, Steve; their grown children; and their first grandchild. She's not one to take this blessing of a sweet family for granted. But probably the most defining thing about Ellen is her purpose. In this life stage, Ellen has felt a calling to be an encouragement to other women of all walks of life.

Ellen believes that a fulfilled, content woman is vital to our society, our work-force, and most important to our families. A woman who purposefully chooses to live intentionally makes for a productive employee, a strong marriage partner, and a positive role-modeling mother. Her desire is to inspire confidence and motivate women to live to their full potential—with *uncommon* joy—for Christ.